AGAINST SOCIALIST ILLUSION

GW00494392

Also by David Selbourne

Plays

THE PLAY OF WILLIAM COOPER AND EDMUND
DEW- NEVETT (Methuen)

THE TWO-BACKED BEAST (Methuen)

DORABELLA (Methuen)

THE DAMNED (Methuen)

SAMSON and ALISON MARY FAGAN (Calder & Boyars)

Non-fiction

AN EYE TO INDIA (Penguin Books)

AN EYE TO CHINA (Orient Longman)

THROUGH THE INDIAN LOOKING-GLASS (Zed Press)

THE MAKING OF A MIDSUMMER NIGHT'S DREAM
(Methuen)

(editor) IN THEORY AND IN PRACTICE:
Essays on the Politices of J.P.Narayan
(Oxford University Press)

AGAINST
SOCIALIST
ILLUSION

A Radical Argument

David Selbourne

MACMILLAN

© David Selbourne 1985

All rights reserved. No reproduction, copy or transmission
of this publication may be made without written permission.

No paragraph of this publication may be reproduced, copied
or transmitted save with written permission or in accordance
with the provisions of the Copyright Act 1956 (as amended).

Any person who does any unauthorised act in relation to
this publication may be liable to criminal prosecution and
civil claims for damages.

First edition 1985
Reprinted 1985

Published by
THE MACMILLAN PRESS LTD
Houndmills, Basingstoke, Hampshire RG21 2XS
and London
Companies and representatives
throughout the world

Printed in Great Britain by
Antony Rowe Ltd
Chippenham

British Library Cataloguing in Publication Data
Selbourne, David
Against socialist illusion.
1. Socialism
I. Title
335   HX73
ISBN 0-333-37094-5
ISBN 0-333-37095-3 Pbk

Hitherto men have constantly made up for
themselves false conceptions about themselves,
about what they are and what they ought to
be . . . The phantoms of their brains have got
out of their hands. They, the creators, have
bowed down before their creations. Let us
liberate them from the chimeras, the ideas,
dogmas, imaginary beings under the yoke of
which they are pining away.

> Karl Marx and Friedrich Engels
> Preface, *The German Ideology*

Tell me where is fancy bred,
Or in the heart or in the head?

> William Shakespeare, *The Merchant of Venice*,
> Act Three, Scene Two

Contents

Prefatory Note

To keep the argument of this essay as clear as possible, sources, evidence, corroborating and conflicting positions have been rather ruthlessly consigned to the notes. The material there can be read or not, according to the taste of the reader. But examination of these notes will show that I have paid attention to certain socialist and anti-socialist texts above others, texts from a vast literature and chosen especially for the distinctive quality of their perceptions or follies.

In the body of the book I have had no choice but to use those unavoidable short-hand terms – including 'left' and 'right', and 'socialism' itself – whose problematical meanings, conventionally accepted, themselves demand serious question. Despite reservations about most of them (explained in Chapter 3 in regard to 'working class' and 'worker' for example) I have tried to avoid placing these terms in inverted commas, though I would prefer always to have done so. Indeed, only repeated qualification and explanation would properly justify their use at all in most cases; this is obviously not possible. But wherever unease has been too strong, I have had recourse to quotation marks, even if the irony which is often signalled by them can become irritating to the reader.

For the socialism of the Soviet Union and Eastern Europe, I have used the term 'real' socialism, rather than the perhaps more customary but more cumbersome term 'actually existing socialism'. The terms 'left' and 'left movement' I use to signify socialist activity in general, without discrimination as to the degree of its radicalism. That is, I use these terms in much the same way as the 'right' uses them: to categorize the whole spectrum of socialist thought and action. But where 'left' means merely the 'left wing' of a socialist party or movement, either I adopt the term 'left socialists' or the context will make my meaning plain.

This book is a fuller exposition of arguments first touched upon in *New Society* (12 November 1981), the *New Statesman* (2 July and

22 October 1982) and the *Guardian* (21 December 1981 and 20 June 1983). I am grateful to Paul Barker, Hugh Stephenson and Richard Gott, respectively, for encouraging the trial of my ideas, for which they can bear no responsibility. But if the genesis and development of these arguments were to be fully accounted for here, I would have far too many personal, intellectual and political debts to acknowledge. Above all, I am grateful to my wife for originally helping to form my ideas on, and sharing with me her understanding of, many of the subjects raised in this text; as well as my past and present students at Ruskin, the college of the labour movement, whom I have been trying to teach and who have been teaching me for nearly twenty years. I must also thank David McLellan and Leslie Macfarlane for help in tracing elusive references, Sybil Brooke for typing from my manuscript with exemplary skill and speed, and the staffs of the Bodleian, Social Studies, Nuffield and Ruskin libraries in Oxford for their assistance.

Oxford   D.S.

1   The Politics of Illusion

Illusion is a tenacious force in the life of any society, and political illusion, like any other work of the imagination, can exert a powerful attraction upon citizens tired in one way or another with the given. Indeed, like the utopian impulse, its first cousin, it can serve beneficent or innocent purposes. But where it gives rise to settled taboos and right or left limits-of-mind which inhibit political truth-telling, it becomes a menace as well as a consolation.[1]

Thus, to many on the right in Britain, the illusion of the nation's inherent majesty and prowess protects them from the truths of its economic decline to the status of second-rate power;[2] yet – with its *folie de grandeur* – it can plunge the rest of us into the South Atlantic adventures of a Drake, in the age of the atom and mass unemployment. Likewise, the left, in its own cloud of unknowing, is prevented from seeing that existing forms of socialist theory and practice are thoroughly exhausted; or that the accession to political power of the working class is not on 'the agenda' of Western capitalism, and least of all in Britain.

Such truths as these are necessarily unpalatable or shocking to those whose emotional and intellectual security, together with their political sense of direction, is sustained by wishful thinking, or whose time is occupied in shadow-boxing with phantoms. Free of illusion, few could doubt that it is in the unfolding of events, whose historical roots are deeply embedded, that Britain should now have become a net importer of manufactured goods for the first time since the industrial revolution; or that the political thinking of such large numbers of the Western working class, however constituted, should be anything but socialist, however defined.[3] Yet the assumptions, even if at bottom uneasy, of eventual industrial capitalist revival in Britain, on the one hand, and of a socialist renaissance in the working-class movement on the other – each of them equally implausible – remain in each case fixed poles of right and left orthodoxy. Indeed, left and right share

3

illusions about the latter, the one as hope, the other as
apprehension.

In general, however, it is the political inventions which reassure
that are most gratefully received by their respective partisans and
aficionados. 'Full employment', Anthony Crosland announced in
1956 in *The Future of Socialism,* 'has replaced depression.' Jarrow
'was condemned . . . to a decade without jobs', he wrote, because
of decisions taken by 'private monopoly bodies' to 'close down the
shipyard on which almost the whole town depended for its
livelihood . . . Today . . . capitalist business', he went on, 'has lost
this commanding position . . . Few firms . . . would even try to
repeat the Jarrow story', since 'traditional capitalist ruthlessness'
had 'largely disappeared'. Instead, 'capitalism itself' had been
'reformed almost out of recognition'. In consequence, a 'repetition
of 1931' was 'unthinkable [*sic*] . . . The national shift to the left,
with all its implications for the balance of power, may be accepted
as permanent.' But, 'of course, if unemployment . . . were to
reappear, then the full employment theme would provide all the
dynamic needed to sweep Labour back into power with an
unambiguous programme.'[4] Political illusion and political rhetoric, of left, right or centre, march in step together.

Yet, it is not as if the fact of the general weakness of the British
economy, whose symptoms began to appear a century ago, were
not known to the right, and the cause in broad outline not
understood; or as if the conservative political temper of the British
working-class movement were not a matter of historical record
and, for the left, of continuous dismay and *dis*illusion. The
problem is rather of those illusions on both right and left which
replace, and compensate for, this knowledge. Those of the right
are in general organized around the necessity for, and solace of,
stability and continuity; those of the left in general around the
notion of progress, whether revolutionary or reformist. Of course,
the ways in which such displacements of the empirical world, and
of its dense complexities, may be expressed vary greatly: they may
be timid or magisterial, pacific or violent, cautious or apocalyptic.
Moreover, concepts of 'continuity' on the one hand and 'progress'
on the other are themselves stereotypes, for the purpose of
argument; they exclude all those hybrid structures of illusion of
which middle-ground, or centrist, political fancies – oscillating
between a desire for, and a dislike of, change – depend.

Nevertheless, it is clear enough that left thought on our society and economy has at its optimistic heart the idea and promise of progress, in one form or another; and that this idea of progress has proceeded – alike through two world wars, the slump of the 1930s, 'decolonization' and the post-war 'reconstruction' – in tandem with the contraction of the national economy and the gradual reduction of the nation's political influence. It, rather than the unwelcome truths of economic and cultural stasis, has been the assumption on which socialist planning has rested; it has been the premise of left political endeavour, and it has been the point of departure for all but the most backward-looking and sentimental of contemporary socialist historians, whose golden age now lies in the past instead of the future.

Thus, Raymond Williams agreed (with Crosland) in *The Long Revolution* – its content as portentous and windy as its title – that 'the objectives for which many generations worked have been quite generally achieved'; and that 'our whole way of life is being profoundly affected by the progress and interaction of democracy and industry'.[5] That is, a 'long revolution' was under way, although towards what is unfortunately nowhere made clear and is made no clearer in his latest work, *Towards 2000*.[6] But it would be comprised, so much is plain, of 'democratic, industrial and cultural revolutions',[7] in which the onward and assured march of industrial development is seen, classically, as the precondition and promoter of the progressive democratization of our institutions, and of ever-rising standards of education and cultural achievement.

Though such a proposition (itself a specific cultural construct) was nonsense then, and is more plainly nonsense now, its well-established intellectual pedigree has suffered little from being founded on little more than decade-by-decade reiteration. One short step back to R.H. Tawney, for instance, brings us to the like argument that the gradual, and again progressive, widening of public provision was the 'natural consequence of the simultaneous development of an industrial civilization and of political democracy'.[8] And behind this lies Edwardian and Victorian Britain's utilitarian faith in 'industrialism'[9] and progress, a faith in general remarkably little disturbed by war, poverty, urban squalor and colonial subjugation; further back, stand Marx's own roaring 'forces of production' and the certitude of the proletarian revolution; and behind them the argument of Andrew Ure's *The Philosophy of Manufactures*, for example, with its eulogy of 'the factory system, replete with prodigies in mechanics and political economy, which promises, in its future growth, to become the great minister of civilization to the terraqueous globe'.[10]

Unfortunately, the prospect of 'machine-produced plenty' and of 'consumer utopias with luxury for all'[11] on the 'terraqueous globe' was and is as naive as the associated Marxist belief that the working class would itself become 'the great minister of civilization'. Yet, structured as they are around rooted ideological conceptions of progress, given institutionalized forms of expression, and with vested political and intellectual interests attached to them, such illusory beliefs have acquired great power to cast their shadows over other forms of perception. Against them, and the premises on which they rest, rival truths fight an uphill battle. That the long-term technological contraction of employment will never be made good by new forms of 'job creation'; or that the detritus of industrial development and decay has made an irrecoverable wasteland of large swathes of Britain; or that the vision of 'democratic wealth' was a mirage;[12] or that the working-class movement has neither the will nor the strength for a struggle for political power, must themselves struggle for attention, however obvious the nature of the empirical evidence which supports them.

No doubt, intellectual response both on left and right to this evidence, most of which has been truly evident for an unconscionably long time, now shows a deepening sense of dislocation. But the larger discomforts are assuaged, as ever, by alibis and scapegoats. Thus, on the one hand, a near terminally weakened trade unionism can be resurrected, by the levitational force of the right's illusion, so as to displace the true causes of our industrial disintegration.[13] On the other, the left's sense of media conspiracy has become as pathological as the right's mirror-image fantasies of subversion. And some may retreat, as they always have, to higher reaches of illusion, making a transcendental fetish of race or class or nation, while others may seek to blame history for delivering us in Britain with the 'wrong' kind of state, or the 'wrong' kind of working class, or whatever. Perhaps the *locus classicus* for this means of hiding from the real in the name of an ideal is Perry Anderson's 1965 essay on 'The Origins of the Present Crisis'. It was, certainly, an early response to the subterranean malaise of the left, of which the over-production of illusion has for twenty years been a symptom. But it is itself an intellectual subterfuge in which each successive event or process in British history is judged to have failed to come up to Marxist expectation. The inadequacy of the seventeenth-century English revolution was that it 'left almost the entire [political] structure intact'; the disappointment of the industrial revolution, that it created the first modern proletariat too soon – that is, before Marx's Marxism; the tragedy of the growth of empire, that it stifled the 'consciousness' of the domestic working class with its ill-gotten gains and national ardour; and the defect of victory in two world wars, that it helped to preserve the continuity (and complacency) of British institutions.[14]

That these are characteristically middle-class socialist compensations, themselves demanded by false intellectual premises, is a subject to which I will return in detail later. Moreover, through the dark web of invention of which they are a part, little of the even darker truth can be seen clearly; least of all that the whole 'socialist project', given the discredit which 'real' socialism has attracted, hangs by a thread of conviction which the discarding of such illusion would make even more tenuous. Indeed, all manner of increasingly complex equivocation is now required to preserve it, including – latterly – the silent replacement of the utopia of continuous (if uneven) economic progress with the utopia of continuously extended political 'participation'.[15] In fact, the present disarray of the left in Britain is in part attributable to those who have moved to this 'new' ground, but often without abandoning the illusions which inform older and more orthodox notions of the 'road to socialism'. Thus, the great majority of socialists still cling to the assumption that economic and industrial development, miraculously revived under Labour, will once more bring in its wake gradual social, educational and democratic progress; and that out of this progress an improved social order ('socialism') can little by little be constructed.

But it is precisely because the idea of socialism-as-gradual-social-progress – rather than the even more utopian socialism-as-working-class-seizure-and-command-of-the-means-of-production – is so general in our culture that Britain's economic and social decline is so politically serious for Labour. Continuous ameliorative change in the condition of the people, usually measured by levels of consumption, is after all predicated on the continuity of economic progress. In its absence, and given the recoil of working people from any real struggle for political or state power, this kind of socialism can only take refuge in more energetic and despairing forms of wishful thinking, or abandon the field altogether. 'The principles and barriers of an inherited kind', Raymond Williams once wrote – confidently surveying the future from within this web of illusion – 'will in any case go down. It is only a question of whether we [*sic*] replace them by the free play of the market, or by a public education designed to express and create the values of an educated democracy and a common culture.'[16] Whatever the latter option means, 'we' have never really come within reach of such values; and it seems to be too late now, as the tide of 'unwanted labour' rises. Yet without honest explanation of what went wrong with one set of socialist illusions – those based upon the the prospect of plenty and of socio-economic barriers 'in any case' coming down – a new wave of socialist wishful thinkers is now at work in the ideological market, offering us the political goods and services of 'democratic accountability', 'self-management' and 'participation', in part-exchange for the economic or consumer ones. Moreover, if economic decline historically portends not only a restriction of democratic rights, but also an enforced contraction in cultural and educational resources – as it ought, logically, to do for those who earlier connected them in a unison of progress – there has been a remarkable silence on the subject from the left, even though the right has won two successive elections by insisting precisely upon such a connection.

But these and other contemporary difficulties in launching effective socialist counter-arguments in a sea of ideological troubles are not really so perplexing. Indeed, to begin to measure it, we need only look to the intractability and scale of the social and economic developments with which socialist illusions and mirages have collided. Thus, the hieratic forms which advanced technical changes are in fact taking, but which 'ought' to have promoted democratic progress under the old socialist rubric, have not only generated huge waves of unemployment; they would be incapable of being rendered democratic even under conditions of 'workers' power'. In addition, the evolution of the 'labour market' and changes in the division of labour (quite apart from the effect of cross-class political hostility to the trade unions) are helping to decompose rather than to develop the forces of labour organization.[17] Again, unemployment, most present forms of which are permanent and 'privatized'[18] by welfare, undermines and does not enhance social cohesion; while the world of manual workers – the basis of the old labour order – is atrophying, with nothing of its like to replace it. And after 200 years (at least) of capitalist industrialization in Britain, in which at no point has there been a trial of strength for political power between capital and labour, the steady contraction of Britain's manufacturing industry has arguably set the seal on such a prospect.

There are naturally very few on the left, 'gradualists' included, who can face up to this. In large part, this is because the human beings whose interests socialism and the labour movement set out to prosper are still there, with many of their needs and aspirations unanswered, and their latent and real skills – though rapidly diminishing in range – squandered. Moreover, the fond belief still remains general on the left that some turning of the economic tide, or the return of a Labour government under a new leader, or the starting of a new Labour newspaper, or even withdrawal from the Common Market, will serve to revive the socialist project with the 'mass' support of working people. Even those on the left who know, but do not say, that full employment and unemployment, trade union strength and trade union weakness, boom and slump, peace and war, have made no fundamental difference to the long-term debilitation in the West of socialist theory, and the regression of its prospects in practice, hang on for dear life to such notions. It is no wonder, either, that the necessary redefinition in each historical period of what is meant by 'left' and 'right', by 'democratic' and 'progressive', and by the term 'socialist' itself is not yet seen to be urgent. Instead, the 'challenge from the right' and the 'weakness of the left' are held to be the consequence of 'the current crisis', whose end will restore strength to the trade unions, Labour to power, and (for some) reactivate the class struggle.

This perspective is trivial. The world-wide 'recomposition' of capital – and of classes and electorates – the transformation of the 'old machine and "smoke-stack" industries',[19] the highly-concentrated development of new micro-electronic methods of production-control and control-over-knowledge, and the 'state-supported quiet desperation of the growing surfeit of populations'[20] – most of these phenomena not confined to the capitalist system – beggar such analysis. Indeed, traditional forms of industrial manufacturing and mass production, where labour has been strongest and Labour recruited its forces,[21] can never be resumed. And, likewise, the left's equally traditional forms of social and economic understanding of this evolution – Marxist forms included, as I shall argue later – have run out of steam, equally outmoded. Similarly, growing scarcity of personal resource, of living space, of job opportunities and of political and technical knowledge has changed the terms on which socialist discourse, if it is to continue at all, must be conducted. In fact, in the mid-1960s it was already long out of date, and merely to foster old illusion in Britain, to argue that we were living in an 'expanding' culture.[22] Instead, under the pressures of an economic and social decline which have promoted a sharpening neither of class conflict nor of the acuity of the left's analytical responses to what is actually happening, we have reached a new stage of our national history without the intellectual means, on left or right, to order and encompass it.

A large part of the reason for this on the left is that it is too bitter a matter to reject, as the premise of the argument, that the whole (teleological) notion of the 'long revolution' is false; that the prospect of a progressive humanization of the social order by means of a democratic expansion of wealth and culture is a phantasmagoria; and that fear of unemployment, or any other feature of the economic crisis, is a wholly inadequate explanation for the fact that the readiness and will of the working-class movement to defend its own basic democratic rights has faded. Meanwhile, the alleged skill and subtlety with which the British ruling class manages its 'hegemony', and 'contains' latent class pressures against it, has served for fifty years, in one 'sophisticated' form or another, as an intellectual alibi of last resort for the defeat of middle-class socialist expectations of working people.[23] As for the strident exhortation which seeks to arouse flagging working-class spirits against their wills and choices, it merely serves to compound all our problems; in the rhetorical din of it, the possibility of political ratiocination vanishes.

Rather, what has to be grasped is that the various historical turning-points in the prospects for socialism, of one kind and another, have usually passed by long before most socialists in each era, including Marx, have been able to perceive the true nature of the social and economic changes taking place around them. Thus, in every phase of our social and economic development, successive illusions, whether revolutionary or reformist, have given way too late to a realistic appraisal, always in retrospect, of their errors of judgement: whether about the temper and mood of the working class, the commonest form of error, or about the feasibility of this or that socialist programme. From, say, the socialism of a 'socialist workers' commonwealth' – the prospects for which can be held to have passed with the defeat of Owenism in 1840[24] – to the socialism of full employment and widening public provision still being advocated in the present period, the same kind of anachronism has dogged socialist footsteps. Indeed, changes in the technical division of labour, or changes in the nature of the means of production, or sociological and cultural changes in the class composition, and 'consciousness' of the people, have constantly outpaced the romantic but slow-thinking socialist utopian, as well as the 'hard-headed' yet cautious gradualist who always believes that he has his finger on the pulse of the nation.

Moreover, as I shall argue later, middle-class socialist thinkers have consistently misjudged the consequences, positive and negative, of the development of the industrial capitalist system on working people. In particular, the latter have not needed to have their own experiences 'explained' to them by socialist intellectuals, whether Marxist or any other. The effects of 200 years of employment (and unemployment) in factory capitalism have been hated, adapted to and welcomed in ways which have not fitted well – or sometimes at all – into the matrix of socialist theory and practice; and least of all into orthodox socialist and Marxist notions of class, class consciousness and class organization, many of which are based upon middle-class fictions quite remote from actual working-class experience. Indeed, so extensive now is the disjunction between them that it is arguably beyond the reach of the left to arrive at an illusion-free redefinition at all of what 'democracy' or 'progress', let alone 'socialism', can mean in such circumstances; circumstances which do not now allow the left, if they ever did, any unproblematical equation between 'socialism' and what the (usually) middle-class intellectual perceives to be 'working-class interests'.

Instead, setting aside as *prima facie* inadequate, or wrong, elaborate alibi explanations for the long failure of socialist expectations in our culture – whether explanations of our historical misfortunes, of the vice-like grip of ruling-class 'hegemony', or (most commonly now) of conspiracy by 'the media' – we must also ask in what other ways we might account for the strange fate of the socialist project in the home of the industrial revolution. How is it, in more than a century and a half of wrecked hopes, that the working class, or at least the overwhelming majority of it, has not raised recognizable socialist objections to 'the way things are' in a capitalist society? And even where it has, why has it not done so very often, or been unwilling to act for very long upon those objections? Could there not be, also *prima facie*, something seriously wrong in our times too, and growing wronger, with the 'socialist alternative' – however formulated – which disables, and perhaps deservedly disables, all those expectations to which I referred earlier?

After all, in the current twenty-year phase of British socialist illusion and disillusion, up to and including the 1983 general election, there has been a steady falling away of support among *Labour* voters, let alone among the millions of others, for basic socialist principles, as presently understood.[25] The appeal, for example, of more public ownership, or of lower military spending, or even of the defence of the existing rights of trade unions, has been fading. Indeed, by 1983, it had reached the point where there seemed to be large minorities, and even substantial majorities, among *Labour* voters in favour of stricter laws to regulate the activities of trade unions, in favour of the reduction of supplementary benefit to strikers, and in favour of giving council house tenants the right to purchase; that is, in favour of key *Tory* policy objectives. Even on issues like reducing income tax for the higher paid, or selling off parts of state-owned industries, it has appeared that opinion is more or less evenly divided for and against them among *Labour* voters. So that even though it may be true that 'there is . . . no inevitable . . . trend towards a more Conservative working class',[26] it seems to be even more true that, especially among working people, whether they vote Labour or not, and whether Labour is in or out of office, there has been a marked refusal of political sympathy – noted since the mid-1960s – for most of the socialist notions which have been incorporated in the programmes of the Labour Party.

For the purposes of this argument, these are more important indices than, say, that the Labour Party has only one quarter of the number of members of the National Trust;[27] or that the average share of the constituency vote which went to Labour in the 1983 election was the lowest since the party was founded, or that the Labour Party in 1983 could not claim even to *be* the party of the working class, in so far as 'the working class has ceased to be largely Labour',[28] splitting its vote in three ways, with only 38 per cent of manual workers voting Labour, and coming third among white-collar trade union voters. Shifts and trends of judgement about socialist policy, particularly if such trends are deep-seated, are more important than mere election statistics, since there is always the possibility – on the psephologist's swings and roundabouts – of a turn in electoral fortunes. But a working-class political rejection, albeit complex and very disparately composed, which in its implications seriously questions the legitimacy of the socialist alternative – even in its attenuated 'social democratic' form – is a different matter. That is, it not only poses a problem which far transcends, especially in the longer term, the more local issue of the electoral vicissitudes of the Labour Party, but also challenges left socialists in ways which cannot be evaded with feints into further illusion.[29]

This is because the general problems of socialism and the socialist alternative, and the problems of the Labour Party, are deeply connected; even if pure cant should insist that 'the Labour Party . . . is not the carrier of a socialist ideology. It is not, in fact, in any meaningful sense whatever a socialist party.'[30] Yet fifty years and more of armchair criticism of the Labour Party – sometimes on the part of the idly privileged, who have subsequently sought to join it – have rightly throughout been arguments about socialism. And they have been equally rightly directed at the only 'mass' party of the working class that there has ever been, or now will be, in Britain. Indeed, those who have castigated the Labour Party since its foundation for 'opportunism', or 'immobilism', or 'Fabianism', or 'revisionism', or whatever, have all along known and admitted it, if only in private. More confusingly, the main issue behind the criticism of the Labour Party for its political failures, the very force of the criticism has itself served to obscure: namely, that it is yet another intellectual alibi for the fact that the working-class movement, with or without the aid of Marxists, has never really considered itself a serious oppositional force to the capitalist state, and least of all in our present period. Labour's difficulties as a party, the failure of Marxism to take root in the political culture, and the general debility of the socialist project in all its British variants, are part of a common problem. The more or less equivalent exchanges of recrimination between the various sectors of the socialist movement which have punctuated its history since the beginning are themselves evidence of it.

In addition, all the political and ideological crises which have plagued the international socialist and communist movements – crises of socialist definition, crises of militarism and war, crises promoted by the negative impact of 'real' socialism, current crises in the socialist sense of direction – have all been played out inside the Labour Party, in one way or another. It may be true, as I shall show, that the task of formulating a socialist programme has been historically subjected to peculiarly acute difficulties in the Labour Party. But it is not *sui generis* for all that. It bears the same political stigmata of socialist success and failure as every other Western socialist party, including those parties which are 'more' socialist; even if it has suffered some unique wounds, unerringly self-inflicted.

Thus the question of whether socialism is the replacement of the 'free market' by the nationalization of the means of production, the social control of investment and generalized state planning; whether it is workers' self-management and libertarian anti-statism; whether it is no more than the enlightened Benthamism of the public school liberal; whether it is capitalism plus the National Health Service; or whether it is an egalitarian moral aspiration, a fraternal ethic and the construction of the new Jerusalem, has bewildered and divided the Labour Party, and its most engaged followers, in the best socialist tradition.[31] Riven in a dozen directions, it contains those who are in essence reconciled to capitalism, and those who are not; those who, if capitalism were 'reformed', could become reconciled to it, and those who could not; and those who, like Anthony Crosland, do not think we live in a capitalist system in the first place. For some, socialism is confined to the widening of opportunity, the redressing of misfortune, 'a broad human movement on behalf of the bottom dog',[32] and the defence of welfare; for others, it means a fundamental reordering of society and the 'comprehensive direction of the social process'.[33] For some it is a 'commitment to production, liberty, care and peace';[34] to others, 'disarmament, devolution, abolition of the Lords and subsidized fares on the buses'.[35] In the Labour Party, as in every other Western socialist organization, there are those whose utopia is a classless social order, and others whose socialism is predicated on the 'mixed economy' and a plural political system.

At their most elementary (and incoherent) theoretical level, these disparate beliefs constitute an internally irreconcilable chaos. Yet many of them increasingly have their correlatives even within Marxist parties and grouplets – or provoke their fragmentation. Indeed, they provide the most basic evidence that it is the nature of the 'socialist alternative' itself, and not the inadequate 'consciousness' of working people, to which the left must turn its attention if it wishes to understand the reasons for its own ideological and political failures, as economic and social crisis deepens. For the inevitable consequence of this disarray of essential theory and purpose is publicly visible confusions and contradictions at the level of political practice. The attempt to shrug off these difficulties, as those of a 'broad church', or, as G.D.H. Cole put it, those of a 'socialism almost without doctrines' and 'so undefined in its doctrinal basis as to make recruits readily among persons of quite different types',[36] merely makes matters worse. Indeed, it is this which, *inter alia*, has latterly invited and earned political defeats at the hands of an opponent who has ridden head-on into its divided and floundering ranks.

And yet in this ideological mêlée of unhorsed socialist riders and riderless socialist horses, trampling their own ground into a morass – unless or until (temporarily) curbed by a new leader – it is the ambivalence and indefensibility of fundamental Labour positions, many of them thoroughly socialist, which become always more obvious. Their pedigree is also a pure one. It was Eleanor Marx who, in 1891, wittily described the Fabians as 'middle-class folk too honest to be contented with the present conditions of society; too educated to throw in their lot with the Salvation Army; [and] too superior to identify themselves wholly with the profane vulgar.'[37] The ambiguities to which these remarks point are plainly crippling; understood for a century, they are as crippling as ever, yet overlaid by unrepentant illusion. On another flank, to choose at random, Engels, from 1890 onwards, was enthusiastically implicated in the 'reformism' of electoral politics; in 1893 he even described the election of socialists to the British, French and German Parliaments as a 'landmark in world history'.[38] It was nothing of the kind. But that a revolutionary should have thought and said so itself points into the depths of an irresolvable socialist contradiction.

There are many others from the sublime to the ridiculous, but all of them in their own ways crucial. There is the brute fact, for example, that socialism as a fundamental reordering and transformation of the capitalist system cannot possibly come about by constitutional and democratic methods. Yet it is those methods alone which most socialists – and certainly nearly all Labour voters – are prepared to countenance.[39] The result of this dilemma is, as ever, stasis and recrimination, particularly in times of economic crisis. Moreover, equally obvious (and in its own way ludicrous), the amount of political freedom which could or would be permitted to reformist socialists for the purposes of controlling private enterprise and interfering with the market, 'must be severely limited in a capitalist system'.[40] In consequence, those socialists who have no intention whatever – and make their lack of intention plain – of proceeding to the logical political conclusion of their tentative acts of market restraint, are disarmed in advance. Yet they must also feign political outrage at the inevitable (and, by their own rights, legitimate) acts of self-defence by the vested interests they have half-heartedly threatened. Indeed, it is court masque, not class struggle; in which such socialists must cry foul at the first signs of the very counter-action by their more 'class-conscious' opponents which they themselves have provoked and anticipated.

This kind of organic political disability is the result of an ambivalence of purpose which cannot be blamed on the vacillation or frailty of individuals. It is, rather, the result of irreconcilable aspirations, whose irreconcilability has multiplied over time rather than diminished. Thus, we can think straightaway of another triple incompatibility: of socialism-as-a-social-ethic of brotherhood, as service and the husbanding of resources, with socialism-as-the-good-life, rising standards of living and economic equality founded on material well-being, and of both with the miasmas created by 'real' socialism. Even the moral basis of the socialist impulse is a battleground, condemned and mocked as it often is by Marxists as mere 'bourgeois' sentiment, or as 'only [sic] . . . a moral crusade propelled by emotions of outrage at injustice and suffering'.[41]

Thus, the 'rainbow-light called "socialism" '[42] itself contains all the colours of the moral spectrum: as self-denying struggle against the evils of competition, as the solidarity of the exploited, as uneasy middle-class altruism, or as more public spending on the welfare system – and with its own pantheon of British *avatars* and heroes, from Robin Hood to Keir Hardie, Christian the Pilgrim to Anthony Crosland. Not surprisingly, there is a precarious relationship between, say, middle-class socialist aspiration compensating for its privileges and/or for inherited moral indifference on the one hand, and the righteous anger, however repressed, of its working-class victims on the other. So there is, too, between the heroic passion for a heavenly justice on the one hand, and the 'down to earth' or 'common-sense' desire – often equally moral – to do for others what is 'practical and possible' under the circumstances, on the other. Though these particular moralities are not entirely irreconcilable, there is tension and unease in them also, as when Labour practice shows its Janus-face, aspiring high and achieving little. It was Tawney who described the 'impulse behind the [Labour] movement' as 'obstinately and unashamedly ethical'.[43] But the bluff approval of the Labour Party's politics at its foundation in 1918 for containing 'a version of socialism . . . not too sublime to be turned into prosaic sections, sub-sections and schedules of Acts of Parliament'[44] was Tawney's also.

This form of a familiar ambiguity of purpose is relatively minor, and can be posed much more sharply. For instance, if socialism is a 'moral crusade', as some deeply believe, how can it be fought with, say, import controls, or an expansion of the bureaucracies of the public sector, or the block vote of the trade unions? Or, worse, if the labour movement should lose its claim to represent a traditional moral majority in society – that of the employed working class, the unemployed, the old, the poor, the badly-treated and disadvantaged – on what popular basis, and on what ideological imperative, would the politics of socialism-as-moral-crusade then rest? Hitherto, Labour's orthodox reformist version of the socialist alternative, with its particular moral history and popular support, has not had to face the possibility of political recession on this scale, though in 1984 it has appeared to be at hand. Certainly, in a 'broad church' with a shrinking congregation, Labour's appeal would begin to echo with increasing hollowness. Indeed, it would start to face some of the same intellectually ruinous dilemmas as have now driven Marxism and Marxists to the wall in Britain. In the last depression of the 1930s, the vigour of Marxist counter-analysis made a considerable impact on socialist and Labour Party thinking, and further afield on informed public opinion also. Fifty years later, the same cannot be said, despite contemporary Marxist illusion to the contrary. Instead, three decades of destructive political sectarianism, the increasing abstruseness and irrelevance of Marxist analyses, and romanticizing illusions about the working class – whether about the heroic class struggles of the past, the present 'balance of forces' or the political prospects of socialism in the future – have justly taken a disastrous toll of Marxism's intellectual reputation. And from it, we can see how severe would be the consequences for the Labour Party of a political rejection on a similar scale to that suffered by Marxism, on the part of the constituency it is ostensibly serving.

For eventually what happens is plain from the Marxist experience, as political isolation and intellectual illusion proceed together. The minority, and the exceptional cases, tragically come to be mistaken – in Marxist history of the working class, for example – for the majority and the general rule. (The 'silent majority' is not, and never has been, a figment of the right-wing imagination.) Likewise, Marxist intellectual privatization, the consequence and further cause of political isolation, has incorrigibly given rise to equally private languages, incomprehensible to outsiders. Even where exceptionally it does not, the inhabiting of an unreal world of fancy makes it increasingly difficult to call real things by their real names. The authentic vocabulary of a truly human creation becomes a matter of intellectual embarrassment, and withers with inhibition; the skills of language and the practical methods required to communicate plain truths about the world atrophy; essential moral and political questions as to means and ends – questions of ultimate purpose – are displaced by strenuous intellectual competition, within a closed and airless space into which real human beings can no longer be admitted. The tragedy of this kind of socialist endeavour, of Marxist ink spilled to no purpose, has veritably consumed the last decades. Even the question *'cui bono?'* comes to be rarely asked, let alone answered. Behind all this, there has been a justifiable Marxist desperation which has for long afflicted the Labour Party too, though in different and less cerebral ways. It has been based, for decades, on the impossibility of reconciling belief with discovery: the dreaming *belief* that socialism is, in some sense, immanent in history and that the working class is its bearer, and the nightmare *discovery* – awesome for any Marxist – that capitalism, despite (because of?) its crises, has not created, and is not creating, the conditions for its own transformation. For the socialist gradualist, although he/she does not really seek the transcending of capitalism, the problem is no less severe. 'Content to administer the existing mixed economies in a liberal spirit', as Eric Hobsbawm has described it, 'the old Social Democratic parties', like the Labour Party, 'now find that few such economies are still prosperous enough to allow them to do even this . . . It is by no means clear what else they aim to do.'[45] The answer must be, very little.

What has gone wrong for the socialist alternative, left, right and centre – for their real prospects and illusions alike – is thus very serious indeed. Nor is it just a simple matter of the defeat of socialist expectation, with which socialists, in particular Marxists, have lived and died for a long time. After all, it was in August 1871 that a correspondent of the *New York Herald* asked 'Dr Marx': 'Do you expect to succeed soon in England?' 'Sooner', he replied, 'than in any other country.'[46] In May 1925, Trotsky, fifty-four years of waiting later, wrote that 'Britain is heading at full speed into an epoch of great revolutionary upheavals . . . The contradictions undermining Britain's social organism will inevitably intensify . . . it ['upheaval'] will be measured in terms of years . . . at the utmost in terms of five years, not at all by decades.' (For good measure, he added: 'we Marxians understand the tempo of development of the British Labour movement, and foresee its morrow . . .'.[47]) Fifty-nine years later still, the 'social organism' is still not 'undermined', but in the same stasis as it was in 1925; or in 1871, for that matter.

No, the dilemma is much more fundamental and stands, as it has for a century, at the very heart of socialist confusions. To simplify, it is this: do we believe that capitalist crisis in general promotes socialist consciousness and endeavour, and that capitalist prosperity in general impedes it? Or do we believe the exact opposite? And on the basis of which belief do we act, or fail to act? Damagingly, Marx himself, like his successors, faced both ways on the question. In the 1848 *Communist Manifesto*, written with British capitalism most in mind, he (and Engels) conflated the contradiction of capitalist wealth creation and proletarian pauperization into an optimism that, out of this contradiction, the birth of revolution was not merely certain but imminent.[48] Yet only two years later, composing his *Class Struggles in France* with the same evidence in hand, and referring specifically to England, what was to become a chronic doubt receives its first expression in the socialist canon. 'With this general prosperity', he writes, 'in which the productive forces of bourgeois society develop as luxuriantly as is at all possible within bourgeois relationships, there can be no talk of a real revolution.'[49]

We can follow this fissure, essentially one between illusion and reality, through to Trotsky. 'Britain is heading for revolution', he wrote in the mid-1920s, *because* she has entered the epoch of capitalist decline'; and, 'everything points to the further intensification and deepening of those difficulties through which Britain is at present passing, and *therefore* to a further quickening of the tempo of her revolutionary development'. Yet, only a few pages earlier, Trotsky had shown socialist judgement's other face, that of deep doubt – though masked – on the relation between capitalist crisis and socialist prospects: 'the decomposition of British capitalism *inevitably* leads to the impotence of the trade unions.'[50] The contradiction is veiled by reference only to the trade unions. But the contradiction remains, since neither in socialist theory nor in socialist practice can the question of the strength of the trade unions be severed from the question of the strength of the workers' movement as a whole.

Moreover, to trace this fundamental (and just) doubt down to the present is to confront an impossible proposition for many socialists: that both the power and the well-being – as the right insists – of the labour movement are directly tied to the health of capital. Behind the dismay of socialists, Marxists in particular, at the silence of the working class in two world capitalist crises, there lurks the awareness that socialist programmes, of all colours, as means of working-class escape from capitalist disorders have foundered in the very periods of their seemingly most obvious necessity. But few on the left dare pursue to their end the political implications of the premise that when capital sickens so does labour – jobs, organization and socialist convictions together. Instead, the existence of the welfare system, the role of the media, and the demoralization of unemployment serve, wholly characteristically, as today's alibis for the latest defeats of expectation.

Of course, it is clear that most socialist gradualists find it much easier than Marxists do to look away from the implications of their dilemmas. They can cheerfully take the view, say, that 'the strength of the labour movement and the welfare of those it represents depend on full employment'[51] without acknowledging that, in the absence of any desire to get rid of or even challenge the capitalist system, the ultimate logic of their politics must be that of seeking to advance the prosperity of capital in the interests of labour.[52] There is moreover no escape, except by dishonestly fudging the issues, from all the consequences of this position, including the rejection of strikes which, by damaging capital, also damage labour. It is precisely at this point, a point which is broadening in its catchment area, that right-wing socialists, particularly in the trade union movement, hold the same views as their anti-socialist political opponents. But it is not necessary to go so far over to the right among socialists to discover arguments which make a logical nonsense of the socialist case. To take one example: in a *New Left Review* article on the 'transition to socialism', we find the view that 'it is just not possible to strengthen the competitive position of national capitalism and the power of the labour movement simultaneously'.[53] If this is so, its logic points the way directly into the Tory Party.

Obviously, the collapse of assurance in the continuity of progress, whether as the 'expansion of culture' or as the development of the 'forces of production', is destined to bring all those versions of the socialist alternative which were (often silently) predicated upon it to a similar confusion. The benevolent idea of socialism-as-gradual-social-development or as 'the march of events, guaranteed by the ordinary machinery of democracy' – the kind of notion lampooned by Marxists[54] – depends, intellectually and politically, upon there being a sufficient forward momentum in the social and economic process to promote such socialist purpose. In its absence, the socialist gradualist must embarrassingly wait around, devising alternative strategies on paper while secretly hoping for the capitalist economy to revive in precisely the same way as his political opponents. But equally, Marxists too must hang on – increasingly weighed down by the kind of doubts I have discussed – hoping for further, and even catastrophic, depression of the world economy, the exacerbation of capitalist contradiction, the intensification of class struggle, and a Messianic redemption which would emerge from the social storm like Botticelli's Venus emerging from the waters.

Like Edouard Bernstein's half a century before him, Crosland's chosen means of escape from the socialist dilemma – by insisting that capitalism has already been transcended – has once more been sealed off by the scale of the current economic crisis. His confident belief in the mid-1950s that we no longer lived in a capitalist society at all, and that socialism could therefore abandon its 'largely economic orientation' and instead 'direct [its] energies into more fruitful and idealistic channels', has been

hard hit by the events of the real world, which cannot be
substituted for by wishful thinking. The return of mass unemployment and of basic forms of hardship for millions has reduced to
ashes his socialist prospectus for the 'cultivation of leisure, beauty,
grace, gaiety, excitement' and 'all the proper pursuits, whether
elevated, vulgar or eccentric, which contribute to the varied fabric
of a full private and family life'.[55] Here the dilemma I have touched
upon presents itself at its clearest. This is a 'socialism for good
times',[56] in which capitalist economic growth turns out to be the
necessary (and embarrassing) precondition for the achievement
of socialist objectives; in particular, of its aims to enhance equality
of opportunity, redistribute income and wealth, and raise the
standard of living.

But it is not only Crosland's bland expectations which time and
event have refuted. Tawney, for example, held that 'the structure
and mechanism of industry'[57] in Britain had been decisively
transformed by nationalization; in 1949, he quite clearly believed
that though Labour would 'doubtless commit its own blunders',
the prospects for socialism (as he understood it) were set fair in
Britain. At the worst, there might be 'errors . . . in the selection of
services to be transferred to public ownership'; or 'unsuitable
forms of organization' would be adopted; or Labour might be
'tempted . . . to pander to popular tastes' in 'developing its social
services'. Indeed, Tawney felt, it could well be that 'a generation
must elapse before a cordial partnership between the public
bodies responsible for the conduct of a nationalized industry and
the employees in them . . . can successfully be established'. Both
the accent and the assurance, at this distance, seem Edwardian;
the 'proper attitude' to these matters, Tawney wrote, is 'to keep an
open mind'.[58] What he plainly did not envisage is that the whole
caboodle of this and other kinds of socialist aspiration would come
so quickly to challenge and confusion. It is not simply that only
two years after those words were published, Labour was defeated
and Churchill was back in office; rather, that after three complex
decades of decline in political support among the intended
beneficiaries of precisely those once confidently-announced programmes, we can see from today's vantage-point that the whole
enterprise was never secure.

The growing awareness among socialists of every kind that
there is no necessary connection at all between, for example, the
forms of public ownership adopted in Britain from 1945 onwards

and any form of socialism worth having, has served to multiply every dilemma. Even if 'buying the economy from the capitalists, piece by piece, until it [is] all state owned, and therefore all socialist'[59] was always a foolish notion, the results of having attempted in part to do it are still painfully with us. Responses to it vary. Some, like Raymond Williams, have struck empty poses: the nationalized industries 'have so deeply damaged any alternative principle in the economy, as to have emptied British socialism of any [sic] effective meaning'.[60] Others, like Tony Benn, have been no more circumspect – 'the nationalized industries have been a great disappointment . . . [They] have altogether [sic] failed to realize the hopes of those who campaigned for public ownership.'[61] Indeed, for very many socialists, their disrepute, whether as inefficient state bureaucracies, or (for Marxists) as instruments of 'state capitalism' in which there has been no fundamental change in the 'relations of production', has been an increasing burden to socialist arguments, however just, against their privatization.

Weighed down by other (seemingly) related political albatrosses – such as the incubus of guilt-by-association with the state socialism of Eastern Europe and the Soviet Union – it is not surprising that the socialist alternative is now on its ideological knees. No less surprising is that, in reaction, some socialists have been provoked to new levels of political stridency, and intellectual quackery, to rescue what seems for good reason a desperate situation. One such essentially compensatory line of argument, which I will discuss in more detail later, is now being promoted by the over-driven rhetoric of socialism-as-self-government; or, in Tony Benn's words, of 'the winning of democratic control . . . on a majestic scale', so that the people can 'take control of their own destinies'.[62] Under the pressure of a despairing excess, induced by the socialist (and not just the economic) crisis, Britain even becomes the 'last colony in the British Empire', which faces – and requires – nothing less than a 'national liberation struggle'.[63]

In fact, Benn's political bark is much worse than his bite. For behind the braggadocio is an old familiar and worthy socialism-of-Christian-virtue, 'decent human values' and social justice.[64] It is the deeper political ambivalences, magnified versions of some of those I have already mentioned, which are much more important. It is not simply that the people's 'taking control for themselves' can quickly become – in alternative statements – 'political power shared more widely',[65] an entirely different notion; but that, astoundingly, Britain as the 'last colony' becomes, elsewhere, so free that 'most people in the world would give their eye teeth to have the rights we have won'.[66] If this is so, the need for the 'majestic winning of democratic control' is simply hot air, and the whole prospectus an ideological South Sea bubble. Yet this kind of fundamental intellectual incoherence has spread widely as social-ist desperation has developed. To take another example at random: a 'radical strategy for Britain's future', prepared in 1981 by Francis Cripps, John Griffith, Peter Townsend and others, similarly calls, on page 18, for the 'liberation of Britain by a Labour Government'; but sixty pages later is declaring that 'we are fortunate to live in one of the more free societies in the world today'.[67]

At the very least, this reflects a disabling degree of political muddle, in which realism and illusion jostle uncomfortably together. Here, socialist bewilderment is centred – or fails to centre itself – upon the issue of whether Britain is or is not democratic, and thus whether democracy is to be restored, transformed or defended. Indeed, in one and the same socialist argument, it is possible to find the radical urge to transcend, and the conservative desire to defend, the *status quo* woven inextricably together; the call for 'strong government to protect us' combined with that for the maximum 'decentralization of power';[68] and the will to see the people 'take control for themselves' in a 'liberation of Britain', with a belief that it is 'of central importance for the maintenance of confidence in our system of government that [the] process of . . . social change can be made to work effectively' – the first a revolutionary call to arms, the second a straightforward utilitarian nostrum, and to be found within a few pages of each other in Benn's *Arguments for Democracy*.'[69]

Yet it is from within precisely such fundamental contradictions among left socialists that the critique of Labour 'revisionism', 'corporatism' and so forth are directed at others. According to it, moreover, a weakened commitment to the very ideas which Labour voters reject is attributed with 'undermining the credibil-ity of . . . socialist values and the party itself'.[70] In consequence, a further ambiguity, equally ruinous, dogs the critics. Is the Labour Party socialist or not? The answer, expectedly, is that it is and it isn't. On the one hand, it is socialist both in having had socialist aims *ab initio* and in having latterly 'rediscovered' them; on the other hand, 'the link between the Labour Party and socialism is so tenuous' that a 'clear socialist alternative' is constantly called for.[71] The Labour Party manages thus to be both damagingly 'revisionist' and still socialist; we can even find that 'it has not changed',[72] despite often simultaneous argument to the contrary.

In the teeth of the evidence, heroic illusion can discern the 'spirit of Labour reborn' even in the severest political recession; the working class can be held to be 'represented by no other party';[73] and 'winning the working class to socialism' can still be inscribed on the ideological orders of the day, when neither the class nor its destination can be known and spoken of in such simplistic terms any longer. It is, in fact, a Quixotic world of large gesture and timid action, in which poor Rosinante, knackered, becomes in the inflamed imagination a white and handsomely-caparisoned charger. Such invention can – but only with the pen and on the platform – transform weakness into strength; or rhetorically turn defeat into victory with mere heroics; and make of every minor event a disaster or a triumph. It also represents a classical escape from real socialist dilemma into the oratory of mind over the obstinacies of matter.

However, since Tony Benn, for example, is not a Marxist, his free-floating (and often wild) form of utopianism is relatively little troubled by, or anchored in, beliefs in some kind of historical 'trajectory' inscribed in the progress of events themselves, and which is bearing us through crisis towards a socialist haven. But those Marxists, albeit shrinking in number, who are beholden to an intellectual absolutism which must ultimately envisage a society without a state or a market, are inescapably plagued by the need to 'explain', or explain away, the socialism-of-the-Soviet Union. Indeed, whether it is 'state socialist', a 'deformed workers' state', 'social imperialist' or whatever, is more than an intellectual predicament. However defined (or disavowed), its political example has served to crush under its weight the Western socialist alternative in all its variants; an ideological effect for which the alibi of media conspiracy is a wholly insufficient explanation. In consequence, even at the relatively insignificant level of Marxist theory, the labyrinth, or web, of complexities created by decades of old left and new left rationalization for practical political failure – East and West – itself now defeats summary or description.

But it is at the point of political collision between the idea of socialism as a new historical stage of human development, and

public knowledge of the actual world of 'real' socialism, that the
socialist project is most obviously threatened with ideological
catastrophe. Such a concept of socialism, as long as it was not yet
realized – or not yet claimed to be realized – for nearly a century
possessed the immunity from challenge by the humdrum which
all transcendental notions about a 'morally alternative future to
the present'[74] deserve to possess. However, once the ideal socialist
virtues of 'harmony, association, community and co-operation'
came to be looked for, as in the case of the Soviet Union, in the
actual and empirically verifiable outcome of a generation of
bloodshed, sacrifice and struggle, the human wilderness which
was found instead – indices of real economic progress notwithstanding – broke the heart of the socialist movement. Instead of
the transformation of capitalism's way of life, there was only its
attempted reproduction, in inferior copy; instead of the mastery of
industrialism, mastery by it; instead of a model for emulation, the
darkest political shadows thrown across the path of Western
socialist prospects.

To deal with it, illusion was once more driven to take flight to
the topmost boughs of fancy, while everything from historical
circumstance to the aberration of individuals was invoked in
explanation. Alternatively, it could be held that socialism, 'in its
full critical and philosophical sense – as the realm of freedom, the
final [sic] triumph of man over necessity and alienation'[75] – had
not remotely been realized in the Soviet Union or any other
socialist country. Nevertheless, as late as 1965, Perry Anderson
could argue that 'in a minimally-ideal [sic] sense, these countries
are socialist . . . their economies [sic] are socially and not privately
appropriated, and the ideology which regulates their operation is
a socialist one . . . The Russian Revolution and all that follows
from it forms part – an immense part – of the common heritage of
the whole socialist movement. It cannot be renounced or evaded
by any working class party in Europe.'[76] But this in turn is the very
reason, among others, which has made it increasingly difficult for
the Western socialist movement to sustain and legitimize its
domestic opposition to capitalist inequalities and unfreedoms;
able only to turn its back, stand on its head, shut its eyes or do the
splits when faced with the socialism-of-the-Soviet Union.
Moreover, the form of certain internal polemics and upheavals
in the world of 'real' socialism has merely confounded Western
socialist confusion. Thus, in their advocacy of wider political

democracy, or a multi-party system, or independent trade unions, or the reintroduction of market incentives, some, have shakingly seemed to come round – after a long historical detour – to the espousal of what recognizably approaches the mixed economy and its liberal democratic institutions, yet (most often) still in the name of socialism and workers' power.[77]

Such convergence, far from confirming the validity of non-Marxist socialist theory and practice, has added to the left's ideological difficulties in general, since it has served to strengthen the right's ironic or crusading objections to the whole socialist project. But that Marxism itself should thence be driven into particularly tight corners – from which the only escape is deeper into the intellectual labyrinth – is politically insignificant, when set against the general public impact of popularized versions of what is made to seem like a socialist urge for capitalist freedom. For the grim truth, which illusion flees, is that Hungary, Czechoslovakia and Poland have each been way-stations in the last thirty years of discomfiture of Western socialism of all colours; whatever position individual parties or individual socialists may have taken up on the interpretation of events in those countries. Nor does it take much analytical effort to see that the decline of support for the socialist elements in Labour policy, among Labour voters, has developed during precisely the same period as that of the turmoil in Eastern Europe. Whether its impact is held to be close or distant, the conjunction is not fortuitous.

This is because the claim of the socialist alternative, however Marxists may insist upon a sceptical moral relativism, stands *inter alia* upon a moral ground; and this remains so even if the Victorian high seriousness which used to characterize socialist debate about means and ends has gone for a Burton in Britain. The moral reduction of the Labour Party and labour movement has been more notable even than the contemporary decline in its political fortunes, whether as an instrument of working-class representation or as the 'natural party of government'. Yet twenty years ago, just as this very tide was turning, even the Marxist left seemed to share Harold Wilson's illusions about the party he was leading. In 1965, the 'present conjuncture [*sic*]' was said to offer 'such opportunities to the Labour Party'[78] that it was being enjoined to 'step . . . into the void left by the perishing of the old order' – something it seems in fact to be doing, though not in the way the author intended. 'The situation', Tom Nairn wrote (in orthodox

fashion combining his optimism with abuse of the party) 'is
perhaps more promising than at any time since the formation of
the Labour Party sixty years ago.'[79]

But then that was when manufacturing employment was at its
peak, and socialist fortunes also. Both the 'white heat' of the
Wilson prospect and Marxist ardours were at the same height of
strenuous expectation, as capitalism appeared to prosper. That
the Labour Party's 'class base' was at the same time eroding, and
that the long history of its dominant political and economic
representation of the 'interests of the working class', as a majority
of the British population, was also in jeopardy, was much less
obvious. Today, hindsight has made this visible. But even the
Labour Party's recent history of increasing ideological confusion,
the receding in 1982 of its electoral strength back to the industrial
north and Scotland, where the ILP a century ago was also
strongest,[80] and the discovery of its chronic political 'juniority' as
a national party during the Falklands crisis,[81] are still held at a
distance, by illusion; or re-perceived, even if uneasily, as a
temporary setback, which a new manifesto and a new leader will
sooner or later mend in office.

The complementary assumption on the left that the popular
base of the right is itself unstable doubtless has its own truth. But
even if true, it cannot mask the larger fact that the new British
Jerusalem visualized in 1918 and 1945 will not now be built,
whether brick by brick or by sudden revelation. 'Socialism',
Tawney wrote in 1952 (in an essay called 'British Socialism
Today') 'ought to mean something vital and inspiring in the lives
of the great majority of workers.'[82] That it now does not, and on
the old basis cannot, signifies that a phase in our history is surely
over. Indeed, the lingering expectation that the socialist alternative can be revived around the old political constituency, and
around the old constellation of socialist ideas, however refur-
bished as 'workers' self-management' or the politics of a glib
'participation', needs to be firmly resisted. To promote illusions
which have already failed, or projects which time and circumstance are in the process of disqualifying, is merely to block the path
for genuinely new forms of radical critique of our world and its
institutions. Certainly, the historic moment has passed for good
when even a Matthew Arnold could without qualification describe the labour movement as 'a great working-class power';[83] or
a John Stuart Mill could see, and say, that 'the working classes

have taken their interests into their own hands, and are perpetually showing that they think the interests of their employers not
identical with their own, but opposite to them'.[84]

The pessimism of the right has always been held to have a
profoundly tragic dimension. What has not so readily been
admitted is that the optimism of the left is tragic also, as
generation after generation of socialist travellers have set out to
wander in the same deserts of ultimately unrequited expectation.
Rather, as a modest step to recovery of purpose, socialists now
have to acknowledge not only that capitalist progress has hitherto
been the precondition for the élan of those opposed to it; but also
that today's limited working-class and trade union resistance to
the right's social and economic policies can no longer be
conversely blamed on the capitalist crisis. To transfer to unemployment and all its consequences, however socially serious, the
main burden of responsibility for the disablement of socialist
purpose simply permits the resumed pursuit of old chimeras at the
earliest economic provocation. Instead, the scale of socialist
re-evaluation of orthodoxy (of all kinds) which is required to
understand what I shall broadly call the 'appeal of the right' is
very wide and deep indeed. The historically advanced nature of
the British experience itself – first in its industrial revolution, first
in its industrial decline – ought to have enabled us to see this
before others. It ought also to have taught us that, fitful and bitter
conflicts between capital and labour notwithstanding, a coherent
and organized working-class basis for mass socialist opposition to
private property and its dominion cannot now be reconstituted.[85]
Moreover, the simple or naive idea of working-class agency[86] in
the transcendence of Western capitalism and militarism is what it
always was: a utopian reduction of the actual enormity of the task
of such transcendence to intellectually-manageable proportion.
Indeed, if we look closely, we will see that the (essentially
middle-class socialist) project for the overthrow of capital by
labour is nothing more than the rhetorical reflection of the
practical working-class role, within the division of labour, of doing
the dirty work.

To know or discover this will have great ultimate value,
especially for those who call themselves Marxists. For it will
eventually permit the thorough redefinition of those terms – 'left',
'socialist', 'progressive' – whose unchanging parameters now
enclose an ideological cemetery of dead abstractions. At the

micro-level of the British political experience, the gradual ebbing of the appeal of even dilute socialist ideas among Labour Party voters, trade unionists and working people in general also allows critical intellectuals, especially of the coming generation, to escape the labyrinths inhabited by the present one. In any case, it will be long overdue. For at the very time, nearly 150 years ago, when Marx was formulating his notions of the capitalist working class as mankind's liberators, the forms of working-class militancy and mobilization on which he rested his extravagant intellectual expectation were already losing ground, energy and purpose. Hence, it is to other notions of working-class interest and organization that we must turn our attentions, however embarrassing the outcome. We will have to learn how to accept that most of the orthodox features both of Marxist and 'revisionist' socialist analysis in Britain are now beached like whales, and expiring in very thin air indeed, with their bundle of misperceptions about the working class on the one hand, and their medicine chest of utilitarian economic potions on the other. Harder still, but equally necessary, to recognize is that even the buoyancy of the best and most romantic socialist illusions has itself evaporated, while the high moral ground where Labour speculation was once at home has been almost entirely vacated. William Morris, Ruskin and Tawney himself might never have existed. Even a plain, common-or-garden understanding of what has gone wrong, and of what might be done about it, is being newly threatened by old wishful thinking, and by banal forms of rhetoric. And, worst, the most obvious of all local political truths has been missed: that Britain, for good reasons already implicit in the arguments I have begun to offer, has been governed since 1979 not by 'authoritarian populism',[87] but by an authentic version of working-class Toryism, founded upon the bedrock ethics of nonconformist labour.

2   The Appeal of the Right

Since the industrial revolution, intellectuals have rarely been able to understand (how could they?) the complex nature of the impact on working people – on their lives and 'consciousness', on their minds and bodies – of industrialization and of industrial work; to say nothing of the effects, now, of industrial decline and unemployment. In particular, socialist thinkers have constantly misjudged, because they have had motive to misjudge, some of the most crucial aspects of the historic relation between capital and labour, and of the impact of the one upon the other. To take an immediate instance of this failure: the social consequences for the working class of the supposed post-war revival of the British industrial economy are not adequately represented by such (middle-class) terms as 'consumerism' or 'welfarism'. Similarly, the alleged destruction of 'working-class culture' is based on largely middle-class premises which are remote in fundamental ways from working-class experience.

It is from this kind of misperception that so many further analytical errors of the left follow. As a result, the lack of working-class enthusiasm for the socialist project comes to be attributed to whole sets of wrongly imagined causes. Thus the same constituency is variously reduced to inertia by television and aroused to 'populist' reaction by 'the media'; frightened away from socialism by ruling-class conspiracy, but at heart awaiting a 'genuine' socialist programme; hostile to capitalism yet, puzzlingly, as, or even more, hostile to Labour. To solve the problem of such 'contradiction' – itself a convenient term for rationalizing intellectual incoherence – a theory of 'crisis' is invoked. Boiled down, it declares that the times are economically and politically out of joint, and that the citizen has lost his wits in consequence.

Yet, as I have already pointed out, the phenomena in question are older than the 'crisis' and its 'contradictions'. Moreover, it is overdue for us to recognize that there is no monopoly of wisdom on the left about either the historical process or the nature of freedom;

and that agnosticism in relation to, or actual refusal of, the socialist project is cross-class and deep-seated. Indeed, it is only by this route that we will see clearly why rising unemployment, and attacks on the welfare system and the trade unions, have promoted neither an acceleration in class conflict, nor made existing forms of the socialist alternative any more viable ideologically, despite the crisis. But such a route still lies beyond the normal intellectual bounds of socialist comprehension. In the meantime, both socialist utopianism and socialist utilitarianism are in the course of being historically overtaken not simply by transient party regroupings of the right and centre, but by new constellations of political and moral notions which old labels do not fit.

It is precisely because socialists have been so slow to grasp these and other related truths that the current Tory version of the 'market philosophy' has been able to proceed so far, despite continuing economic failure, against its more bewildered opponents. Even questions of the nature of the general good, or of social and moral progress, have come to be increasingly dominated in the West by arguments from the right and the centre. In the special case of Britain – special because leading the capitalist world in the scale of its industrial reversal – local socialist failure to understand its own industrial history and culture does not even permit it to grasp the most obvious of its ideological problems. The close political and moral relation between the 'self-interest' of capital and the 'self-help' of labour is only one of them. Failing to understand it permits very little understanding of the particular forms of the socialist crisis in Britain.

Instead, the left takes refuge in familiar intellectual consolations. Some await the future revival of class 'consciousness', while others dream in their archives of past heydays of the proletariat. To avoid the real issues, emphasis can also be shifted from the fact that the working class may once and for all have 'ceased to be largely Labour'[1] to the proposition that the 'new right' is itself engaged in an intensified form of 'ideological class struggle' as capitalism totters.[2] Intellectual residence can also be taken up in a (paranoid) world of 'carefully orchestrated moves' and of 'reactionary mobilization'.[3] That 'a major party has seldom penetrated so deeply into the political thinking of the other side's staunchest supporters',[4] as Tory has with Labour, gives way in analytical precedence to hectic assertions about the 'radical and traumatic restructuring of . . . relations between Capital and Labour',[5] which Tory policy is allegedly designed to effect. Elsewhere, the profound long-term historical discomfiture of socialist values – expressed in local form by, say, the unpopularity of the trade unions with very large numbers of trade unionists and Labour voters – is offset by the (relatively) trivial notice of 'ideological disarray' in the Tory Party.

The range of left misjudgement about 'Thatcherism', moreover, could not be wider. A reductionist misnomer, as I suggested earlier, for a cross-class politics with the deepest roots in the world of labour, it becomes a 'despairing last throw by the right, a final attempt to hold the Tory electoral coalition together'.[6] Like 'the right-wing in British politics generally [*sic*]', it is variously 'bankrupt'[7] or 'yearning for the values of Dickensian Britain'.[8] It is as if the fact that 'conservative values are spread throughout the whole working class electorate, regardless of which party they vote for'[9] could somehow be diminished or concealed entirely by lampoon and satire. Thus, the demand for a 'return to "Victorian values" ' is reduced, under such pressure, to no more than a 'rhetorical gesture'; and 'thrift', 'family morality' and 'law and order' are deprived of their overwhelming ideological resonance across the classes by a flick of the wrist which is itself no more than an idle left flourish.[10] Such shallowness of perception about 'ruling-class ideology' has of course as long a pedigree as related failures to understand 'working-class culture'. Thus, to Crosland, for example, Conservatism lacked 'a faith, a dogma, even a theory';[11] to Perry Anderson, arguing the same position from the other side of the socialist spectrum, 'capitalist hegemony in Britain' is founded on 'an ideology of stupefied traditionalism and empiricism, an anti-ideology which is the enemy of all [*sic*] ideas and all calculation'.[12]

It is little wonder that the intellectual left can gain no ground in the labour movement – let alone in the political culture – when it is thus disarmed in face of the truths possessed by its opponents; especially when those truths are shared on such a scale by those to whom it is appealing. Yet despite this, what Tawney once called the 'oldest and toughest plutocracy in the world',[13] and ruler in its time of a world empire, is perceived as lacking 'any systematic major ideology', its 'hegemony' instead 'diffused in a miasma of commonplace prejudices and taboos'.[14] Saddled with such self-deluding assumptions, it is simply not possible to make any sense of our politics; indeed, any socialism founded ideologically upon them deserves to be defeated. For if the socialist alternative *does,* conversely, constitute a 'systematic major ideology' – of and for the working class in the bargain – it says little for it if mere 'commonplace prejudices and taboos' have triumphed for a century and a half over its persuasions.

But socialist misperception of the strength and reach of what is, in fact, a cross-class and national political culture is as deep-rooted and hoary as the culture itself. Moreover, intellectuals who are not on the left do not make the left's disparaging (and foolish) errors about the allegedly threadbare content of 'bourgeois ideology', whose notions necessarily express – albeit often at a high level of abstraction – the governing ideas of this culture. Thus John Rawls has justly called Hume and Adam Smith, Bentham and Mill 'social theorists and economists of the first rank', something which the left denies at its increasing peril. 'The moral doctrine they worked out', Rawls argues, was 'framed . . . to fit into a comprehensive scheme'; and 'those who criticized them often did so' – in their own times, as now – 'on a much narrower front', while themselves failing to 'construct a workable and systematic moral conception to oppose it'.[15] By dismissing Bentham as the 'leather-tongued oracle of the commonplace bourgeois intelligence of the nineteenth century',[16] Marx himself made the kind of intellectual error which permits today's Marxists their satires on the ruling class's 'basic stupor of outlook'.[17] Moreover, it is the product of a left vision much more myopic than that possessed by the objects of its observation, and which, had it been true, ought long ago to have established the ideological priority in the minds of working people of a theory and practice devised in their interests.

But above all, it is the organic historical strength in the working class of a wide range of (coherent) popular versions of non-socialist and anti-socialist belief which have always been at the heart of Labour's chronic dilemmas; and it is precisely these forms which the left tries in vain to keep at a distance by reducing them to the 'unsystematic' or the 'commonplace'. Yet they have proved politically immovable, these commonplaces, and for good reason. More embarrassingly still for the left, in the worst of times – times of insecurity, hard, near-the-knuckle times – it is the ethics of labour, not capital, which defeat socialist expectation, even if left wishful thinking, seizing as ever on the minority for its archetypes, would have it otherwise. Why this should be so, and what these 'bedrock' ethics consist of, I will come to. But what we can see at the outset is that, in recent combination, the Tory right's moral earnestness, its appeal to self-reliance, its homilies drawn from home economics, and its continuous celebration of 'individual freedom' are no more an 'anti-ideology' than was the utilitarianism of Bentham. Even less are they 'Conservative Podsnappery';[18] and neither are they a grandiose 'restructuring' of the relations between capital and labour, nor (least of all) that 'authoritarian populism' which is allegedly media-dependent and halfway to fascism.

The truth is, rather, that the very ordinary form of working-class Toryism which we have before us is so serious and complex a business for socialists to deal with, precisely because of the greater frailties of their own theory and practice. Indeed, it has shown up, with disastrous effect, the especially threadbare version of Labour Benthamism – tricked out with a few bespoke utopian flounces – to which the socialist alternative has been reduced, for at least a quarter of a century, in the hands of Labour. Moreover, only a form of working-class Toryism, in a period of mass unemployment, *could* have taken such a large part of the moral ground once so confidently held by Labour. There are deep non-socialist *allegiances* in it too, which pre-date those to Labour, and which many socialists seem wilfully to have forgotten. Under such promptings as these, the implicit or explicit rejection by millions of working people of vain socialist expectations of the economy, and of its resources for expanded public provision, begins clearly to have its own logic. And it matters not at all that Tawney once could argue that 'civilization . . . is to be judged not by the output of goods and services per head, but by the use which is made of them'.[19] For across the classes and deep into the labour movement, the proposition of the right that without 'wealth creation' there can be no enhancement of the quality of life or 'civilization' in the first place, plainly has its own ideological capacity to gain access to popular assent; and socialist illusion, in crisis, equally evidently lacks it.

Left mockery may justly excoriate the hypocrisy of it, or jeer at the right's claims that an unproblematical 'common sense' supports it. Yet socialists, heads in clouds and consistently misjudging both history and the humdrum, are on increasingly dangerous ground when they choose the 'down-to-earth' as their battlefield. The right's prospectuses may themselves represent a 'counter-utopia',[20] to make good the failures of socialism in theory and practice; but the Western left's historic inability to correct its own theorems to the actual conditions, experiences and beliefs of working people – and to the kind of politics which would express them – disqualifies such condescension. The argument that the 'appeal of the right' is merely an appeal by default, is also a precarious consolation. For a large area of socialism's own intellectual ground has been irreparably ravaged by Marxist metaphysics, while the world of nineteenth-century liberalism's social and moral concerns has today been largely surrendered to socialism's opponents.

Thus nothing much now remains on the left of Ruskin's old concern to achieve a 'right understanding of what kinds of labour are good for men'.[21] Instead, the general Victorian engagement with questions of 'moral culture' seems almost completely out of date in today's socialist wasteland. It is as if the disputants over these and related matters had all dispersed or died out, and the debate was over; or as if it had been entirely subsumed for the left within the argument about 'exterminism' and nuclear weapons. But in fact, moral debate about means and ends, even if sometimes conducted in a new conceptual language, rages on as ever, but decreasingly on the ground of the left's own choosing. The failure in the West of socialism's ideological reach in matters of peace and war, shadowed as it is by the militarism of the Soviet Union, has been such that the left's moral politics of nuclear disarmament has made relatively little practical progress, in the thirty years of development of the capacity for universal destruction, even against the barbarism of arguments for a mutual 'balance of terror'. Socialists now find themselves unable, for the same reason, to challenge effectively the right's moral inroads, spuriously based or not, on the critical question of individual freedom. The Marxist left, of course, has always been fatally shy of joining issue over questions as to the essential nature of liberty and equality as such, on the ground that both are broad moral abstractions – even 'bourgeois' abstractions – whose practical meaning is determined, and masked, by specific economic interests. It is unsurprising then, with its back half-turned on the battle and weakened by a century of its own narrowing economic preoccupations, that the socialist alternative as a whole should now be failing to pass muster morally, even in the midst of severe social crisis, and at a time of great fear of nuclear annihilation.

Tawney justly called the dismissal – as 'bourgeois morality' – of 'ordinary human virtues, from honesty to mercy', a form of 'chicanery'.[22] To attribute such a dismissal to Marxism, is itself a distortion of Marxist argument; yet it is nevertheless true that the 'conception of individual freedom' as essentially 'petit-bourgeois' – and 'linked with voting for the Liberal or the Conservative Party', as Trotsky put it[23] – is still disastrously pervasive on the left, in one qualified form or another. An intellectually up-market but deeply authoritarian version of this ideological crudity might pronounce the concept of the individual to be an 'essentialist abstraction [*sic*] based on the notion that persons . . . are closed, demarcated beings, with fixed boundaries between them'.[24] But in the face of this apparently profound assertion, who would be bold enough to insist that the real world has always been inhabited by precisely such 'demarcated beings with fixed boundaries between them', one of whom is the author of the proposition which denies it? Nevertheless, the negative quality which all such morally-impoverished left ideas have in common is clear; and it is one which has helped to disable even the libertarian socialist case against right-wing doctrines of 'market freedom'.

Other consequences of socialism's moral failures, at the level of both theory and practice, have been no less serious. Indeed, it makes much less ideological difference than it did whether a narrowly individualist self-interest does or does not lie at the centre of the capitalist ethical system. For when set against the dire moral record of 'real' socialism, the argument that capitalist individualism is the best morality for the strong who wish to increase their strength, and also serves to justify their acquisitions and powers, can be true without being persuasive. After all, in the era of the Gulag, protest at the destructive precedence in Western culture of an ethic of self-interest over other moralities, whether of sacrifice or self-denial, cannot make the moral headway of the past, when socialist hopes were in their springtime. Yet the incorrigible attractions of wishful thinking continue to hound even moderate left political discussion. As recently as 1977, C.B. Macpherson felt able to argue that 'the democracy of a capitalist market society' was 'over [*sic*]'; or 'so nearly finished that one may presume now to sketch its life and times'.[25] Such error, of course, has its own complex history, which will one day have to be written. But it is so self-evidently wrong that it indicates, as it stands, why the left has been unable to mount an adequate political and intellectual challenge to the certitudes of the right, however banal or in their turn dishonest. Indeed, no Milton is required here to give the best of the argument to Satan; left error suffices.

Failure of left political judgement is, of course, especially disastrous when its subject is the nature, limits and purposes of individual freedom, the most important in practice of all moral-political issues. Its writing-down as a 'petit-bourgeois' concern would be risible if it were not now politically catastrophic; particularly in our times, and particularly in our culture. Worse still for British socialists, tempted by such reductions, is that the suspicion of what are perceived to be state encroachments on the 'rights of the individual', however illusory the rights and however ambivalent the suspicion, crosses all political boundaries. Indeed, it establishes an ideological kinship between ostensibly opponent interests in the culture which no version of the socialist alternative has ever seemed likely to sunder. Whether expressed in the form of trade union 'voluntarism', or working-class 'self-reliance', or the 'freedom of the market', or as 'the Englishman's home is his castle' a common core of moral belief and political commitment holds them embarrassingly together. Indeed, Matthew Arnold knew more than most socialists, in his and our times, when he wrote in 1869 that the working class, 'pressed constantly by the hard compulsion of material wants, is naturally the very centre and stronghold of our national idea that it is man's ideal right and felicity to do as he likes'.[26]

Furthermore, the left has failed to take seriously the evidence in our culture of an *idée fixe:* namely, that in the world created by 'industrialism' a 'genuine' self-development of the individual is not to be found, whether under capitalism or socialism, in prosperity or hardship.[27] But unless such a notion is incorporated into left perceptions, it will never be possible to understand how certain ideas of personal freedom can be invested, across class boundaries, with a moral primacy which holds the world of merely economic and political arrangements at a distance. What is at stake is nothing less than fundamental failures of left comprehension of the very issues closest to its concerns, indeed under its very noses. Among them, for instance, is the fact that right-wing 'anti-statism', in the name of 'freedom of the individual', is not automatically seen by working people as an alibi for the unleashing upon them of exploitative forms of ruling-class licence – even if socialists are perfectly justified in fearing it as a consequence. More damaging still to socialist, and in particular collectivist, versions of the politics of freedom is that, historically, the very core of radical working-class libertarianism has been essentially conservative. Rooted in concepts of the natural rights of the individual – and in ideologically crucial respects also anti-egalitarian – such libertarianism is in its foundation not merely pre-socialist, but anti-socialist also. Romantic socialist historians, with the aid of the evidence of the minority and a fertile imagination, may need to make something different (and false) of the historical record. But the bitter and incontrovertible truth for socialists remains that, in our popular political culture, 'liberty' has much more to do with claims to individual economic independence than the fond prospect of socialist transformation; while 'equality' has above all signified equal citizen rights (including to private property), and equality of opportunity rather than of outcome.

Additionally handicapped by the burdens of 'real' socialism, socialist misperception of these matters is such that even the most cynical argument on the right can now run rings around its opponents, if it chooses to make an issue of individual independence and personal freedom. 'A competition with the Conservative Party', John Westergaard wrote in the mid-1960s, 'is almost always likely to work in the latter's favour, if the terms of reference are those of "legitimacy" of authority, "respectability" and "efficiency".'[28] The same, twenty years later, is now clearly true of the question of freedom, as popularly understood in our culture; and with a third political party, born from the side of Labour, to deny Labour's socialists their claimed monopoly of libertarian wisdom. The fact that the right's proclamations of the virtues of self-reliance are obnoxious to socialists, at a time when public provision for job creation, for welfare or for reflation have political and ethical priority in the socialist scale of values, is no more than obvious. But merely to reiterate, in conventional socialist fashion, that the right has shamelessly nailed the colours of freedom to its political mast, notwithstanding or because of the economic crisis of capital, no longer meets the case, or the political challenges socialism faces. Instead, socialists must fight first on the ground chosen by the right, and with its weapons. The right's version of the nature and purposes of individual freedom will not dissolve merely because of reflex moral objections to it, however worthy.

Indeed, Marxists are even more hindered in engaging with the
right's positions by their prior ideological commitment to the view
that 'real' personal freedom is contingent on the conquest of
political power, and of the economic means of production. But an
indefinite millenarian prospect of a general liberation cannot be a
response to the immediacy of socialism's growing crisis.

Behind all this there are other and deepening political difficulties which have contributed to the flagging of socialist purpose on
the one hand, and to the strengths, in difficult times, of the passive
defenders of the *status quo* on the other. Thus, even where some
Western socialists fight in the van of the struggle to defend civil
liberties, and to control the abuse of individual freedom in their
own and other societies, they do so in the name of an ultimate
political purpose – socialism – about which there is increasing
unease and no socialist agreement. Then again, socialist
attempts to constrain the capitalist market in the pursuit of social
justice are bedevilled, particularly among the working class, by
the general equation of property-right with freedom. On top of
this, Western socialism's compromises with the capitalist polity
and economy have sharply reduced its room for decisive man-
oeuvre, and incorrigibly muddled its perspectives. A crude British
political translation of this dilemma might read as follows: given
that another Labour government would once more unsuccessfully
pursue economic policies not greatly different from those of the
Tories, given that there is lacking any general momentum of
working-class support for 'genuine' socialist measures, and given
that the right is easily capable of being ideologically perceived as
the defender of much-desired individual citizen-rights to personal
ownership and possession, the scope for a coherent Labour
alternative to the politics of capital itself comes into serious
question.[29]

Moreover, socialists cannot and would never want to escape the
fact that the promise of self-determination, whether of class or
nation or of the individual person, has always been at the very
centre of their impulse. Yet it is in this very promise that Western
socialists are most vulnerable, particularly in an epoch when
socialist forms of liberation, above all as they affect the individual,
have fallen into such discredit. Hence it is increasingly simple,
even in the teeth of the memory, say, of Vietnam, for the cause of
individual emancipation – whatever it may be said to mean – to be
given a 'right-wing' as well as a 'left-wing' gloss. Furthermore, to

express this promise of self-determination in absolutist and utopian terms is to emphasize not socialist strengths, but socialist frailties. Thus, against the ideologically plain claim to individual private property or possession, the proposition that 'liberty for all is unattainable unless *all equally* have access to *control* over productive property'[30] has little fathomable or practical meaning. Similarly, against the 'common sense' 'facing of uncomfortable facts'[31] about inflation, say, the imagining of a 'classless, fundamentally egalitarian society with a social structure that is *completely fluid* from one generation to the next'[32] seems to speak from a cloud-cuckoo land which can promise neither freedom nor order.

The (usually middle-class) socialist depressive who first sets up his own bogeys – 'our democratic rights have been taken from us'[33] – and then prescribes a utopian emancipation from them also serves only to confuse every issue. 'The establishment of a free press', thus declares Tony Benn, 'will . . . have to be a priority in the plans of a future Labour government.'[34] That we already have, by any political standards – and particularly by existing socialist ones – a profoundly free press (with its consequently gross defects), and that there are very few British socialists who do not benefit from it in one way or another, seriously disables the left in meeting the challenge of the right-wing libertarian. Moreover, in its objections to the 'populism' of the right's espousal of the values of 'freedom', the left's own cant – for example about the 'liberation' of Britain by a socialist government[35] – is fully its equal. Indeed, this abuse of language, and therefore abuse of the truth, is a symptom of the left's political incapacity to face the unwelcome actuality of what Marxists like to call 'lived experience', but which for two centuries has itself defeated socialist expectation. Harold Laski's blunt, or crude, assertion that 'without economic security, liberty is *not worth having*'[36] is of the same order of political misjudgement. The trouble is that the socialist is likely to believe it essential to hold some such view as this, if the socialist project itself is to have any purpose. That a substantial degree of economic insecurity may, in practice, be commonly regarded as a price worth paying for the preservation of certain kinds of individual freedom to which all in the culture are habituated, and which very few would willingly surrender, is impossible for most socialists to acknowledge.

In this respect, John Stuart Mill was much subtler and much

wiser than Laski. 'After the means of subsistence are assured', he
wrote in 1849 – one year after the *Communist Manifesto* – 'the next in
strength of wants of human beings is liberty.'[37] There is a political
world of difference in this seemingly like judgement. Moreover,
behind its *ex cathedra* confidence there stands one of the classical
assumptions of the social liberal, but an assumption increasingly
uncomfortable for socialists who must bear the cross of 'real'
socialism everywhere with them. It is the premise that liberal
democratic freedoms under capitalism, however unequal their
expression, can provide for the individual of all classes a sufficient
quantum of political 'good' to overshadow all theoretical objection, every left demonstration of their lack of substance notwithstanding. Indeed, if sufficient numbers of the economically
disadvantaged have now come decisively to accept such a liberal
democratic assumption themselves, then the socialist project
could scarcely take another step forward; particularly in circumstances where the right to profit from the vulnerability of others is
perfectly well understood to be the corollary of the right to pursue
one's own advantage to the disadvantage of others, yet where the
disadvantage is then discounted by the victims!

Socialists, of course, wish to argue that the right-wing libertarian case is itself nothing more than a despairing device,
'designed' to help the ruling class extricate itself ideologically
from the capitalist crisis by shifting the political focus to argument
about freedom, national pride and family virtue. But even if this
could be shown to be so, the general moral (and therefore
political) appeal of the need to 'frame the plan of our life to suit our
own character', as Mill puts it, is unlikely to diminish in our
culture. This activity he considers to belong to the 'region of
human liberty'.[38] And socialists who have abandoned this ground
to the discourse of others, or who have only long-failed countervailing argument to offer, can now make no headway against it.
Moreover, and much more dangerous for the socialist alternative,
it seems to be something like this formulation – rather than the
banal but also potent 'market freedom', or 'freedom to choose', of
a Milton Friedman – which comes closest to expressing what the
right intends by individual freedom.

The trouble is that the notion, however illusory, of the *free*
formulation of the individual's own purposes in life now weighs
more heavily than ever in the ideological balance than socialist
objections – shadowed by 'real' socialism – that the exercise of

such a right is so economically restricted, for so many, as to have no substantial meaning in practice. Indeed, the socialist alternative is in political difficulty across the class spectrum, not least because it is widely seen itself to threaten such freedom. Worse, it is a perception which is easily bolstered by the belief, first, that socialism's prior concern with the circumstances and conditions which constrain its enactment is, in fact, an alibi for unconcern with its immediate value here and now; and second, that the possibilities of its exercise are more reliably available now, under the *status quo*, than could be vouchsafed in socialism's ideal utopia.

Moreover, the modern left's own compensatory but uneasy post-war, and post-Stalinist, concerns with the subjective meanings of self-determination have thrown the whole ideological relation between the socialist ideal and the idea of individual freedom into ideological confusion.[39] It is a confusion which, in general, the right does not share. To take a basic example: neither on left nor right could anyone seriously dissent from the view, whatever its provenance, that human conduct cannot be adequately accounted for without invoking the concept of individuality.[40] But the difficulty is that in socialist practice regard for such 'individuality' is seen as *prima facie* subordinate, and even antithetical, to a 'true' socialist purpose. More revealing still is socialist discomfort with the reduction of Marxism to a vulgar determinism; indeed it is already a century old. So that many of today's forms of socialist uncertainty in the encounter with right-wing libertarianism are themselves based on a long-standing disarray about, say, the role of the individual in history, the nature and limits of free will, and so on. Thus socialists of all colours themselves know very well – though not all choose to admit it – that, as Andre Gorz has put it, 'individual existence can never be entirely socialized'.[41] Marx might argue that 'man is an animal which can develop into an individual only in society',[42] but most of today's Marxists, increasing their own dilemmas and exposing their flanks to the right, cannot argue so simply. Nor can they permit such a premise to lead them back into the determinist wilderness. Indeed, the view that 'there must exist a sphere of autonomous activity in which the individual is the sovereign author of actions carried out without recourse to necessity'[43] cannot really be disputed by any socialist. But it is also ground which must be shared with the right. Embarrassingly for the left, the right got there first and is deeply entrenched in it.

Hence, as socialists stare moodily across the political barricade which separates them from the view that 'property, possessions and free choice allow us to differentiate, express and realize ourselves as human beings',[44] many may now have begun to realize that the problem such a view poses is not that of its truth or falsity. Instead, it is its ideological rootedness, and the potency of its appeal over rival socialist definitions of freedom, which present the left with its greatest challenge. Moreover, an Adam Smith has the formidable political advantage of every plain speaker over the socialist who is driven into intellectual convolutions by the need to disown any social theory which is posited on an unchanging 'human nature'. For even if Adam Smith was wrong, his blunt moral presumption that 'the desire of bettering our condition . . . comes with us from the womb, and never leaves us till we go in the grave' possesses the kind of general legitimacy in the culture which alternative socialist readings of human motivation have never mastered. 'In the whole interval which separates these two moments [of birth and death]', he declares insidiously, 'there is scarce perhaps a single instant in which any man is so perfectly and completely satisfied with his situation, as to be without any wish of alteration or improvement of any kind.'[45]

Yet this kind of morally subversive worst-case – as it appears to many socialists – is not the typical form in which today's libertarian right presents us with its theses about the *homme moyen* and his 'natural' ambitions. Instead, they are customarily hedged around with the kind of disclaimers and qualifications which make them unexpectedly elusive targets for accurate socialist fire. Thus, what the left sees as the licensing of individuals to think only of themselves and the accomplishment of their private purposes is alleged *not* to be the right's mode of freedom. Likewise, says Hayek in *The Road To Serfdom*, 'nothing has done so much harm to the liberal cause as the modern insistence. . . on certain rules of thumb, above all the principle of *laissez-faire* ' and the 'defence of anti-social privilege'.[46] Thus, though the left may insist that the individualism of the right seeks merely to legitimate the 'entirely selfish actions of individuals',[47] the right itself insists, as Milton Friedman puts it, that 'self-interest is not myopic selfishness'. Rather, it is 'whatever . . . interests the participants, whatever they value, whatever goods they pursue'.[48] Indeed, according to Hayek, the right's notion of individuality 'does not assume, as is often asserted, that man is egoistic or selfish, or ought to be'.

Instead, 'the recognition of the individual as the ultimate judge of his ends, the belief that as far as possible his own views ought to govern his actions . . . forms the essence of the individual position'.[49] Cant this may also seem, or be; but even if dishonest, such a definition of the ethic of *laissez-faire* gets clean away from left categorizations of it as 'inhuman'.[50] And even if it be argued by the left that 'the opportunity of knowing and choosing between different forms of life'[51] does not exist in practice for more than a privileged minority in a world ruled by capital, the left knows that it also does not exist in that 'real' socialist world which is nominally ruled by labour.

Moreover, socialist conceptions of freedom do not themselves gain any greater legitimation by transposing the argument to the 'deformities' wrought in popular consciousness by 'market values'. First, the very range and source of these values escape such reductionist classification. Second, their ideological force at every level – whether that of philosophical abstraction or of unformulated daily perception – is a force which itself rests upon material foundations. Third, and above all, the belief that no complete ethical code can, or should, displace individual moral judgement and action represents an invincible cultural commitment. The prospect that 'bourgeois' freedom of thought might suffer, under any form of socialism whatever, the fate which E.H. Carr called 'the nationalization of opinion'[52] – however nationalized by the market our own thought-forms may already be – is sufficient to halt the socialist project entirely. In addition, admission to the ranks of those moral doctrines and values which are culturally legitimated with the imprimatur of 'common sense', however banal or ethically tawdry, is very difficult to achieve for whatever is ideologically perceived as 'idealistic'. It is a difficulty disastrous to most kinds of socialist aspiration. In this 'practical' light – a practice no less rooted in working-class experience than the 'praxis' of the Marxist – the Rousseau who holds that true liberty is freedom from self-interest, not the pursuit of it, is no doubt worthy. It is his perceived unworldliness which is his undoing.

Thus, at the outset, we can see that there are many levels at which socialist objections to the arguments of the right-wing libertarian fail, or falter, particularly those objections which are ill-thought out, and ill-founded. Even the simple equation which socialists establish between 'market freedom' and ruthless capitalist appropriation is harder than usual to establish on the terrain

of British capitalism's general lethargy and decline.[53] Paradoxically, even the reduction by today's Anglo-American shopocracy
of Humboldt's conception of freedom as 'human development in
its richest diversity'[54] – to a mere question of supermarket freedom
of choice – ensures it a wider cross-class reach than more
grandiose forms of the same proposition could achieve. After all,
even Tawney, with the ambivalence to which I have already
referred, wrote down, perhaps had to write down, the 'venerable
abstractions' of liberty and equality to what he called the
'pedestrian requisites' of which each consisted.[55] Yet, in any
cultural competition between such reductions on right and left,
the left's dreams of what does not yet exist – other ways of living
from the empirically given – wither on the vine once translated
into the 'pedestrian'. But the defence and legitimation of what
already is demands (and gets) vernacular and commonplace
expression. Thus the freedom of *homo economicus* is readily turned
into the domestic language of the bargain. And simple truths or
homilies, which confirm and conform with immediate experience, make easy way against even the best of the left's struggles
to uncover the true nature of things, behind the veil of illusion.[56]

Hence, the 'proletarian' dispossessed of the means of production, and dependent for his survival on the sale for a wage of his
'labour power' – the only 'commodity' he can benefit from –
appears to bear the whole gloomy burden of (Marxist) history on
his back. The 'free agent', however, buying and selling in the
market place, can be made to seem a much less encumbered
figure. Moreover, that wealth has rights which are denied to
poverty, and that money gives access to other men's labour, can be
simply evaded – however cynically – under the very rubric of
freedom. And if left protest is pressed, the worldly-wise maxim
that in life the rough must be taken with the smooth can always,
and still does, come to the rescue. The doctrine of individual
self-development, even at its noblest, may be utterly blind to
oppression; 'free' systems may depend on the most stringent
control of economic and political behaviour; monopoly may be the
necessary outcome of competition.[57] Yet should an Adam Smith
once declare that 'it is not from the benevolence of the butcher, the
brewer or the baker that we expect our dinner, but from their
regard to their own interest', or what he calls their 'self-love',[58] the
socialist must lose himself in history, Marxist economic theory
and moral philosophy to find the arguments to meet it.

Indeed, the 'new right's' restatements of Adam Smith's assertions about 'human nature' and the market, made in the hindsight of nearly seventy years of 'real' socialism – including that of the Chinese – have become an increasingly formidable political proposition. We should note, too, that thirty years ago a socialist could confidently assert that 'the dogma of the "individual hand" ' and the belief that private gain must always lead to the public good . . . failed entirely to survive the Great Depression'.[59] But today, especially in its popularized or gutter-press versions, even the crude proposition that a free market is a 'necessary condition for political freedom'[60] has the power to open up the very ground the socialist tries to stand on. 'Unless voluntary exchange has been its dominant principle of organization', Friedman tells us, 'no society . . . has ever achieved prosperity and freedom.'[61] And when the left argues back (trading insults about South Africa and the Soviet Union) that it is 'the struggle against market capitalism' which has led to the 'extension of individual liberty',[62] the right's second wave of argument is now deeply destructive of socialist positions. For, on the one hand, a 'predominantly command [sc. socialist] economy' rests on 'tyranny'; on the other, we are shown that in 'real' socialist economies, because 'the economic cost of eliminating them would be too high', 'voluntary market elements flourish'.[63]

On a second crucial ground of contention, where Friedman makes much larger and more sweeping claims, the socialist case does not fare any better. Indeed, it arguably fares worse. 'A society's values, its culture, its social conventions', he insists, 'all . . . develop . . . through voluntary exchange, spontaneous cooperation, the evolution of a complex structure through trial and error, acceptance and rejection.'[64] No, says the left, firing in the wrong direction and forced into falsehood: 'the free market can provide neither material nor moral civilization . . . Only the existence of some kind of public authority and spirit of community can do that.'[65] If so, argues Friedman in turn, it must be a 'cooperation among individuals' which rests upon 'no external force, no coercion, no violation of freedom';[66] for it is in and through 'structures produced by voluntary exchange' that 'language or scientific discoveries or musical styles or economic systems'[67] develop. Socialists of every kind might well feel deep intellectual unease at this. After all, Marx himself spent most of his life obsessively trying to fathom the mechanism, or 'laws of motion', of precisely such an economic system.

Moreover, this true sense of the organic nature of social and economic processes – which, to the right but not to the left, 'develop a life of their own' – is not effectively countered by the left objection that the forms of this development are contingent, say, on the mode of production. For changes in the mode of production are themselves the consequence of Friedman's 'exchanges'. More specifically, the just objections that much economic and social exchange under capitalism is *involuntary*,[68] and that where it is voluntary it is inefficient, have proved ideologically to be no more than pinpricks in the hide of a politics well prepared to withstand them. Certainly, it is bold – or brazen – enough to assert that 'the great achievements of capitalism have redounded primarily to the benefit of the ordinary person';[69] or that 'by the beginning of the twentieth century, there can be no doubt that its [Western capitalism's] success surpassed man's wildest dreams . . . of material comfort, security and personal independence'.[70] The argument can be met with readings from the grim record of colonial exploitation, indices of crash and crisis, inflation and mass unemployment. But against the left's equally crude insistence that libertarian individualism is merely a synonym for a proto-fascist or at least Hobbesian survival of the fittest, the right has an easy time of it. In addition, the left's blind urge to assimilate the right's individualistic ethic entirely to a callous disregard of public duty is itself met by the fact that the 'market system' has for nearly a century coexisted – whether willingly or under political pressure here makes no substantial ideological difference – with extensive public provision.[71] In any case, the right as a whole (and not simply its utilitarians) knows very well that individual action, however multiplied, cannot possibly displace most of the functions assumed by state institutions. And when the left terms this 'state capitalism', and a parody of the 'free market' system, it will merely hear the right agree with it.

Furthermore, wherever it can be shown – and it always can – that 'persons do not have equal access either to money or to the market' or that behind the forces of the 'free market'[72] stand other darker forces of economic and political compulsion, the socialist project of 'controlling' or 'replacing' the market comes under the equally dark cloud of an anticipated coercion and violence. Against what Tawney called 'a society in which some groups can do much what they please, while others can do little of what they ought',[73] the prospect of 'breaking the stranglehold of market forces'[74] promises, in the shadow of 'real' socialism, not the overcoming but the reinforcement of state power. Indeed, Tawney's own ironies at the expense of Hayek (the 'nervous professor'), who is attributed with 'paroxysms of alarm' at the 'menace to individual freedom involved in every extension of the activities of public bodies',[75] now have a much reduced capacity to persuade left, right or centre. In such a predicament, as I have already suggested, abuse of language – which in turn does further abuse to perception – relieves the blockade of socialist expectation. Under its pressures, the 'free market' can itself come to embody the very principle of violence. Even Habermas has alleged that 'the general public' has 'realized that social violence is practised in the form of exchange', and that the market system is, in consequence, in the throes of a crisis of 'legitimation'.[76]

Wishful thinking of this and even more extreme kinds, which always mistakes the thought for the deed, is itself a symptom of socialism's own much deeper crisis. It also enables the right to claim for itself a monopoly of ideological reason, at a time when capitalism's disorders have in any case damaged the politics of capital much less than those of labour. For it is the defenders of the market and of the 'freedom of the individual' who then remember what the left, for equally good cause, prefers to forget: that the historic development of a market society did indeed promote the establishment of certain fundamental democratic freedoms, and (worse) that the moral priority which is given to those freedoms in the culture constantly outweighs objections to the inequities which flow from them, crisis or no crisis. The right has also been politically quick to exploit its own awareness of what socialists can never admit: that the struggle for those forms of socialism which were historically perceived as the 'final' consummation of the struggle within and against the capitalist market, a struggle for always greater popular freedoms, has clearly come – temporarily or permanently – to the end of its ideological tether.

At the heart of the problem of freedom is a redoubtable truth which socialists in the capitalist world can no longer overcome with any of their existing forms of theory and practice. Simply put, it is that there has been successfully conflated within liberal democracy's particular forms of freedom and unfreedom a sufficient universality of meaning and value to have seen off, ideologically, all its even more inadequate rivals. It is not that the

only possible meaning of freedom is its own. Far from it. It is
rather that the answer 'no' to the question of whether a 'free man
who owns large scale means of production [is] the same kind of
free man as one who does not'[77] has decisively lost its ideological
force, *pari passu* with the loss of political legitimacy of 'real'
socialism's counter-definitions. Moreover, their fall from ideological grace has been the greater for the greater historical claims
made for the virtues of socialist and communist forms of human
emancipation. 'Communist society', Marx wrote, is 'the only
society in which the original free development of individuals
ceases to be a mere phrase'; indeed, the communist revolution is a
'general condition' for such individual human development.[78] But
very much more than this is promised: the rehabilitation of man as
a social being, complete freedom from material constraints, the
ending of alienation, and so forth.

Yet no more of this prospectus has been achieved, or is likely to
be achieved, by 'real' socialism than by real capitalism, and, in
certain respects, much less. Moreover, what has been materially
achieved in such socio-economic systems has been at equally great
cost in human exploitation, above all of working people.[79] Indeed,
it is the political understanding of this, however manipulated,
which for millions of the Western working class has inevitably lent
legitimacy to the very institutions and values which their
organizations are (ostensibly) attempting to overcome. And, at a
more parochial level, the particular form of British socialist
compromise with capital has created a political theory of labour
which depends upon, and in turn corroborates, the ethics of the
liberal democratic form of the market system. It speaks essentially
the same political language, and means the same things by it.
Thus, when Keir Hardie at the inaugural conference of the ILP in
1893 argued that 'the demand of the Labour Party is for economic
freedom. It is the natural outcome of political enfranchisement',[80]
the assumptions which informed this demand were much nearer to
Locke's than Marx's. Tawney's assertion, likewise, that 'freedom
implies the possession by individuals of a genuine, if partial,
power of self-determination'[81] has more in common with classical
liberal than with socialist definitions of freedom.

In fact, the closer one looks at the mainstream formulations of
British socialist purpose, the plainer it becomes that most of their
fundamental political and economic premises assume – and even
demand – the retention, in whole or in part, of the capitalist

market system. It is not simply that an unabashed 'revisionist' like Crosland could speak the fluent market language of 'the consumer' as 'the best judge of how to spend his money';[82] or that an Attlee could speak of socialist aims so exclusively in Lockean terms as to suggest a search for a socialism which could entirely avoid being socialist.[83] For it is in Keir Hardie as well as in Ramsay Macdonald; and, choosing at random, as clear in Richard Titmuss's celebration of 'the right to choose between satisfying different economic and social wants',[84] as in Tawney's belief that 'a more positive content' would be given to personal liberty if 'firmer guarantees' were provided, *inter alia,* to 'opportunity'.[85] The point is not, of course, that these positions are objectionable, nor that they are presented without (at the least) a political doffing of the hat to more recognizably socialist notions. It is rather that their deep and uncomfortable political ambiguity – however justifiable – reveals the force of the gravitational pull of liberal democratic values in the culture. Potent enough to transmute into liberal market terms most versions of the socialist alternative, they also serve to drive intransigent left socialists into a desperate utopian rhetoric to protect themselves from political contagion. It is little wonder, then, with socialists themselves so publicly uncertain in their sense of analytical direction over the most fundamental of issues, that it should be the simple panaceas of the 'free market' which are ideologically the most pervasive.

The time is long past for political hesitation about what all this implies politically for the socialist prospect. The voter knows, as well as the philosopher, that since there cannot be absolute freedoms, the crucial moral-political issue becomes the question of their better or worse allocation. Hence, the clear signs of a general cross-class political preference in the culture for the view that 'market freedoms' are a 'prerequisite of, or a substantial part of, the full enjoyment and development of the human essence', must at the very least be accorded high political status, whether we like the outcome or not.[86] This is particularly so, if the scale of such preference seems to be constant, if it survives (or is even prospered by) economic crisis, and is accompanied by a substantial rejection in the working class of what are perceived to be non-market or anti-market alternatives. We are also not simply dealing here, as I have indicated, with the corner-shopkeeper's freedom of choice of grocery items, nor with crude 'petit bourgeois'

claims to unlimited consumption; even if the left would prefer that
we were. For we also have to do, *inter alia*, with sober preferences
for 'individual freedom of choice of work and reward',[87] whose
moral-political significance in the culture reaches far beyond the
narrow boundaries of socialist reduction of their meaning.

But the lynch-pin of this cross-class refusal of anti-market
political theories is plainly the general ideological legitimacy of
one right above all: the right to property of all kinds, most often –
including in the sight of the majority of working people – without
regard to its extension. I have already referred briefly to the
historically fundamental role, played since at least the mid-
seventeenth century in our culture, of radical democratic claims
for the extension and equalization of the citizen-right to individual
property. It was also a claim which stood at the heart of the
cross-class cry for 'liberté' in the French Revolution, it was a basic
assumption of early nineteenth-century working-class Jacobinism
in Britain, and it was the premise of the organized bargaining
power of the trade union movement at its Victorian zenith. This is
not to deny that a (very small) minority working-class tradition in
favour of collectivism and the communization of property has
always coexisted with it. But despite the inflation of its true
magnitude in the imaginations of socialist historians, it has always
been dwarfed in fact by the overwhelming scale of the political
acceptance, across class boundaries, of non-socialist and anti-
socialist property-centred notions of what is meant by individual
freedom.[88]

It is on these rocks above all that the socialist boat has
foundered, even to the extent of making false a key element in
Marx's general theory: that pre-industrial artisanal property-
interest would be overtaken – as the result of the development of
factory capitalism – by the proletarianized interests of a 'class of
producers in general'.[89] It was among them that the commitment
to individual property-right was expected to give way to increasingly socialized forms of life, labour and political 'consciousness'.
Instead, the belief in the legitimacy of exclusive individual
appropriation – not just possession or consumption – has not
merely survived in the modern working class, but has been
constantly strengthened and generalized, to the point of being
very near to a political and moral universal in the culture. Indeed,
it constitutes the principal political reason why the ethics of
capitalist accumulation, however obnoxious to middle-class

socialists in particular, cannot be – and never have been – seriously called into question by the working-class movement.

This incorrigible truth, we can see, has many unpalatable but logical consequences. First, the deep ideological legitimacy which attaches to individual appropriation in the culture as a whole has further prevented the organic growth and development of genuine philosophical and political alternatives – whether socialist or any other – to the 'common sense' of the capitalist system, come hell or high water. Second, it has plunged British socialists of all kinds and for over a century into inextricable errors of political judgement, both in theory and in practice: from the sublime Marxist folly of perceiving socialism in essence as a struggle towards the light of a general liberation from the private ownership of the means of production, to the simple (but disastrous) Labour mistake of seeking to prevent the sale of council houses. Third, it gives us a clue to that other history of working-class struggle, a secret history to socialists only: the struggle to escape from the 'point of production' entirely, and to get free of wage labour and the working-class condition altogether.[90] And for those who do not succeed, or have not yet succeeded, or do not attempt it, there remains the right – bitterly fought for even at the coal face – to 'property in the job', a right which is once more Lockean, not Marxist.

More awkward still for the socialist, the cross-class belief in the legitimacy of individual appropriation does not rest on classic distinctions between personal and private property, nor is it overmuch qualified by moral differentiation between ethically just and ethically unjust degrees of it. Indeed, I have stated the case in such general terms because an uncritical ideological acceptance of the right to property is itself general. It is so general that the concept of socially-owned public property – and therefore, the principle of defending public ownership – has an entirely inferior ideological and moral status. There is nothing in any of this as grandiose as Hegel's belief that property is a manifestation of 'the will to appropriation'; only a commonplace near-universal acceptance, overriding socialist objection, that what (and how much) the individual citizen owns, rich or poor, product of capital or product of labour, is primarily his or her private business. A Tawney might speak without irony of 'promoting industries to the dignity of public ownership',[91] but the notion of such dignity – however just – is no match for Tom Paine's own much deeper-rooted version of these matters; according to which 'every man wishes to pursue his occupation, and to enjoy the fruits of his labours, and the produce of his property in peace and safety'.[92]

Ireton's voice in the Putney Debates of 1647, declaring that 'liberty cannot be provided for in a general sense if property be preserved'[93] has not been stilled, but it has always been the voice of dissenting protest against installed beliefs so deep and broad that they remain largely unspoken. Nor does the political right itself always grasp their popular meaning correctly, transforming the vernacular of common assumptions into its own self-serving political theory. Thus private property, to a right-wing ideologue, becomes 'the essential *guarantee* of the independence of the individual',[94] or even the means of 'making men both virtuous and free'.[95] But more humble popular belief – working at a different moral level – would be more likely to see in the 'redistribution of wealth', for example, the taking away (from those to whom they belong) of private accumulations, for a suspect and even invalid political purpose. Indeed, it is precisely in such responses that there is expressed a popular conception of social justice, however inchoate, of which socialism as hitherto understood knows nothing. Moreover, even if we discriminate analytically, as we must, between *private* property (property which can be turned to profit by its owner) and *personal* property (property which is for the personal use of the owner), such discriminations make heavy political weather in the face of popular failure to accord them recognition. Similarly, the reformist socialist who is embarrassingly saddled with the need to distinguish between capitalist profit as the rich man's unearned surplus income – 'deserving to be squeezed' – and capitalist profit as a surplus for productive investment – 'deserving to be enlarged'[96] – will not get much popular political help in his dilemma if the distinction is itself seen to be ideologically incomprehensible or offensive. In fact, the entitlements of ownership are seen, by the light of the ideological consensus, to attach equally to a mansion or a council house, to a pair of old boots or a boot factory; to retain their legitimacy whether exercised by their owners or conferred (in any way they choose) on others; and to be an equally-shared cross-class right, however unequal the appropriations. It is almost exactly as Locke but not Marx, and as the Declaration of the Rights of Man but not the *Communist Manifesto*, intended.

Indeed, though Marx, with Engels, addresses himself pungently to the question of personal and private property – and the differences between them – he takes positions and makes errors of his own which have rebounded against him. 'Communists have been reproached' he declares, 'with the desire of abolishing the right of personally acquiring property as the fruit of a man's own labour.' To meet this charge, a trumped-up one in the first place, Marx distinguishes between 'hard-won, self-acquired, self-earned property', which, he says, 'there is no need to abolish', and *private* property, or capital – 'that kind of property which exploits wage labour', and which a revolution will be required to overturn. There is 'no need' to abolish *personal* property, Marx argues (though only by avoiding the further reaches of the issue), since 'the development of industry has to a great extent already destroyed it, and is still destroying it daily'.[97] But it is the very opposite dilemma which has helped to bring Western socialism to its ideological impasse: that of the daily creation and retention, albeit unevenly and insecurely, of 'hard-won, self-acquired, self-earned property' by working people, poverty and unemployment notwithstanding. Thus, on the one hand, Marx's projections excluded the possibility of such acquisition. But, on the other, he failed to foresee that the legitimacy – which he necessarily recognized – of personal appropriation ('for the maintenance and reproduction of human life'[98]) would come to attach itself to *all* forms of appropriation, both personal and private, as the capitalist mode of production extended its purchase, and as the notion of community of property became culturally more marginal than ever.

Marx is correct in asserting that capitalism – like 'real' socialism – has deprived the individual of direct access to the means of his own survival, through the concentration of ownership in the means of industrial and agricultural production. But the logical outcome of this long historical process has been to strengthen, not weaken, the ideological preference – especially among working people – for individual forms of appropriation. Thus, it is true that property in capital is more a franchise than a freedom, and that property in one's own labour is a mere parody of the rights of capital. Yet 'labour property' in the job, in the right to work, in the wage, in consumption, in welfare entitlement and, above all, in 'self-earned' personal property acquired through work – however threatened – has acquired in the culture a sufficient ideological equivalence to the property of capital, to stop

the socialist alternative dead in its tracks. It has, of course, not
helped to distinguish between one kind of property and another
that some formulations of socialist purpose, reflecting precisely
the ideological mutations I discussed earlier, have so emphasized
consumer over producer values as to obliterate almost every last
trace of their difference. 'What socialism really means', John
Strachey wrote (in *Why You Should Be A Socialist*), 'is giving
nine-tenths of us a chance to get at least ten times as much
individual private [*sic*] property – ten times as much clothing,
houses, gardens, motor-cars, supplies of food, furniture and the
like as we ever get today.'[99] If this is so, then Milton Friedman's
philosophy must be socialist also.

It has not helped socialist prospects for some socialists to have
made the same ideological errors on the issue of 'consumerism' as
have been made on the question of council-house purchase.
Indeed, socialist objections – many of them over-fastidious and
again picking the wrong targets – to popular forms of post-war
consumption have served primarily to corroborate what are
perceived to be the democratic virtues of the 'free market'. Thus,
the increasingly familiar (and increasingly mistaken) left judgement – rooted in Richard Hoggart's sentiments about the
subversion of 'working-class culture' – that the 'material concessions' of capital to labour have 'all been a vast swindle',[100] merely
offends, with its seemingly illiberal disdain, those who have
worked for and value material improvements in their condition,
however precarious. In any case, nostalgia offers no way out of the
socialist impasse. No doubt, Crosland's reproof that 'those
enjoying an above-average standard of living should be rather
chary of admonishing those less fortunate on the perils of material
riches'[101] can be held to be that of a socialist sybarite; and in any
case, 'riches' are not the issue. But it is not wrong for all that, even
if it points back into the ideological nest of vipers we have just
passed through. Furthermore, in political argument with the right
about the vices of market freedoms, socialist intellectuals who
seem to deny to the working class, in the name of socialism, what
they have themselves – of possession, privilege, leisure, individuality and autonomy of personal action and consumption, and
at levels usually beyond the reach of working people – can make no
ground at all. Indeed, they decisively lose it, and fairly so.

Yet the deeper truths on this question are quite different. First,
because 'the sphere of individual sovereignty is not based upon a

mere desire to consume',[102] as Andre Gorz has justly asserted. Indeed, only middle-class condescension would presume it, while seeking to distinguish qualitatively between its own preferred forms of individual expression, and the supposedly baser levels of working-class aspiration. At its very worst and most authoritarian – for example, in the work of the libertarian socialist Wilhelm Reich – this has led, in the name of working-class emancipation, to over fifty years of middle-class denunciation of indiscriminate 'mass consumption'; and even to allegations of the 'collective mutilation of the class mind', as a consequence of its form of individual appropriation.[103] Second, the socialist dislike for 'consumerism', quite apart from the general political misjudgement which it expresses, is made worse by being so often empirically quite unwarranted. In conditions of unemployment, poor housing and a deteriorating urban environment, the term 'consumerism' cannot be applied to the recourse to such material compensations as there may be – however impoverished – for deprivation and social disadvantage. Third, beyond this lies the real difficulty for socialists. There may indeed be no route to a worthwhile freedom merely through increasing consumption, and certain chosen forms of it can truly be held to be demeaning; yet, for all that, the ideological perception of the 'free choice' of objects and materials for consumption as a defining characteristic of freedom-in-general remains too deep-rooted to be shaken.

In any case, for socialists to deny the right to consume according to choice would be a draconian folly, with or without the prescription of a sumptuary limit; and whether such right be the correlate of efficient socially-organized production in 'real' socialist conditions, or a 'natural' citizen liberty in mixed economies, where the function of meeting every need of the consumer is allocated between the market and public provision. The true reason for socialist travail, especially but not exclusively in capitalist societies, is deeper: that the right to consume 'freely', the right to individual appropriation, and the general legitimacy of private and personal property – whatever its extension – constitute *one single ideological matrix*, none of whose parts is separable from the whole. Hence, though it is true that 'per capita consumption of materials . . . can rise to infinity without . . . a leap into the realm of freedom for the consuming individuals',[104] as Rudolf Bahro has put it, the ideological conviction at which such a truth points the finger of accusation suffers no real disturbance. Nor does it, even more obviously, when misplaced puritan zeal assails the particular forms of consumption which citizen-right has 'chosen'. Moreover, this matrix of beliefs is itself linked to a conception of 'natural rights' ideologically more secure than ever it was in the days when Locke had to plead for it; and which sees in the citizen-rights to life, liberty and property much more than a 'bourgeois' apologia or a licence for selfish possession.

So strongly – and fearsomely for socialists – is this the case in the culture that the ideological status of each of these rights can be said to be equal. Indeed, their perceived equality, as I have already suggested, has the force of discounting socialist objection that the second and third are incompatible with one another. Thus, we can see why the fundamental socialist notion that want, or unemployment, or other forms of social and economic dis-advantage lead to a loss of freedom as such, carries such surprisingly little ideological weight; why restrictions on freedom are almost exclusively identified with political 'interference' rather than economic deprivation; why Tawney's view that 'the liberty of the weak depends upon the restraint of the strong'[105] is seen primarily in moral terms, as at most an ethical reproof rather than a ground for interventionist political action; why the majority of those with lesser amounts of property, or none at all, respect the rights – and the persons – of those with more, socialist incredulity, exasperation or denial notwithstanding; and why there is a profound ideological predisposition to equate the freedoms of capital and the 'freedoms' of labour, and to subsume both within a democracy of consumption, however unequal. It is in 'exchange' for such forms of personal freedom as I have discussed, for the continuities of 'custom and practice', and for the security of personal accumulations that there is forged and reforged, equally securely, an implicit social contract between capital and labour. It may be appalling to the socialist temper – and be falsely termed 'apathy' – but it is the ground of political obligation in the culture.

The socialist arguments are, of course, incontrovertible that a right remains a political abstraction without adequate means to exercise it, and that some liberties are in practice no more than privileges of the rich; privileges 'brazenly called rights',[106] in the words of the Abbé Sieyès. Yet the prospect of the denial of these same rights, however unequally exercised or illusory they may be, is itself ideologically perceived as a threat to freedom. Thus, even the right to buy the labour time of fellow citizens, and to profit from it, is overwhelmingly seen across the classes – and however grudgingly – as no more than a right among others in the ideological matrix of which I have spoken. This is a crucial reason why socialist theories of exploitation, even when their moral case is made, have had such an uphill political struggle. Indeed, though it may bewilder socialists, even gross forms of economic exploitation are capable of being seen – including by the exploited – as at worst the result of the misuse of a legitimate freedom, rather than as the very denial of freedom itself. More difficult still, the ultimate source for the validation of what to a socialist cannot be validated, and certainly not ethically, is itself an essentially ethical issue: namely, that the abuse of the right to individual appropriation weighs less in freedom's scales than would the abolition, or authoritarian circumscription, of such right in the cause, say, of the socialist ownership of the means of production.

The strength of such a non-socialist and anti-socialist philosophy of freedom gains weight from the ideological attribution to the whole matrix of ideas to which it belongs of a 'natural' superiority over all other definitions. Continuously confirmed by the material and political failures of 'real' socialism, there necessarily arises a belief in the non-class universality of its wisdom. More awkward still, the corollary that there is no feasible non-utopian alternative to its prescriptions, whatever their own defects, logically follows. Indeed, it is here that we find the explanation for what John Rawls turns into an elaborate philosophical conundrum: that at the level of the social and individual prosperity attained by Western capitalism – recurrent slump and, in Britain's case, gradual decline notwithstanding – citizens of all classes would not willingly surrender their basic, or even their less basic, liberties for 'an improvement in their economic well-being',[107] if such a choice were hypothetically to be presented to them. (In his *Theory of Justice*, Rawls invests what both he and John Stuart Mill call the individual's 'plan of life' with a crucial ideological importance in the culture. Pursued 'without the incentive of evident reward', it is motivated not by crudely selfish or Hobbesian endeavour, but by the desire for 'self-respect' and for the exercise of our individual capacities and 'natural powers'.[108]) In this mild variant of the cross-class consensus I have been discussing, a further main proposition can be extrapolated: that the notion of equality has a much lower ideological status, including among working people, than that of freedom, whatever its definition. If this is so, and I believe it is, then the socialist promotion of the former by means of any substantial curtailment of the latter, including of the freedom of individual appropriation, will find no greater favour among the working class in capitalism (or socialism) than among any other classes.

Behind this stand fixed conclusions, true as well as false, drawn from 'real' socialist experience. They have, *inter alia*, thrown into confusion in our own culture even the socialist conviction – fully justified by the British history of public provision – that individual freedom can be increased, as well as diminished, by state action. Indeed, the ideological equation between 'real' socialism and the denial of the political rights of the citizen has now become so firmly established culturally as to have begun to discredit even the most innocent and necessary forms of centralized social intervention. In his 1948 preface to *Roads to Freedom*, Bertrand Russell saw the 'problem' of 'preserving as much liberty as possible under Socialism' as 'even more urgent' than it had been in 1918, when the book was first written.[109] Nearly forty years further on, the 'problem' unsolved has carried much of socialism down with it. It is no wonder, then, that at the level of popular ideological perception, the right of individual appropriation should itself be so free of political odium; or that theorists of democratic freedom, such as C.B. Macpherson, should have come to the conclusion that 'the absence or severe restriction of civil and political liberties ... diminish[es] men's powers' more than does the 'market transfer of powers' brought about by the inequalities of the capitalist system.[110]

Indeed, when Marx distinguished between the feudal and the capitalist economic process, characterizing the former by its largely compulsory and even servile forms of obligation, and the latter by its 'free' wage-labour, it was the confident prospect of truly emancipated socialist forms of life and work which above all validated his critique of the capitalist system. But in the absence of any genuinely liberatory socialist transcendence of the capitalist mode of production – above all for the working class – the ironic quotation marks around the word 'free' become merely irritating. That this should be so is a true ideological disaster, not merely for Marxists but for socialists of all colours. Moreover, it is this which enables the right to counter Marx's fully justified arguments against capitalism – for example, that 'it is not within the competence of capitalism to plan its production to meet the needs of the community of producers'[111] – with attacks on socialist *dirigisme*, planning failure and political oppression. Similarly, the right feels confident to argue that the 'apportioning of resources by administrative action' in 'real' socialism merely shifts the forms of capitalist competition to 'another field', in which rival bureaucratic and other interests vie for 'the favour of the state'. 'It is difficult', say Joseph and Sumption, 'to see why this should be a more acceptable form of competition.'[112] Again, confidently admitted inequalities of wealth in capitalism are said to be replaced under socialism by inequalities of power which confer on the few rights unavailable to the many. And emboldened by socialist failure, the right can even be found taking the offensive on the left's own ground, arguing that 'brotherhood is not necessarily destroyed by inequality, but it is necessarily destroyed by the abrasive measures which are required to make men equal'.[113]

But, at its most effective, the right now makes no bones about the fact that some of the capitalist institutions which 'real' socialism originally set out to replace were, and are, 'unpleasant'.[114] It is their replacements which are held to be more unpleasant still. Thus, 'real' socialism – often misnamed 'communism' in right-wing polemic – is perceived either as a form of autocracy, or as a fictitious party-collectivism; while under their cover, individual self-interest is seen to be competitively pursued through a minefield of constraints on personal and political freedoms. In this kind of presentation, socialism no longer fulfils the simple role of a Manichaean alternative to capitalist achievement – though the cruder right's demonologies insist precisely on this – but is seen as a failure in its own terms. As such, the nature of its defects can then be used propagandistically to shed light on the supposed universality of capitalist values, *including* those which are 'unpleasant'. That is, in the argument at its best, we face much more than the right's familiar objections to the employment of tyrannical means to overcome the injustices of the 'free play' of market forces, or to secure the enforcement of socialist ideals against political and class opponents. Instead, and however cynically, 'real' socialism is 'charged' by the right with having failed, at great cost in life and liberty, effectively to transcend market forces, or to liberate its own proletariats, or to create the economic and political forms with which the Western working class would want to replace the market system.

As early as 1849, John Stuart Mill was already speculating with remarkable prescience about the socialist prospect. 'We are too ignorant', he wrote, 'of what individual agency in its best form, or Socialism in its best form, can accomplish, to be qualified to decide which of the two will be the ultimate form of human society.' (And so, still, are we.) But, he went on, 'if a conjecture may be hazarded, the decision will probably depend mainly on one consideration, viz. which of the two systems is consistent with the greatest amount of human liberty and spontaneity'. And then – nearly seventy years before the Bolshevik Revolution – raising one of the central themes of this chapter, he argued that 'the restraints of Communism would be freedom in comparison with the present condition of the majority of the human race . . . But it is not by comparison with the present bad state of society that the claims of Communism can be estimated.' Instead, the ultimate tests – as befitted a Victorian liberal – would be those of 'asylum left for individuality', the 'multiform development of human nature' and the toleration of 'a variety of intellectual points of view'. But above all (in the weight of Mill's argument) was the warning that any general 'requirement' on the part of the people to 'exchange the control of their own actions for any amount of comfort or affluence, or to renounce liberty for the sake of equality' would run counter to 'one of the most elevated characteristics of human nature'.[115]

Here, and most difficult of all for socialists to accept, is something more than the expression of mid-Victorian 'petit-bourgeois' scruple, classically generalizing its interests in terms of 'human nature'. Rather, it is the political writing on the wall which has set socialists the almost impossible ideological task of providing evidence, whether drawn from 'real' socialism or anywhere else, of the existence of a 'necessary connection between socialism and democracy'.[116] For without such evidence, the ideological matrix to which I have referred cannot be deprived of its political primacy in the culture. Indeed, unless such evidence is forthcoming, the 'connection' itself 'remains . . . largely a declaration of faith'.[117] And as long as it remains such, it will be constantly swamped by alternate 'facts' or arguments which suggest that the known world of capital, though not the only possible one in theory, is the best one in practice. Equally important, against the immediacy of the political challenge from the right, and without adequate countervailing evidence drawn

from socialist practice to meet it, the left's own critique of the free
market falls on deaf ears, not because it is false, but because it is
perceived at best as a truism, the ideal alternative to which is
utopian.

It is in such circumstances that the right has been increasingly
presented with opportunities to exploit the very knowledge which
socialists themselves dare not concede: that an overwhelming
majority of working people invest the right to individual appropriation with a legitimacy which is denied not only to compulsory
expropriation for socialist purpose, but also to more benign forms
of social ownership of the means of production. In turn, it is this
which now permits the right its confidence in denying the political
or intellectual validity of collective and social definitions of
economic virtue or political justice;[118] and this which allows it to
rest the defence of privilege upon the existing structure of social
and economic inequalities, when such inequalities are ideologically preferred to the prospect of social disorder in pursuit of a
never-yet-attained purpose. Indeed, many classical right arguments against socialism and its dilemmas have increasingly been
made redundant by the very weight of popular approval in the
culture for the essential features of the capitalist state, capitalist
economic relations and the capitalist ethical system. There are, of
course, negative advantages in this, since more immediate
political contradictions, such as those in the Labour programme –
on which powerful right arguments could be founded – now
attract diminished critical attention. Thus, to choose at random,
the Labour movement's commitment to state action in almost
every economic sphere except that of wage regulation is unsustainable in logic, whether socialist or any other. Or, again, many
indefensible forms of public spending which serve no socialist nor
even useful purpose are defended as an act of (misplaced) socialist
faith, or out of the inertia of vested bureaucratic interest. These
issues do indeed go to the heart of gradualist socialism's
intentions; yet they are made relatively insignificant when set
against the general ideological refusal of socialist arguments for
equality, or against the cross-class legitimacy which is attached
both to the matrix of rights I discussed earlier and to the consequences of their exercise.

Above all, it is in political practice that we can see what happens
when the necessary political action to correct the more oppressive
of these consequences possesses a lower ideological status than do

the rights themselves. One blunt example suffices: the myth that
the Englishman's home is his castle, a myth which goes to the root
of the national culture, has towering ideological precedence over
the practical problems of the homeless, and those living in
substandard housing. Indeed, it is not difficult to see why inaction
(on the part of governments of right and left alike) even in matters
where the most fundamental forms of inequality are at issue,
should itself be considered as relatively insignificant, once the
general ideological notions which govern cross-class perceptions
of the nature of equality are correctly identified. The most
important of them, first, is a culturally overarching one: that in so
far as the richer have a fundamental right to their (greater)
appropriations, and the poorer have a fundamental right to their
(lesser) appropriations, then in this ideologically crucial respect –
even if in no others – they are considered to be equal. And
secondly, if neither 'interferes' with the other, they are equally free
in the bargain. Such is the tenacity of these linked beliefs, among
working people in particular, that where a disproportionate
freedom from restraint is demanded and exercised by capital, and
a disproportionate self-discipline demanded of labour, even this
fails to promote the credit of alternative socialist notions of
equality over those ideological attachments which I have been
discussing.

In the same way, socialist notions of equality are handicapped
by precisely those factors which have vitiated the ideological
prospects in the culture for socialist definitions of freedom. Thus
what is perceived to be the former's essential utopianism is
compounded by the general (cross-class) knowledge of the
degrees of political, economic and social inequality – both of
opportunity and result – which exist in the world of 'real'
socialism. That the nature (and limits) of socialist egalitarianism
are mischievously falsified and misrepresented by the right is an
additional burden. But it is not made lighter by absurd left
demands for 'absolute'[119] and impossible forms of equality – such
as for 'equalized employment' or 'equalized personal income'[120] –
which the real world, whether under socialist or capitalist
management, could not deliver. Yet Marx, his own utopian
egalitarianism notwithstanding, made perfectly clear in his
Critique of the Gotha Programme, for example, why wages could
not be equal even under socialism, in the course of rejecting the
programme's declaration that 'the proceeds of labour belong

undiminished with equal right to all members of society'.[121] As for 'revisionist' socialist confusions on the subject, which are essentially the product of political recoil from the implications of pursuing egalitarianism in practice, even theoretical attempts to find a *via media* between a minimum equality of opportunity and a maximum equality of outcome run into great intellectual difficulty. Trotsky himself can be found on one occasion arguing that socialism was concerned 'only to ensure to all people similar material conditions of existence',[122] a proposition untrue to much socialist theory, and one to which even a Milton Friedman might give his assent.

But the greater truth is that philosophical arguments about the possibilities of, and differences between, equality of circumstance, opportunity, consideration, entitlement and outcome are justly subordinated in socialist theory, of all kinds, to political and moral objections to exploitation. Yet it is because neither equality of circumstance, nor opportunity, nor outcome is attainable – if attainable at all – in a capitalist market society, and because none of them is ideologically perceived to have been attained in 'real' socialism either, that the right's objections to the pursuit of equality *tout court* have taken on a sufficient plausibility to earn them a comfortably-sustained ideological approval. It is an approval which in turn continues to damage socialist egalitarian theory in all its (conflicting) versions. So much is this the case that for over a decade argument has logically shifted – as in the work of John Rawls – to determining which *inequalities* can be morally or otherwise justified; on the assumption, which empirical evidence drawn from 'real' socialism can do nothing to refute, that such inequalities are 'inevitable' in any society whatever.[123]

The further trouble here for the socialist prospect is that the left, disabled by utopian illusion, cannot follow very far along this route without seeming to abandon its most cherished principles. The abstract idealism on the subject of equality which stops such 'compromises' is fundamentally incompatible with the kind of realism about absolutes which could have been expected above all of socialist materialists. Nevertheless, it stops them. In consequence, the question of the moral worth and political legitimacy of this or that distribution of *inequality* – a central practical question – can never be engaged with on the left. We must be content, instead, with the measurement of the rooms in one socialist castle-in-the-air after another. In further consequuence, it is the ideological right and centre which gain ground, able in addition to build – as I have already shown – on basic cultural predilections. Moreover, the left obviously cannot bring itself to acknowledge that inequality in wealth has not merely coexisted in a market society but even been consistent with 'a substantial equality in liberty and personal rights',[124] however flawed this equality might be. Such actual or practical experience of this truth as is obtained at the level of daily life serves only to confirm the right's claim to a monopoly of 'realism' and 'reason'. The left counter-argument that, for example, '*any* accumulation of private capital is detrimental to equal liberty, and equality of opportunity'[125] thus not only clashes with the cross-class legitimacy given to individual appropriation, but also with 'lived experience'. And from here it is a short step to ideological acceptance of the right's basic positions, especially if couched in a popular idiom: that 'it is not "fair" to take away from others benefits which they worked to acquire',[126] or that those who are 'equal at dawn [are] unequal at dusk',[127] and so on.

Indeed, it is precisely the right's growing knowledge of the hidden depths of its ideological support which has encouraged it to push its more 'intellectual' arguments against socialist egalitarianism even further. Thus, 'there is no natural right to equality'; 'equality is an ideal which promises what it cannot give'; 'to suggest that, by treating men as if they were not selfish, we can somehow do away with the consequences which follow from the fact that they are, is surely absurd'; or 'because men will tend when they are made equal to become unequal again after quite a short time, it is necessary to preserve equality by the same despotic means which were employed to create it. An egalitarian must either suppress, or frustrate, human ambition: there is no third alternative.' And even, 'Man has fallen. Original sin exists.'[128] These arguments, answerable as may be, are made more redoubtable by the tangle of disparate socialist aims and values which confronts them. Equal opportunity (of becoming unequal) and 'absolute' equality of outcome, 'fairer' distribution of wealth and 'equal' access to control over the means of production, the moralities of human fellowship and a national wage minimum (or maximum), variously compete for socialist attention. And even in circumstances in which the egalitarian formulation is itself clear, it is much more often for the attainment of ends which themselves remain vaguely utopian or entirely unspoken; as if the means themselves were sufficient, and the ends beyond question.

Yet even equality of opportunity may be ideologically judged, by the potential socialist constituency itself, to be obstructed by socialist practice; for example, as threatening the prizes to which successfully achieved inequality is held to entitle the winner. Or attempts to equalize wealth by state regulation may be seen – and not just on the right – less as a justified attack on plutocracy than a 'politically-motivated' general incursion on the individual right of appropriation. Moreover, the arguably insuperable problem of the unequal use to which equal entitlement (supposing it could be arranged) can be put, requires no ideologue of the right to point to. In addition, both in theory and in practice, at an abstract level and at the level of popular perception, the classical socialist definition of *liberty* as *'equality* in action'[129] – including the elimination of 'special privilege' – begs more political questions than it answers. This is particularly clear when necessary erosions of the first in the interests of the second fall foul of ideological priorities, which underpin the whole national political culture. 'An indifference to inequality', Tawney himself once wrote – and even what he called the 'esteem' in which *inequality* is held – 'is less the mark of particular classes than a national characteristic . . . not a political question dividing parties, but a common temper and habit of mind which throws a bridge between them.' He also described this as turning a 'blind eye on privilege'. And who can doubt it, with an unreformed House of Lords and a monarchy buoyant, over 300 years after both were abolished in the English Revolution?

'Who does not recognize', he asked – and the answer must now be, 'most of the socialist intelligentsia' – 'when the words [sc. economic equality] are mentioned that there is an immediate stiffening against them in the minds of the great mass of his fellow countrymen . . . as though economic equality were a matter upon which it were not in good taste to touch?'[130] What we have to do with here is not an ideological phenomenon contingent on decades of socialist failure, as the left would doubtless prefer to believe, but the very cause of it. Indeed, it points to an incorrigible ideological commitment which must be seen for what it is, rather than being enveloped in the shadow of the left's own conscience. For it is in the darkness of left misjudgement and taboo about the permissible limits of what can be intellectually conceded that the right gets away with murder in defence of privilege; itself occasionally ready even to admit the fact (though not the extent) of 'the restriction of opportunities open to the poor in a competitive society',[131] as Hayek impassively describes it. But it is, above all, against the generalized desire of working people, already referred to, to escape the point of production and 'get on', that the right is the more easily able to press its objections that socialist measures taken 'in the name of equality of outcome' have 'restricted individual liberty' and 'failed to achieve their objectives'.[132] With 'real' socialism to aid them, the right's drastic proposition that 'only a very small percentage' of the people in the world of Western capitalism 'would voluntarily choose a system enforcing equality of outcome', in preference to a system 'characterized by inequality [*sic*], diversity and opportunity'[133] under capital's aegis, rides clean through socialism's broken defences. Even the best 'real' socialist efforts at social transformation are cynically reduced to an 'officially enforced inequality',[134] to which the inequalities which arise 'spontaneously' in the market are held to be ideologically superior.

But socialist theorists have now made too many political and analytical errors themselves about the world they inhabit to have any easy – or perhaps any – redress against even the worst of the right's distortions. As long as equality (like liberty) is correctly seen by popular ideology to be a relative not an absolute notion, the cultural value-judgement which underlies political preference about the most desirable balance between them will continue to work against socialist prospects in Britain. This will be so, at the very least, until there is an entire reworking of socialist notions of individual right and social justice. Certainly, as long as contemporary British socialists in a serious political manifesto can urge that 'the concept of equality between women and men, managers and workers, black and white, healthy and handicapped should . . . be *complete and absolute,* without any notion of superior merit or entitlement on one side or the other',[135] political argument with the right will be deservedly lost. A preliminary corrective to this kind of thinking might be that Marx himself, once more in his 1875 *Critique of the Gotha Programme,* rejected the idea 'in present-day [sc. German] society' even of an 'education equal for all classes'. (I will return to this in Chapter 4.) Indeed, the 'democratic belief in miracles'[136] on which such a proposal – together with the rest of the Gotha programme – rested, according to Marx, was based upon the same kind of socialist misreading of the Germany of the 1870s as we ought now to see has been a large cause of British socialist failure a century later.

What have been the deeper reasons for such continuous error of judgement? Obviously, socialist 'wishful thinking' is not in itself sufficient explanation for holding, in the teeth of the evidence, that 'there still exists widespread popular support for the socialist goals of redistributing wealth and power',[137] or for a new programme of militant state acquisition. Nor can we gain any consolation from the bitter truth that much socialist political theory, socialist history and socialist political science – in its often gross, and sometimes highly sophisticated, disregard for empirical evidence and for common experience which refutes its theses – will be discarded by the future in much the same way as the present has discarded Lysenko. For what is required is to shed light on the central weaknesses of British socialist, and especially Marxist, analysis of its own culture; and it is socialists themselves who must do the work, if there is to be any remedy for the failure of the socialist project to become that 'national-popular' force which is the precondition for its political progress. It is also urgent; political ideas which are neither believed in nor acted upon by those who 'ought by rights' to act upon them must lose their legitimacy, and deservedly lose it.

In fact, as I shall further show in the next chapter, the sources of socialist misperception run so deep as to be fully worthy of the scale of socialist failure. They are to be found in absolutely fundamental, and essentially middle-class, ignorance of working-class life and labour.

3   Middle-class Socialism and Working-class Politics

The 'crisis of the working-class movement' is as much the crisis of intellectual failure to grasp its true nature as the crisis of 'the movement' itself. To impute to 'the working class' and its alleged defects of 'consciousness', responsibility for the failure of the socialist project (and its projectors) is to deepen every illusion. Indeed, to use fundamentally middle-class concepts of the working class and the 'proletariat' as the organizing principles of socialist theory and practice is to have been at odds from the beginning with the self-identification of 'working' people themselves, whether as citizens, appropriators, consumers or as individuals. For these are concepts, the only ones we have, which are not only narrow, authoritarian and reductionist, but based on an ideological perception *de haut en bas*. In its light, the usually middle-class socialist intellectual who theorizes about (and for) 'the working class' almost always sees himself as a distinctive, free and independent individual in relation to the mass-object – the 'masses' even – of his observation and analysis. Against the appeal of the politics of individuation, self-interest and self-reliance, it is as if socialist categories of class and mass hold 'the worker' even more deeply and impersonally snared than the mode of production itself. They do not merely *define* the individual in relation to his role within the division of labour – as the term 'middle' in 'middle class' does not – but *confine* him to it in a hated thraldom supervised both by capital and by the socialist intellectual. Conversely, it is as if escape from class and the point of production – whether objectively in actuality, or subjectively in imagination – is to gain an ideological freedom from subordination to the world both of capital and labour.

'Plenty of people will try to give the masses, as they call them', Matthew Arnold wrote in *Culture and Anarchy*, 'an intellectual food prepared and adapted in the way they think proper for their actual condition.' 'Working on the masses', he sardonically (or bitterly) called it.[1] Largely in consequence, and especially in our political culture, the subterranean struggle of many working people to disown socialist definition itself is as much part of the 'class struggle' as any other. It is a struggle in which it is the socialist intellectual who must insist, against increasing ideological odds, upon the superiority of his analytical premises over all others. Yet he is also insisting upon laws made of the same iron as Adam Smith's, and upon the authoritarian designation of the human-as-worker,[2] or proletarian, which is as severe (and destructive) a contraction of political and social identity, in its manifold social relations, as any which 'bourgeois' political theory has invented. This does not at all mean that, say, 'propertyless producers of the means of life' do *not* constitute a 'proletariat'; or that 'the working class' is incorrectly defined as being essentially composed of all those who sell their labour power as a commodity to capital and its agents, and who only have their labour power to sell. Instead, the growing weakness of the socialist alternative – and paradoxically, unemployment helps to reveal it – is that the human-as-worker is trapped by socialist, and especially Marxist, theory within categories and structures of argument which have always referred only to part, and a shrinking part, of individual function. Socialist practice, especially in its 'real' socialist forms and despite its universalizing rhetoric, is caught up within the same trammels.

Indeed, the intellectual necessity, magnified in socialist theory, to reduce often incoherent multiplicity and diversity to analytical order has been the source of over a century of truly tragic political error. Under its pressure, the conflation of individual wills and perceptions within the will and perception of 'the working class' – 'class consciousness'[3] – together with the conception of 'the class' as an actually or potentially single-bodied actor on the 'stage' of history, remain, for all their truths and power, the impositions of intellect upon the raw materials of an actuality whose density and variety evade every such framework. The class becomes an 'ideal type'; labour and the labour process are fetishized; the interests of the human-as-worker become not merely his exclusive interests, but the general interests of the class to which he belongs. Against such conceptual reductions, countervailing evidence – however overwhelming – struggles in vain, or is itself harshly sifted for corroboration of the *a priori*. Thus, to take one crucial example, the argument that factory organization of labour may have served to

undermine, in the real world and in practice, the social foundations of collective action must be discounted against the demands
of socialist theory.[4] Similarly, worker 'cooperation' becomes (to
a middle-class socialist) 'the reality of the industrial labour
process';[5] the 'idea . . . whether it is called communism, socialism
or cooperation' becomes one 'we properly associate with the
working class'; and 'working-class culture' becomes 'the basic
collective idea' together with 'the institutions, manners, habits of
thought and intentions which proceed from this'.[6] To challenge,
let alone to unthink, these fixed and taboo notions – on the basis of
evidence which points strongly, in each case, to the opposite
conclusions – becomes in itself unthinkable.

Instead, the bitter history of their empirical refutation, of
working-class individualism pitted against the collective, or of
'reaction' against 'progress', is as veiled and mystified as is the
world of exploitation which Marxist materialism once entered the
intellectual lists to combat. Not even the fact that modern – that is,
nineteenth-century – socialism was an essentially middle-class
doctrine for, rather than of, 'the working class' has taken on any
greater resonance now in the epoch of its increasing 'working-
class' rejection. The truth is that socialist intellectual readings of
the complex forms of impact of capital upon labour, for all the
dialectical reach of the Marxist variant, have always been deeply,
and self-damagingly, partial. And the working class, embarrassingly, has itself played a far more important role for socialist
theory (and for socialist theorists) than vice versa! At their very
worst, middle-class fantasies about the class potency and class
consciousness of the proletariat have been analogous, even if
inadvertently so, to the prejudices of racism.[7] Class has been
insisted upon as the defining unity of working people in the
manner of nineteenth-century anthropologists of imperalism who
insisted upon the tribe as the defining unity of black people.[8] It is
precisely under dictates such as this, however unwished and
denied by socialist intellectuals, that the human-as-worker comes
to be perceived first as a member of the working class, and only
secondly as a man or woman; just as the black man or woman is
first seen as a black, and only secondly as whatever else he or she
may be.

Indeed, what George Orwell once mordantly called 'transferred nationalism' – the nationalism of intellectuals who disown
their own nation and transfer their impulses of loyalty to another –

is also one of the factors deeply at work in the vicarious attachment of middle-class socialists to a 'proletariat' which is ideologically basically of their own creation. 'The making over of the workers' cause into the intellectuals' cause', Raymond Williams once wrote – but has evidently forgotten – 'was always likely to collapse.'[9] Instead, the complicated forms of intellectual (and emotional) dependency which it expresses have the power to survive even the discomfiture of seeing the human-as-worker refuse in action socialist identification of his 'true' or essential nature. The intellectual who absurdly 'remember[s] discussing equality . . . over a bacon sandwich in the lumpers' canteen in Grimsby docks during the 1966 election campaign'[10] – or the middle-class socialist who, in search of the 'salt of the earth', speaks in terms of a 'reverence'[11] for working people, and for whom to be 'very' working class is a *summum bonum* – may be, from one point of view, both innocent and worthy. But from another, the socialist romanticization of 'labour', whether sublime or ridiculous, is predicated on a complex set of projections on to 'the proletariat' of usually middle-class hopes, guilts and fears which are politically deeply misleading. Indeed, such projections have always had the capacity to resist the fact that this same working class rarely acts in ways which accord very closely with what the middle-class socialist holds to be the former's 'class interests'. It is plain, therefore, how large a part of such notions is subjective.

At its grandest, or most inflated, the 'historic role' wished upon the working class – a role which it has at no time wished upon itself – is truly cosmic: a 'historic world mission' to liberate the 'whole of humanity' beyond all possibility of fulfilment, or even to 'dissolve the existing world order' and 'found society anew'.[12] But though it is easy to argue that it was 'an Hegelian error to have burdened a particular class with the fate of humanity as a whole',[13] it is much harder to undo the disastrous political and ideological consequences for socialism and socialists of having 'dreamed of a proletariat', as Sartre put it, 'in absolute conformity with our own wishes'.[14] If it is true that individual liberty or a 'free society' can have no 'real' meaning without the 'liberation of the working class', and yet the working class itself refuses its 'world historic mission', then the socialist alternative is ideologically disarmed in the face of the right's 'down to earth' conceptions of freedom, whether of the market or any other. A middle-class mythology of the working class, together with the particularly uneasy and alienated relation to real manual labour which is obviously at its heart, cannot provide a secure basis for a philosophy of universal freedom, even supposing that such a philosophy could have practical meaning.

But there is another equally debilitating consequence of the middle-class attribution to the working class in capitalism of a transcendental historical role which is unfulfillable by its very nature. It is that its inevitable non-fulfilment is then perceived as an empirically explicable 'failure' to achieve the (impossible) ends prescribed for it. And worse still, the necessity to 'explain' such (inexplicable) 'failure' then in turn necessitates prodigies of useless intellectual labour, whose largely metaphysical character is determined by the metaphysical nature of the problems to which they seek a solution. At the lowest political level, however masked by intellectual sophistication, they can descend to disappointed abuse of the working class for having failed to live up to middle-class socialist expectation. Theories, as we have seen, of 'consumerism', of the 'deferential' working class, of the 'long catalepsy'[15] of the British working-class movement, of a 'class consciousness' 'subordinate' in its very 'texture' to the 'hegemony of the bourgeois', [16] all have silently inscribed within them the figure of a politically defective proletarian who is the obverse of the archetypally active class hero of socialist romance, first cousin to Dryden's noble savage. To some, it is the 'late arrival' of Marxism in Britain which is mainly to blame for the political inadequacies of the working-class movement; to others, the 'absence' of a 'vanguard party'; to others again, 'the British proletariat . . . has been kept in terrible ideological backwardness by the bourgeoisie and its Fabian agents'.[17] 'History', Trotsky wrote in the mid-1920s, 'turned its nether parts to these gentlemen [sc. Fabians], and the writings that they read there became their programme.'[18] Thus, whether under the 'hegemony of Fabianism',[19] whether in 'unconscious' thrall to 'single-minded concentration on the bourgeois virtues',[20] or whether surrendering to individualistic right-wing populism, the working class – because it has read the wrong books, or followed the wrong leaders – is seen as less than it might be, or ought to have been; that is, in one way or another, it has betrayed its 'real' essence.

Yet to turn the telescope round upon the socialist intellectuals responsible for this kind of thing is to give a truer perspective for understanding their judgements. Obviously, there is, as I have already suggested, fear and guilt – as well as Carlyle's pity and anger – in many of the sentiments as to proletarian virtue and proletarian purpose. There is also that 'mixture of puritanism and paternalism' which 'the Webbs . . . typified to perfection';[21] as well as the complex hypocrisy of the socialist (whether middle-class or working-class) who is socially a Lockean in his aspiration or behaviour, but politically does not admit it. There is too, the prosperous Marxist intellectual, who, face-to-face with the human-as-worker, may believe he must seem down-at-heel or out-at-elbows. Behind the disguise will lie a motive in fact little different from that which Trotsky attributed to the 'socially-minded philanthropic bourgeois', who out of 'compassion for the poor' makes 'a religion of his own conscience';[22] and out of that, we can add, a political economy, a social or socialist history, and (less frequently) a philosophy of action. In much of this, as I have indicated, there will be a complex revulsion from and awe of manual labour. At worst, there will be guilty compensation for even stronger middle-class feelings, which George Gissing almost alone in literature openly expresses, when he writes of the 'disagreeable lower classes' who, he adds violently, 'with their grotesque accents' are 'often repulsive, sometimes hateful'.[23] 'And to think that at one time I called myself a socialist', he wrote (of himself) in *The Private Papers of Henry Ryecroft*.[24] But however extreme, this is merely one form of the deep underlying ambivalence of that middle-class socialism which can celebrate the labour of others, make a hero of the human-as-worker, but avoid the life of labour itself as the worst of all conditions. For itself, it can privately welcome and cheerfully exercise the right to individual appropriation in the market, but deny intellectually that the same right could or should have the same legitimacy for others. And it can bemoan 'impoverishment of the working class spirit [*sic*]'[25] by the very cultural and economic forces from which it itself picks and chooses, evidently without ideological contamination, but which are a snare and delusion to others.

It is able to do this, and commit other like offences against truth and reason, in large part because middle-class intellectual assumptions about the hydra-headed 'mass movement' of humans-as-workers have provided Marxists and non-Marxists alike with a (false) bird's eye view not only of what the working class 'is', but also of what it allegedly does and does not yet understand. Thus, 'true practical class consciousness lies in the ability to see' –

as the middle-class intellectual allegedly can see – 'beyond the divisive symptoms of the economic process to the unity of the total social system underlying it';[26] and it is by these means that the individual human-as-worker may obtain a 'correct' perception of his place in the social and economic scheme of things. The ulterior purpose of such 'unalienated' knowledge is that, through the overcoming of the 'devastating and degrading effects of the capitalist system'[27] upon the very perception of the human-as-worker, he will at last grasp the full truth of the relation between capital and labour, and act upon this relation to change it. (That the worker may already understand this relation from life, and yet not act upon it as he 'ought', is either an entirely taboo subject, or discounted as in some sort a limited form of awareness which time, leadership and the next crisis of the capitalist system will remedy.) In its most extreme form, middle-class socialist condescension – especially in its Marxist variant – can believe that 'millions of people are now *dumbly* enduring the pain of living in an inhuman society, *unaware* even of the possibility of an alternative existence';[28] or, likewise, that 'many British working class people are not yet aware of their condition, and don't understand what's happening because the media prevents them from doing so'.[29]

What underlies this extraordinary (and truly 'hegemonic') readiness to discount, as politically and even morally inferior, the widely prevailing forms of non- or anti-socialist knowledge gained by so many millions of humans-as-workers – with or without benefit of 'the media' – from their own experience? It is the assumption, or rationalization, that the *experience itself* is 'alienated'. Such an assumption permits Henri Lefebvre even to argue (conveniently) that 'alienation [is] so powerful that it *obliterates all trace of consciousness* of alienation'.[30] Indeed, it is arguments like this which license the socialist, above all in his speculations upon the human-as-worker, to depress even more deeply the political status of the latter's allegedly 'false' knowledge. The truth is, rather, that just as (usually middle-class) objections to working-class 'consumerism' are in fact aesthetic judgements about *bad taste*, so conclusions which are drawn by the human-as-worker himself about the 'unity of the total social system' and his socio-economic and other interests within it, are held to be 'false' if they do not accord with a (usually middle-class) socialist ethic of what constitutes 'truly class-conscious' perception. Yet 'class consciousness', whatever else it is, is no transcendental matter. It is a question, first and last, of 'what is going on inside the heads'[31] of real, not abstract, individuals. Thus, except to a Marxist metaphysician of class – itself a contentious category of political economy – it is, and can only be, 'an expression of the effects of every-day life',[32] in which experience and the consciousness of it is shaped by a world of forces, both personal and social. To compose, for the purpose of socialist analysis, an abstract proletariat from real human beings is one thing; to confine the real human being, for the same purpose, to the human-as-worker, is another; but to make consciousness of class the highest criterion of authenticity of response-to-life in the human-as-worker (but in no one else) is a final reduction of the nature of human activity, experience and knowledge.[33] It is also a reduction which the intellectual, especially the socialist intellectual, would not permit of his own case; or not without a struggle.

The socialist cause under capital has of course paid dearly for it. Indeed, the very reductionism of class analysis has itself helped, over time, to promote the politics of individual escape from its categories into culturally already dominant moralities of self-interest and self-reliance. Moreover, any inflexible intellectual commitment, however principled, to a straitjacket of schematic social and economic assumptions, some of them deeply false in the bargain, could never reach a constituency itself in flight from, or marginalized by, the very world within which socialist theory and practice seems to promise only further confinement. It is a political and philosophical dilemma of truly tragic proportions. Yet in the longer term, as I shall argue later, there may be hope in the truths which stand behind it. But what is clear is that the political, social and economic activity and thought of the human-as-worker are determined by factors much denser and deeper than 'class', and that therefore such activity and thought are not capable of being understood and ordered by such a concept, unless it is radically transformed and extended. It is clear, too, that humans-as-workers see their own interests in ways which rarely accord with the narrow politico-economic presumptions of the theory of 'class struggle'; and that, as further consequence, many of the ends which humans-as-workers seek in practice do not, and are not intended to, advance such a struggle.[34]

It is the failure to grasp this which has made a ruin of so much of socialist 'history' in particular; or rather, transformed most of it into a multicoloured fiction. At certain times it has mistaken for the 'class struggle' what has in fact been the complex, rearguard defence of the individual right to appropriate; at others, imputed progressive democratic aspiration to utilitarian forms of self-interest; and seen socialism in embryo, or even approaching full term, in the politics and economics of essentially capitalist forms of economic self-reliance. In the process, it has foisted onto the present romantically false notions of past heydays, or golden ages, of class conflict. As one result, the contemporary becomes – like the working class itself – a mere pale shadow of what it once was, or might have been. Constantly, and out of an eternal wishful thinking, such history mistakes the minority for the majority, the minor for the major, the historically eccentric for the archetypal, and the exceptional case for the general rule. The political damage which this has done to the possibility of reaching an ideologically secure socialist perception of the nature of the present cannot be overstated. For what is at stake is nothing less than the already deeply compromised status of socialist 'truth' itself, in the battle against those (wrongly) despised forms of 'empirical' or 'common sense' knowledge on which the right claims to ground its own case. Indeed, as I have already indicated, the confidence of the latter in face of its own systemic crisis in part rests on exactly such socialist frailty; prevented, as the result of left misperceptions of the past and present, from mounting an effective ideological challenge to the right's own forms of unreason.

Moreover, even when socialist inquiry deals in a plethora of empirical or archival detail, 'true to life', its discoveries are too often informed by false left certitudes and too often compressed within them. Their instinct – despite the Marxist theory of contradiction – is to reduce multiplicity to one dimension; to confine the disparate to what can be managed by theory; and to contain the disconcerting variety of human event and purpose within intellectual bounds which such variety is always escaping. Through the narrow mesh of socialist concepts the greatest complexity can be winnowed into system and order; purely intellectual reproduction can multiply the few into the many; the defects and defeats of the past can be made good by effort of mind alone, and in so doing help to make a nonsense of the present. Thus the *a priori* assumptions which guide so many socialists to their evidence – above all, that the action of the 'proletarian' will in general be inspired by the sense of the collective, and that of the 'bourgeois' by self-interest – may time and again break down, in deeply complex fashion, against the densities of the record. But left judgement can, as if by intellectual instinct, refuse to accept it, or subconsciously reorder its meaning as (in one way or another) aberration.

That *many* working-class struggles and grievances, for example, have been and continue to be struggles among working people, in which the better or more powerfully organized triumph not against capital but against weaker sections of labour was admitted (at least in part) by Marx. Yet it remains a source of intellectual discomfort not only for latter day Marxists but most other socialists also. But it is palpably and inevitably a truth, the denial of which – as if it were a political hostage to fortune – foolishly surrenders the ground on which it stands to the right's misuse of it. The even more difficult problem – which Marx did not, because he could not, concede – that *most* working-class struggles and grievances have nothing (in intention, implication or outcome) to do with socialism at all, however defined, is almost entirely passed over in silence. Instead, socialist desperation is still capable of insisting that 'history and the working class as a whole [*sic*] will decide what is and what is not left-wing or socialist'.[35] Or, whenever it suits it better, it is ready to displace uncomfortable but obvious evidence of continuous historical differentiation in class structure, class relations and the 'consciousness' which accompanies them, with an a-historical or trans-historical pro-letariat so idealized as to be entirely immune from the real historical process. 'In our old Chartist time', Thomas Cooper reported, 'you would see [Lancashire working men] in groups discussing the great doctrine of political justice, or the teachings of socialism. Now you will see no such groups. But you will hear well-dressed working men talking of cooperative stores, and their shares in them, or in building societies.'[36] The idealized proleta-rian, however, resists them; or, if he fails to resist them, can be 'rescued' and partially restored to a pre-Adamite state of grace with 'determinist' explanation of the causes of his fall from class perfection. The issue, simply, is one of cant; and therefore, of a search for the possibilities of intellectual freedom from it, which the myth-making of so much socialist history and theory has helped to inhibit.

It is a harsh transition to escape from this world of (essentially middle-class) left make-believe to the crude assertion that, for

example, 'most [working class] gut feelings are not socialist but
Tory'; or that the 'virtues of . . . thrift, self-reliance and individualism', together with 'harsher feelings about personal failure,
scroungers and the workshy'[37] are more representative than any
others of the ethical system of most working people. Against such
propositions the single-minded socialist, scrambling into ideological action, will be most likely to defend his positions – and
himself – with intellectual images of a righteous struggle for the
soul of labour between, say, the values of the market society on one
side, and the fellowship, probity and self-respect of 'authentic'
working-class morality on the other. It will be a dramatic or heroic
encounter, in which the working-class pilgrim of a Bunyan-like
fable either stoutly defends the good and the true against the
blandishments of the market, or is himself consumed alive in the
act of consumption. In the light, or darkness, of this simple vision,
it is difficult for a socialist to see that 'self-interest' and 'fellowship'
may coexist within one constellation of virtues in real individuals; that 'class solidarity' and the aspiration for self-
advancement, however contradictory intellectually, are not in the
real world mutually exclusive; and that the ethic of mutual aid and
self-denial can as well be turned to anti-socialist as to socialist
purpose. It is hardly surprising if, at the domestic political level,
socialists should then find puzzling the widespread support
among working-class *Labour* voters for the sale of council houses,
or for cuts in social benefits to the families of strikers, or for
reduction in the size of the civil service, all main features of
contemporary Tory economic management; and if they should
least of all know that such a politics appears to the voters
themselves not as vice but as virtue, and even class virtue in the
bargain.

     As I have already suggested, one of the main reasons why British
socialists are so unable (and unwilling) to grasp much of this is
that they grasp so little of the truth of the ideological history of
their own movement. Thus working-class hostility to the state, the
perceived virtues of 'voluntarism' and the belief in the moral
superiority of individual and small-group autonomy over the
coercions of large-scale organization, whether of capital or labour,
are not simply 'Victorian values'. Neither is the resistance among
working people to all but the most modest forms of mutual aid, in
the event of the failure of self-reliance, met by socialist satire on the
moralities of the 'petit-bourgeois'. Instead, to begin with, they are

inscribed at the very heart of the history of the trade union movement. Moreover, it is the practical day-to-day experience – through generations of working-class effort and labour – of precisely these forms of self-determination which is itself the ground of working-class notions of freedom, in which a politically unsupervised personal liberty is held to be the highest good. In addition, out of a knowledge of necessity unshared by most socialist intellectuals, it makes deep connections – which no socialist theory can disturb – between the problem of economic survival and practical struggles for self-improvement. And both, in turn, are linked in mind and effort to precisely the kinds of domestic economic management which the right, for its own purposes, glibly terms 'wealth creation'. Indeed, although alternative socialist ideas – as to the preferability of social ownership, or public provision, or state planning – may complicate perception of these virtues, and even intermittently promote support for socialist forms of collective and state action, such ideas and such action have always possessed relatively little ideological or moral significance when set against these prior 'values of labour'.

It is not knowing this – or worse, knowing, but not admitting it – which leads socialists of all kinds into error after political error. Thus, the complaint of a Hoggart that working-class aspirations are now mainly 'material', where once they were largely 'ideal', is the same old Manichean error, and rooted in a misjudgement whose outlines now become clearer. So, likewise, does the extent to which today's Tory policy, miscalled 'Thatcherism', expresses much and perhaps most of the true spirit of British labour. Even if Labour were to be returned to office, it is precisely this spirit which, *inter alia*, would come with it. So would, for instance, the ethical priority of self-reliance over the defence of welfare provision, or the now widespread working-class conviction that since there can be no significant difference in the physical conditions of labour under capitalism and socialism, capitalism is the lesser of two evils. Not even an understanding of the shared inheritance of 'nonconformism', for all its range of meanings, will do justice to the extent of the ideological common ground of perception not only between the classes, but between the worlds of capital and labour. When the unitarian John Trevor, for instance, established his Labour Church Union in 1893, and proclaimed that 'the religion of the Labour Movement' was a 'free religion'

which left 'each man [*sic*] free to develop his relations with the
Power that brought him into being', the resonances of his
declaration are larger than can be contained in either a history of
religion or of labour. For here is the secular ethic of voluntarism,
the philosophy of working-class freedom, the morality of self-
reliance, the 'fear of God' and the sense of a collectivity composed
of individuals, all together. To take it in context is to spread the net
of reference wider: to a belief that it is not only with the power of
God, but with that of Mammon also, that the individual must
make his peace according to his conscience. Further, the
'Emancipation of Labour' is held to depend upon a 'hearty
endeavour' to obey the 'Economic and Moral Laws of God'; that
is, upon a righteous balancing of the books on earth as in heaven.
It depends on the 'development of Personal Character' too, as well
as (last and least) 'the improvement of social conditions'.[38] This is
no curio of the socialist canon, nor can it really be reduced to it. In
its combination of respectability with duty, and modest social
progress with individual self-improvement, it points us into a
working class world discomforting to the (middle-class) socialist
intellectual. It is a world whose citizens were the majority of the
working class, yet whose 'theory and practice' could never be
confined within the intellectual's boundaries between class and
class, or interest and interest. But it is from this standpoint alone
that we can see – with whatever distaste – that 'Thatcherism', as
well as representing the power and interests of capital, can also
simultaneously recall labour to some of its own half-forgotten
virtues.[39]

Thus, left irony at the expense of the right's reinvocation of the
'Victorian values' – of 'hard work', say, or 'thrift' or 'independence' – is to miss the ideological heart of the matter. For it
mistakes those values as the values of capital alone, or as the
inauthentic expression of a *'displaced* radical nonconformity',[40]
instead of its very essence. To berate the 'daughter of a
comfortably-off shop owner, uttering the limited conventional
wisdom',[41] is to overlook the fact that most of it is also the
'wisdom' of labour. In any case, the Grantham shop owner in
question was a methodist lay preacher in a town which was
'almost entirely working class'; in which 'the traders were of the
same stamp';[42] and in which working-class Toryism and working-
class Labour shared, as they always have, a large part of a
common ethical system.

In fact, it is because capital and labour have for so long inhabited the same ideological and even moral universe – and never more so than now – that Samuel Smiles, for instance, is as much the archetypal expression of the one as of the other. 'Help from without', he argued (of the truly cross-class virtue of self-reliance), 'is often enfeebling in its effects . . . Whatever is done for men or classes, to a certain extent takes away the stimulus and necessity of doing for themselves; and where men are subjected to over-guidance and over-government, the inevitable tendency is to render them comparatively helpless.'[43] Indeed, its theme is a cultural constant, that of 'free and independent action'.[44] To Mill, in like fashion – the very same fashion of the London Corresponding Society, or of early nineteenth-century trade unionism – the preconditions for the 'well-being of the people' were the 'self-government' of the citizens and 'the virtues of independence'.[45] 'Employ them', wrote Samuel Bamford, poet and weaver, of the Lancashire working class, in a letter to Thomas Acreland in 1844,

> pay them, and give them an opportunity for feeding, clothing and sheltering themselves. Watch over their interests, be regardful of their worldly welfare . . . Do these things, and I may defy all the fire-brand demagogues that ever flared away at torch-light meetings, to estrange one heart from its affection towards you and your order.[46]

It is one world of perception, in which such ideological differences as there are between the classes are generally those of degree, not kind. More important, common conceptions of virtue not only cross or criss-cross boundaries of class, but also those between the secular and the religious. From the 'spirit of self-help' of a Smiles – and the 'help from within' which 'invariably invigorates'[47] – to the morally improving socialism seen (by Keir Hardie) as the 'embodiment of Christianity in our industrial system',[48] is a mere handspan's distance. But the ideological abyss which separates them both from the world of collective expropriation of private wealth, 'vanguard' political leadership or the dictatorship of the proletariat is one beyond bridging.

Nor is this anything so plain and simple as Arnold made of it, with his rough-and-ready assertion that 'at the bottom of our English hearts' is 'a very strong belief in freedom and a very weak belief in right reason'.[49] For the notion of liberty-as-independence and self-determination, even if real for some and less real for others, is underpinned by common assumptions, many of them both complex and inexplicit. Their range touches the public realm and the private – including, above all, the ethics of individual appropriation – and they have their own political coherence. Worse still (for socialist prospects), these assumptions have not simply coexisted for a century and a half with antithetical socialist aspiration and organization, but have actually been combined both in theory and practice with them. The ideological consequence is a rich flora and fauna of political hybrids which are equally deeply rooted. Thus, if we look – freed of socialist schemata – we can find democratic and monarchic principles not merely grafted but growing together; a commitment to brotherhood flowering on the same political stem with the practice of racial discrimination;[50] simultaneous struggles for working-class unity on the one hand and the maintenance of wage differentials on the other; and nostalgia for the Pax Britannica with an ethical rejection of political violence. The accusation of 'hypocrisy', being merely abuse, will not cover it; 'contradiction' (too often a descriptive not an analytical term) begs the central questions; 'bourgeois hegemony' is at worst untrue, at best a truism. For, in it all, there is an implicit theory of the state, of natural rights, of property, of liberty and order, derived not from capital but from the life of labour, and a system of values based on its own deep-laid premises, however objectionable these may be to the socialist intelligentsia. Indeed, they can only be added to, not subverted, by socialist principles.

In the previous chapter, I briefly discussed the terms, profoundly unsettling to socialists, of the political contract in our culture between capital and labour. It is a contract which has shown itself well capable of riding every assault from right or left upon it. But there is an economic or industrial contract also whose fundamental elements can equally be identified. It is governed by the same implicit theoretical premises, however illusory, of the equivalent legitimacy and autonomy of the rights of capital and labour; is similarly sustained by a general belief in the rights of individual appropriation and in the virtues of individual self-determination. Hence, its content in practice involves for socialists a catastrophic – because essentially voluntary – acceptance by labour of crucial limitations on its own powers. For once capital's fundamental rights have been conceded by labour, as they clearly have been in our political culture, labour's own rights in turn contract to a travesty of what they could (and for socialists should) become. The 'right to work' becomes essentially the right to work for capital and for the state which manages its interest; a 'fair day's work for a fair day's pay' (from capital and its state) becomes the basic meaning of economic justice; and humane treatment and good working conditions define the limits of labour's democratic entitlement at the point of production. Likewise, the right to express the claims of labour to capital and its state, to extract concessions from them by bargain and, if disappointed, to stop working for short periods – with or without penalty – become the outer perimeters of labour action.

Yet, this implied contract is so central and so deeply institutionalized in the ideology of labour that all serious political opposition from its own left flank to the rights of *capital* will be deterred by the labour movement itself. Indeed, the established relation between capital and labour is usually defended with much more ardour by the latter than by the former; worse, often with more ardour and sense of urgency than the rights of labour themselves will be defended by the leaders of the labour movement. And it is here that we come to one of the best-kept secrets of all in the hidden politics of labour: that its own collective rights have a lower moral status in its own eyes, political rhetoric notwithstanding, than does the contractual relationship itself between capital and labour. The reason for this is simple, and is implied in all my earlier argument. It is because the legitimacy of individual appropriation, which is at the very heart of the capitalist system, is also at the heart of the ethic of labour self-reliance and self-determination. Once more, the socialist price of not seeing this – or at least, not acknowledging it – is error upon error. Thus, to a socialist illusionist, 'the primacy which Mrs Thatcher gives to self-help' becomes the expression of 'business liberalism'[51] rather than of this common ethic. Similarly, a Tawney can speak, with familiar puritan zeal, of the need for socialists to 'grapple' with the 'idolatry of money and success' – 'this demon', he called it[52] – when the universal legitimacy of individual appropriation in the culture, whether presented as the 'thrift' of labour or capital's 'wealth creation', leads both capital and labour not merely in the same general ideological direction, but into the arms of exactly the same 'demon'.

Indeed, there was never a more glaring discrepancy between 'middle-class socialism' and 'working-class politics' than that displayed in Tawney's idly expressed desire to 'make it contemptible to be rich and honourable to be poor'.[53] As a misdirection of purpose, however nobly conceived, it is grounded in the kind of wrong socialist judgement which perhaps has no equal in British socialist writing. It is not just a question of what Raymond Williams once called 'the workers' envy . . . to have the same kind of possession' as 'middle-class man'; and thereafter to 'go on being themselves'.[54] For to acknowledge this casually, as Williams (once) did, but not then to trace out – beyond the crude 'envy' – its full ideological implications for the socialist project, is to set the hare running but not the greyhound. It is as if a fundamental characteristic of labour values could simply be arbitrarily reallocated by socialist theory, and quietly placed in the category of the superficial or contingent while no one was looking. Richard Hoggart, less socialist in intention (or pretension), has in consequence come closer. 'The debilitating invitations [sc. of the market]' are 'successful', he has argued, because they appeal to 'established attitudes' among working people.[55] But even this is much too cautious, not only because the 'invitations' are not ideologically perceived to be quite so 'debilitating' as they appear to the middle class, but because the 'established attitudes' are themselves much more than 'attitudes'. They are interests, not merely 'attitudes'. And yes, class interests, too; with a 'consciousness' of those interests expressed in the very acceptance of 'invitations' which the middle-class socialist finds 'debilitating'. What does this mean? It means that working people – like any other people – perceive and pursue their interests in ways which, more often than not, have nothing at all in common with socialist judgements of what their interests ought to be, or of how they ought to act upon them.

These errors are, however, obviously much more than simple errors of judgement. For they go to the root of socialist misperception itself, reaching deep into problems both of socialist method and of its most fundamentally wrong first principles. We can see where they begin. 'It is not a question', Marx wrote, starting a history of intellectual disablement in the face of truths which socialist theory cannot encompass, 'of what this or that proletarian, or even the whole proletariat, at the moment regards as its aim. It is a question of what the proletariat is, and what in accordance with this being [*sic*], it will historically be compelled to do.'[56] So, as we have already encountered, the real proletarian –with his own aims, and his own (intellectually) inconvenient ways of regarding them – is displaced by an ideal proletarian constructed, on paper, out of rigorous intellectual artifice. The contemporary left's castigation of British 'empiricism', noted earlier, in fact expresses a like impatience with things as they are. But it does not merely prefer – usually for the best political reasons – something other than the given. Instead, in the name of an intellectual anti-conservatism, however justified, it displaces the real, in mind, long before its nature has been grasped. Moreover, it in general replaces it with the ideal and the empirically non-existent. Yet it is on the battlefield of everyday life, amid the 'ordinary' details of daily experience and the perception of them, that the socialist alternative, whether Marxist grand theory or non-Marxist well-meaning, loses so many of its struggles. 'You are misled', Alexander Herzen warned his deaf nineteenth-century socialist contemporaries, 'by categories not fitted to catch the flow of life.' His is both a tragic and necessary vision. 'You can be as angry as you like', he told them, 'but you will not change the world to fit a programme. It goes its own way.' Life, he said, in his finest assertion, was 'infinitely more stubborn than theory'.[57] Moreover, this is neither the 'pure empiricism' nor the 'common-place prejudice' of jejune socialist criticism. It is a realism which socialist artifice, much of it grounded in 'bad faith', can never master.

For British socialists, and especially Marxists, to be thus felled at the first hurdle of method is easy. It is made easier still by the fact that the indigenous 'empiricism' so dangerously despised by many Marxists is not merely skilfully presented to, and accepted by, the culture as 'common sense' philosophy and 'common sense' method, but is itself deeply materialist in foundation. Indeed, it is much more materialist in its intellectual procedures than most contemporary Marxism. It was John Locke himself, in his persona as scientist and doctor, who contrasted 'accurate practical observation'[58] – that 'work of time, accurateness, attention and judgement'[59] – with 'speculative hypotheses' which 'fill the world with useless though pleasing visions'.[60] It is as if we see, 200 years before its time, much of socialist theory pass in judgement before him; while with the 'learned empty sounds' which 'possess no precise, determinate signification'[61] every reader of modern

Marxism has fought, and most with increasing anger. Closer still
to the bone of that intellectual immodesty, or authoritarianism,
which *imposes* mind upon matter, Locke also points to the 'waking
dreams' with which 'men warm their own heads', and which 'pass
into unquestionable truths, and then the ignorant world must be
set right by them, though this be beginning at the wrong end,
when men lay the foundation in their own fancies'. Yet, he
consoled himself – and us – 'experience destroys such systems'.[62]
This too is no simple or 'bourgeois' rationalization for 'vulgar
prejudice'; but even if it were, to insist upon it could make little intellectual or political progress in the culture against so powerfully
and justly entrenched an opponent.

   Nor is it a merely theoretical problem, since it is the practice of
liberal democracy which is prefigured by Locke, and that of
socialism which is sustained by intellectual constructions, most of
whose 'pleasing visions' have been 'destroyed' by 'experience'
precisely as Locke suggested. The popular rejection of what
Trotsky (approvingly) called an 'iron systematization . . . scientifically known'[63] is one thing. But the failure of domestic socialist
theory and practice even in their more modest forms to 'relate not
only to the practical needs, but to the mental and moral traditions
of men and women, as history has fixed them',[64] in the words of
Tawney's injunction, is a much more serious matter. Superficially
at least, it is also more puzzling; after all the indigenous socialist
tradition is as much informed as any other in the culture by
Lockean cautions against intellectual extravagance. Indeed, most
British socialists know, without being told, that reality – 'more
stubborn than theory' – makes its own irresistible demands on
them. No, the deeper difficulty is that the task of making popular
sense of such demands, and turning them into ideological
convictions, has come to elude the grasp of socialists in particular.
The larger reason for this I have already made clear: the world of
British socialism, dogged as it is by 'real' socialism's disasters and
dominated by false notions about the working class, cannot or will
not come to political terms with the ambiguous labour moralities
I have been discussing; moralities which are now more ambiguous
than ever.

   But it is seriously wrong analytical first principles, shared (in
attenuated form) between non-Marxists and Marxists, which also
cast their own lengthening shadow. At their head, stand three
fundamental and related intellectual errors of Marx's own

political economy, which I will deal with briefly in Marx's own terms. First, *all* developed economic activity beyond that of simple exchange consists essentially of 'commodity production', secured by the sale and purchase of labour power.[65] The law of value, the role of money and the functions of capital and surplus are, *in essence*, constants of the economic process. That is, commodity production and class societies are universal, whether under conditions of capitalist ownership or socialist management; while those who control the 'surplus social product' control, as they always have and always will, the whole social order. Thus, the 'social relations of production', in real – and even in imaginary – socialist production systems cannot be qualitatively distinct from those under capitalist conditions. Second, therefore, it is by no means the private ownership (or otherwise) of the 'means of production' which is the ultimate, or even the main, determinant of social and economic distinction. It is the division of labour. 'Real' socialism suggests quite clearly that 'who *does* what' is an even more important general criterion, in the last analysis, than 'who *owns* what' in determining the social and economic pecking-order. It is this division – roughly that between 'middle-class' 'mental' and 'working-class' 'manual' labour – which stands at the heart of every social system and its hierarchies. Third, the 'working class', whether in socialism or capitalism, can be 'emancipated' only by means of the abolition or radical transformation of this division of labour, as Marx himself of course indicates. But what he does not, because he cannot, concede is that the (utopian) dissolution of the division of labour – unlike the abolition of the private ownership of the means of production – would bring down the whole social and economic order in ruins. Indeed, since the whole structure of society, whether under socialism or capitalism, must always rest on the backs of working-class labour, the working class can only be more or less exploited. And of the two major forms of economy which historical evolution has produced, one does precisely this in the name of capital, the other in the name of labour.

Working people the world over have, of course, always known this bitter truth better than any intellectual. And they have known it despite the mental and physical obstacles set in their way, not the least of which have been the hindrances to perception thrown up for at least a century and a half by middle-class guilt projections of a 'work-free' technological utopia. The ideological consequences of this universal understanding, whether openly acknowledged or held in secret, are truly enormous. Indeed, it is here that there can be found the hidden clues to working-class aspiration at its profoundest: to *escape*, not to control, the means of production. Moreover, it expresses a desire for a realm of freedom centred upon the security of individual, not upon the power of social, appropriation. It is here that we again see the site of socialism's Waterloos, past, present and future: in a 'working-class' knowledge of the universal 'labour process' which is derived not from theory, but from the kind of practical experience which eludes all the categories of socialist, and especially Marxist, intellectualism. Thus 'the real barrier of capitalist production', in Marx's words, may (or more truthfully, may not) be 'capital itself'.[66] But even if this were the case in Britain now, and a socialist mode of production were to replace it, unemployed working people themselves know that the price of re-employment would merely be identical forms of 'socialist' labour. And beyond this knowledge lies the awareness, however inexplicit, of the increasingly anti-social and violent ends to which the universal 'means of production', again whether under capitalist ownership or socialist management, are now being put. They are ends which the intellectual can no longer argue to be functions of one socio-economic system rather than another.

In addition to all this, other kinds of uncomfortable truth, hitherto turned to falsehood by the political need of socialists to refuse them, have begun to reassert themselves as increasingly difficult to controvert, or incontrovertible. For example, and at random, there is the dilemma that market institutions in 'real' socialism have the same essential form and substance as in the world of capital, even if their scale differs; or that Adam Smith was correct in practice – and Marx wrong to refute in theory – that it was 'the higgling and bargaining of the market' by which the 'exchangeable value of all commodities' was 'commonly estimated'.[67] Indeed, the unease which all such propositions provoke reaches to the very foundations of socialist thought. For they suggest, between them, that the capitalist social order is too complex to be amenable to a production-based analysis of its class relations, or for its state to be perceived as housed in a ruling-class fortress, awaiting seizure by opposing proletarian forces. It is not that these sources of unease are unfamiliar; far from it. Rather, it is the exhaustion of conventional socialist rationalizations for them which now constitutes one of the left's most formidable burdens. Moreover, it is the accelerating rate of intellectual disavowal of (some) previously unquestioned socialist assumptions which is itself a source of deepening dilemma. Thus, it is not only that socialism's old alternative world, in which the 'associated producers' would 'regulate their interchange with nature rationally . . . and accomplish their tasks with the least expenditure of energy and effort',[68] can be seen as an Atlantis of the middle-class imagination, historically ignorant of the real nature of productive labour. For matters have proceeded much further; and in conditions of growing socialist confusion, some socialists – Marxists included – have even been driven to abolish 'the proletariat' altogether.[69] But it is itself no more than a consequence of the head-on collision between life and theory; while the recrimination which has accompanied the heresy threatens not only to destroy truth together with falsehood, but to restore the proletarian concept in the name of 'solidarity' or mere organization.

More serious has been the slow but growing discovery by socialist intellectuals, for example through the work of Fernand Braudel, that the true history of the world development of trade and commerce dwarfs, and even dissolves, the importance of classical socialist preoccupations with the meaning of 'feudalism' and 'capitalism', and with problems of the 'transition' from one to the other.[70] Again, that the 'industrial revolution' (and even 'factory capitalism') is an intellectual's misnomer for a process without end or beginning, is a truth to appal any socialist still wedded to categories, schemata and periodizations which new empirical knowledge is gradually undermining. Indeed, if it should turn out, as now seems likely, that Marxism itself will one day be seen by socialists themselves to have been an essentially idealist regression from the scientific (and empirical) thought-processes of the seventeenth and eighteenth-century enlightenment, then an era of analysis and expectation will truly have ended in rediscovery and disaster. The socialist sceptic may always have doubted, or dismissed, the transcendental 'dialectical' process, which links present to future (and class to class) as religious metaphysics once linked man to god and earth to heaven. But it is the messianic idea of human 'liberation', whether or not through the struggle of classes and in however dilute a form, which gives socialism its deepest legitimacy and socialists their deepest and justest purpose. Without it, socialism itself would be reduced merely to minor schemes of utilitarian amelioration, which could as well be carried out in the name of another purpose and which could also be carried out by others.

   Neither can the sense that such a fate – or something like it – faces the Western socialist project be met any longer through the nearly century-old (Leninist) device of rationalizing socialist failure under capitalist conditions by shifting the focus of socialist analysis and effort to economies subordinated to the interests of capitalist empire.[71] This is because such a transfer can do very little to reach the deepest and most complicated inner truths about the economic, political and ideological relations between Western capital and Western labour. And even if imperialism and all its outworks were really the missing links in the explanation of metropolitan socialist failure, to ascribe the defeat of expectation so wholly to exogenous causes can do nothing to relieve the domestic political effects of these causes. In addition, this transfer of Western political and intellectual interest has persistently minimized the truth of the steady reproduction, through indus-trialization in the 'Third World', of exactly those ambiguous relations between capital and labour which we have observed in this one. Yet, confusingly, a central (if false) assumption of Western socialist thought and its internationalist tradition – that there is 'a direct coincidence between European working class interests and those of the rest of humanity'[72] – has been overlaid, and even silently abandoned, in the process. But more important for us is that the arbitrary (and even whimsical) displacement of socialist energies from one arena of the world to another, on the grounds that it is demanded by the urgency of the worldwide contest with imperialist domination, can provide no more than an illusory escape from the gathering debacle of 'First World' socialist theory and practice. Indeed, there can be no simple haven in the 'Third World' from any of the leading truths of this one; including the truths that 'hegemony over nature has given man the illusion of creating order', or that the 'chaos and disordering which now takes place as a consequence of man's activities are far greater than would occur through natural processes'.[73] Rather, they confront the itinerant internationalist at every step in his Cook's tours of the struggles – of others – against economic bond-age and basic physical deprivation. They are truths which warn labour the world over that the 'socialization of production', under socialist as under capitalist conditions – and whether in the 'First' or the 'Third' Worlds – has nowhere given the producers real or secure command, for rational ends, over their own means of production. In fact it becomes more clearly so, from China to Peru, as technology advances.[74] In addition, 'creative social labour', as both means and end of socialist endeavour, is overshadowed – even in the enclaves where it struggles to express itself – by its universal abuse for the purpose of mass destruction. And the socialist dream of transcending the given, and reaching a 'higher stage' of authenticity in human relations and social organization, is constantly defeated by the reduction of the workers of the world at worst to unemployment or starvation, at best – under whatever system – to the status of a mass of wage-earners.

But as I have pointed out, it is as much the forms of (largely middle-class) socialist theory and aspiration as the material recalcitrance of the real world of real human beings, or the powers that command it, which are responsible for socialism's failures. Nevertheless it is also too easy to argue, as the right has always done, that Marx's is a 'vision of the City of God'[75] like all the others; offering, like all the others, only an historically recurrent escape from the present, in Marx's case into a classless social perfection which is as finally inaccessible or as unreal as More's Utopia or the 'New Harmony' of Robert Owen. It is too easy an argument even if it be true that socialists, like everyone else, tend in general to acknowledge 'only as much of reality as they find reassuring'.[76] For Marx's own analysis, like much modern socialist theory, is directed without flinching to empirically real economic processes and systems of production, as well as being intended to celebrate their (real) producers. Yet the awesome paradox for socialists is that it is precisely here – in the world of production – that socialist, and especially Marxist, understanding is slightest. The reason is now entirely incorrigible, and expresses the very essence of middle-class socialist misjudgement. For the heart of it, as I have already indicated in passing, is in *the false view of manual work* itself, and of the manual worker who does it. It is the source, the *fons et origo*, of every other socialist error. Thus, it is not a worker's truth, but a middle-class intellectual's uneasy admiration of working-class labour, which speaks in Marx's hymns to industrial machinery in *Das Kapital* or the *Communist Manifesto*. Its 'body' 'fills whole factories' with a 'demon power'; which, 'at first

veiled under the slow and measured motions of his giant limbs, at
length breaks out into the fast and furious whirl of his countless
working organs'.[77] However, this is a description not of a real
machine-shop, but of an industrial fairground. Indeed, the
rhythms in it are not of toil, and of the desire to escape it, but of a
Rossini overture or a Chopin mazurka. Even Bentham, free of a
guilty conscience and the bad faith that goes with it, knew better
than Marx that 'aversion . . . is the emotion – the only emotion –
which labour, taken by itself, is qualified to produce'. To the much
wiser utilitarian, that (vicarious) 'love of labour' which middle-
class socialists carry on their sleeves and in their manifestos was
nothing more than 'a contradiction in terms', as Bentham put it.[78]
The poor Manchester silk-weaver might tell a House of Commons
select committee in 1835, thirteen years before the *Communist
Manifesto*, that he had seven sons, 'but if I had 77 I should never
send one to a cotton factory'.[79] But to have said so, was – and is – to
lose (middle-class) title to the status of 'genuine' proletarian. For
however 'alienated' or oppressive manual work may be – and
Marx himself asserts it[80] – the Bentham who knew that 'cessation
from labour' was one of the 'principal enjoyments of . . . human
nature'[81] knew more than Marx and Engels could ever admit
about work and the worker.

   Instead, fatally for socialism of all kinds, and much worse than
mere error, Marx defined the very meaning of 'self-realization' as
'precisely, labour'.[82] It is a judgement which may be true to the
working experience of the intellectual, or to the author of *Das
Kapital*, but one which few factory workers have ever accepted in
these terms, and rightly so. It is part of what I earlier called the
socialist fetishization, as a heroic virtue, of the (preferably)
manual labour of others; that is, labour from which, except as
'exercise' or diversion, the middle-class 'mental' worker feels
precisely Bentham's aversion, yet which with much less aversion
he will applaud in others. Moreover, it is here – and only here –
that the middle-class socialist and anti-socialist tellingly have
their world views in common: whether in the form of the capitalist
work ethic or as socialist 'self-emancipation' through labour, or
even, most terribly, as the *arbeit-macht-frei* of the Nazis. Not all
middle-class socialists, of course, have been so stupid. William
Morris, for example, showed that he knew that 'whatever pleasure
there is in some work, there is certainly some pain in all work',[83] a

plain perception of truth which (ruinously) can be found nowhere in Marxism. Even Oscar Wilde, aesthete of Victorian aesthetes, was wiser than the very architects of the world's labour movements on the question of 'pleasureless' labour. 'To sweep a slushy crossing', he wrote (free of socialist guilt) in 1891, eight years after Marx's death and in the lifetime of Engels, 'on a day when the east wind is blowing, is a disgusting occupation. To sweep it with mental, moral or physical dignity seems to me to be impossible. To sweep it with joy would be appalling.'[84]

There are still very few socialists, especially of the middle class, who would dare to agree with this in public. Indeed, that they concede it only *in pectore*, if then, is part of socialism's squeamish failure. The argument that much industrial work degrades and abases those who do it is either held to be a symptom of 'reaction' – like Southey's use of the term 'unqualified deformity'[85] to describe the social and cultural consequences of industrialization – or is discreetly hidden under the camouflage of theories of alienation. Most socialist and especially Marxist intellectual theory has preferred to turn its back on such embarrassing political issues. It has taken refuge instead in sentiment about the past, or in arcane and scholastic forms of intellectual competition, much of it sound and fury signifying nothing. Distracted by both sentiment and competition, hurried middle-class obeisances to the working-class here-and-now tend to become highly ritualized and formal. For they neither derive from, nor have much to do with – at first- or even second-hand – the experience of real working people or the conditions of their existence. Even the term 'working-class' itself serves, in such usage, as a distancing term. It, and other cognate terms, can keep the real world at bay and replace it with mere words and abstractions, having 'no precise determinate signification'; to which the 'working class' is in any case not listening. Marx himself was rougher with such Marxists than socialists today are, even in the fiercest polemic. They were, he said in 1878, 'professional socialist riff-raff', 'non-entities in theory and useless in practice', who 'concocted their socialism according to university recipes, palatable to the petty-bourgeois'.[86] By 1879, they had become 'bourgeois converts from the universities', 'one more confused than the other', each with 'a private science of his own' but with 'an absolute lack of real educational material, whether theoretical or factual'.[87] Years before, he had called it 'theoretical bubble-blowing'[88] and 'the brainwork of individual pedants';[89] at the end of his life, he was still fulminating against them.

Indeed, the need to mask the defeat of Western socialist expectation, while avoiding the real issues of labour, has for nearly a century called forth mountainous (middle-class) intellectual effort, with a very small molehill of practical consequence. The 'hair-brained chattering of magpies', Ben Tillett once called it; it was 'wearisome futility' to Tawney.[90] But for twenty terrible years the world of the middle-class socialist intellectual has been more than ever a world of mannerisms, in which socialist discomfitures have been hidden behind a screen of increasingly elaborate artifice. The analysis of class relations has given birth to the language of 'horizontal imbrications' and 'convergent mutations';[91] the Labour Party has been turned, or contorted, into the 'inert, serialized unity of the British working class';[92] while for two wearying decades, socialist intellectual protest has been directed, in one form and another, at the 'nullity of native intellectual traditions'.[93] Thus, utilitarianism has been judged to be 'stunted',[94] the 'corporative tendencies' of trade unionism 'primitive' or 'instinctive',[95] and indigenous socialism (always) 'inadequate'.[96] Conversely, socialist thought 'in Europe' has throughout the whole period undergone a 'profound and creative renovation';[97] the intellectual grass on the other side of the Channel has been for ever greener, or redder. It is a distorting lens this, which has consistently minimized the scale of its own fundamental errors of perception; and, by looking through the wrong end of the political telescope, it has often magnified into 'massive' proportion the relatively (or even absolutely) insignificant. Thus, at random, 'whether socialists should or should not belong to the Labour Party' becomes 'the debate of the decade';[98] the picket of Saltley Gate becomes a 'proletarian *revolt*';[99] and the miners' strike in 1972 a challenge to the government 'by means of *force*'.[100] And politically dressed-up before the same mirror of compensatory make-believe, Tony Benn, for example, is said to give expression to '*immensely powerful* social forces',[101] while the Labour Party is seen (in April 1982) to be capable of turning itself into a '*gigantic* lever of popular mobilization'.[102] It is, most of it, a whistling for success in the dark of socialist failure, while the world of labour turns on its own social and political axis, and as far out of reach as ever of the socialist intelligentsia.

It is not really difficult to understand why there should be this distance. The reductionism of the term '*working* class' itself, and the intellectual misperception of the supposed dignities of manual work are, as I have indicated, cause enough for severe ideological discomfort between the parties. But these are essentially problems of theory. Translated into incoherent practice, they open up a chasm, which grows wider at periods of economic crisis, between the moral and political concerns of the middle-class socialist – naively ignorant of the world of work – and the everyday economic preoccupations of working people. It is not just that employment on a missile silo remains employment, while (essentially middle-class) demonstrators, with their own ethical discriminations about the legitimacy of one kind of work and another, besiege the gates of Greenham Common. Nor can the deep hostility of wide sectors of the trade union movement to what is perceived to be a left radicalism sustained by middle-class privilege be taken lightly; and even less be written off by fundamental intellectual error as mere 'philistinism' or 'reaction'. Rather, there are ideologies, interests and contradictions here of which Marxism, especially, knows nothing. Why? Because, to start with, many working people are dependent for their immediate livelihoods, in ways in which the socialist intelligentsia in general is not, on the very forms of industrial work and reward against which socialist theory and practice are (in principle) pitted. This divergency of condition fissures to its very foundation the common ground on which socialists think they are standing. Moreover, in economic decline, it is not merely an abstract economic dependency or insecurity which increases. For the perceived necessity of defending not only the traditional right to work for capital, but 'the system' itself, also becomes practically more urgent. And all the while, in the depths of recession, Marxists in particular are to be found looking in the wrong direction, and with an uncomprehending puzzlement of their own making, for the appearance of a quite different set of 'contradictions', whose nature is largely derived from intellectual speculation.

Indeed, trade union militancy in defence of jobs is not at all the expression of the 'class consciousness' which socialist intellectuals firmly believe it to be. It is not so simple a matter. Rather, as the foregoing analysis prepares us to see, such ostensible 'class' action – for example, against factory closure – is founded upon dilemmas unknown to (or unadmitted by) socialist theory. Instead, a thwarted and visceral desire entirely to escape the hated world of production into self-employment, and the irreducible need to secure the means of individual appropriation – by restoring the relation between capital and labour – will be woven with fraternalism into the complex web of purpose. But socialist theory, because of the narrowness of its primary focus on the human-as-worker, cannot even grasp that most industrial wage-work, whether in the name of capital or labour, never has been and never will be chosen voluntarily, under whatever conditions. Nor can it absorb the fact that the wage, under capitalism or socialism, can never be more than compensation (not reward) for such labour. In the absence – particularly in 'real' socialism – of the means of escape from it into an autonomous economic and social existence, characterized ideally by self-employment, individual appropriation becomes the principle end of labour. To sum up, it is in this complex of circumstances that the real truth of contradiction in the 'working-class condition' must be located: in dependency, in the struggle to escape into autonomy, and in the desire for uninterrupted appropriation.

We can now see why the making-over of such circumstances as these into a coherent socialist purpose (as hitherto understood) is not possible except in intellectual fantasy, where everything is possible. Moreover, this particular contradiction – one of many from which socialist theory is excluded – is not contingent on the present condition of the capitalist system. It is rooted historically, as I have indicated, in the oldest responses of working people to the industrial process. Indeed, the obstacles now to the redefinition and effective reorganization of radical objectives, let alone socialist ones, around increasingly complicated and contradictory 'working-class' interests are multiplying; and not merely because of local economic crisis. Furthermore, these are problems which reach to the very heart of socialist theory, whose premises and *raison d'être* are bound up with, and even buried in, the labour process itself. Thus, what the term 'working class' means when large numbers of 'workers' are not working, when larger numbers seek, as they always have, to vacate the point of production entirely, and when the nature of many kinds of work is itself changing, is only one such question which socialist theory now cannot answer.[103] The fact that, in practice, the capitalist crisis has served to strengthen, rather than dissolve, the 'social relations of capitalist production' among those in employment, while consigning millions of other workers to an alternative dependency upon the welfare system, is another dense problem which socialist theory is ill-equipped to face, particularly after a century of simplifying error on the nature of the proletariat, its interests and its aspirations. The further trouble is that, on this kind of question, non-socialists have made many fewer errors. In 1862, when Herzen declared that 'the working man of every country is the petit-bourgeois of the future,' and that 'the manners, ideas and habits of life of the middle-class appear as the one goal to strive for',[104] the miseries of Victorian labour for millions of working people justified socialist derision at Herzen's proposition. But when, in 1931, Tawney – himself a Victorian liberal dressed in socialist clothing – argued (circumspectly) that capitalism was maintained 'not only by capitalists but by those who . . . would be capitalists if they could',[105] we do at least come closer to the kind of crucial discriminations about working-class purposes which socialist theory has avoided.

It was the much-despised 'revisionist' Edouard Bernstein who hinted most mordantly at the historic reasons for this (usually middle-class) socialist refusal of facts which challenge fiction. 'We have to take working men [*sic*] as they are', he wrote at the end of *Evolutionary Socialism*. And, according to him, they were 'neither so universally paupers as was set out in the *Communist Manifesto*, nor so free from prejudices and weaknesses as their courtiers wish to make us believe'.[106] The banal but complex expressions of this middle-class socialist 'courtship' of working people – a crude word, but a just remonstration – are various, but they all stand in the way of reason. Sometimes we have seen it, however refracted, in the strenuous romanticization of the labour process, in origin an inverted (and contemporary) form of Carlyle's hero worship. Sometimes, contradictorily, it underlies the disappointed castigation of the working class for failing to fulfil the transcendental expectations allocated to it by Hegelian Marxists. Sometimes it is in the antics of those 'intolerable intellectuals', as Ernst Toller, the playwright and leader of the Bavarian Soviet Republic described them, who 'idolize the proletariat, make a regular cult of it, and teach the workers to despise all other cults except their own'.[107] Indeed, handicapped by one or the other blindness – or more usually, by all of them together – it is precisely *not* 'taking working men as they are' which has allowed Western socialist intellectuals to avoid seeing why their own projects have constantly foundered. Worse, in the last fifty years it has concealed truths much more damaging to socialist prospects than, say, that of the working-class desire for self-employment; the essentially plebeian nature of fascism is perhaps the direst of the phenomena which socialism has never admitted. Thus, the middle-class socialist 'non-worker' who guiltily feels that he benefits from the exploitation of working people has much more than merely local ideological contortions to answer for. Indeed, the misperception of the nature of fascism was a tragic historical flaw worthy of classical drama; at its catastrophic height, when Hitler came to power on the backs, and with the knowing support, of most of the German working class, intellectual puzzlement as to why deepening 'capitalist contradiction' had not promoted the 'class consciousness' of the 'proletariat' was the inexorable (and fatal) outcome of a long chain of fundamental error.

Moreover, the intellectual refusal to accept that in our culture the defence of the capital–labour relation takes ideological priority among workers, particularly in times of economic crisis, over political support for socialist alternatives has been less excusable than ever in the last half-century. For it is particularly since the 1930s that the conscious acceptance, however grudging, of the legitimacy of the capitalist system has been reinforced, year upon year, by the ebbing of such working-class commitment as there has been to the socialist prospectus. Indeed, it is a process of change which stands in sharp contrast to the constancy of those older pre-industrial and non-socialist allegiances among working people to the virtues of economic voluntarism and political 'autonomy' of which I have spoken. Yet from the 1930s, too, came the rapid general growth, especially in Britain, of a new level of (non-Marxist) contradiction: the pledging of labour to capital through the development of mortgage and hire purchase systems. This development, characteristically, has been largely overlooked by socialist theory, which is rarely able to embody daily event and the incidents of 'ordinary' existence.[108] But what we face here is of crucial importance. At one level, plainly, it signifies the social institutionalization of debt to capital and to the capitalist production system. Beyond it are the compulsions involved in the necessity to work for the repayment of such debt, through efficient and repetitious performance of labour of one kind or another. Above all, financial mortgages by 'easy payments', in the case of the house mortgage for a lifetime of labour, promote an unbreakable 'ideological mortgage' to the values of the capitalist economic process. But the real difficulty for socialists is that such a system of obligation, although deepening every dependency and intensifying the treadmill round of life and work for millions, is itself interwoven with the even more fundamental fact of the claimed right to individual appropriation, which this system simultaneously expresses and reinforces.

Marx, for example in *Wage Labour and Capital*, approached the essence of all this – but in 1849 could not come near enough to it – in one of his most basic assertions about capitalism: that 'as long as the wage-worker is a wage-worker his lot depends upon capital'. Indeed, for Marx, the 'much-vaunted community of interests between worker and capitalist',[109] urged *ad nauseam* by the right (usually in defence of privilege), was no more than this dependent relation, the other side of which was that wage-labour produced the wealth of those who ruled over it. But what Marx, and Marxists, cannot argue – because the former was unable, and the latter unwilling to see it – is that the essentially compulsory relationship between labour and capital in exchange for a wage, and between 'house-owning' labour and the building societies in exchange for house purchase, has become part of an accepted *set* of relations between capital and labour. And not only is it this *set* of relations which *as a whole* has gained ideological legitimacy over all other possible relations; the gradual expansion of the economic –ideological mortgage system has coincided historically with the steady contraction of 'real' socialism's perceived virtues. In 1847, Marx was able to argue (justly and on behalf of tens of millions of workers) that 'the loss of the old social system . . . is not a loss for those who have nothing to lose by it, and in all contemporary countries this is the case with the greatest majority. They have, rather, everything to gain through the ruin of the old system;'[110] but drawing up today's political profit-and-loss account is a much more complex matter.

Indeed it is the conscious (that is, *knowing*) rejection of precisely Marx's proposition by the same 'greatest majority' which has turned the tables on the socialist project in all its present versions, in particular upon those predicated on the 'ruin of the old system'. Moreover, intellectual attempts to refute this, if honest, cannot merely theorize their way around the problem. For even the coercive nature of the relations between capital and labour, including in their mortgaged form, has been preferred to socialist beliefs about what constitute the preconditions for a true freedom. 'It is one thing', Trotsky wrote in the 1920s, polemicizing with Stanley Baldwin, 'to work in workshops, factories, yards and mines belonging to capitalists, and another [for the working class] to work on their own property. There is a great difference in that, Mr Baldwin!'[111] But the truth is that there is no essential difference (except to an intellectual speculating on it, in the old familiar way) between working in a capitalist or a socialist 'yard', and no essential difference – for a miner – between a capitalist and a socialist coalface. This is bad enough for socialist projections. But that a preference for working on your 'own property' could have become true in a sense Trotsky never anticipated or intended, is an irony still beyond most middle-class socialist perception.

So too is the irony closely related to it: that the nature of 'working-class interests', as conjured up in (usually) middle-class imaginations, bears little resemblance to what they are, or have become, in the real world which working people inhabit. It is here that (usually) middle-class lamentation over the destruction of 'working-class traditions' – for example, that the 'old defensive working-class culture', with its 'dense and guarded richness' has gone, 'drained', 'pared away', 'gutted'[112] – encounters a dry-eyed world, as deeply traditional as any, which is alien to socialist theory. Its most important feature, in this context, is that working people are to be found in practice defending what they have always defended: rights, jobs and freedoms, however illusory or precarious, against everything that appears to threaten them, and, where it seems necessary, against the socialist alternative also. The fact that further (non-socialist) contradictions play across the surface of this (non-class) struggle does not alter the simple and fundamental truth of it. Nor does the fact that socialist values, as I have already indicated, can even coexist – in whatever transmuted and weakened form – within this complex of working-class interests. And, in further deep contradiction, essentially middle-class socialist enthusiasms and (vicarious) political and cultural priorities continue to battle it out, inside every Western socialist movement, with working-class anxieties over problems of economic security and economic survival. Indeed, the ideological struggle among socialists is as bitter as, even bitterer than, the struggle with the forces ranged against them, precisely because of differences of perception and interest such as these. Perhaps the ultimate irony is that the conflict within the movement between the ethics of middle-class socialism, making all its errors about the interests of working people, and a working-class politics founded upon economic necessity and forms of labour of which the intellectual can know little or nothing, is itself as close as any to the concept of class struggle.

Its highly complex history goes back not merely to the foundation of the Labour Party, where it was the submerged cause of multiple kinds of estrangement, but to the very beginnings of the early nineteenth-century socialist movement. Moreover, the forms in which this 'internal class struggle' have surfaced from the depths have varied greatly. It is in Keir Hardie's description in 1892, at the ILP's first conference, of the 'absence of the learned' as the 'hope of the Labour Movement'.[113] It is in the TUC's Glasgow conference decision in the same year to recognize among its delegates only *'bona fide* working men';[114] and in the resolution presented to the first Labour Party conference in 1900 to 'restrict Labour candidatures to members of the working class'.[115] It is hidden deep in the intricacies which made the primarily middle-class socialist political groups of a century ago, and not the trade unions, the moving force in bringing the Labour Party into being in the first place. It can be heard now, with much else besides, in the disparagement of middle-class constituency parties; or, say, in the declaration by the 'real Bermondsey Labour' candidate in the February 1983 by-election, that 'the people here are not socialists. They are Labour.'[116]

And where such conflict has historically driven some socialists into extremes of anti-intellectualism, it has driven others into becoming 'honorary proletarians'. Likewise, it has always made it difficult to find a political *lingua franca* within socialist parties and organizations which can cross internal class division. It has also forced some socialists to invent their origins and others to deny them; and made of 'speaking for the working class' a comic (or vulgar) ventriloquism in some cases and deaf middle-class monologue in others. In the babel of misperception, there can be heard 'grass-roots' or 'rank-and-file' cries about the 'betrayal' of working people by 'elitist' politicians;[117] militant – and even middle-class – demands to reclaim the party 'for the workers'; and mutually exchanged accusations of 'parasitism', 'conspiracy' or 'carpet-bagging'.[118] In complex (and practical) ways they express what is fundamentally a socialist class division, even if on either side of it are to be found socially-disguised representatives of the other. There is genial enough farce in it, too, as middle-class socialists, with deep-buried condescension, pursue the 'salt of the earth' or 'hearts of gold' among 'real' workers; or as 'real' workers act out to the letter the proletarian role allotted (in the middle-class script) to them. But there are deeper undercurrents also, since middle-class intellectual patronization has always played with fire, or ridden a tiger:[119] above all, the tiger of plebeian hatred, often just, of the hypocrisy of middle-class socialist privilege, or of its complex forms of emotional manipulation of working people. In this class labyrinth, one of whose exits has historically brought the most bewildered to fascism, it is often impossible to see where any of the actors are going. But that it is not towards socialism is at least certain.

Yet, even if persistently false notions of the world of work and working people have prevented socialist theory from grasping the nature of its own crisis, particularly since the 1930s, the ideological hold of the most mischievous forms of error has not weakened. Thus, a concept of proletarian 'virtue' has continued to be *prima facie* attached to the actions of 'workers'[120] – we encountered it earlier as a middle-class analogue of racism. But this is only one expression of a traditional socialist incapacity to suspend belief when an article of faith is in question. Nevertheless, it is an incapacity which threatens every prospect of socialism's theoretical renewal, because it threatens the discriminations which are its precondition. This is not a question of making moral distinctions in the abstract between political vice and virtue, but of distinguishing, say, between the *plebs* (the commonalty, the mob, the common people) and the *proletariat* (working people, wage-workers). Marx himself did not, in this respect, suffer from the same ideological handicap; he is not held back by condescension, fear or habit. Indeed, his fierce account of the French 'lumpen proletariat'[121] in the 1848 Revolution is afflicted by none of the frailties and timidities which have made contemporary socialist responses to our political culture so anaemic. This is the more disabling since socialist, and especially Marxist, analysis is ostensibly *founded upon* the capacity to make true class distinctions. It is as if those Marxists who feel (however foolishly) let down by history in general, and 'the working class' in particular, were capable of 'blaming' them either in the abstract or in private; but too fearful of what they might find to translate their malaise about the latter into honest inquiry. Instead, to evade it, newly fetishized forms of 'contemporary working-class culture' have been fashioned by socialist intellectuals out of what Marx would almost certainly have perceived as 'lumpen' violence or the destructively 'plebeianizing' effects of mass unemployment.[122] Alternatively, such issues have been entirely avoided with simpler and intellectually less laborious expedients: by concentrating on, say, the 'class enemy' or the 'global crisis'.

The consequences of such avoidance have been large and ideologically debilitating. Marxist socialists who have taken refuge from the political storm, for example under the catch-all umbrella of 'bourgeois hegemony', have simply failed to see how large an area of the national political culture – let alone the 'culture of the working class' – has in fact been 'plebeianized'. The *Sun*, in the vulgar (that is, common) stridency of its prejudices and ardours, both expresses and appeals to it. But so does the *Socialist Worker*, bending to the pressure of the same forces in its carefully calculated but equally vulgar vernacular reduction of socialism's political vocabulary – to meet the same plebeian market. Indeed, both are written in that pidgin English which the middle-class traveller has always reserved for the 'native' or 'alien'. And if he or she does not understand, the preferred solution has always been to speak louder and more slowly. That all this, in a highly complicated fashion, derives from and is addressed to the brackish mainstream of labour is doubtless a difficult truth. But to see and hear it depends upon a readiness to get beyond 'classist' perceptions of the human-as-worker, which are as narrowing in their sentimentality (or scorn) as the view of the human-as-black, and as little else, is racist. And once beyond their boundaries, political anger or despair at unemployment, at welfare dependency or at urban squalor no longer dangerously appear – under the distorting lens of unexplored concepts of class and class consciousness – as somehow 'socialist' in their expectations. Then, too, the mass plebeian support for the Falklands war might be seen to have overwhelmed whatever (little) proletarian resistance there was to it, in yet another subterranean form of the 'class struggle' unknown to today's socialist theory. Moreover, a sensitivity to such differentiation might at last begin to show us how and why unemployment has plebeianized the 'grass roots' of the labour movement. It would make visible some of the political consequences of deep-rooted antipathies within the trade unions between proletarian and plebeian; and, in an informed way, put us on our political guard not only against the historic plebeian appeal of non-socialist and anti-socialist doctrines, but against those forms of pseudo-socialist rabble-rousing, left and right, which attract the plebeian and plebeianized in every political culture.[123]

On such a basis, we could also begin to judge the extent to which the terms 'left' and 'right' have broken down against the densities of allegiance and of interest in the real world of real human beings, not least among humans-as-workers. Indeed, where intellectuals – who often have their own vested interests in the distinction – magnify the ideological difference between 'right' and 'left', 'ordinary' perception may more often (and more correctly) see identity and convergence between them. Thus, the notion of a 'left' movement being led by a 'right'-wing nationalist will seem a contradiction to a socialist intellectual, where the idea of the Labour Party led by an Enoch Powell would seem much less paradoxical to many working people. But to get to an understanding of how this could possibly be requires that a fetishized view of the 'working class' be replaced by one closer to what actually exists in the real world. The nearest that 'classist' socialist intellectuals come to it, for fear of giving offence, is in distinctions between the 'respectable' working class and the rest, whose nature usually remains discreetly hidden. Alternatively, 'unrespectability' can be translated, or romanticized, into raffish forms of rebelliousness.[124] Or 'the crowd' – as, for example, in the work of George Rudé – can be transposed to the safe distance of, say, the French Revolution. Marx's own sub-distinction between the 'advanced' and 'backward' sections of the proletariat, taken over gratefully by Marxists in preference to his denunciations of the 'lumpen', is itself insufficient. It glosses over the analytical possibilities of deeply conservative instincts and interests in the former, and the converse in the latter.

Moreover, any form of illiberalism in the human-as-worker can come to be discounted, or recycled, as an aberration from the norm of a supposedly instinctive, or class, predilection for progressive, fraternal and democratic solutions to social and economic problems. That history does not reveal the latter unequivocally, to put it mildly, is inconvenient. Indeed, illiberalism is as much an ideological choice of direction as any other, and more explicable, in conditions of insecurity or fear of unemployment, than many. But, once more, it is middle-class socialists who lead the way in strenuous search for unnecessary alibis, usually buried deep in the economic process, to explain away in the political and moral behaviour of working people, what only a 'classist' would think needed explaining in specific terms in the first place. Hence, 'missing social purpose'[125] – that is, purpose which does not coincide with the ideal stereotype – will be diagnosed as the product of alienation or 'anomie' in one historical phase, and of 'consumerism' in another. Yet, all the while, behind such a posing of false questions and the discovery of false answers, real and authentic purposes, both social and a-social are (obviously enough) being pursued in the real world; purposes of which such theory grasps little. Thus, unbeknown to it, the sheer extent of the culture of individual appropriation not only dissolves in practice much of the distinction between 'proletarian' and 'plebeian' interests, but also much of the distinction between 'left' and 'right' with it. Equally awkward for conventional socialist assumptions is that social purpose and social organization – *for the sake of appropriation* – are to be found precisely where socialists urge that they have been most disrupted, including in conditions of 'alienated' labour and allegedly 'anomic' disarray; or in that Slough of Despond inhabited – in socialist imaginations – exclusively by inert 'consumers'. This is precisely why, say, interruptions of the productive process, which seem to threaten not only the most basic means of personal security but the right to appropriation itself, will be feared or opposed across class boundaries with an energy which has nothing in common with 'missing social purpose'. This opposition is usually seen by socialists as 'backward'. Yet it is also fundamental in its own way to the defence of individual rights; rights which are not class-specific and the outcome of whose exercise is an unequal one; but rights which in our culture will often be defended *equally by capital or labour*, and by means which are in no other sense democratic.

And on the other side of these (non-socialist) contradictions lies the general urge to escape the point of production entirely. Indeed, the deep and legitimate hostility of many working people to their own occupations, except as a means to appropriation, is variously expressed. It is to be found, at one remove or another, in the 'reactionary' objections of workers to the 'excessive powers' – powers never more reduced than in this period – of their own trade unions, in refusal of the term 'working-class', or in voting against Labour. Moreover, this desire to avoid the 'proletarian condition' has to be coupled with the contemporary phenomenon of the plebeianization of the national culture, if any sense at all is to made of the 'absence' of the kind of 'working-class consciousness' which middle-class socialists have been seeking in vain since the nineteenth century. In fact, it constitutes an increasingly powerful *presence*, displayed through and reinforced by the popular media, by the atrophy of artisanal skills, by the growth of unemployment, and by the failures of the post-war education system, to go no further. As I have suggested, it is a form of 'plebeian consciousness' which dominates ('hegemonically') large areas of the national culture and its ways of thinking. Marxists and other socialists, looking to a working class whose ideal forms of consciousness they have largely created themselves, have seen little or nothing of it.[126] Instead, unrequited socialist reliance on 'the working class' and its organizations, as potentially dependable democratic bulwarks against the more extreme expressions of national sentiment – which are no less appealing to the human-as-worker than anyone else in the social order – has been based for nearly two centuries on all those false judgements I have examined. And the world of permanently 'unwanted labour'[127] which we have entered now makes such left myopia more politically dangerous than ever.

But what is the very first step towards an analytical cure for failing to recognize that the working class, together with the work it does, is not what socialists think it is? Or for failing to recognize that it will never be what they believe it ought to be? In its logic, the answer is immediately awkward: that, like it or not, it is not only the 'consciousness', but the very *sense of identity*, as well as the modes of existence and forms of organization of working people which have been derived from the capitalist system itself and from its social order.[128] A second step is to grasp that it is not only out of a 'passive' dependency upon the capitalist division of labour, but upon the active acceptance of the legitimacy of its organizing principle – the right to individual appropriation – that a national (cross-class) political culture has been erected in every Western capitalist country. To term it 'bourgeois' is a *reductio ad absurdum*. Indeed, as a system based like 'real' socialism on the exploitation of wage-labour, capitalism could not have weathered its recurring economic crises had not the generality of citizens, above all wage-workers and the 'propertyless proletarians' themselves, given priority to what they perceived to be its 'liberties' over what they have always known, from experience, to be its forms of subjection. A third step is to recognize that whenever intermittently challenged, however half-heartedly, by socialist redistribution, the structure of (unequal) private appropriations has been relatively easily defended, *especially* at the 'grass roots' where socialists direct their appeals. Fourth, this defence has been conducted by the political organizations of both capital and labour, and around the same argument – rarely made explicit – that this structure of inequalities, subject to minor adjustment, is the just price to be paid for the 'preservation of freedom'. And fifth, the promotion of any form of state-supervised equality, in the name of socialism, encounters in our culture as an ideological adversary principles of self-determination and self-reliance which are expressed in the very ethics of the labour movement. (I will return to this subject in Chapter 5.) The political victories of the British right, despite the gross failure of its management of the economy, become unexceptional in terms of all the foregoing. Equally, the return of Labour would be a return not merely to precisely the ideological terrain I have mapped out, but to the strictest circumscription within it.

What other basic analytical understanding, if any, is required of socialists, if they are to make sense of this? One, in particular: the recognition that 'real' socialism, such as it is, is to be found only in societies where the 'liberal democratic' form of capitalist order – the modern 'liberal bourgeois' state of Marxist theory – had never existed at all, or had been overthrown by external military force rather than popular force, or had been precariously built on the shallowest foundations. And beyond this is the plain truth that in the British historical circumstance, a politics of (make-believe) socialist 'liberation' from the toils of a liberal democracy, however deeply flawed, can hardly be invested with the ideological urgency which was once brought to the storming of the Winter Palace. More awkward still, much of the countervailing British radical tradition, necessarily invoked against the cross-class allegiance to values and institutions which uphold a world antithetical to socialist purpose, is itself more compatible with individualist than with socialist ethics. Appeal to the example of the Levellers, Tom Paine or, indeed, the Chartists,[129] is – tragically for socialists – to militant conceptions of individual citizen-rights which, in their own times, overshadowed alternative socialist principles of belief and organization. Thus, to ask, as Christopher Hill has done, why 'the English Labour Party is virtually the only working class party which is not Marxist even in name',[130] is simply the wrong question. Better to ask, rather, why the Labour Party and its intellectuals have failed to understand that it is *itself* the political inheritor of 'rank-and-file' working-class beliefs in the legitimacy of the relation between capital and labour. It is, of course, wounding to socialist self-respect to have to concede, or even consider, that it is on old and profound allegiances shared with the ruling class that fraternal struggles for the amelioration of social conditions have all along rested. But better this disillusion than the continuous seizing upon the wrong evidence in diagnosing the essence of 'working-class' aspiration. Moreover, what appears in a true rendering of the case to be a mere confusion of class purposes – that is, when tested against a socialist 'ideal type' – has its own internal coherence and deep material roots too; a coherence fatally unshared in the culture either by socialist theory or socialist practice.

Even at the most superficial level, we should long ago have learned more than we did from the way in which a sense of national, not class, solidarity has historically been promoted in the tension of political or economic crisis, both real and imagined. The most recent evidence of it is as telling as any. For what (middle-class) socialist intellectuals saw locally as the petit-bourgeois 'jingoism' of Mrs Thatcher's crusade to the Falklands, was characteristically approved by the overwhelming majority of working people as itself the work of a 'self-made, ideological believer in country'.[131] It is a truth which points straight back to all those severe ideological tests failed by socialist theory. At one level, Tawney's fleeting sight of the fact that 'the class which is the victim of economic exploitation . . . is precisely the class which attaches most importance to . . . elementary decencies'[132] gives us a glimpse of something perfectly benign. But, at another level and at certain critical historical moments – as when 'national interest' is brought sharply into issue – it can also produce a 'proletariat' which very readily identifies with its own 'bourgeoisie' rather than with the 'proletariat' of other countries, and without benefit of theories of the damage wrought by imperialism to the 'class consciousness' of working people. The fact that 'Henry Dubb . . . in becoming a socialist . . . has no intention of surrendering his rights as a citizen'[133] is itself a large enough truth of a related kind to warrant the rewriting of most orthodox socialist expectation. For it similarly directs us to the heart of a 'class consensus' which owes nothing whatever – the suggestion is politically insulting – to bourgeois conspiracy or manipulation by the media. Indeed, when Matthew Arnold hesitantly referred to 'Englishmen of all classes' who possessed 'more than one class instinct at the same time',[134] he was wiser than most Marxists even in his handling of class theory.

Yet middle-class socialists continue in some cases to call for, and other cases to presume the existence of, a common *socialist* culture. Instead, we already have a deeply-embedded common culture of capital and labour; its effects all encompassing, and with its own ideological rationality, contradictions and multiple dimensions – including a shallow socialist aspiration. Moreover, it is within and not against its confines that most political conflict between 'left' and 'right' is enacted; a common culture whose most distinctive ideological capacity is its capacity to defeat socialist ambition. So that while the left may argue that the 'post-war consensus' has been subverted by the right, or 'destroyed' by unemployment and economic failure,[135] the much deeper general consensus (of which the 'post-war consensus', has been merely one variant instance) has been wholly unaffected. Marxists, too, may dream of an 'articulated [sc. Marxist] ideology' which can 'bridge the gulf between working-class habits and values, and middle-class culture'.[136] But such a 'bridge' already exists. It is expressed alike by 'working-class Toryism' and, less effectively, by the traditional politics of the Labour Party. Much more important, however, is that no other kind of socialist politics can cross it – or, if it does, it will be thrown back by capital and labour together.

'Be just towards them in respect of their civil rights', wrote Samuel Bamford, the weaver, of his fellow working men, to Thomas Acreland, 'and fear not.' It is the voice of a condescension which also crosses classes. They would 'not be elbowed out of their place by a trifle', he continued, but neither – god help the socialist cause – did they 'wish to mount into yours, you may depend upon it'. Instead, said Bamford, pointing plain and straight to what I have dignified as 'the legitimacy of individual appropriation', 'they . . . want what they have a right to have, a good living for their right good labour; aye! and they will have it too, either with labour or without it'.[137]

It is the not knowing of this – or the not wanting to know it – which marks that real political chasm in the culture across which no bridge has been discovered; the chasm between the worlds of middle-class socialism and working-class labour.

4   The Dilemmas of Public Provision

Implicit in all that has preceded is that the welfare state has never been accorded, especially not by working people, any real or lasting ethical priority over the perceived virtues of 'self-reliance'. In general, welfare benefits have the ideological status of mere supplements to what can be gained from 'normal' methods of individual appropriation. Yet it is precisely the deep contradiction in practice between the ethic of public provision and the all-embracing world of private appropriation which is consistently avoided in socialist analysis, as if it did not exist. But without an understanding of it the left will never be able to see why the conception of welfare *rights,* so dear to (usually middle-class) socialist utilitarians, suffers such widespread ideological reduction in the eyes of beneficiaries and opponents alike, throughout the culture.[1] Health provision is, justly, the great exception to this general rule. But even after nearly forty years of the National Health Service, it has done little or nothing to redress the general cultural perception, deepest of all among working people, that the benefits of social provision through public agencies are unearned surrogates for, or inferior alternatives to, what is acquired through gainful employment. So powerful is this notion that it has served for decades now to drive to the margins of ideological awareness the countervailing knowledge – grasped much more readily by the middle class – that all such rights and benefits are paid for and overpaid for, out of taxation on income; and, ironically, disproportionately so in the case of working people themselves. The 'real thing' is that which is earned through labour; public benefits are reliefs, 'charity' and hand-outs – not rights – of one kind or another.

'True' rights are seen to be of an entirely different order, itself antithetical to the whole principle of welfare, as I have indicated. Indeed, this is a large part of the reason why there has been such half-hearted resistance to current erosions of public provision. Moreover, on the one hand, Labour socialism has become little more than a system of welfare provision; but on the other, the working-class audience to which Labour addresses its welfarist appeal is the very one in which such an appeal arouses the greatest subterranean class discomfort. More difficult still, it is clear that much of Labour's constituency discriminates in the matter of welfare in ways in which welfare socialists generally do not. Thus, the argument that 'the health service . . . may be seen as pure socialism',[2] or that it is the 'mirror of our socialist principles',[3] is one thing, and justly persuasive. But the proposition that there is an ethical imperative, dictated by the same socialist principles, to pay social benefits to the families of strikers or, say, dole to long-term unemployed 'immigrants', or to provide free health service treatment for visitors to Britain, has plainly proved to be another. Indeed, even the special status of national health provision has come under increasing, and highly damaging, ideological pressure as some trade unions have themselves chosen private systems of medical insurance and treatment for their own members. But these are relatively trivial instances, however magnified by the right for its own political ends, of a serious and growing cultural problem: the general rupture between the purposes and perceptions of benevolent Beveridgeans of left, right and centre, and the ideological world inhabited by beneficiaries dependent upon welfare provision. In fact, the more dependent, the more problematical the relation. The right, of course, capitalizes ideologically on the (small-scale) misuse or abuse of such provisions. But left counter-polemic, for example on the gross scale of tax avoidance by the wealthy, merely bypasses the issues which 'welfarism' raises. Indeed, much of the left's own uncritical commitment to the moral principles on which the welfare state stands, without regard to their complex social outcome in practice, is itself increasingly obscurantist.[4] Thus, the implications of the widespread *non*-use of benefits by those most in need of them – and, conversely, the evidence of disproportionate and redundant advantages gained from public provision by those who do not need it – are matters which cannot any longer be avoided.

Instead, left taboo and the circumscription of socialist debate, as circumscribed here as that of the right, again prevent engagement with exactly those issues which haunt socialist prospects. Thus, the argument that high standards of housing, health and education are crucial not merely to the well-being of the human-as-worker, but to that of the whole nation, has largely disappeared from sight politically, in the face of increasingly blind commitments on the left to 'build up the welfare state'[5] as if no social, cultural or economic dilemmas attached to such a programme. It could of course be – as the project of welfare socialism implies – that an efficient system of social services, combined with basic democratic rights and the removal of removable inequalities, is actually the highest (as well as the only realistically achievable) goal of socialist endeavour. But not even here can the necessary arguments be joined, so long as welfare provision is crudely seen by a minority of socialists as capital's most insidious instrument of labour manipulation, and by others as the expression of authentic socialist virtue threatened by this same capital's reinstatement of 'Victorian values'.

As it is, there is plainly a cat's cradle of contradiction in such completely opposed judgements. Indeed, the disarray itself points to a deeper ideological unease about public provision which, fatally, is not allowed to surface. Instead, simple polarities cloud judgement, equally on left as right. For the left, they mostly concern the practical inadequacies of, and the threats to, the welfare system; for the right, the supposed damage wrought to the fibre of the nation by the allegedly all-too-adequate scale of its provisions. More seriously for the left, such simplicities obstruct the long-overdue recognition that in crucial respects welfarism and socialism may have nothing whatever to do with each other. Nor does it help the left that faults and failures can easily be found in the attempt to organize 'universal' welfare provision. The polemical exaggerations which such failures provoke in socialist criticism merely assist the right to its contempts for the left's intellectual procedures. Thus, the 'poverty trap', the restored use of the means test in provision for the long-term jobless, or widening forms of disqualification from welfare entitlement are serious issues. But for inflamed imaginations (which know nothing of the 'Third World') to discover '*mass* poverty'[6] in the indices of increasing deprivation and desperation under Western capitalist conditions is to mock the truth and the truly poor together. Yet this too is a minor matter. For all such follies are dwarfed by the largest folly of all: that of welfare socialist expectation itself, in a social order still ruled by capital, not labour. Institutionalized disabilities and inequalities – of opportunity, access and treatment, to say nothing of outcome – are organic and functional within its system of controlled exploitation, and cannot be undone, or even substantially remedied, by the huffing and puffing of the welfare-minded.

Indeed, the make-believe incredulity of the latter's protests at the forms of poverty which coexist with privilege in a capitalist order, as they do in socialist orders also, does not itself deserve to be taken seriously. For the premise which underlies such exasperations – if they are to be treated as more than false ingenuousness – must be either that capitalism no longer exists, and mere problems of maladministration or political malice stand in the way of the egalitarian satisfaction of citizen needs; or that, if capitalism does still exist, welfare socialism can amend, and above all has a political *right* to amend, its effects upon the individual. Both these notions are false, and in similarly naive ways. The first, as we have seen, is *inter alios* Crosland's error. The second is an illusion founded upon a classical form of utopian thinking about the real world. Tawney's view that 'even a slender and reluctant measure of redistribution' could produce significant results in the fields of health, social security and education – and whose influence on the population was a 'cumulative' one – is at least founded upon a more careful kind of realist judgement.[7] But he too was caught by taboo, and could only hint (as I shall show later) at reservations which welfare socialism will now have to admit, if the true nature and social cost of mistaken intentions in public provision are to be re-evaluated.

Some problems are immediately embarrassing, and the fact that it is the policies of the right which have helped to reveal them does not make them imaginary. The most obvious dilemma is that, under the real constraints of economic contraction and decline, the growing pressure to renege upon irreversible welfare commitments – including those which have nothing to do with socialism – threatens governments of both left and right with even worse social consequences than their satisfaction has already promoted. Again, whether it is true or false that the welfare state has 'paid too much attention to universal benefits' and 'too little to . . . special cases',[8] the ideological need of socialists to defend the welfare system *as a whole* against those who oppose *some* of its provisions has already had one clear effect: it has further reduced the possibility of essential discrimination on the left between the good, the bad and the indifferent in public provision. Yet, as the right correctly argues,[9] the welfare state in the course of its decades of development has proceeded far beyond the bounds of basic citizen-protection in matters of social and economic need, however inadequate provision even for those needs can be held to be. That is, it has assumed responsibilities which reach to the outer limits and purposes of social organization, whether in a capitalist or a socialist system. But the complex issues which such a development has raised cannot begin to be debated as long as state provision itself is the subject, on left and right, only of the simplest forms of political recrimination. And woven into this ideological cat's cradle, as I have called it, is the long hostility of working people to what is perceived as dependency on public provision. Moreover, if we can readily find in the culture an historical insistence 'from below' upon equality of individual political freedom, we will *not* find any similar historical enthusiasm for equality of individual economic entitlement, which some of the main benefits of universal welfare provision offer. However, for one contradiction in particular the left reserves its deepest silence, or unawareness, though it is the key to understanding all the other dilemmas which flow from it: that the moralities and expectations which inform public provision, at its best and worst, are in essence incompatible with the economic laws and values of the capitalist market process.[10] And because social provision and the market system are at bottom incompatible, they produce in combination an incoherent political dispensation whose logical consequence is the continuous moral and political undermining of the former by the latter.

'Letting parents spend money on riotous living [*sic*], but trying to prevent them from spending money on improving the schooling of their children',[11] is merely one mischievously-formulated expression of a real contradiction which goes destructively to the very heart of socialist travail. For we are here outside the walls of a capitalist Jericho where the egalitarian spirit can be found, armed only with the trumpet of high moral intention, blowing in vain at a fortress of material purposes; purposes themselves defended by a legion of forces, drawn from all classes. Political surprise that state provision – at an economic cost beyond calculation – has not fundamentally diminished either inequalities of opportunity or of outcome, is itself even more surprising.[12] So too has been the fond and foolish expectation that decades of such provision would produce a new 'welfare socialist' man and woman, whose social and cultural attainments would help to build the new Jerusalem upon Jericho's ruins. Instead, welfare benefits, under the pressures exerted by market values, on the one hand become 'supplements' to the latter in the way I have already suggested; and, on the other, the noblest of intentions in theory are persistently contradicted in practice by a world in which public provision is, ideologically speaking, a mere drop in the ocean. Tawney, almost alone among British socialists, once saw part of this, even if taboo – or the optimism of 1919 – stopped him drawing the more difficult conclusions from it. 'If men have been taught', he wrote in an essay on John Ruskin, 'that the whole meaning of economic activity is to accumulate profits for a private employer, they are not likely to listen – why should they? – when they are told that they ought to show a tender solicitude for the interests of the community.'[13] The dilemma is not well stated, yet it is the correct one. For it points not to the glib truism of a Galbraith that 'private affluence' coexists with 'public squalor', but to the much more important truth that integrity of purpose in public provision will be continuously defeated by the greater legitimacy which attaches across the classes to the right of individual appropriation.

The second-rank ideological status which thus attaches to public property – and which has finally blocked the route through extended public ownership to a socialism which 'commands the heights of the economy' – can now be seen in fuller context. Indeed, the proposition that 'industry . . . is a social function', whose reform can achieve the subordination of 'individual and corporate interests to those of the community',[14] has not even been made good, because it cannot be, in the 'nationalized' enterprises themselves. In any case, they are no more than islands 'publicly owned' – the category itself is a juridical fiction – in a sea of private competition. And inevitably in a capitalist society, it is the community's needs, for example for a cheap, efficient and convenient transport system, which have themselves been subordinated to the 'corporate interests' of nominally public undertakings. Thus, there can be no real ground for surprise, or dismay, that the latter approximate in few respects to the ideal conditions of 'partnership', 'professional zeal' and 'public spirit'[15] which it was hoped public service – in a capitalist system founded upon social 'wealth creation' and private appropriation – would attain. Yet the impossible expectation continues, at the very same time as capitalist criteria of profitability increasingly determine planning decisions in the public sector, as they are bound to do under governments of whatever colour.[16] The Sankey Commission inquiry into the pre-nationalized coal industry, for example, envisaged that under public ownership there would be 'more economical use of technical knowledge'; that there would be continued working of less profitable seams and a 'reduction in administrative expenses'; that 'full information' would be given to miners on costs, prices and the general financial situation of the industry; that miners would 'serve the public direct', and so on and forth.[17] That this is not a description of today's nationalized coal industry is obviously not in question. But much more to the point, objections to existing forms of public ownership, whether from right or (increasingly) left, on the grounds of 'inefficiency' or 'bureaucracy' or whatever, are largely misconceived and misdirected. For they point to failures of public sector enterprise, within an encompassing private enterprise system, which administrative amendments alone, however energetic, cannot possibly master. To pretend otherwise is not only political deception; it is self-deception also. But then there are few socialists who would want to concede that efficient socialist planning of industrial output is impossible without both social control over investments and the direction of labour.

Public ownership itself, when plain first principles are examined, must always remain an economic anomaly within a dominating capitalist order. Thus, for all the special pleading which is invested in uncomfortable praise, from left and right alike, of the 'mixed economy', the public sector is bound to coexist with – and, in fact, to be damagingly subordinate to – a-social purposes which are incompatible with the social principles on which it rests. No matter that welfare provision may be socially indispensable in ways in which some forms of public ownership are not; for it too is hemmed in, and transformed by, its socio-economic context. In consequence, as I have begun to indicate, social rights – to health care, to education, to welfare protection – are themselves reduced by a large number of their beneficiaries to a form of property whose ideological market value, with some exceptions, is far below their intrinsic worth when measured by other standards. I am not here speaking of circumstances in which, for example, an old age pension is an individual's only revenue, and the right to it a critically important personal entitlement.[18] I refer, rather, to those multiple social rights which reach across the whole spectrum of public provision, but which the morality of private appropriation prevents from being perceived as a collective or communal endowment. For the welfare state is at best a form of collective property[19] – yet the public use of such a term would itself ensure ideological rejection, for the reasons which I have given. Indeed, that which is publicly owned seems (ideologically) to be ownerless, and therefore not really property at all; and that which is socially provided, to possess *reduced* value for the very reason that it is social wealth, a form of wealth inferior to that of individual appropriations unmediated by public or state organization. Hence, public spending, whether modest or 'excessive', attracts an odium in the culture which private spending does not, even where the former is for beneficent social ends and the latter for plainly anti-social purpose. Yet the reason, as I have made clear, is not far to seek, even if most socialists do not seek it. It is that public provision and private market cannot exist without mutual social injury; an unequal relationship in which, despite arguments to the contrary by the libertarian right, it is the former which suffers much the greater damage, both in perception and in practice. And here, once again, the simplest truth of all is the least acceptable to socialist judgement: that socialist forms of organization cannot coexist with, and expect at the same time to improve upon, the economically and politically more potent forces of the market, not even during the latter's recurrent disorders.

Indeed, it is illusory left beliefs to the contrary which help to invest the right's arguments against the socialist case with an ideological rationality they would otherwise lack. Moreover, in the continuous collision between the ends of public spending and the (dominant) ethics of the market, many of the terms of the wearying debate between right and left about their respective virtues have been falsified by repetition and attrition. Thus, Britain is not a country with a particularly high level of public welfare spending, or an especially cumbersome civil service apparatus – on the contrary – yet the right insists upon it. Conversely, the spending of a significant proportion of national resources on public provision obviously depends on the availability of such resources, yet the left is equally driven to ignore or deny it. And with fundamental argument resting on institutionalized falsehoods of one kind or another, public spending and the private market become, each in turn, invested with vices and virtues which neither of them possesses. As for the maladroit forms of reasoning which pass for proofs on either side of the main ideological division, they merely serve to hide truths to which they all point together. Thus, the right fails to concede or even debate the absolute social and political necessity for many forms of public expenditure, emphasizing only the need for economies in provision. But this is no more dishonest than the left's refusal to accept that the capacity of any society to meet such obligations is 'dependent on the total amount of its wealth, however distributed'.[20] Yet, though all such evasions are equally perverse, it is the left which suffers the greater, and increasing, ideological harm from them, for an inescapable reason I have already given: that the socialist project, in all its current gradualist forms in the culture, depends upon and must cohabit with the 'capitalist mode of production' since it plainly does not propose to overthrow it. In the welfare socialist literature there are of course no more than oblique hints of where this truth leaves us. But then the conclusions which flow from it could never be drawn, since they would require intellectually that such versions of socialism be themselves abandoned. Tawney, characteristically, is both oblique and honest enough. 'Obviously', he was writing by 1952 – that is, after the defeat of the Attlee government – 'the speed at which anti-social inequalities can be removed depends on *the surplus over necessary costs available for the purpose,* and that surplus, in turn, partly on the aggregate output, partly on the relative urgency of the different demands upon it.'[21] But then that is precisely the Tory argument.

This incorrigible dilemma, in its surrounding matrix of dilemmas, can of course be stated in other ways. But the preferred method of drawing a veil across its furthest and darkest implications – by simply shutting the eyes to them – hardly varies. Even the better perceptions consistently stop short of the central political issues. Thus 'the modern welfare state does still [*sic*] rely on capitalist incentives', Macpherson writes delicately, skirting the truth in the act of conceding it, 'to get the main productive work of the society done'. What follows? That 'so long as this is so, any welfare-state transfers, from owners to non-owners, cannot offset the original and continuing transfer in the other direction', that is from labour to capital, non-owners to owners.[22] What does *not* surface in the wake of this assertion is any sense of the scale of its political and economic significance. Above all, what is avoided is thoroughgoing analysis of the confusion inherent in a 'democratic socialist' project which is *dependent on* – and not merely failing to 'offset' – precisely these latter 'transfers in the other direction'. No wonder, then, that what is known to the right by the ruthless euphemism of 'wealth creation' should take ideological precedence in the culture over all such woolly and wishful thinking. It cannot be a surprise, either, that welfare benefits should be perceived by their recipients across the classes as subordinate forms of private appropriation; nor that their receipt should be seen to depend less (or even not at all) upon taxation than upon the 'health' of the capitalist system. Obviously, socialists can be found who know that 'despite welfarist institutions . . . Adam Smith's "invisible hand" still rules . . . in the world of individual performance',[23] as it does to a large degree in 'real' socialist societies also. But how are socialists to deal with the greater truth that both the material well-being of individuals in capitalism, and the vulnerable socio-economic progress of capitalist society as a whole, will always depend under capitalist conditions far more upon the 'invisible hand' than upon the 'inputs' of public provision? Certainly, such a proposition can never be conceded by those socialists who look to increasing state intervention for an escape from their own theoretical confusions. Yet when the left insists upon the alleged inviolability of welfare provision in gradually declining economies like the British, it is also advancing, sometimes cap in hand, a non-existent 'natural right' claim against capital on behalf of labour. And this is not done innocently, nor *in vacuo*, but in a capitalist society which most of labour has no real thought of changing! Against such arguments capital's realpolitik, denying such 'rights' or expectations, has a relatively easy political time of it, and in a sense deservedly so. After all, it is essentially to the determining 'discipline' of the market and its rulers – what and whom else? – that those who reject 'undemocratic' socialist solutions, or the strenuous prospect of socialist controls exerted over market forces, must hand over their own 'demands' for economic and social justice.

None of this, of course, was faced up to when illusory welfarist expectations were being promoted in the heyday of Beveridgean social planning. On the one hand, deterrent poor law reliefs, arbitrary decisions as to individual moral worth which were made by other individuals unfit to make them, cruel forms of means-testing and the systematic humiliation of the destitute, gave way to conceptions of social rights and universal entitlement to them, irrespective of means, class and status. They were to be replaced by a system based on standard benefits and standard contributions. But, on the other hand, passed over in silence was the fact that such social rights – above all, to protection against the consequences of sickness, old age and unemployment – even if 'ranged alongside political and civil rights as the rightful possession of all citizens',[24] could no more 'modify the play of market forces'[25] in a capitalist society than Canute could stop the tide rising above his ankles. Even 'guarantees of subsistence',[26] understood without illusion, contradict the real priorities of the capitalist system. Thus, though the necessity for such guarantees is *absolute*, as measured by criteria derived from an entirely different value-system, this necessity can give rise to no equivalently absolute right in a social order founded and dependent upon the 'ethics' of the profitable exploitation of some by others. Similarly, the benevolently utilitarian argument of a Bentham, which presumes that 'the greatest happiness of the greatest number' is a precondition for general economic and social progress, can only be true – and unreliably true, at that – in certain favourable conditions in a capitalist system. In addition, the principle of universality of entitlement regardless of need, when the existence of need could be the only *raison d'être* for attempting to meet it in the first place, was doomed to invite troubles in practice.[27] The worthy but weak second-line proposition that 'needless' benefit arises from the entitlement of rich and poor alike to public provision and 'confers on everyone a badge . . . of citizenship',[28] entirely lacks the ideological reach needed to match (market-influenced) objections to it in a market system. In any case, it is the better-off and their political representatives who know, better than anyone else, their own capacity to pay for what is provided out of public resources. So that, whatever their cynical ulterior motives are alleged by the left to be, their own objections to universality of provision are, in this respect at least, grounded upon a true knowledge. The left itself knows, of course, that no market system has of its own accord ever provided, or ever could provide, for the general health and welfare of the whole people irrespective of individual ability, or lack of it, to buy in the market what is made available through state provision. But the belief that a structure of public remedies erected to make good this defect can indefinitely hold at bay, or suspend, the 'operation of market forces' in a capitalist system – and even help to pave the way from one social order to another – is again illusion. And it remains so, despite the equally illusory fears of the right that a socialism red in tooth and claw threatens to spring upon them out of the dense thickets of public provision.

The truth is, rather, that the pursuit of social justice and the attempted provision of universal welfare under capitalist conditions do not constrain but, with increasing incoherence, supplement the market sector; their benefits are *correctly* perceived by the beneficiaries as supplements to private appropriation. No matter how far or hard labour's morally just demands against capital are pushed – for increases, large or small, in 'social income', for a wider reach of 'socialized public services', for the more effective 'social control of work' and so on[29] – the cross-class acceptance of the superior legitimacy of individual over social appropriation blocks the way in the culture to any real or lasting enhancement of the status of the latter. This is so even, or perhaps especially, in times of crisis. But the causes of the particular ideological failure of the British welfare state, reflected most acutely in the relative weakness of the popular will to defend its benefits from erosion, are also more parochial and shallow. They can be traced back, in part, to what Richard Crossman called the 'intellectual vacuum' in Labour's original intentions for welfare provision. In 1945, he wrote, Labour ministers – their own plans for post-war welfare Britain 'vague' – were 'almost automatically committed to the Beveridge system', coupled with a 'continuance of war-time controls and rationing', in lieu of new forms of social planning. As a result, 'socialism . . . became disastrously identified in the consumer's mind with shortages and austerity; and industrially with bureaucratic interference from Whitehall'.[30] These are, of course, relatively trivial matters of means, not ends; and in any case, the real moral and political problem is that universal welfare provision is incompatible with capitalism's own impetus, the impulse of the market. But such formulations of its social purpose as were attempted – for example, to 'reduce and remove barriers of social and economic discrimination', as Titmuss put it[31] – were no less perfunctory, being grounded in familiar intellectual muddles and disagreements as to whether the welfare state was synonymous with socialism, a way-station on the road to it, or even one of capitalism's own blind turnings.

Yet perhaps the greatest error of all as to public provision is one which has pursued us for four decades without remission. It is an error based on the post-war Labour supposition that in a society still ruled by capital and the market, 'social services' would by definition socialize; that democratically-intended and democratically-supplied provision would create a democratically-minded people; and that socially progressive policy could be translated *pari passu* into real social progress. The imagined 'evidence' of an exactly opposite correlation is the stuff of the right's own intellectual fantasies, but the left itself must come to terms with a truth of the right which it can no longer evade, unless it wishes to fail further: that 'high moral motives', such as those which informed the projects of the welfare system – Crossman's 'intellectual vacuum' notwithstanding – do not necessarily promote the 'highest virtues'[32] in others, particularly when the boulder of capital is for ever rolling downhill upon the Sisyphus of labour.

It is an old truth, but most of the left has either not wanted, or been unable, to grasp it. Karl Kautsky, for example, before the modern phase of welfare provision, shared the very premise of welfare socialism which events have most consistently and bewilderingly falsified. The 'slightest reform', he wrote in *The Social Revolution*, could be 'of great significance' for the 'physical and intellectual rebirth of the proletariat'.[33] But the 'great significance' of four decades of social reform through public provision in our own culture has actually been a great deal more complex and a great deal less social than the left ever anticipated, or than it has subsequently admitted. The political cost of this outcome is a large one, and will grow larger. For it is common ground that the very notion of 'socialism', whatever its variant meanings, must contain at its heart the aspiration for the 'social'. Therefore, any evidence that socialist-inspired conceptions of social progress, social development and social education have seriously failed to enhance the status of a social over an individualistic ethic – whether under favourable capitalist or favourable socialist conditions – must strike a chill into all socialist purpose. After all, no truly social order, as socialists understand it, can be founded upon widespread a-social individual impulses. Or to put it another way, a social ethic and socialism are not merely philosophical and political close relations; the latter, at least in aspiration, is the political embodiment of the former. And when we find welfare socialists working to egalitarian conceptions which are not only intellectually and morally inexplicit, but which also have little or nothing to say of the quality and purpose of this equality, a truly social impulse cannot be extrapolated from such confusion and silence merely by wishful thinking. Indeed, most of today's welfare socialists rightly cannot envisage any society in which complete equality of opportunity, let alone of outcome, is attained. Instead, they seem to seek the equalization of nothing more than entitlements to enhanced public provision, many of them increasingly tawdry in content in an economy which is declining. Moreover, this socialization of entitlement is for the achievement of social ends which remain unweighed and un-spoken. This is not simply to reduce the meaning of equality, in very rough and ready fashion, to a narrow and practical enough compass; but to reduce it to an 'equality' in which the job centre and the social security office, like the soup-kitchen and the workhouse before them, define the outer perimeters of a social purpose which is not merely shrunken, but itself a-social. It is here, of course, that the absence of any necessary connection between welfarism and socialism is at its most obvious. But even when the boundaries of welfare socialist aspiration are pushed further outwards, the social uses to which egalitarian opportunity and entitlement are to be put generally remain in the laps of the gods of capital. In fact, it is all little more than the making of a political mare's nest; but it is also the point at which socialist failure under capitalist conditions is inscribed most clearly. It is true, of course, that equality in a market system can rarely mean more in practice than a superficial and essentially unsupervised equality of opportunity to become unequal. Yet not even this can explain, nor justify, the extent of British welfarism's contraction of the moral purposes of socialism to the small change of public benefaction.

Indeed, after forty years of welfare, the 'intellectual vacuum' to which Crossman referred is arguably more void than ever. To take a larger example at random: the slogan of 'social services for all', offered in a socialist manifesto, shows how far down the narrowing road of market reductions of socialist aspiration even the Labour left can travel. Thus, in 1982, Cripps and Griffith, without intellectual qualm conflating 'goods, services and responsibilities' together, were concerned with how 'types of consumption which contribute to people's 'well-being' – including the 'consumption' of free or cheap public transport – 'might be extended'.[34] And yet it is the right which is generally blamed by the left for exactly such reductions. Thus, it is accused of perceiving even medical care to be a 'personal consumption good',[35] or charged with applying 'consumerist' criteria to the welfare system as a whole, in order to 'challenge the existing acceptance of social provision'.[36] But in the left's own vacuum, both the purposes and the effects – social, cultural, moral – of public provision are largely taken for granted. Accordingly, the project of 'building the welfare state' becomes as unproblematical in its outcome as it is unfocused in its intention. Yet as Hayek has argued and as the left must argue also, 'the welfare of a people, like the happiness of a man, cannot be adequately expressed as a single end',[37] particularly not an end which is no more than a general slogan. Even if Hayek's argument were a false one, socialism's universalizing aspiration for a common rule for all to live by places a particularly heavy ideological burden on its formulations of purpose. Why? Precisely because general and systematic social provision is given priority over individual preference and private 'choices'. That is, the more random 'play of market forces' can tolerate as part of its logic the seeming absence of overarching ideological intention. Socialist projects, which ostensibly aim to master 'irrational' market forces in the name of socialist coherence, cannot. Indeed, lacking a clearly understood and popularly accepted social and moral purpose, a socialist programme – whether under capitalist or socialist conditions – can never make its ideological way against individual predilection, without inviting continuous political defeat in the first case, and demanding coercion in the second.

Moreover, planning for social and economic justice raises difficulties of theory and practice which provoke easy attack from the right on the left's often less well-guarded ideological defences. Indeed, under capitalist conditions, the left is a sitting target. Thus, public provision is seen to be for ever (and impossibly) repairing 'strokes of misfortune', 'disappointments' and 'defeats' sustained in 'market competition'. In consequence, socialists are held to be 'unable to refuse responsibility for anybody's fate or position'.[38] Or going back to first principles – and theories of human nature – the right can be heard asking the left, with growing confidence, 'if man [sic] did not, driven by self-interest, care for himself and his family, then who would care for them?'; and less scrupulously, 'if others are to care for him while he [sic] cares for others, what purpose will be served?'[39] But even if such questions are held by the left to parody the true nature of individual motive and social provision, the knowledge that the great majority of working people would agree that 'a man's first duty' is 'to support himself' and 'not depend on others'[40] should long ago have been a corrective to the left's own forms of glibness. The left, in turn, can justly seize upon the many cynicisms of the right; but it has been prevented from seeing or acknowledging that the right can normally get the better of it, even on the ground of moral argument, wherever the latter's positions are ideologically perceived to be 'more realistic' or truer to public experience. Take, for example, the dispersal and contraction of the family to a nucleus of the parents and their dependent children, together with the reduction in the scope of inter- and intra-family assistance. It is a general cultural phenomenon of which the great majority of the population has the directest kind of knowledge. Now it is this complex social process which has arguably been both cause *and effect* of historically-increasing expectations of welfare provision and of its 'communal shouldering of obligations'.[41] But this argument certainly cannot be met politically (or intellectually) by reflex left recoil from the whole notion of 'individual responsibility' and, by extension, of family provision. It is a recoil which is not shared by its political constituency. Indeed, it is precisely at the point where public policy intersects with personal circumstance that, paradoxically and disastrously, socialist moral argument often turns out to be least persuasive. Thus, a socialist will hold that it is an 'essential part' of public provision to shield the citizen against 'the contingencies of life'.[42] But right objections, often dismissive, that it is not part of the function of government to seek to protect individuals from 'the vicissitudes of fortune',[43] themselves appeal to a 'sense of the practical', confirmed by daily experience, which in turn reads utopian impossibilities into left aspiration. The left's own ironies about the politically disabling nature of such 'common-sense' beliefs, as if 'common sense' were by definition inferior to other forms of knowledge, are themselves much more disabling. Indeed, after two centuries of ideological counter-effort, and four decades of post-war welfare, Adam Smith's ruthless proposition that 'nobody but a beggar chooses to depend chiefly upon the benevolence of his fellow-citizens'[44] would still command overwhelming assent across the classes – notwithstanding left protestations that 'benevolence' and the welfare system have nothing in common.

It is not really surprising, therefore, that the right's often false criticisms, whether of the 'inefficiency' or 'impersonality' of public provision, or of the alleged moral harm which is done to its beneficiaries – 'wards of the state', Friedman has harshly called them[45] – should now have such a reach in the culture. Indeed, Gradgrind objections to welfare provision, some trivial and others of great substance, could not be pressed far by the right without the confidence that its leading ideological assertions – for example, that 'moral responsibility is an individual matter, not a social matter'[46] – were widely shared and deeply grounded; so widely shared that it has arguably become superfluous today for the right to urge so strenuously that 'paternalistic' provision 'reduces the incentive to work, save, and innovate' and even 'limits our freedom'.[47] More modest forms of intelligent reservation are threatening enough to welfare socialist arguments. Yet it is also the demagogic or 'popular' objections to public provision and its administration which are the most difficult for the left to counter, precisely because they contain truths which the left refuses to acknowledge. 'The poor', Milton Friedman insists, mischievously posing as the defender of their interest, 'tend to pay taxes for more years, and receive benefits for fewer years, than the rich – all in the name of helping the poor.' Or again, 'the middle- and upper-income classes have conned the poor into subsidizing us on the grand scale'; especially in higher education, where, Friedman claims, those who obtain its benefits are subsidized 'at the expense of those who do not'.[48] Dangerously for socialists, such argument directed against the principle of universality of contribution and benefit is ostensibly derived from a concern – hitherto the monopoly, in its own eyes, of the left – for securing greater social and individual justice in public provision. It is dangerous because, in so far as Friedman's assertions are true, they again expose the Achilles heel of the welfare socialist case: namely, its own ideological refusal (morally justifiable as may be) to countenance selectivity of provision based on need, for fear of compromising its whole project. Yet such refusal is short-sighted, especially when careful ideological judgement is demanded of the left, as never before, in meeting the right's challenge. Moreover, it is merely to compound two of the dilemmas to which I have referred: that there is no necessary connection between every means of welfare provision and the ends of socialist aspiration, and that meeting need is the object of all such provision in the first place! Above all, it assumes without more ado what remains to be

proved: that universal provision is democratic or egalitarian in its
effects under capitalist conditions, merely because it is democratic
or egalitarian in intention.

This is a complex set of circumstances, and not only because the
right blurs the issues by pretending to solicitudes it does not really
share. Furthermore, the right's own corpus of positions is by no
means simple or coherent, permitting certain kinds of ameliorative
public action on utilitarian grounds, those of a right-wing realpolitik, while rejecting others 'on principle'. But welfare socialists
themselves cannot see that the Benthamite aspiration for 'the
greatest happiness of the greatest number' – a notion which they
themselves espouse – was historically an illiberal antidote to the
ideological threat which was posed throughout Europe in the
wake of the French Revolution; an attempt to meet the politics of
the Declaration of the Rights of Man, and the slogans of 'Liberty,
Equality and Fraternity', with the enlightened benevolence of the
reformer. Thus, it was logically consistent that Bentham, the true
philosophical progenitor of the purposes of the welfare system,
should have held the doctrine of the 'natural rights of man' to be
'nonsense'.[49] It is therefore also consistent that today's left should
appreciate that the right has a strong case, albeit mobilized for its
own political purposes, when it urges that Benthamite welfare
provision 'limits our freedom'. Indeed, it is a case which any
reexamination of the political arguments of the French Revolution
will reveal to have even more to say to the left than to the right.
Yet, by left default, as I pointed out earlier, the right has
succeeded in taking much of the high ground of philosophical
debate about the meanings of freedom. At the very least, the left
could begin its counter-attack by conceding as much as the
dogmatic libertarian right has conceded in its admission that
'some security', provided by state action, 'is essential if freedom is
to be preserved'.[50] Thus, the left needs in turn to recognize that
there is no necessary connection, to put it modestly, between every
kind of welfare provision without discrimination and the enhancement of those forms of liberty which socialism has historically
sought to promote. The noble attempt to provide citizens with
'security against unmerited misfortunes, caused by forces which
individuals . . . are powerless to control'[51] is one thing. But the
plethora of difficulties, social, cultural, political – some real,
others imagined – which is held by the right to ensue from such an
attempt is another, and the left can no longer afford to baulk at

them. It might learn instead from Mill, who as early as 1859 fastened with unwonted vigour on what he saw as the risk of 'conversion' of 'the active and ambitious part of the public into hangers-on of the government'.[52] Of course, in our own times, there are new views – though not very new – of these old problems. They range, broadly speaking, from the claim that 'the more remote the services . . . the less interest . . . people [take] in them',[53] to the assertion that the 'moral base of community life' is not 'reproduced' when 'public authority' displaces 'community effort'.[54] But implicit for over a century in all such arguments has been the consistent proposition that certain kinds of social provision can have serious a-social consequence. Indeed, socialists who now contemplate the social and cultural wasteland at the heart of the welfare system can less than ever avoid such arguments; least of all when their own deepest theoretical assumptions as to the inevitable enhancement of social progress through public provision have been to such a large extent refuted in practice.

Of all left responses, however, the decrying of 'concern for self and responsibility for self',[55] under conditions of economic decline and growing urban squalor, is the most serious ideological mismatch with popular – and especially working-class – perceptions. No doubt much of the 'evidence' which the right adduces as to 'welfare dependency' and its supposed (and real) passivities, is false, unjust or over-heated. But it can provide no legitimation for equally great or greater left errors of judgement. Thus, there can be no real grounds for incredulity that Labour in office launched an 'official campaign against "scroungers" ',[56] when Samuel Smiles's belief that 'where men are subjected to over-guidance . . . the inevitable tendency is to render them comparatively helpless'[57] is probably more widely believed among Labour's working-class and unemployed consitituency than anywhere else in the culture. Certainly, what the right, for its own ideological purposes, regards as the release of personal initiative is more, not less, likely to appeal politically to 'dependent' beneficiaries of public provision than enhanced welfare protection is. Indeed, the left would be ideologically better equipped to face its opponents if it took it as axiomatic that the longer the individual citizen required 'help from without' – 'often enfeebling in its effects', as Smiles scornfully described it[58] – the greater is the ideological appeal of 'responsibility for self'. Yet most of the left blindly

persists in equating such notions with the competitive self-interest
of the market. Instead, the just recoil of the individual from a
welfare relation between state and citizen could well have more in
common with a search even for socialist meanings of freedom than
most socialists themselves are now able to recognize. Moreover, in
so far as the welfare relation is itself invested by socialists with no
ulterior moral purpose, its rejection might be counted a step
forward. In any case, the time has already come – and may even
have passed – when 'helping . . . men to elevate and improve
themselves by their own free and independent action'[59] needs to
be reclaimed from the right as also a main purpose of the socialist
pursuit of social justice; and not least because it is a notion deeply
embedded in the ethics of labour. Socialists might then see that
the true significance of mass unemployment *to the unemployed* is
neither that it brings the 'contradictions of capitalism' to a new
and acute stage, nor (even less) that socialism's moment ripens in
economic disaster, but that it excludes the unemployed from the
'free and independent action' – however illusory in practice –
which Samuel Smiles celebrated.

In fact, there can be no informed discussion of the reasons for
working-class ambivalence about the benefits of public provision,
without continued reminder of the ways in which notions of
self-help and social autonomy are institutionalized in the labour
movement itself. It is in the ethic of 'voluntarism', in the rights of
'free' collective bargaining, and in the long history of resistance to
'state interference' with trade union self-regulation. For labour's
perceived right to make its own 'free' bargain with capital, on the
basis of self-organization, has much more to do with claims to an
independence from state power than with a challenge to it. And
though the self-organization takes a collective form, it is most
accurately understood as a means to the end of acquiring such
independence.[60] (To confuse this kind of instrumental collectivism with the collectivism of more obvious socialist purpose – for
example, that which is directed at the collective ownership of the
means of production – is a separate and additional error, to which
I will turn in the next chapter.) Indeed, the concept of political
and economic 'autonomy' which informs such aspiration rests
upon a political theory of the *'private' rights and interests* of labour
and the trade unions; rights and interests which must be advanced
and defended by means of social organization because there are no
other practical means to advance and defend them. Thus, in our

culture, working-class self-organization is not for the most part what socialists, and especially Marxists, have wanted to make of it – an expression of socialist means, and socialist 'consciousness', for socialist and even collectivist ends. Instead, it is the social expression to capital of the 'private' interest of labour. Thus, we can begin to see from yet another vantage point why the world created by public provision and public ownership – even if objectively in the general interests of labour – should have earned such inconstant ideological regard from working people. But the virtues of 'self-help', or 'self-discipline', or 'responsibility for self' require no special pleading, nor equivalent political effort, to justify them.

If one looks across the socialist literature, past and present, on the question of state provision, Marx's work included, a fragmentary sense of all these formidable difficulties posed to socialist purpose can sometimes be made out. But at best it is a matter of hints and suggestions whose logical implications are never pursued very far, and for good reasons. Thus, at random, 'those who have been benefited most', Titmuss wrote in 1960 of welfare provision, 'are those who have needed it least'.[61] This is Friedman's point also; but what is left candour in the first, becomes right reaction in the second! Even the Webbs can be found arguing, in 1948, that 'the fact that sick and unemployed persons were entitled to money incomes without any corresponding obligation to get well and keep well, or to seek and keep employment, seemed to us likely to encourage malingering [*sic*], and a disinclination to work for their livelihood'.[62] But this was a retrospective judgement, and one given no priority in their Fabian practice. In his *Equality*, Tawney, too, thought that public provision should be 'adequate in amount, but its use should be discriminating, and the more it increases, the greater the need for discrimination becomes', especially in circumstances of unemployment. Why? 'The reason', he answers, 'is not the occurrence of individual malpractices, which are statistically unimportant. It is the danger of encouraging . . . social malingering.' (The alternative he offers is 'treatment of a different type' and a 'drastic change of regimen', though what this means is not spelled out.)[63] But it is not the use, in both these cases, of a term like 'malingering' – a form of harsh reproof normally associated with 'reactionary' assaults on the 'workshy' – which surprises. It is rather the speed at which the profound social issues, standing behind the form of the argument itself, are dropped; not the sound of the propositions themselves which puzzles, but the silence which follows, a silence in which the right makes all its advances. There is a similar silence, fatal to the legitimacy of socialist purposes, in Raymond Williams's merely passing mention of the 'hostility' among working people 'to one's life being determined in a dominative mood, by whatever idealism or benevolence'.[64] Yet it is a premise of welfare socialism, and other socialisms too, that precisely such idealistic or benevolent 'determination' should work upon the individual's life. If the working man or woman is truly 'hostile' to it, as Williams correctly admits, such 'hostility' cannot be left merely to hint at the reasons for welfare socialism's ideological failures. More recently, the unsatisfactory raising – and swifter dropping – of left 'suggestions' which reach to the core of welfare socialism's intentions has gone still further. Thus, 'welfarism' can even be openly asserted to 'reduce consciousness, awareness and general political education';[65] but the drastic implications for present socialist plans and prospects which such a proposition holds, if true, are sedulously avoided.

Marx, at least, did not hesitate or equivocate in these ways, even if his politics seems – and sometimes is – very much closer to where the libertarian right rather than the left now stands, Marxists included. 'The proletariat', he wrote in 1847, one year before the *Manifesto*, 'not wishing to be treated as a rabble, needs its courage, its self-respect, its pride and its sense of independence even more than its bread.'[66] Such a sentiment cannot of course be squared with much of what has passed for socialist theory and practice since. But it is fully compatible, and indeed exactly expresses, those forms of belief among working people which I have been discussing. Moreover, in the *Manifesto* itself, Marx took the view that 'the bourgeoisie . . . [was] unfit to rule because it cannot help letting him [sc. the proletarian] sink into such a state' – we might call it the welfare state – 'that it has to feed him, instead of being fed by him'.[67] The remark is a complex one, and has been historically unregarded. Yet it points directly to Marx's healthy distaste for precisely what welfare socialism holds dear. Indeed, in his *Critique of the Gotha Programme*, more than twenty-five years later, Marx went much further, attacking fellow socialists for what he called their 'servile belief in the state'.[68] Marx's own attitude to the state, like that of all socialists, is contradictory and inconsistent. But the meanings which he gives to the embattled and exploited 'independence' of labour under capitalist conditions have nothing in common with welfare socialist intentions.

The continuous hints, in the more recent literature, of suppressed (and confused) left anxieties about 'dependency' on welfare and its social consequences – like those which attach to 'consumerism' and its supposed effects – are themselves some measure of the correctness of Marx's own fierce judgements. Nevertheless, the left cannot follow the right, without complex sociological disguise, into the latter's underworld of argument about the 'feckless' poor, or about the harm to 'the sense of personal responsibility for one's own actions' which the right alleges is suffered by the beneficiaries of public provision. Yet, at the same time, largely unexpressed unease about 'welfarism' has itself created an ideological labyrinth of left inhibitions, from which political escape with a clear sense of social direction is extremely difficult. Left objections that there is more extensive welfare provision, and of higher standards, in other countries, or that welfare cover in Britain is so inadequate in practice that the very term 'welfare state' is a misnomer, do not meet any of the essential reservations I have noted. In fact, they compound the unresolved difficulties by proceeding further still into the existing dilemma. Certainly, the times are long gone when what Tawney (strangely but significantly) called the 'dividends' from 'investments' in the social services could be unproblematically held to include 'strengthened individual energies and an increased capacity for co-operative effort'.[69] Indeed, I believe that the left now covertly shares with the right forms of alarm about welfare precisely because experience has so largely refuted Tawney's expectation. But the trouble for much of the left is that its ideological, even psychological, resistance to engaging with any terms which have about them the remotest association with 'private' enterprise – since they are the tainted political monopoly of the right – damagingly alienates it from its own knowledge. Three relatively innocent decades ago, as the welfare system got into its stride, there was little embarrassment and therefore less difficulty in a socialist arguing that the 'effective enforcement of public responsibilities' had to be combined with the 'preservation of personal initiative'.[70] Today, as deepening left uncertainty paralyses open discourse, it would be immediately and wrongly identified as an argument from the right. Yet paradoxically, there is no shortage of left objections that we live in a culture of 'lost identities' and

'substitute satisfactions';[71] nor, for example, that 'the struggle of
the working class for power [*sic*]' has been reduced to 'the welfare
state taking care of working class needs'.[72] But since the area of
right-wing ideological appropriation – that of individual freedom
in all its various meanings – has become largely a private preserve
where the whole of the left fears to trespass, it is confined in despite
of itself to its own political ghetto. Moreover, the quarters
occupied by welfare socialism can invite the citizen only into a
world of never-ending social provision, the socialist fireman's
rescue of the economically and socially trapped from their
immediate tribulation, and the insurance salesman's packages of
welfare policies at times of election.

Sixty years ago, in an earlier phase of economic crisis, Trotsky
perceptively saw the British unemployed not as 'a "normal"
reserve army' but as 'a kind of permanent social stratum'. They
were also what he called, struggling for correct judgement, a
'gouty growth in the social organism, a morbid change of tissue'.[73]
But the orthodox 'dialectical' socialist in him impelled him to
insist, wrongly, that 'the insurance of the unemployed' not only
passively protected the jobless from what would otherwise be
intolerable and inevitable deprivation, but 'intensified the
strength of resistance of the working-class'.[74] For this, in Trotsky's
meaning of the words 'strength' and 'resistance', there is no
evidence whatever. Yet the paradox of the left – of which this kind
of 'dialectical' wishful thinking is a symptom – is that, because
labour in a capitalist system has no absolute rights against capital,
the social protection of the interests of the former against the
latter, by whatever means available, must be a first priority of
socialist action. In consequence, even when it is found that vital
remedies against vulnerability and exploitation themselves multiply some labour dilemmas while resolving others, the human and
political imperative which lies behind recourse to public provision
takes precedence over all other considerations. It is a question of a
fatal necessity; including the necessity which dictates silence, or
(at best) creates ideological confusion, on the subject of the social
consequences of such provision. Thus, Trotsky's dialectical
optimism and the welfare socialist's undiscriminating 'building of
the welfare state' are driven by the same political compulsions.
They are very little different from those mortgages to capital
which I discussed in an earlier chapter.

It is therefore easy to see why scruples about joining the right's criticisms of state action should stop left argument dead in its tracks, or push it in false directions, even at the cost of the increasing jeopardy to socialist prospects. It is also not surprising that today's commonplace and 'a-political' visions, medieval in their intensity, of an 'enormous dependent population',[75] culturally impoverished by technological change and economic crisis – and suffocated by public welfare – are not inviting to the left. And this is particularly so if they seem to impute blame to the victims. Yet the greater intellectual danger to the left is if unfamiliar forms of moral anxiety about the future, heretical inquiries into unquestioned socialist assumptions, or uncomfortable empirical evidence about the social effects of public provision should come to be rejected together by ideological reflex action, merely because they are not 'recognizably left' in their provenance or presentation. There can be even less intellectual confidence in such rejections when we consider how far the criteria of worth and truth by which they are rejected have already failed both past and present. Similarly, there are great political dangers for the left in discarding the libertarian right's beliefs in the virtues of 'individual moral action', or in doubting its professed hostility to the 'totalitarian', merely because of the depth of the left's just objections to the right's essentially ruthless view of labour. An intellectually near-automatic process, which refuses all discrimination between principles of different kinds, can now do the left no credit, particularly at a time when it has found itself more than ever unable to establish ideologically the moral validity of its own beliefs in freedom. Put another way, welfare socialism's commitment to public provision has turned out (like the commitment to nuclear disarmament) to be an insufficient condition in itself for the ideological success of the socialist project under capitalist conditions. Moreover, it has failed specifically to furnish an ideological antidote to the moral appeal of an anti-welfare 'politics of freedom'. Instead, by refusing to face the dilemma that much welfare provision is seen, however cruelly, as little more than an inadequate and/or temporary surrogate for frustrated private appropriation, the welfare left, carrying Western socialism's most prominent banner, continues to march boldly in the wrong ideological direction. Worse, where Mill could see that 'the spirit of improvement is not always a spirit of liberty' – for, he argued, 'it may aim at forcing improvements on an unwilling people'[76] – the left prefers to blame some of its political defeats on its own 'weakened commitment to the ideals of the welfare system'.[77] The left, like the right, even begins to complain that public provision is 'over-bureaucratic and officious'.[78] But millions of its benefi- ciaries may be much more tired of *needing and taking* what is provided, and more anxious to escape a client status into 'independence', than to have the 'ideals of the welfare system' freed of bureaucratic encumbrance.[79] But to grasp this, as I have indicated, demands an understanding of those convictions, espe- cially working-class convictions, which are alien to every socialist premise; in particular, the belief that labour's right 'freely' to work for capital, or capital's state, is (in general and on balance) of greater moral worth than most of the rights created by public provision.

In fact, it is because the sense of the moral reduction of the beneficiary of such provision is felt most strongly among working people, and is rarely felt at all by the middle-class socialist intellectual, that left misperception of popular values is so widespread. Thus, what the middle-class critic sees as the growing problem of, say, a return to means-tested benefit, or of bureau- cratic insufficiency in public provision, ranks as a relatively minor irritant when set against more serious working-class fears and reservations about the whole welfare-and-benefit relation. That the penal style and recriminatory aspects of the old poor law administration now flourish once more throughout large areas of the welfare system, simply serves to confirm a class recoil rooted in much deeper objection. Moreover, where the 'social right' of the citizen is reduced, as it often is, to a casual and perfunctory transaction between donor and recipient – teacher and pupil too, and doctor and patient – this is itself an effect of profound social causes beyond mere administrative explanation; 'bureaucracy' is an effect of the same causes. That is, we have to do here with the expression in many forms of a deep cultural discomfort, most powerful in the working class, with all that seems to compromise the morally preferred values of what Marx himself called the 'sense of independence'. Thus, a distanced or 'alienated' bureaucratic relation between welfare state and welfare citizen on the one hand, and non-use or misuse of social provision on the other – whatever else they can be said to represent – share a com- mon origin. Moreover, donor and recipient are in general per- ceived to be fundamentally unequal in the transaction. Indeed, the latter is ideologically felt, on both sides of the counter, to lose part of his or her citizenship at the very moment of benefit; precisely the same moment when the architects of the welfare state believed he or she would gain it! In fact, this sense of inequality between the parties at the point of benefit is generally stronger even than in the case of the truly unequal relation between capital and labour at the point of production. Four decades of the post-war welfare state have failed to undo this perception. Rather, they have intensified it, but bureaucratic authoritarianism, or condescension, has not been the prime mover in the process of deterioration. Instead, what is regarded by most working people, taxation notwithstanding, as 'free' welfare appropriation – or non-contractual appropriation of benefits at below market value – has not been accorded the cultural status it would have received and deserved, if such deep and complex reservations as I have referred to had not been present. Moreover, these reservations are at work even where the most necessary and desirable forms of social benefit are implicated. Obviously, habituation and a cumulative disregard have played their parts in it. But they too are effects before they are causes. It is true that the status of the system of health care is higher than that of other areas of public benefaction; true, too, that (very modest) forms of protest greet (some) erosions of welfare provision. Yet none of this can meet, let alone refute, the evidence of much profounder ideological unconcern among most of the beneficiaries as to the general welfare of the welfare system.

It is only by this route, and what lies further beyond it, that the largest problem of state provision – the increasingly serious failure of the state education system – can begin to be adequately analysed. The subject which is most hedged around by left ideological prohibitions, it is also the arena in which there converges almost every social and cultural dilemma of public provision, in a welfare capitalist system ordered by competition and under conditions of economic contraction. Whether the problem be the long-drawn-out dying of Jude the Obscure, or the struggle for literacy on the battlefields of inner-city schooling; whether the issue be education for social equality, 'citizenship' or 'personal fulfilment'; and whether the defence of 'working-class culture' or the safeguarding of 'educational standards' be held to be most at stake, it is on the terrain of the educational system that these issues are raised and met with a diminishing coherence. Incoherent, in part because old Victorian and Edwardian certitudes, or seeming certitudes, as to the moral, intellectual and

social purposes of education have not held under the fire of social
change, partisan commitment, pedagogical discovery and the
movements of fashion. Thus, for a Matthew Arnold, with his
belief in 'self-discipline through culture', the purpose of education
was held to be 'to make the best that has been thought and known
in the world current everywhere'; and not to 'try to teach down' –
as many 'comprehensive' schools have done to their own and the
community's disaster – 'to the level of inferior [*sic*] classes'.[80] In
1931, 'universal schooling' was expected to 'bring face to face for
the first time labour and culture, and effect a marriage between
them'.[81] Whatever such a prospectus can be held to mean, few
(even on the left) would argue that it has happened, either in its
own terms or in any others. There has, of course, been mountainous social and intellectual effort, for decades, on the part of an
army of teachers and pupils. But the more towering disadvantages
of class and sex – to say nothing of race – upon which the social
order is founded, have not only survived, but been confirmed in
ways beyond all statistical assessment. 'No one', says a characteristic left judgement, 'would want to gloss over the difficulties some
schools have experienced';[82] and then, as has been the case on the
left now for three decades, the text proceeds to gloss them over.

It is a corrective to false socialist notions about 'universal' or
'comprehensive' education to examine the development of Marx's
own little-known and less-analysed arguments on education, to
which I briefly referred in a previous chapter. Carefully considered, they embarrass almost every position taken up by contemporary socialists, and especially by Marxists. In the programme of
the *Manifesto*, in 1848, there is of course the famously simple (and
familiar) demand for 'free education for all children in public
schools'.[83] But by 1850, in his *Class Struggles in France*, comes the
first clue to a more complex or ambiguous position on the subject.
In the course of his account of the 1848 Revolution, Marx declares
mockingly that 'the smallest reform of the old social disorder' was
regarded by the opponents of reform as 'anarchy' and 'socialism'.
He then ironically identifies some of the political responses on the
part of reaction to the reform programme, as follows 'Regulation
of the state budget – socialism! . . . Freedom of the press, right of
association, *universal public education* – socialism, socialism!'[84] The
inference is clear enough, even if the reference is oblique: the
opponents of reform have wrongly assumed, as so many of today's
socialists equally wrongly assume, that 'universal public educa-

tion' *is* in some sense 'socialism'; or at least that there is some
necessary connection between them. But by 1866 Marx had gone
very much further, though deeper into ambiguity also, setting out
in that year unashamedly *unegalitarian* proposals – by today's
standards – for a two-tier educational system. 'If the middle and
higher classes neglect their duties towards their offspring', he told
the delegates to the provisional general council of the First
International, 'it is their own fault. The case of the working-class
stands quite different. . . They are unable to act for themselves. It
is therefore the duty of society to act in their behalf.' This
declaration then serves as the basis for a proposal which, on
scrutiny, is closer to educational sophistry than political sophistication, but which has had a long run for its money. The working
class, Marx argues – but not the 'middle and higher' classes –
needs 'mental education', 'bodily education' and a 'technological
training which imparts the *general principles of all processes of
production*'. That is, the children of working people, though no
others in Marx's scheme, require something near to the syllabus of
the old technical schools, while the 'higher classes' make their own
provision. But where the latter do *not* 'neglect their duties to their
offspring' – much the most obvious circumstance, as Marx would
have known well – and instead purchase a high standard of
education for them, Marx, like the modern Labour Party in office,
has no counter-proposals to offer. In fact, the whole issue remains
unmentioned. And how can this be justified or rationalized?
Because, Marx continues – along a tortuous intellectual path no
socialist could take today – 'the combination of paid productive
labour, mental education, bodily exercise and polytechnic [*sic*]
training will raise the working class far above the level of the
higher and middle classes'.[85]

At the meeting of the First International, three years later in
1869, it can be discerned from the minutes that Marx, the mature
Marx, maintained his consistently ambivalent position. It is a
position which has become familiar over more than a century of
similar middle-class intellectual doubts about the possibilities in
practice, especially in a society ordered by competition, of a truly
egalitarian education. Marx's own wrestlings with the problem, a
socialist Jacob's wrestling with the Angel of utopianism, are
merely the first and clearest. 'Marx', says the record of the
meeting, 'was not in favour of free college education.' His
arguments are not given. But in a crucially important discussion

of the issue of 'compulsory state education' – under capitalist conditions' – 'Citizen Marx said there was a *peculiar difficulty* connected with this question. On the one hand, a change of social circumstances was required to establish a proper system of education. On the other hand, a proper system of education was required to bring about a change of social circumstances. We must', he concluded unsatisfactorily (or 'pragmatically'), '*commence where we are.*' [86] But the equivocal caution of it is itself instructive, when today's political expectations of 'comprehensive' education impose on it such burdens and duties as could never be fulfilled in a society ruled by the cultural values and social ordering of the market. In 1875, only eight years before his death, Marx held his ground. But he was now much more vigorously, almost violently, opposed to a contemporary socialist programme for 'universal and equal education by the state', even at the elementary level. '"Equal elementary education"?', he protested; 'what idea lies behind these words?' And there then follow two further questions, no doubt astounding to today's educational wishful thinkers; questions which would not now even be asked in public, let alone answered, where socialists – and especially Marxists – were present. 'Is it believed', he exclaimed, 'that in present-day society (*and it is only with this one has to deal*) education can be equal for all classes?' 'Or', Marx asked, 'is it demanded that the upper classes also shall be compulsorily reduced to the modicum of education – the elementary school – that alone is compatible with the economic conditions . . . of the wage workers? The paragraph on the schools', Marx admonished his fellow German socialists, led by Lassalle, 'should at least have demanded technical schools' – for the working class – 'in combination with the elementary school.' And the passage ends with Marx's description of 'elementary education by the state', or what he also calls 'the state as educator of the people', as 'altogether [*sic*] objectionable'. Instead, 'government and church should . . . be equally excluded from an influence on the school'. Indeed, the 'whole programme' of the German party, 'for all its democratic clang' – and how much today's welfare socialism under capitalist conditions has suffered from this 'clang' – was 'tainted through and through by [a] . . . servile belief in the state, or, what is no better, by a *democratic belief in miracles* . . . both equally remote from socialism'.[87] This sequence of declarations, amusingly, would now be held, especially by Marxists, to be 'reactionary'; but they are also Marx's reactions.

In fact, these are judgements for obvious enough reasons among the least regarded, but also the most urgently instructive, in all Marx's writing. They warn socialists in unmistakable terms against precisely the kind of political illusion which has afflicted every 'socialist' strategy of state provision in market systems, from that of the Germany of the 1870s to the Britain of the 1980s. Indeed, it is exactly that 'democratic belief in miracles', as Marx put it – tragic in the impossibility of its social and cultural expectations of education – which in 1942 led the Labour Party to see as a feasible political objective the provision of 'educational opportunities for all which ensure that our cultural heritage is denied to no one'.[88] And after forty years of the (increasing) failure of such an enterprise, however objectively necessary and for reasons which Marx makes all too clear in the passages I have quoted, Labour's 1982 'socialist alternative' in education is still baying for the same socialist moon in an essentially unreconstructed and declining capitalist system. 'The education system', it declared, and how Marx would have roared in derision, 'must give all people the skills and confidence to help shape society – to be the masters [*sic*] and not the servants of their environment.'[89] But if political illusion and error on such a scale, imposed alike upon educators and the to-be-educated, were confined to hopes, demands and theories, they would in some measure be governable as Marx in 1875 sought to govern them: by political counter-argument and alternative forms of pedagogical reason. Our problem is different. It is expressed in the forty years of a losing educational battle against social, economic and political forces entrenched in a social order ruled by capital; fought out in the raising of buildings, in the reform of curricula, and in socialist lives misspent and exhausted by heroically misguided effort in the classroom. For the education system is charged with a task it desperately attempts, and equally desperately fails, to fulfil: no less than to 'break down', in a capitalist order which builds them up and is based upon them, 'the divisions in society . . . of class, sex and race'.[90] So, for one Labour socialist, education must actually *be* the 'solvent of class division and personal disadvantage'.[91] For another, it must be a main instrument in 'equalizing' the 'social distribution of life-chances'[92] in an unchanged world which Marx would have instantly recognized, and where capital rules labour. And for yet another, education in

Britain is the 'main channel of social mobility',[93] in a society almost uniquely marked by a fundamental class stasis.

It is precisely thus that education is set unfulfillable social and political tasks, as Marx was too wise to do. For there is transposed onto the backs of teachers a large part of the political burden of securing a radical reordering of the socio-economic system. And error is then heaped upon error, like Pelion upon Ossa, in the institutionalized misdiagnosing of the reasons – which Marx would have found obvious – for the educational failures which inevitably follow. Yet, undeterred, socialist educationists, sociologists, psychologists and statisticians rack their brains over the simplest of all matters: that the educational system at every level, especially the 'comprehensive' level, continues 'to reflect, to defend and to perpetuate the division of mankind into masters and servants',[94] and in ways which are organic to the socio-economic system as a whole. There is nothing contingent about it, nor in the last analysis is it remediable by however many structural rearrangements of the educational system. A socialist of our times – more egalitarian but less politically wise or realistic than Marx – echoing the empty cries of the Lassalleans, can urge until he bursts that 'the children of all classes in the nation' should 'attend the same schools' or that 'a special system of [sc. private] schools' is a 'grave national misfortune'.[95] But the sententious solemnity of it merely points to lifetimes of backbreaking teachers' effort – and the continuous reorganization of institutions – in the vain search for solutions to problems wrongly posed. Moreover, 'socialist' expectation tends to bring in its wake only greater political misfortune. And it again raises, in acute fashion, the central dilemma of public provision in a market society which has been brought under welfare socialism's aegis: that of resources and energies spent in the name of socialism on state-promoted intervention, but in a social order where a higher ideological status attaches, across the classes, to the values and rewards of private appropriation than to the benefits of public action. Indeed, other welfare socialist dilemmas pale into insignificance beside it. Thus, shrinking allocation made to educational (or any other) provision, however mischievous in intent or destructive in outcome, merely compounds those problems which are set to society by the 'democratic clang' of the whole welfare socialist project, education included. Thus, it is precisely a 'belief in miracles' which pretends to itself – and others – that the 'input' of more resources, or more elaborate surveys of socially-determined educational disability, or even the abolition of the private education being acquired by Marx's un-neglectful 'higher classes', can transform educational provision into what it is politically incapable of becoming. But it is now quite clear that post-war resources, whether increasing, falling or constant, have proved unable to meet what Marx euphemistically called the 'peculiar difficulty' of providing egalitarian educational provision in a market order. Indeed, throughout Western capitalism the 'social circumstances' to which Marx referred have proved structurally impervious to such attrition, even when access to educational qualification has been expanded to the limits, and even when the purchase of special privilege has been much more sharply restricted than in Britain. Rather, the 'peculiar difficulty' remains after more than a century of social change since Marx first referred to it, despite multiple forms of educational innovation. But this is itself an understatement. For the failure to secure egalitarian educational advances of any substance, together with deteriorating relationships in the classroom, have been on a scale beyond every prediction. Moreover, a low and even falling ideological esteem for public educational provision can only be partly explained by negative comparison with coexisting private education, or by the harm caused by cuts in resources. The greater truth is that though there have been substantial 'material improvements and educational advances',[96] including the wide expansion of popular instructional provision by radio and television, certain forms of greater social poverty have gained ground, year by year, over educational endeavour. Today, the Matthew Arnold who wrote, in 1869, that 'the idea which culture sets before us, of perfection . . . is an idea which the new democracy needs far more than the idea of the blessedness of the franchise',[97] seems a remote and alien figure. For he is speaking in an entirely foreign language, now beyond translation.

Yet, on one side and the other, wrong educational questions are plied without cease, and wrong answers given. Almost invariably, the most wrong are socialist, for reasons Marx long ago made plain. 'Why is it that education seems to have done so little for working class children?' asks one.[98] Or, complains another, the question of why 'the expansion of education has not itself led to a more rational, egalitarian or viable society' has 'bewildered reformers'.[99] The truly socialist counter-questions, the ones which

Marx would surely have asked – 'why should it?' or 'how could it?' – are neither asked nor answered. Instead, education and the educational process have been invested with an instrumental political purpose, foredoomed to failure, as a surrogate or alibi for those actions against state and class power which the welfare socialist has no intention of taking. At the same time, precisely as the right argues (for its own purposes), falsely egalitarian welfare-socialist actions have damaged, even wrecked, wide areas of educational opportunity and achievement in demagogic pursuit of the impossible ends for which Marx belaboured the Lassalleans. It has been a sorry and benighted business. And it has not been redeemed, but made worse, by the intellectual efforts of socialist inquiry, scientific and unscientific, to find explanations – or *ex post facto* rationalizations – for the inevitable social consequences of preceding error. Thus, Titmuss was eventually to write, in 1964, of 'socially malnourished' school-leavers 'barely able to write a letter or read a book';[100] and to confess that 'we failed to grasp the importance of the connections between, for instance, bad housing and the inability to profit from education . . . We did not see that the task . . . of getting them [sc. 'the poor'] to use and benefit from health, education and social services was a far more formidable one than most reformers imagined.'[101] He attributed the 'not grasping' and the 'not seeing' to failures of 'social analysis'. But in fact, the understanding of this 'inability to profit from education' is not only beyond the scope of what Titmuss meant by 'social analysis', but also now quite outside the terms of socialist discussion. To repeat, what we should see instead is, first, that wild socialist expectations of education under capitalist conditions and of the general 'ability to profit' from it, are themselves the product of a 'democratic belief in miracles'; and, second, that Titmuss has fleetingly raised, but characteristically not pursued, the dilemma of the failure in our culture of 'universal' educational provision. It is no wonder that the right, with the reproductive powers of the whole socio-economic system to sustain them, should be able to run ideological rings around their opponents. The latter may object, hands druidically raised to the heavens, that 'a confused society' has 'done little by way of education to deepen and refine the capacity for significant response';[102] but it is Marx's 'peculiar difficulty' which characterizes the 'confused society', the educational system and the 'significant response' together.

Thus, as Marx knew in his own time and would know now,

'common educational provision'[103] continues to *prepare* the children of working people on the one hand, and the children of the 'middle and higher classes' on the other, for the 'social circumstances' of a structurally unchanged socio-economic order. Indeed, for all the exceptions of the 'upwardly mobile', it is essentially what it was when Marx attacked the Lassalleans. But our problem has been made much greater by the fact that, during all the intervening decades, this preparation of the classes has been conducted under precisely those false rubrics and false colours which Marx refused to encourage. Above all, it has set up false expectations in the classroom which, for the great majority, are dashed outside it. It cannot therefore be surprising that so much educational provision, and those who provide it, should be discounted – and even despised – by those who receive it. At the same time, the gradually diminishing ideological regard in which public educational provision at school age is held increases the pressure on the morale and sense of purpose of the educators. And when their struggles to prevent a downward momentum then flag or fail, the esteem of parents and pupils for what is already regarded, openly or covertly, as a form of 'second-best' provision in the educational market falls with it. To this educational vicious circle we must add the largely successful 'socialist' attempt to erase grammar-school education and the survival in strength, for obvious socio-economic reasons, of more exclusive private provision for the 'middle and higher classes'.[104] Thus, the theoretical failure to understand what Marx meant by education's 'peculiar difficulty' in the 'social circumstances' of a market system ordered by inequality, is one thing. But the educational folly upon folly which has ensued in practice, and of which the victims have been a generation of teachers, parents and pupils, is quite another. It has given us a comprehensive education which is not comprehensive, and which has set false aspiration before teachers and false expectation before pupils; it has reorganized (and broken) certain institutions, good, bad and indifferent, of middle-range educational privilege and achievement; and it has left unscathed others at a 'higher' and even more privileged social level. Yet, it has not for all its pains achieved very much of that 'advancement and diffusion of knowledge'[105] – or 'enlightenment' – among the 'common people' – which progressive nineteenth-century opinion, Marx excepted, saw as the virtue and hope of universal education.

In 1943, Tawney, while arguing the case for educational

change, praised the general standard of public-school education. He went on to urge that it was 'obviously important' that reform, 'whatever shape it may assume', should not 'impair [the] educational values' of the public schools, but 'should preserve and extend [*sic*] their influence'. At the same time, he made clear (or protested, lest he be misunderstood) that he was not speaking of what he called the 'social idiosyncrasies of the schools in question'.[106] In the disordering of four decades of educational reform which has followed Tawney's warnings, the public schools' 'social idiosyncrasies' remain, but the influence of their 'educational values' has not been extended; indeed the suggestion that they ought to be would today be regarded as deeply regressive. Instead, the 'disparity of esteem'[107] between public and private educational provision has widened. Yet, on a simple measure alone of the intellectual energy devoted to the attempt, by tens of thousands of teachers and administrators, to create a democratic educational system, such a system ought by now to have been securely founded. Unfortunately, however, the precondition for such an achievement would have been a socio-economic and cultural vacuum in which to build it. In the necessary absence of such a vacuum, even more havoc has been wrought (by the 'social circumstances') upon Labour's schemes, than Labour's schemes have themselves wrought upon the general school system. Indeed, the claims to coherence of post-war socialist educational policy can barely be sustained at all when, in a competitive society, free and uncompetitive universal access to educational opportunity stops at the school gate; leaving millions of children – of the working class – stranded in exactly the same socio-economic positions, within the ordering of a market society, as they would have been in if democratic public provision had not existed. 'Of course', wrote Anthony Crosland, 'some degree of educational "eliteness", resting on the Universities, the sixth forms, and simply the fact of staying at school until 18, is *inevitable*.'[108] Or, as Titmuss put it (in parenthesis) in an essay on the welfare state in 1965, 'the principle of universality cannot be applied to higher education in any country of the world in this century'.[109] So that, as far as the school gate of comprehensive education, and only so far, there would be in Tawney's words 'easy, natural and unselfconscious contacts between young people of varying traditions and different social backgrounds'.[110] That this daft description bears no resemblance, and never did, to those conditions in the real world which Marx called 'commencing where we are' – in Birmingham, say, or Liverpool or Glasgow – is not the immediate issue. Rather, it is that we are dealing here with the children of welfare socialist fable, not of the inner city. It is a fable composed of grim delusion. For, in the real world, it is at the school gate that a whole generation parts, to take its separate places either in the division of labour or in the dole queues. It is 'only with present-day society', Marx wrote, that 'one has to deal'. And it is present-day society, now as then, which has made a shambles of socialist dreams of education as the 'solvent of class division'.

It must always be so where disproportionate effort is directed at effects, not causes. Nevertheless, after decades of (objectively necessary) public provision and protection against the social and economic consequences of living by a market order, the illusion has been fostered and institutionalized – at the expense of formidable levels of public investment – that to deal with effects *is* somehow to deal with causes. The overwhelming evidence that it is not is confirmed, decade on decade, by social inquiry. However, even this has done little to disabuse belief that, like a socialist pearl in a capitalist oyster, some kind of egalitarian order can be installed, and can expand, by means of ever greater public provision within a market system. Yet, taking the field of education as a continuing example, 'non-selection' at eleven cannot substantially amend – let alone overcome – much more deeply-rooted processes of social selection. For they are processes upon which the political order itself depends for its maintenance and reproduction. The resilient survival of a hierarchical educational system is merely one of the most obvious symptoms of it. The essentially class-based 'streaming' in 'non-selective' schools – to the point at which, in most 'comprehensive' schools, there are at least two schools in one – is a much more telling social phenomenon even than the 'gap in social prestige'[111] between the public and private sectors. The sad truth is that what Victorian benefaction could not achieve, enlightened state provision, its political successor, cannot achieve either. So much is this the case that criticisms (usually *parti pris*) which are too narrowly confined to the educational standards of 'comprehensive' provision are themselves misconceived and misdirected. Thus, as Marx at least understood, it is simply foolish to expect of 'universal public eduction' anything other than what Crosland, for example, indignantly described as 'the appallingly low quality of parts of the state education system'.[112] Similarly, to object – on the grounds of its 'inequity' – to the 'purchase by wealthy citizens of so overwhelming a social advantage'[113] as private education, can be no more than false ingenuousness when 'inequity' is itself the principle of the social order.

Worse, a century of false expectations of 'mass' education as a means to cultural progress (or, more naively to a new 'way of life' based on a 'common culture')[114] is increasingly being corrected by a newer species of educational error. It merely compounds every problem. Paradoxically, it is marked by an essentially middle-class form of (pseudo-democratic) philistinism towards what have come to be dismissed as 'narrow and specialized academic disciplines'.[115] It is as if the failure of 'universal' educational provision to achieve its intendedly egalitarian ends could somehow be made good by vulgarizing – or plebeianizing – the means of achieving them. The fact that this is being done allegedly in the name of 'breaking down' the 'bias' towards 'specialisms', on the grounds that such 'specialisms' 'reflect the class-based dominance of professional people',[116] is not at all persuasive. For it is precisely such 'professional people' of the left, including some of its leading university intellectuals, who can be found urging such a 'breaking down' of 'bias'. But there are wider issues here than that dishonest demagogic purpose. These are, after all, times of widespread 'de-skilling' of the human-as-worker, which is a cultural as well as a 'purely' technical matter; times, too, of the development of increasingly refined and inaccessible forms of specialized knowledge. A middle-class intellectual populism of the left, pretending crudely to 'undo the damage' of an 'over-academic curriculum'[117] by avoiding 'specialism', must therefore threaten to add failure to failure. Moreover, our real educational problems are of low levels of school-age literacy and numeracy, of connectedly low levels of adult political education, and of even lower levels of debate on the left and in the labour movement about them. But they cannot be met by a misconceived scorn, usually middle-class itself, reserved for the appropriation by the middle-class of precisely those kinds of knowledge which are the sources of a large part of its authority in the division of labour. Rather, a populist left evasion of this issue merely ensures that universal educational provision in a market society will continue to reproduce existing hierarchies of knowledge, and privileged access to them. Indeed, so falsely conceived is much of the left's educational purpose that, in familiar fashion, it gives to the right's own 'repressive' pedagogy a legitimacy which it would not otherwise deserve. Worse still, when set against the seeming desire of at least some on the left actually to leave the field, or scorch the earth, of 'narrow . . . academic discipline' entirely, even some of the educational right's authoritarian remedies – through the restoration of discredited teaching methods, for example – might begin to be counted as socially more progressive than the left's original reaction, and overreaction, to them. Certainly, a spurious egalitarianism advanced by the already highly educated can promise only further intellectual and social impoverishment to others; including, in the avoidance of 'specialism', the impoverishment of every technical skill. Such an educational philosophy, in fact, has no moral worth of any kind. To *add* to disadvantage, in the name of equality, is merely a bad joke. And the fact that this promise is usually presented in terms of 'broad' or 'basic' provision of 'high quality'[118] – yet without any sign of the high seriousness of purpose which once informed socialist debate about education – makes it no better than the empty huckstering of the car salesman.

Moreover, in our decaying urban landscapes, snaked by the queues of the jobless, and in the wilderness left behind by a recession much more than economic, the knowledge of 'what is really happening',[119] and the capacity to act in different ways upon it, remain as ever functions of a humane, technically efficient and 'disciplined' system of education. And what of the current transfer of utopian socialist expectation to a theoretically egalitarian order – within an inegalitarian one – founded upon 'accountability' and 'participation'? Would it not also demand for its practical fulfilment precisely those virtues of judgement, informed and technically expert, which the left's educational populism can only undermine? Instead, what do we find? Idealized paragons of a revived democratic process are *imagined*, not educated, into existence; paragons able to resist the rhetoric of the right, or the blandishments and disinformation of 'the media', by the force of innate character and capacity for discrimination alone. 'We must never accept', Tony Benn has argued – flying in the face of a long socialist tradition from Winstanley to Morris – 'that democracy can be limited by the educational qualifications of the rank-and-file.'[120] This folly enough; yet to go further and seek to replace, with meretricious shortcuts and 'broad' provision,

the technical long march to 'specialized' knowledge – and general
knowledge goes with it – is to invite new degrees of future
political failure. Moreover, as the middle-class intellectual of left
and right knows full well, the traditional criteria in the culture for
distinguishing between the 'educated' and the 'uneducated' have
largely survived intact. And even where they have changed, they
have worked *increasingly* against the status of unskilled and
semi-skilled knowledge of all kinds. The arousal of expectations,
through education, which the social order is incapable of fulfilling
is one thing. But to reduce expectation, while leaving an
increasing number of school-leavers lacking in basic intellectual
and technical skills of every kind, is another. That a 'broad'
pseudo-egalitarian (or worse, 'socialist') impulse to 'break down
specialisms' should be contributing to the latter brings back
Marx's diatribe against the 'democratic clang' of the Lassallean
education programme with a vengeance; but as a form of social
failure which threatens democracy itself with its death-knell.

The defensive reiteration of left commitments to educational
theories and practices which have been failing for years in their
purpose, in place of debate about this purpose itself, is not tenacity
but blindness. Indeed, the very need to defend public provision
from its assailants has made the prospects for such debate, at least
a decade overdue in education, even remoter. Yet there comes a
point – and we have reached it – where the issues are no longer
those of party. After all, left illusions and left populism are fully as
damaging to educational progress as the right's economic assaults
on the public education system. Moreover, it is the limits of
educational possibility which must be redefined, as well as its
ulterior purpose. Thus, an Adam Smith might urge, on utilitarian
grounds, only that 'in every informed and civilized society'
government must 'take pains to prevent' or to 'counter' the
depressing 'mental and moral effects of the division of labour'.[121]
But socialists must themselves learn that education in a market
order can do nothing in itself to amend its structure. Nor does
Marx's belief that 'if man is shaped by his surroundings, his
surroundings must be made human'[122] give any licence to hopes
that universal education can in itself defend the environment from
destruction, when it is the advancement of knowledge, harnessed
to productive ends, which has done so much to destroy it. Rather,
the left must still be able to see now, without fond illusion, what de
Tocqueville saw in Manchester in the 1830s: where 'civilization

makes its miracles', he wrote, 'a civilized man is turned back almost into a savage'.[123] A century of progress later, in Nottingham, the same 'man-made England' which D.H. Lawrence saw as 'so vile'[124] the left must have the courage to recognize also. Why? Because unless it has this kind of knowledge, it will never be able to mount a resistance – especially in inner-city Britain – to everything masquerading as the 'broad' and 'basic' in 'comprehensive' provision. For these terms are themselves no more than an alibi for the depression of self-regard and intellectual attainment, including at truly basic levels of literacy, numeracy and the dignities of self-expression. In 1859 Mill strongly opposed, on the grounds of preferring 'diversity' of provision, the principle that the 'education of the people' should be in 'state hands'.[125] Sixteen years later, Marx's attack on German socialist illusions brought him to (superficially) similar conclusions. Yet even Mill's arguments speak, albeit negatively, to the left's dilemmas. 'Such establishments', Mill wrote, as were 'controlled by the State' should only exist 'for the purpose of example and stimulus, to keep the others up to a certain standard of excellence'.[126] And today we know to our cost that a great deal of state educational provision, especially at school age, has failed – for reasons Marx would have understood – to provide in 'present-day society' any semblance of such 'stimulus, 'excellence' or 'example'. Socialists can no longer ignore it. For though the basic apparatus of state provision, despite Marx's strictures, is in fact now irreplaceable by any other system, it is the right which increasingly benefits from the left's 'democratic belief' in *educational* 'miracles'. Indeed the former is able to advance the most banal forms of snobbery – that, say, 'conformity to majority tastes' is 'scarcely a cultural virtue'[127] – against the left's combination of sentiment and falsehood about the supposedly inherent superiority of institutions which are visibly failing in their purpose. Moreover, the fact that the right has resisted every extension of educational provision from the Education Act of 1870 onwards is itself an exhausted alibi. For the focus of debate has justly shifted to question hard-won (and hard-worked) democratic entitlements, both as to their actual effects and, more dangerously, as to their intrinsic merits.

But once more it is left avoidance of the issues which invites the right – with Marx's 'peculiar difficulty' to assist it – to argue that 'spending on education has been sky-rocketing, yet by common consent the quality of education has been declining'.[128] It even

permits the right to take from the left, by intellectual default, what
should have been the left's own case: that 'a system dedicated to
enabling all children to acquire a common language . . . to giving
all children equal educational opportunity' has in practice
'exacerbated the stratification of society and provided highly
unequal educational opportunity'.[129] Here, the Friedman of 1980
and the Marx of 1875, like the Marx of *Das Kapital* and the Adam
Smith of *The Wealth of Nations*, move close together, across however
wide a chasm of purpose and explanation of causes, in at least
seeing effects without blinking; or worse, shutting their eyes to
them entirely, as most of today's left does, out of embarrassment at
their meanings. Instead, the left must have the courage to agree
the right's case, as Marx would have done before proceeding, that
the education system 'now helps to shape a life of misery, poverty
and crime for many children of the inner city'.[130] Even the
'nullification' of the 'advantages of talent',[131] which the right
ignores when the cause of it rests in the chronic disabilities of
social under-privilege, the left cannot itself ignore when it is the
consequence of the false egalitarianism – within a competitive
market society – of its own socialist projects.

   Moreover, there are other equally ignored wider issues,
implicit in the cumulative moral and ideological failures of
decades of public provision, which go to the very heart of socialist
purpose. The incompatibility with socialist prospects of a-social
or anti-social impulses – and all that fails to check them, whatever
their democratic intention – is simply the most obvious of them.
Thus, today's reincarnation of what Arnold at the height of
Victorian 'wealth creation' called the 'sunken populace of our
great cities',[132] raised only to be depressed again in each recurring
cycle of economic failure, should not merely challenge the right to
actions of containment and pacification. It should challenge the
left, too, to recognize the enormity of the political and ideological
problems which confront it; and especially if socialist progress is
thought to depend upon Labour votes from the cultural waste-
lands of the industrial revolution. For it is precisely here that the
values of private appropriation – often in degradingly competitive and even violent conditions of social and economic decline –
are more than a match for 'broad' and 'basic' social provision,
whether of education or any other public good. That is, it is the
social relations of unemployment, of 'unwanted labour' and of the
'division between workers and non-workers'[133] which have re-

placed for millions the social relations of production as the context both for individual and for social, or a-social, action. Moreover, where only thirty years ago it could be seriously held that 'material standards are rising to the point where we can spare more energy, and more resources, for beauty and culture',[134] our generation – with 3 million 'indictable offences' recorded every year [135] – can see clearly the scale of damage done to place and person by the ravages of industrial growth and industrial contraction. To invoke, in hope, the virtues of community in compensation for this knowledge, looking for a red phoenix to rise from these grey ashes, is to underestimate the huge extent of the social, economic and ecological disaster which has now overtaken the old industrial areas of Britain. It is an epic of waste and recession, and it has claimed the very skills, technical and social, which are alone capable of rebuilding a living world in its ruins. When the machines are stilled, and the chimneys no longer smoking, we can see how little of lasting worth or value – in goods, or minds, or institutions – was created by it. Public provision, especially 'broad' and 'basic' provision, can never make all this good; and welfare protection is no exchange for those functions, within the now outmoded technical division of labour, to which generations of working people were trained and shackled. But at the same time, contrary to socialist expectation, no social philosophy worth having can be founded upon, or flourish in, these conditions either. That is, the very conditions of economic decline and social neglect to which most socialists contradictorily look for their vicarious hopes of class rebellion, are precisely those in which unskilled, a-social and unemployed fears all prosper together. And even *in extremis*, one social principle stands out in our culture above all others: the sense of the legitimacy of the existing market order.

To sum up, the measure of welfare socialism's continuing political failures in such conditions is that in 1949 Tawney could argue that 'social solidarity has been strengthened as the essentials of civilization, once the privileges of a minority, have increasingly become a common possession'.[136] Instead, with the right to public provision in our culture inevitably subordinate in status to the right to private appropriation, welfare entitlement does not have to be brought into question by cuts in public spending, or by the right's celebration of self-reliance, for the 'democracy' of the welfare state to be ideologically undervalued.

Therefore, it is not simply the confident post-war expectation that
welfare benefits would be themselves construed as 'an enlargement
of freedom'[137] which events have falsified. Rather, economic
prosperity and hardship alike, whether communal or individual,
have not made – as election results, for example, reveal – any real
political difference to the cultural esteem or disesteem in which
public provision is held. Of course, it is not difficult to see that in
conditions of prosperity most social rights in a competitive society
will lack the prestige of 'private' economic rights, whether of
capital or of labour. But what has been more awkward for the
socialist case is that in hardship, especially the longer it lasts for
working people as mere time-killing, even the most valuable social
benefits begin to represent a form of necessity, not a form of
freedom. Hence as I have argued, to the beneficiary such benefits
will speak of the preferable means of appropriation in the 'free'
market, and not of the vices of an unstable economic process,
whose social destructiveness state benefit must endlessly seek to
balance. Moreover, neither in prosperity nor in hardship
are the virtues of universal provision generally associated with
specifically socialist intentions and meanings. (In fact, only public
ownership reliably attracts such ideological recognition.) Indeed,
despite those measures which have 'socialized' the state, the
'socialized' citizen cannot be said to have emerged from the social
progress which they have promoted.[138] It is this case which the
right now argues, but Marx himself anticipated it, from an
entirely contrary position, as the necessary outcome of futile
expectation under capitalist conditions. Yet even if it were not
futile, today's welfare, or gradualist, socialists have little enough
intellectual energy with which to address all those burning issues
of social purpose which, in their different ways, Carlyle, Ruskin
and Morris addressed in their own generation. Instead, lacking
even the popular press of an 'educated democracy',[139] we inhabit
a political culture which is already a world away from that of
Labour's post-war reconstruction. Moreover, a new kind of
popular 'rank and file' is in process of formation. 'Working class'
as may be in origin it is increasingly remote from the concerns
and perceptions of yesterday's Labour Party, let alone those of
alternative forms of socialist intention.

   What Arnold, in his *Culture and Anarchy*, called the 'fermenting
mind of the nation'[140] now moves in wide plebeian channels,
unmapped by existing socialist theory. Indeed, the most impor-

tant losses to labour, and Labour, are to be found sunk in its muddy waters, swollen by the loss and waste of skills and by long-term unemployment. Against this 'mind', there can be no remedy – on the contrary – in extending the scope and scale of public provision.

5   The Private Interests
of Labour

In the political culture of the market, the trade unions are above
all the brokers of the private interests of labour, the producing
class, and not the opponents of the capitalist system. Brokerage is
their social and economic function: they could not avoid it even if
they chose to; and they do not choose to. That is, labour
organization in a market society furnishes the collective or social
means to the end of individual appropriation of economic and
social goods, however precarious; and labour, like capital, is not
the less a private interest for organizing itself socially in the labour
market by the only effective means available to it.[1] The very term
'trade union' historically signifies the defensive organization of
specific labour interests, trade by trade; precisely as the term
'Labour Party' points not to the political transformation of the
market, but to the defence and advance of a socio-economic
interest within it. Indeed, just as the physical–economic role of
labour is given it, or imposed upon it, by capital and capital's
state, so the role of labour organization is, before everything else, a
market-derived role of economic jobbery in defence of legitimate
socio-economic interest. The historic and present indispensability
of trade unions, as a means of protecting working people from
otherwise unrestrainable exploitation, can do nothing to alter the
objective fact of their circumscription within the bounds, terms
and conditions of the market. Yet socialist sentiment and special
pleading constantly reverse the true order of analytical and
historical priorities. Labour's struggle, such as it is, against the
market is elevated over labour's containment within it; labour's
limited defiance of capital, over the self-defence of its interests in
the market. It is not in question that they are, plainly enough,
'dialectically' connected. But what is not tolerable intellectually,
and is even more mistaken politically, is the left's instinctive recoil
from those truths of the market, and of market powers, which do
not merely give labour its role, but themselves transform and

reshape it. Labour may be the 'alternative' to capital as the organizing principle of the next, or higher, stage of historical development – but it is both the source and bedfellow of capital in this one. And it is with the consequences of this relation that the left cannot deal without the protection of illusion.

For, in a market order, like it or not, the 'bargaining' function of the trade unions is a political, economic and social datum. Moreover, the 'voluntary association' of working people and their representatives, for the purpose of such cross-class bargaining in the market, is not analytically the same as a cross-class collectivism directed at the social ownership of the means of production. That the former may in fact be incompatible with the latter, both in theory and in practice, is an even more awkward issue and one which socialists have in various ways avoided. In addition, it is clear that the trade union function in the labour market can be antithetical even to certain reformist socialist purposes, in particular in the field of incomes planning. These dichotomies are profound, not casual: just as the instability and decline of support among many trade unionists for Labour's social and economic policies have causes which carry us to the depths of basic inconsistencies of labour movement purpose. And how can this be otherwise when the world of 'voluntary association' and 'free collective bargaining' – each word of such terms deserves careful weighing by the left, but never gets it – is ideologically steeped in the ethics of a market in which labour has its price, and labour organization seeks to fix it? It is a world of interests and 'freedoms', where that of making the best private bargain governs other impulses, whether on the part of capital or labour; and where the actions of capital and labour, ostensibly at class loggerheads, are governed by essentially the same ideological assumptions about the basic meaning of what they are doing. That is, 'arms'-length' bargaining power is being voluntarily ('freely') exercised in the market by (nominally) equivalent forces. No matter, either, that it is the skill and time of labour which is being so 'freely' bought and sold. For the ideological perception of it is, in general, subordinate to the sense of the fundamental legitimacy both of the transaction itself between capital and labour, and of the institutionalized trade union function within it. Thus, uncomfortably for the left and whatever its knowledge of the true nature of the relation between capital and labour, the relation itself has an ideological sanction in the culture which takes general precedence over the left's objections to it. Indeed, the ideological and practical prospects for a socialist theory of exploitation can best be measured by the fact that it is labour and its organizations which, on balance, attach an *even greater legitimacy than does capital itself* to the bargaining process! More obviously still, those functions which labour – precariously in a market system – claims as its 'rights' possess considerably less status and legitimacy in the eyes of capital, particularly in times of crisis, than do the rights of capital in the eyes of labour. Hence, the right's historically recurring attacks on trade union immunities are in general perceived by the trade unions themselves as a 'counterproductive' aberration from the norm, according to which the freedoms of capital and of labour ought to be mutually respected. And behind the perceived virtue of 'voluntary association' in defence of the private interests and freedoms of working people, stands that moral commitment to self-organization for political autonomy and economic independence which itself sustains the legitimacy of the market system.

The ambiguities of socialist theory on the subject of the trade unions – the conservative survivors of nineteenth-century radical-ism[2] – though refusing most of these truths, nevertheless uneasily reveal their own dilemmas. Thus, to Marx, the unions were (in 1847) 'ramparts for the workers in their struggles against employers',[3] in 1848 expressions of 'revolt',[4] but by 1865 'applying palliatives, not curing the malady'. They were, said Marx, 'fighting with effects, but not with the causes of those effects'.[5] Likewise for Engels, in 1844, the unions 'direct themselves against the vital nerve of the social order'; as 'schools of war' they are 'unexcelled'.[6] Thirty-five years later, sadder and wiser, they were, wrote Engels, engaged in a 'narrow circle of strikes for higher wages and shorter hours . . . as an ultimate aim' while 'excluding on principle . . . all political action'.[7] In 1899, to Lenin, strikes and trade union struggles were also a 'school of war'.[8] Only six years later, trade unions had become the 'ideological enslavement of the workers by the bourgeoisie', while trade union politics was the 'bourgeois politics of the working class'.[9] But by 1917, the trade union struggle for 'immediate and direct improvement of conditions' was, for Lenin, once more 'alone capable of rousing the most backward strata of the exploited masses'.[10] For Gramsci, in 1919, trade unionism organized workers 'not as producers but wage-earners . . . according to the contours imposed on them by the capitalist system';[11] while to Trotsky, in 1933, trade unions were the victims of their own development 'during the period of the growth and rise of capitalism',[12] which taught them their reformist lessons. Yet neither the left's standard critique of trade union 'economism', nor the greater sleight-of-hand that 'trade unions are dialectically both an opposition to capitalism and a component of it',[13] suffices. For both the aggressive and defensive activities of trade unionism in a market society are predicated upon, and sustain, an ideologically prior political and economic bargain with the rights of capital, to which the 'rights' of labour must in the last resort always be adjusted.

This prior bargain rests on a premise which has been continuously confirmed throughout Western capitalism since the industrial revolution. It is that labour and its organizations accept the fundamental right of property, and of private and state capital, to buy the skills and time of labour in return for the 'recognition' of the latter's own 'rights' to represent and organize its economic and political interests. The legitimacy which labour (and Labour) thus accords to the rights of capital in a market system represents a much more severely self-damaging complicity than does capital's much less reliable recognition of the 'rights' of labour. But such awareness of this as there is on labour's part has made no real difference to the legitimacy and stability of the bargain itself. Indeed, labour's 'rights' are often reduced, in periods of conflict and crisis, even to the point in which the 'right' to bargain is itself questioned. Yet the truth that this is the result (in a market order) of the initial accommodation of the interests of labour to the rights of capital, and that bargaining on such a basis necessarily serves to consolidate the unequal relation between them, has a very low ideological status in the culture. Instead, 'class struggle' at the point of production, in a market society ordered by the private interests of capital and labour, becomes in general a *struggle to bargain*. Thus, strikes will take place because private or state capital refuses to bargain; where, for example, labour will refuse to return to work (for capital) unless capital agrees to bargain with, or accepts the bargain offered by, labour. Conversely, capital may refuse to negotiate with labour, unless labour first returns to work for capital on capital's conditions. Or, labour will refuse to bargain unless a dismissed worker is first reinstated in his work for capital. The fact that, in such circumstances, the trade union is insisting upon nothing more or less than the worker's 'right' to be exploited is discreetly passed over, since the fundamental legitimacy of the basic relation of capital and labour has ideological precedence over all such notions. Similarly, the struggle to maintain the 'closed shop' is a struggle to maintain a monopoly right *to bargain,* in turn in order to maintain the price which labour itself places upon the sale of its skills and time in the labour market. In extremes, easily reached in economic crisis, capital itself may claim – correctly in a capitalist system – that it is under no obligation at all to bargain with labour. In the classical fashion of capital, it will argue explicitly or implicitly that since it purchases the time and skills of labour, and thus 'provides it with the means of survival', it can use this time and these skills as it, not labour, sees fit. But the classical counter-arguments of the labour movement are, in general, decisively not those of the 'class struggle'. (Moreover, they always remain largely hidden.) For labour's objection to capital in such circumstances will in essence be that it does indeed have a 'right' – or, more properly, an interest – to bargain with capital about the price or conditions of its own labour; but as *quid pro pro* for accepting, without fundamental challenge, the legitimacy of capital's property rights, and its right in particular to purchase the skills and time of labour.

Even in the acutest crises of relations – as, for example, in the 1926 General Strike, or in France in May 1968 – the politics of the bargain between private interests has, for two centuries of Western capitalism, overshadowed and overtaken the politics of class opposition to the market nexus between capital and labour. Moreover, in almost every case of crisis, the rights of capital have essentially been restored to it by labour itself, under as much constraint from its own ranks as from any other quarter, so that a new (or old) bargain can be made with it. The left, for obvious reasons, would always rather believe in the simplest fashion that the coercions of state power and economic pressures have, in such events, undermined the 'solidarity' of the 'proletariat'. The role of such pressures can obviously be a large one. But it is surely not as large, in a market system whose values are themselves deeply rooted within the ethics of labour, as that of the ideological legitimacy of the rights of capital in the consent of labour. Furthermore, it is only the most limited conception of the 'rights' of labour, bargaining rights, which is confirmed and consolidated by trade union practice; the trade unions' actual role in the labour market has, obviously enough, established the boundaries of trade union function. And this to such ideological effect that, even without the hostility of capital, serious political proposals from the left to extend the 'rights' of labour (beyond the limits sanctioned by trade union 'custom and practice') encounter powerful resistance from labour itself. So dominating are those limitations upon trade union practice that the 'rights' of labour are no greater in the publicly-owned industries than in the private. That is, the politics of the bargain, and the ideological reflexes of the market system, are fully reproduced in the relations between labour and management in the 'nationalized' industries, as if no change in the form of ownership had taken place at all.

Instead, it was the rights of capital which nationalization most radically affected. The 'rights' of labour remain essentially *what they were* under private capital: private interests, defended by voluntary association and expressed through vigilant market bargains. Indeed, across the whole socio-economic order the same set of dominant labour assumptions is at work, in which an ideological 'realism' dictates acceptance of the rights of capital and its state, and 'common sense' makes the best possible deal with it. It also claims the same private rights for labour and its organizations as it concedes to others; and, on the principle of mutual non-interference, however vain in a relation founded upon exploitation, seeks to make its own 'free' bargains with capital in the interests of labour. But the political market price of securing, in this way, what Bamford called 'a good living for their right good labour'[14] is that labour organizations will themselves deter political opposition from whatever source – left, right or centre – to their manner of (private) defence of labour's private interests, economic and social, within the market. In the same way, the Labour Party, far from advancing the political claims of labour to *be* the 'ruling class', will actually deter and oppose such claims, whether they appear in its own ranks or outside them. Such terms as 'social democracy', 'Fabianism', 'economism', 'labourism' and 'revisionism' are each insufficient for a politics in which the legitimacy of capital's rights, and of the general right of individual appropriation, is itself lodged in the standard but complex practice of labour and its organizations. Indeed, the trade unions embody and express in their own way – whether in their tendencies to monopoly, their competitiveness, their bidding up of the price of labour, and so on – the fact that they are themselves

institutions of the market, part of the market's own forces. So
much is this the case that, whatever the degree of incompatibility
of economic interest between capital and labour, the trade unions
(advancing and defending their members' interests according to
the 'laws of the market') have far more in common, politically and
structurally, with the organizations which represent capital than
could divide them.[15]

The fact that there is an objective necessity in their market
functions is not in question. But that there should be incredulity –
or worse, political abuse from left or right – because much of what
the trade unions do, and the ways in which they do it in a market
system, is 'unsocialist', or 'inflicts severe moral damage on
society' through a 'free-for-all' in pay settlements (in which 'the
devil takes the hindmost' and so forth),[16] is itself foolish. For,
whatever else they may be under the lens of a 'dialectical' vision,
these are market organizations in a market system. Trade union
strikes in the public sector, for example, are vivid expressions of
the logical priority of private interests over public service, in a
social order founded on the former, not the latter. No amount of
intellectually spurious special pleading by socialists – with
arguments which the Marx of 1875 would never have adopted –
can translate the concepts of class struggle to trade union action
which strikes neither at the profits of capital nor at combinations
of private employers, but at public welfare and public provision.
The fact that this brings us close to the arguments of the right
cannot be a deterrent; for it is the refusal, or inability, of the left to
theorize honestly about such action which has been one of the
principal (and just) causes of its own political failures. In any case,
to be inhibited by the fear of being thought to embrace reaction,
particularly when denotations of 'left' and 'right' are themselves
now so unstable, is to invite error. It is also a form of pusillanimity
which, out of intellectual confusion, avoids the related fact that
'incomes policies', for instance, are now the policies of the 'right
wing' of the Labour Party where once they were the hallmark of its
left. The protagonists and opponents of such policies have
changed places, and exchanged their arguments between one
decade and another, but without ever conceding that the trade
unions' own economic actions in the labour market are necessarily
governed not by public need but by private interest.

That this private interest of labour is not only expressed
competitively, but also collectively, does not make it the less

private. Indeed, the separate trade unions' vested (and unavoidable) interests are rooted, union by union on behalf of its members, in particular systems of market brokerage and bargaining, both political and economic. And it is the struggle of discrete groups of workers in and with the market, for market advantage or to prevent market damage, which becomes for each their form of the 'class' struggle; a form shaped by the norms and values of the market, in which the 'class struggle' and market competition blur into one another. In fact, market concepts of the 'freedom to bargain' can even be used to justify (infrequent) collective actions, usually in pursuit of private interest, taken *against* the market. Or, more common and more just, 'civil liberty' will demand the right – Tawney uses the word 'opportunity' – of workers' self-organization as a counter weight to the 'freedom of management' and its otherwise unchecked 'control of the worker'.[17] But what is confusing about such otherwise unexceptional libertarian arguments is that they should be presented in *socialist* guise, when the pressure to balance 'inequalities of economic power'[18] in fact expresses above all the urge for more equal freedoms in the market. Indeed, what is at issue, inevitably in a market order, is the pursuit of labour's private interests through unfettered voluntary association, in which the 'right to organize' is seen as a precondition of economic liberty and trade union 'independence'. The objection that there can be no such real 'independence' for labour in a market system governed by capital is not here in question. Instead, we are dealing with what amounts to a 'socialist' demand for the defence and enhancement of the market freedoms of labour, guaranteed by the trade unions! But it is a demand which itself does no more than express the domination over the politics of labour, and in particular of the trade unions, of the necessary assumptions of a competitive market order. Such demands are, in fact, the translation of the world of capital into the world of labour. And the final irony is that it is a translation which capital has historically obstructed, especially in times of crisis, by seeking to 'curb the powers' of trade unions; curbs on labour's market freedoms which, in the name of democracy (and even of 'socialism'), labour has itself historically resisted.

Indeed, there is no real political escaping, whether 'dialectically' or by any other means, the dilemmas of labour's 'self-organization' in a competitive market system which labour itself has no real intention of radically transforming. For, in these

circumstances, such organization *must* become the institutionalized expression of private interest. The true ideological problem
for socialists under Western capitalist condition is that they have
not been able to admit it, nor the political logic on which it rests.
Trotsky, for example, placed his own knowledge of the dilemma
within the *cordon sanitaire* of inverted commas. 'By means of the
trade union', he wrote in 1925, 'the worker's "individual freedom"
gains immeasurably more than it loses. That is the class point of
view. It is impossible to get away from it.'[19] But an unadmitted
and unintended non-class point of view lurks here also, under
which in practice, despite the inverted commas, thoroughly
non-socialist expectations and purposes inform trade union
organization and action. In 1937, with less or no socialist
pretension, Clement Attlee came a little nearer to the ideological,
if not the real, truth of it. As 'the fruit of long and bitter struggles
by the trade unions', he wrote, the citizen had (allegedly) 'gained
the rights of a free man during his hours of labour'[20] as well as
during his hours of leisure. True or false, individual 'liberty' in
working hours is seen by Attlee as the end of trade union
endeavour. The word 'socialism' and the notion of class struggle
have together and correctly been abolished from the argument;
correctly, since the special interest of labour is by implication held
to be a particular and limited freedom in working hours within a
structurally unchanged market system. But this at least has the
virtue of being true to the overwhelmingly dominant notions of
legitimate trade union function among working people themselves.

The somewhat stronger interpretation of trade union purpose,
as a 'school' of 'democratic' involvement and experience[21] (not
'war') is confined within similar boundaries and assumptions. For
what is implied is that the trade union, engaged in voluntary
actions in the market on behalf of its members, will have its arm
strengthened in the bargaining process not merely by strength of
numbers, but by the quality of their participation. Even in the case
of the most powerful arguments for trade union action – that the
economically weak *must* combine, if they are effectively to
exercise power on their own behalf against superior forces – the
case is no less a market one. The 'power' in question is bargaining
power, such bargaining power will be most often exercised in
rather than against the market, and its purpose will, in almost all
circumstances, be the defence or advance of the particular

(private) interests of the members. Nor, as I have argued throughout, do the trade unions have any viable or realistic alternative. For these are the political and economic dues which labour and its organizations must pay to the market which they accept, and whose values thence bind and determine their own. Indeed, in a market system where 'labour is a commodity rather than a profession',[22] and where non-market criteria of individual worth are powerless to offer their own challenge, the purchase and sale of this commodity, like any other, must in general be regulated by one form of horse-dealing or another. Moreover, even in near-monopolistic conditions, whether in the public or private sector, the ethics of the market bargain govern the determination of the value of labour. And since in only the rarest of circumstances is the actual relationship (of exploitation) between capital and labour really put at issue,[23] capital and labour are 'freely' able, despite intermittent market rancour, to make the deal between them. More important still is the fact that those market conditions and constraints, however harsh, which govern the fundamental relation between capital and labour have not in the last analysis been needed to police the 'class struggle' between them. Rather, labour has for two centuries been largely self-policing; since the industrial revolution generally seeking ends which are either fully compatible, or by bargaining can be made compatible, with the preservation of all the fundamental rights of the private owners of the means of production – or, latterly, with the equivalently wide 'rights to manage' which equally preside unchallenged over the public sector.

That is, labour's own (non-socialist and anti-socialist) ideals of economic autonomy and private appropriation have *in the end* always governed its perception, however intermittently bitter, of its relation with capital and with capital's state. Indeed, nineteenth-century socialist and cooperative programmes for an alternative non-market order were themselves usually closer, even in times of high socialist confidence and expectation, to the spirit of the market system than any other. When William Lovett, the ex-Owenite and Chartist, saw in cooperation a means to the 'gradual accumulation of capital' which would 'enable the working classes to form themselves into joint-stock associations of labour by which ... they might ultimately have the trade, manufactures and commerce of the country in their own hands',[24] he spoke to a general aspiration. It sought, fundamentally, to reconcile socialism with the system of market appropriation, rather than to replace the latter with the former. 'In the days to come', Trotsky promised more than a half-century ago, 'the trade unions will become schools' not of war, but 'of education of the proletariat in the spirit of socialistic production'.[25] But instead, what the trade unions have done since then is what they have always done: to explore, and re-explore, the limited space in a market system within which they can establish their own 'rights'; and in ways which do not jeopardize the exercise of a prior property right, whether that of capital or labour. (I will come to the nature of labour's property rights in a moment.) In such circumstances, the politics of voluntary self-organization, economic autonomy and self-reliance as I earlier analyzed it, becomes the only possible politics which is compatible with the ideal of the freely-made market bargain. But in capitalist conditions, such a labour politics must always be essentially precarious; and always under threat from the right's attacks on the freedoms of the trade unions, despite the fact that the latter are exercised as much with the private interests of capital in mind as the private interests of labour.

Indeed, the very explanation of such attacks is that the market clash between these two sets of private interests – a parody of the class struggle, since they are largely conflicts within and not against the market – cannot be freely tolerated by capital and its state particularly *when the capitalist economy is in crisis.* Yet precisely because the trade unions depend for their functions on the market system, the acceptance of whose legitimacy is itself a precondition for the legitimacy of the claims of labour, attacks on trade union 'rights' by capital necessarily arouse in the trade unions the most ambivalent – and therefore usually the most muted – of responses. With their capacity to bargain threatened, vulnerable because of the scale of their acquiescence with the rights of capital to every charge of illogically impeding the processes of capital accumulation, yet expected by their members to defend their private interests within the market, the trade unions' every dilemma in a market society merely deepens under fire. It is no wonder, therefore, that assault on the trade unions' 'entitlements' to pursue modest claims to self-reliant market appropriation under 'fair' conditions, has proved less a provocation to class struggle than a resented interference with the bargaining process. But every serious political attempt on trade union liberties of action *ought* to remind the labour movement of the low juridical status inevitably accorded to their private interests, in a social order ruled by capital's class priorities and values. Instead, for most labour organizations -- and especially for their officials -- such attempts usually constitute no more than undemocratic acts of bad faith, which disturb a consensus founded upon their own essential acceptance of the market system. That such general ideological acceptance can secure neither permanent immunity nor genuine autonomy for the private interests of labour within capital's own order, is obvious. The problem, rather, is that labour's acceptance of the market system on the unequal terms it is bound to provide, when coupled with a dependency upon capital and its state for the recognition and pursuit of its bargaining function, positively invites restrictions on trade union 'rights' in conditions of economic and political crisis.

Moreover, labour's vulnerability in a capitalist order which it accepts, but does not control, is always to be seen at its deepest within the system of production itself. Thus, on the one hand, it 'militantly' demands an impossible security of work and wages in conditions of industrial decline and closure. But, on the other, it dependently seeks the restoration and revival of industrial processes which capital has abandoned; a contradiction compounded by the fact that its own vested organizational interests are bound up, often inextricably, in a technical division of labour which was created to serve capital's, not labour's, private interest. In such circumstances, made more exigent by labour's many other forms of mortgage to capital, we can see in outline the falsification of one of Marx's most fundamental propositions. For it is the interests of labour, as well as (and sometimes more than) the unjust interests of capital, which can come to be a 'fetter' on technical progress. We may see it when labour organization fights to preserve precisely the areas of the production system which are irreversibly in decline; or when the ethic of competitive self-reliance takes its bitterest precedence over other, historically subordinate, moralities of labour; or when the 'class struggle' is reduced, as it often is, to internal labour conflict over income distribution and sectional advantage. Not even the most efficient fulfilment of the trade unions' market purpose can extricate them from their historic impasse; while the hostilities aroused in the culture, including among working people, by trade union action (successful or unsuccessful) are themselves the expression of an inescapable dilemma.

The political difficulties faced by the trade unions go far beyond the immediate details of familiar – and politically logical – discriminatory legislation. They lie in the history of British manufacture itself, which has given today's labour movement the task of maintaining its claims to social and political authority, but in conditions of economic decline which are themselves the major cause of the weakening of trade union organization. Britain's share of the world's exports of manufactured goods is now less than 10 per cent and falling; at the beginning of this century, the taking of a third share of such trade coincided with the apogee of trade union power. The decline of Arnold's 'industrialism' and of the type and scale of 'producer interests' which were embodied in it, and the decline in the moral status of trade union function, cannot be separated from each other. Indeed, the continuously shrinking range and increasing value of particular technical skills over all others, combined with mass unemployment and the 'unwanted labour' of millions, has exacerbated every problem of trade union purpose, economic and social. The prospects of ameliorative social change through labour movement action, apart from being impossible to achieve in conditions of steady industrial decline, are merely disrupted further by the increased competition in the labour market between favoured and un-favoured labour interests. Yet insecurity in the labour market, as in any other, exasperates the spirit of competition, particularly where it is expressed through bargaining based on voluntary associations, whose strengths and resources are themselves subjected to market pressures. Nevertheless, the 'necessity of submitting' to the 'superior steadiness of the masters', as Adam Smith coldly put it, 'for the sake of present subsistence'[26] is not itself the major cause of the disruption of the labour movement's 'collective' purpose. Rather, it is labour's own historically institutionalized acceptance, in practice, of the laws of competi-tion, together with its own politics of acquisitive self-reliance, which make continuous economic and political defeat unavoid-able under adverse market conditions.

But labour movement orthodoxy, which equally necessarily seeks to legitimize the private interests of labour and the manner of their self-defence, continues to insist that 'voluntary wage bargaining' in the market has reduced the inequality upon which the relation with the market itself rests. Instead, far from having reduced such inequality, the market bargaining process between capital and labour, in a market system ruled by capital, itself serves to confirm it. And it has created a world of essential collusion, not conflict, between capital and labour (whether organized or unorganized), which is necessarily in the predominant interests of the former. Moreover, their ideological commitment to the same ends has led, throughout the whole history of industrial development, to the joint regulation of job recruitment and closed shop exclusions, and of hierarchies of status and reward within the division of labour. Equivalent – but not equal – oligopolies, at work together in the markets of capital and labour, have not only made nonsense of the notion of class struggle; they have collaboratively sought to suspend both the laws of market competition and of opposed 'class interest', in common defence of priorities which themselves derive from the cross-class legitimacy of private appropriation. That 'profit' is the dominant motive in one case, and anxiety over 'job protection' in the other, is a difference more apparent than real. What is really at issue is the joint promotion, by bargain, of the private interests of capital and the private interests of labour, however precarious (and inferior in substance) the latter.

Furthermore, the history of the Labour Party has been marked from its foundation by exactly this impulse. Carried over into the party from the trade unions, it is an impulse unexceptional in a market order whose basic political and economic logic is not in dispute; it is only the manner of exercising particular interests within it which is the subject of compromise and contention. Thus, 'the attitude of the bulk of the unions . . . favouring independent labour representation', at the turn of this century, 'was dictated more by fear for the security of their existing position than by the hope of any millenium. They wanted to hold on to what they had achieved by industrial action.'[27] A half-century earlier in 1847, Marx's proletariat, as we have seen, had had 'everything to gain through the ruin of the old system'. But by 1900, the dilemma of labour – and Labour – was already characterized by the gathering desire to protect existing interest in the existing order, however vitiated by political inequality and economic injustice. Thus, today's trade union and 'socialist' protectionism – of jobs, of welfare, and of the rule-books of custom and practice – is merely yesterday's labour interest under conditions of industrial and political regression. Indeed, when miners are called upon by their 'left' leaders to 'fight for your pits, your jobs and the jobs of your children',[28] there is much more at issue than security of employment. For this is the deeply conservative expression of the worker's 'property' interest in labour,[29] bizarre as it is when dangerous and debasing labour at the coalface is the property in question. It is an interest with its own (market) price and value to labour; in this extreme case even as a form of inheritance for the next generation. It also represents a conservatism as profound as anything the right can offer; while having nothing to do with socialist aspirations to transform, not to conserve and bequeath, capital's system of property and social relations. And even if it could be argued that to invest in and defend job property and its price within the existing order was the best way to secure the private interests of labour, to do so in the name of socialism is quite another matter.

Of course, the claim to job property in wage labour, proprietary or 'capitalist' in form as the claim may be, is no more favoured than any other labour claims which are seen to threaten the interests of (real) capital and its state system. After all, the very conception of labour's economic and social 'rights' and entitlements against capital in a capitalist system, even when such 'rights' are embodied in legislation, can at the best of times be of little real substance. But in times of crisis, or legal confrontation, the labour movement is generally made to pay even more heavily for being disarmed by its own practical acquiescence in the ends of capital accumulation. Indeed, if this had not been so, the absolute need of capital for labour – especially under the most favourable conditions of 'full employment' – would have invested labour with the unambiguous political and economic authority of a class dangerously opposed to capitalist purpose. Instead, struggles to revive dying forms of production, struggles for the right to work for capital, struggles over wage differentials between workers, and struggles to preserve the means of market bargaining and competition – objectively necessary as they may be, from one standpoint or another – have been surrogates for a politics of class opposition to capitalist accumulation. And even if such seeming struggles as there have been for a morally just distribution of the social product between labour and capital are (falsely) elevated in historical significance over the kinds of struggle I have mentioned, they too usually emerge on careful examination as no more than conflicts about income distribution and a fair private reward for productive effort. Moreover, all these market conflicts in the rich industrial countries of the West, whether dignified or not as forms of the class struggle, and however justified when viewed in 'the local context', have for decades been 'fought on the backs of the rest of humanity',[30] ridden in Third World tandem by Western capital and Western labour.

Yet none of this should arouse, on left or right, either surprise or objection – and, least of all, historically uninformed objection. For the forms of trade union struggle, as I have pointed out, have been derived from the ordering of the market system itself. And its goals, even where general strikes have taken place to secure them, have been limited in the last analysis to whatever can be regulated by the bargaining process. Moreover, as Marx pointed out in *Wage-Labour and Capital*, 'the division of labour, introduced by capital and continually increased, compels the workers to compete among themselves'.[31] 'Leap-frogging', and all other such forms of 'competition between the workers themselves', are inscribed in, and part of, the capitalist market order.[32] But what was not envisaged by Marx (nor by any other nineteenth-century socialist) has been the extent of the reduction in practice of trade union purpose to a Wilfred Pickles economics of 'money on the table'. The 'real bedrock, the granite foundation' upon which the aspirations of the trade union movement rest may be held by apologists to be 'values'.[33] But the seeking of 'more cash' – whether from the nationalized boards, the welfare services, the multinational monopolist or the petty employer – has made money-struggle into the main purpose of labour organization. Yet this, too, is the necessary result of the primacy of individual appropriation as a value in the culture, in which the trade union serves (willingly) as a social or collective means to the attainment of ends for which individual means are in general insufficient. The further social consequences of this reduction in purpose are, however, substantial. For the trade unions, historically the organizers of great producer interests battling for market 'rights' and rewards with the even greater power of capital, and in an expanding system of manufacture, now administer little more than the details of the cash nexus, at its meanest and most contracted. Moreover, at such a level all possibility of the survival of the socialist critique of the market order must begin to vanish entirely. For, where Carlyle and Ruskin recoiled, the trade unions are to be found with their purposes centred; and not merely with socialist, but moral purpose itself diminished to the narrowest sense of particular market interest. To Tawney, throwing normal socialist caution on the subject to the winds, the trade unions were 'too easily contented . . . to be bought off with an advance in wages, too willing to accept the moral premises of their masters'.[34] Yet this objection is itself little more than a subject of pained middle-class regret, a matter for correction. Today, when the trade unions are much more deeply lost in a moral-political limbo, from which even the right's attacks have failed to arouse them, we need a different and deeper reading.

The hated wage maximum of the Robespierrist commune would at least be a beginning. Indeed, such was the 'particular hostility of . . . wage earners' to it, George Rudé has written, that when Robespierre was being led to the guillotine, 'workers are said to have shouted . . . *"foutu maximum!"* ',[35] as the tumbrils passed them. A 'freer' economic system and the transient prospect of higher wages were the promises which anti-Jacobin (and anti-egalitarian) reaction offered. Yet because money struggle is propertyless labour's most immediate practical expression of needs – as a demand for access to the only means, for the majority of wage-earners, of their satisfaction – it has always dwarfed other forms of struggle between capital and labour. It is correct, because inevitable, that it should. The middle-class socialist critic of trade union 'economism', for its allegedly unhealthy preoccupation with wages, is rarely driven by such compulsions. But explanation from economic compulsion will not take us far into the politics of trade union action. Nor will the translation to Britain of arbitrary (that is, *a priori*) and schematic Leninist distinctions between 'trade union' and 'political' 'consciousness'. They are schematic because both forms of 'consciousness' are always inextricably entangled, yet the former is always held to be an inferior and limited version of the latter, which is in turn presented as an ideal type closer to the spirit of Max Weber than Marxism. Instead, the overwhelming 'economism' of both trade union and party politics is itself the practical expression of labour's (and Labour's) historic acceptance – exceptions and left rhetoric notwithstanding – of the values, 'rules' and institutions of the market. 'We'll *conquer* them and no mistake/whatever laws they seem to make', sang Preston cotton-strikers in 1853, 'And when we get the ten per cent,/Then we'll live happy and content./Oh then we'll dance and sing with glee/And thank you all right heartily/When we gain the *victory*/And beat the Lords of Preston.'[36] 'Getting the ten per cent' is of course no true political 'conquest' if it is measured by non-'economistic' socialist criteria. Measured by the accepted norms of the market, however, it is most certainly a 'victory' and a characteristic one: that of achieving what seems a just market bargain, economic or political, to which every such struggle, with or without recourse to the strike, aspires. Indeed, a John Ruskin is not entitled to denote such labour aspiration – or the 'singing with glee' which is promised by its successful outcome – as a 'vain, incoherent, destructive struggling for a freedom of which they cannot explain the nature to themselves'.[37] For these are the 'freedoms' and 'victories' gained in battles with (but not against) the market; which labour and its organizations can 'explain to themselves' as well as any, and better than could Ruskin. But then Marx himself was equally capable of misreading labour's true relation with the market. In 1864, he saw the Ten Hours Bill as a 'great practical success'. In labour market terms it was. Yet his innocent claim that it was also 'the victory of a principle' (rather than a successful market encounter), and 'the first time that in broad daylight the political economy of the middle class had succumbed to the political economy of the working class'[38] is pure illusion. Instead, a reduction in the length of labour's working day for capital had been achieved by means of a political market bargain, in which 'middle-class political economy' had by no means 'succumbed' to labour. Moreover, the 'victory of principle' was precisely that celebrated, thirteen years earlier, by the cotton-strikers of Preston.

Nor are higher wages and improved terms of labour (under accepted capitalist conditions of exploitation) what most Victorian, and latter-day Victorian, moralists make of them. Thus, Ruskin saw what he chose to call 'wealth', not higher real income, as the outcome of labour agitation; but then *disparaged* such 'wealth' as the 'only means of pleasure'[39] for working people whose work was itself without pleasure. But this is not only a nineteenth-century forerunner of today's superficial objections to a consumer culture. It mistakes in characteristic fashion the very essence of the role of wages for labour, in a market system to which labour itself is essentially committed. For wages, which can never be wealth, *are* the private interest of labour in the market. That is, they are the main – and, almost always, the only – means, usually derisory, of individual appropriation, to which the forms of public provision I discussed in the last chapter are a supplement. But, however derisory, it is this private interest of labour, whether expressed as the crude demand for 'money on the table' or in more 'sophisticated' bargaining terms, which takes precedence as a

vital interest over all others. Moreover, it is a precedence greatly
reinforced by the political and ideological rejection, by the
majority of labour, of an alternative socialist aspiration. That the
moral purpose of, say, the Tolpuddle Martyrs must be lost in its
shadow is obvious, but this cannot itself be a ground for socialist
'objection' to trade union action. For the claims of labour, once the
terms and conditions of the market have been accepted, cannot be
fundamentally different (morally or politically) from the claims
which capital itself defends and advances against labour. And this
remains true, even if these same claims of labour, judged by
socialist standards, have an absolute moral superiority which
those of capital could never match or justly challenge. Furthermore, in the economics and politics of labour movement
bargaining with capital, no real attack on the rights of ownership
can be effectively mounted, even if it were intended. For the
regulation of labour's market relation with capital, as I have
already shown, depends upon the prior acceptance by labour and
its organizations of the fundamental rights of the latter, even if
such acceptance is not reciprocated. In consequence, the labour
movement's half-hearted acts of collective self-defence against
capital's constant depredations are, however fantastically to
superficial observation, interwoven with an equally constant
commitment to the existing order. Hence, too, it simultaneously
presses for protection for the lower paid and for the maintenance
of wage differentials; demands a 'fair deal' or a 'return to the
negotiating table' while its very freedoms to organize and strike
are being politically threatened; and even seeks to preserve
capital's order in the name of labour. Competition between
workers and the prevention of such competition rub shoulders
together, while the cross-purposes of labour interest, 'opposing'
capital the better to bargain with it, are installed in every trade
union.

   Articles of socialist faith cannot be expected to survive in such a
climate. The expectation itself is foolish. Tawney might senten-
tiously urge the trade unions to 'maintain their dignity' and
'not merely [to] kick the door' of capitalism, 'but consider whether
the edifice itself is not capable of being reconstructed, and
whether, if so, it will not pay [*sic*] them to take a hand in
reconstructing it'.[40] But in the real world of intricate market
bargaining over the price of labour, 'kicking capitalism's door',
though the commonest opening gambit, is not the whole of the

matter. At its basest, and it can be truly base, the question of labour's 'going rate' in the market – that is, 'the rate of pay increase which intelligent men on both sides "think they can get away with" '[41] – itself becomes a term of bargaining art and market speculation. The briefest glimpse into this world, constructed by capital and labour together, suffices. Thus, the answer to the question of what the 'going rate' is can 'in most years . . . be culled from a process of prolonged and exhausting pub-crawling during the September meeting of the Trades Union Congress. It can then be further refined [*sic*] by visits to annual meetings of the CBI, the IPM [Institute of Personnel Management] and a carefully constructed network of personal contacts.' Out of this process, a notional 'collective bargain', mutually acceptable to the private interests of capital and labour, can then be formulated. 'The trick [*sic*] is to combine carefully defined exceptions criteria with a realistic general settlement level and adequate institutions; and to specify the upper limit allowed under each one of the criteria in a given year',[42] and so on and so forth. That this is itself no more than a plebeian version of the equally coarse monetarism of the right – against which the labour movement is in consequence ideologically powerless – is the least of labour's problems. For the money which is thereafter placed 'on the table' is only seemingly the outcome of such expert effort. Instead, despite all the busy manoeuvres of labour's brokers, 'the primary, active and central power over the disposal of resources stays with capital',[43] and with capital's state, in capital's market. But such a truth can never take root, when it is the bargain itself between capital and labour which gives the trade unions their principal functions. Nor has much quarter been given in the labour movement to a century of left objections that a trade unionism 'confined narrowly to wage claims' – as if labour organization had any real choice in the capitalist market – 'can become something of a dead end' or 'alienate public opinion'.[44] For the 'narrow confinement', the 'dead end' and an 'alienated public opinion' are all the necessary result of the bargain labour has struck with the market. They are neither avoidable nor adventitious.

Similarly, the trade unions' resistance to incomes policies, whether such policies are supervised by right or left governments in capital's interests, has nothing to do with a preferred – or socialist – route to the achievement of social and economic justice. It is rather that the central or state regulation of incomes offends market principles in general, and threatens in particular the *raison d'être* of trade unionism in its 'voluntary' brokerage and 'free' bargaining in the market. The left may wish, or need, to argue that trade union opposition to such regulation implies a political refusal of 'one-sided sacrifice by a working class which has not secured control over capitalist profit and investment'.[45] But in the long historic absence – since the industrial revolution! – of any such struggle by the trade unions to 'master the market', we can quite clearly see that it is the demands of the market itself, marginally adjusted to meet the private interests of labour through the bargaining process, which are the trade unions' preferred instrument of income regulation. Moreover, institutionalized wage conflict long ago secured political as well as practical, or necessary, precedence over other non-economic forms of conflict. Indeed, it is precisely *because* the labour movement's relation with the capitalist market is founded upon having acknowledged its legitimacy, that its actions are essentially both economic and defensive of its economic interest.[46] (Conversely, any real struggle by labour to dominate the market would be necessarily offensive, and extend far beyond the narrowly economic.) But wage conflict, even in conditions of capitalist crisis, and however seemingly successful or aggressive, can do no more than sustain the average level of labour's economic and political subordination to the market, once the latter's basic terms and conditions have been accepted. Here, capitalist right and socialist left understand exactly the same kinds of things – and more than labour's own organizations can afford to concede – of the nature of the market. Thus, Rosa Luxemburg insisted upon the impossibility (a 'labour of Sisyphus',[47] she called it) of maintaining the relative value of wages by trade union action; while Milton Friedman equally knows that 'the ability of unions to raise the wages of some workers does not mean that universal unionism could raise the wages of all workers'.[48] The purposes of such argument may differ – in one case, to arouse labour to the need for political struggle, in the other to decry trade union action altogether – but the economic implications are the same. That is, trade union wage struggles in the capitalist market, objectively and practically necessary as may be, can in general achieve only very limited economic gains for their members. Often, too, they secure at best a partial (and usually temporary) advantage for some at the expense of others; while institutionalizing sectional, and in the end a-social, means of guarding private interest. Moreover, the united strength for independent self-help and mutual aid of the skilled worker, skill by skill and trade by trade, remains labour's non-socialist archetype and market model. But although it is a misleading and anachronistic model, since the social and economic circumstances which produced it have themselves ceased to be typical, it continues to govern much of the form and content of labour's selectively bargained relations with the market.

It is no wonder, then, that socialist notions of the working 'masses', or of their amenability to leadership by a political vanguard pitted in collective struggle against market exploitation, should have turned out historically to be impossible to transpose to the world of the 'voluntary' collective bargain with this same market. For its basic law is conservation, not emancipation. It is a world of 'lost jobs'[49] for capital, rather than lost directions for labour; in which, whatever the rhetoric, the governing desire is rather to revive or expand the existing order than to overturn it. And in circumstances of decline, 'keeping everything going on as before'[50] inevitably becomes the best (and forlorn) hope of labour, as capital in its own interest reorders and even destroys the market.[51] 'One can speak of a workers' movement here', Engels wrote of Britain in 1879, 'only insofar as there are strikes which, *successful or not*, advance the movement by not a step.' We are on familiar ground, but the intended permanence of labour's bargain with the market was nothing Engels could have anticipated or conceded. 'To inflate such strikes', Engels continued, 'by which the working class makes no headway, into struggles of world importance . . . can, in my opinion, only do harm. It should not be concealed that at present no real workers' movement, in the continental sense, exists here.'[52] But if the 'present' of 1879 has now lasted over a century, yet there is also still in existence today the very same 'real workers' movement' which Engels in his own time was so unwilling to discover: a reflection of the market, organized by the million, and fluctuating in its strength and weakness as the larger market of which it is a part fluctuates.

In the same way the Labour Party, itself the broker of the labour interest beyond the point of production, is governed not by the 'laws' of class struggle but by those of the political market. These laws – of political supply and demand, and the marginal calculation of political value, for instance – dominate the political economy of Labour, shaping its bargaining strategies, its political manifestos and its electoral choices. Indeed, bargaining alike in the labour market, in the town hall and in the Commons precisely as capital bargains (and even beyond it), and staunchly observing the constitutional conventions exactly as capital observes them, the labour movement 'collectively' does what it must to defend its particular interest in every arena open to it. By these means it makes as much 'headway' as it can, Engels's harsh judgement notwithstanding, against the continuous ebb and flow of its political and economic fortunes in the capitalist market. Moreover, where the state and private institutions and practices of British capital are archaic,[53] so are those of British labour; and where they are in process of change and development, so (ultimately) are labour's, even if much more slowly and with greater resistance to innovation. Hence, unexceptionally, the parameters of the national ideology describe the same outer limits for the interests of both capital and labour, and of their mode of organization and expression.

Yet, because the overarching interest is capital's, not labour's, the latter can in the last analysis never be protected from the withdrawal of capital's always provisional approval of labour, and Labour, acquiescence. After all, the political and economic market bargain which capital makes with labour is necessarily as much a matter of 'free' calculation of the balance of interest as is labour's. Indeed, it is more so, since in general capital – despite all the constraints of monopoly, and of labour's 'custom and practice' – is freer to bargain in its own market than labour and its organizations could ever be. And wherever such calculation of capital's private interest is unacceptably threatened, as by a combination of economic crisis and labour's false expectations of its own entitlements in the market, political attacks on the liberties of the trade unions are likely to follow. Always a latent possibility in a capitalist system, they constitute an attempt to redraw, or even to cancel, the terms of the existing bargain between them. In such circumstances, 'anti-trade unionism' becomes the inevitable, and in capital's terms just, political reflex of one set of embattled interests refusing, or seeking to escape, accommodation with another. Moreover, labour's interests not only possess a lower intrinsic status than capital's in capital's market, but they are interests for which the unstable voluntary bargain with capital can offer no real protection. Ironically, too, such attacks on the trade unions – breaking the bargain or 'consensus' between capital and labour – are an expression of capital's own class struggle with labour, even if it is a struggle for which labour (and Labour) has much less stomach. Thus, under its dictates, capital and the right will periodically restate their own obvious ideological case, political and economic, against labour and its organizations, with (class) arguments both honest and dishonest. The legalized 'powers of the unions' will then become 'the biggest obstacle to raising the living standards of the working class as a whole';[54] or the British trade union movement turns into 'the most privileged trades union movement in the world, commanding a huge conscript army in the closed shop', but which has 'failed its members [and] left them near the bottom of the productivity league, condemned to see the big pay-rises wiped out by inflation'.[55] The trade unions can even be 'the prime source of unemployment' and the main cause of 'the decline of the British economy in general'.[56]

Within the ideological frame of such argument, always mounted when capital seeks strenuously to vary its bargain with labour against labour's determination to maintain it, logical contradiction will be no deterrent. Thus, the 'influence and role of labour unions' will typically be held to have been 'overestimated';[57] that is, they are not as powerful as they think. But at the same time – and often by the same critic – they will be accused of being *too* powerful: 'they have succeeded in getting government to grant them special privileges and immunities, which have enabled them to benefit some of their members and officials at the expense of other workers and all consumers'.[58] Historically, they become a 'throw-back to a pre-industrial period';[59] politically, they are held to 'fear democracy'[60] or to be 'not representatives of the poor people';[61] and economically, their policies are merely 'adjusted to the expectation of rising prices'.[62] Indeed, the 'trade union problem', like the 'ethnic problem' in periods of social crisis, comes to be 'prior' to that of unemployment and inflation. The trade unions can then be perceived, by capital on the offensive, as struggling to defend their interests in adverse conditions which they are themselves blamed for creating. In short, capital in its own market is here reasserting its right against labour to make and remake its arguments as it makes and remakes its bargains; and is as willing, where private interest commands, to rig the one as the other. That trade union

'immunities' from legal restraint are no more than the juridical
reflections of the laws of the market, 'permitting' labour 'freely' to
bargain – and struggle to bargain – with capital in defence of its
own private interest, is easily grasped. And equally obvious, given
capital's ultimate command of (and objective need to command)
the market, is its need in crisis to curb or set aside such market
immunities as seem to work too much in favour of labour's private
interest. Indeed, in its own terms – terms which rule – such actions
against the interests of labour are just; and that labour's market
freedoms should be limited or eroded in the name of freedom, as
capital defines it, also has its own complete logic.

Under political and economic assault, it is also not surprising
that trade unions, compromised by their own intention to do little
more than maintain the network of bargained relations between
capital and labour, should be thrown into the disarray of mutual
recrimination or silence. The fact that the labour-market
strengths of some unions are greater than those of others, enabling
them with more or less success to preserve their market bargains,
does not of course make it any easier in crisis to achieve unity in
ranks so riven. Furthermore, the very forms as well as the values of
labour organization have themselves been determined structurally, skill by skill, industry by industry, region by region, by the
historic location and pattern of growth of capital's interests. Even
the internal competition of one is the internal competition of the
other. Thus, labour's interests have inevitably followed those of
capital not merely into the political and economic market, but in
their actual institutional expression. Bureaucracy for bureaucracy and committee for committee, from the shopfloor to the
national body, labour organization is what capital and its own
organization have made it. Even strikes and lock-outs, the
withholding of capital and the withholding of labour, the cartel of
capital and the 'closed shop' of labour, are less the products of
class struggle than competitive means of self-defence of (unequal)
private interests in the market. But since all these means and
interests have been historically shaped and 'given' by the market,
labour cannot be expected by capital to disavow the practical
methods which it has been driven to adopt to defend its economic
interests. Thus, though it may be true that 'the closed shop has not
altogether helped in developing the consciousness of trade union
members', or that it is itself 'partly responsible for the lack of fight
from members in defence of their own union',[63] it is a mode of

labour organization in the market which the self-defence of private interest has inevitably promoted. As such, it can in logic no more be decried by capital than it should now be nervously disowned by labour.

Moreover, the 'closed shop' is in essence merely an expression of labour's desire for job control – not 'workers' control', which must be given a different political connotation both in theory and in practice – within the system of production. That is, it is merely one form of those 'internal' struggles and aspirations, of which the expectation of a 'property in the job' is another, which are integral to the capitalist order itself and predicated upon its acceptance. The issue which such demands raise is not socialism, but labour's authority over its own role within the existing division of labour. For it is capital's – or management's – excessive and unjust pressure on work organization, or the loss of the job itself, which such demands overwhelmingly seek to resist; not in question is the principle of the capitalist ownership of the means of production, whatever socialist wishful thinkers may need to imagine. In fact, it is precisely because this is so that most conflicts within the workforces of capital take the particular forms they do. Hence, they are most often conflicts between levels, sections and private sub-interests of skilled and unskilled labour about conditions and rewards for work, in which the demands of particularity, hierarchy and competition have taken a continuous historical precedence over the solidarities of collective or 'mass' action. Equally, Marx's socialist ideal of a 'free association among the producers'[64] as the model for, and source of sovereign power in, a new social order is wholly remote from the social and political conditions created by labour's acceptance of the market system. Indeed, it is *against* these conditions that the marginalized socialist project must try to struggle. It is a struggle in which new (or old) conceptions of political rights have to be pitted against a world governed instead by the battle for adjustments of a bargained settlement between capital and labour; a settlement whose terms capital brings into political question much more often than does labour.

In consequence, the nature of these 'internal' labour interests and struggles is such, particularly where skilled work is concerned, that an egalitarian politics, to say nothing of a politics of class, is at a discount in the ethical world created by them. Hence, it is also unsurprising that the Labour Party should itself have such a tenuous political hold upon the allegiance of skilled labour sub-interests, which are themselves organized at the workplace around the competitive defence of one sub-'privilege' against another. At the best of times, of course, any representation in the political market of the variegated private interests of labour, by its own party, must be an uphill struggle in a capitalist order. But to seek to represent in a common *socialist* project labour sub-interests which are in competition with each other is quite another matter. It is no wonder, conversely, that the right should always possess a latent appeal to interests which themselves stand their ground, in internal workplace (or market place) conflicts, on competitive claims to special economic entitlement and social consideration. After all, there is nothing *prima facie* socialist which can be read into the 'collective' action of skilled workers against unskilled encroachment; no socialist ethic in the protection of a property in the job by defensive action against fellow workers, domestic or foreign. Indeed, any resemblance to a 'class purpose' in such actions is coincidental. Yet many on the left continue, out of their own political needs, to mistake the essential nature of much trade union militancy; discerning in its hostilities social and political meanings which such conflicts have never possessed. Consequently, the socialist who for decades has been inspired by falsely-interpreted indices of working-class intention, continues also to be deeply puzzled by working-class resistance to, say, left proposals for greater 'industrial democracy', or for 'workers' control', or for the election of workers to the boards of public sector undertakings.[65] Instead, the majority of the working class has, since the industrial revolution, understood and expressed its own interests in the market in quite different ways from those of left prescription. Moreover, the (continuously-defeated) socialist expectation that 'class-conscious' workers' action will ultimately gain a decisive triumph over the partial sub-interests of labour and the interests of capital together, discounts with blind persistence that the 'social foundations for collective action'[66] by working people, both at the point of production and in the community, are weak and growing weaker. Indeed, even at the nineteenth-century peak of their strength, working people consistently perceived their collective interests, as both Marx and Engels were bitterly aware, less socially and more particularly – group by group, trade by trade, union by union – than could serve a socialist politics of general class unity and generalized class struggle.

Though socialists would have it otherwise, these dilemmas of labour organization are both created and bounded by the market, and by the acceptance of it. In the event, neither dialectical analysis nor dialectical hope has been able to get the measure of the consequences; while labour's collective interests, however arduously reasserted decade upon decade, have been divided by the division of labour itself. But they have also been divided by the different and contradictory effects upon workers of capitalist progress and regression; and divided too by the scale of the desire of each generation of working people to escape entirely from the point of production into individual self-employment. Against such inherent tendencies towards the division of interest, not even the equally inherent relationship of exploitation and injustice, as between capital and labour, has served historically to create the socialist's necessary conditions for solidarity of class perception and action. Indeed, to judge this rightly, the socialist telescope must be reversed: that there has not been *more* hostility to the politics of collectivity, and of socialist aspiration, should be seen as testifying to the negative economic and social effects of capitalism upon the culturally preferred pursuit, by working people, of their own private interests in the market. Moreover, the cultural self-identification – as 'autonomous' individuals – of the members of the putative 'class' which socialist theory insists on seeing in the mass, is itself an act of resistance with which socialism has not yet begun to reckon. In fact, it is arguable that such individuation of working-class perception and interest has been historically promoted, not dissolved, by the development of industrial or factory capitalism itself. For whatever its presumed effect, as hypothesized by Marx, in 'socializing' the 'consciousness' and organization of those engaged in factory production, the impact of capitalist development is at the same time to generalize market conditions and to enhance the aim of increasing individual appropriations within them. Moreover, the process of adaptation of the ends of labour and labour organization to the ends of capital and its interests has been a long and thorough one. Nor, as we can see from British industrial and social history, has the process been determined in the last instance by the immediate success or failure, slumps and booms, of local capitalist performance. Instead, once the ethics and interests of the market have been ideologically domesticated, and deeply institutionalized within labour's own theory and practice, the struck bargain between capital and labour itself becomes resistant, and perhaps impervious, to capitalist 'contradiction', including the severest. In any case, in the latter circumstance – as we can clearly see today – conditions of economic decline, especially in manufacturing, themselves simultaneously reduce the potential of labour organization for militant or socialist opposition to the market. That is, the influence and strength of numbers of the trade unions dwindle together, and at precisely those historical moments when socialists look in vain to their power.

Indeed, the general effect of contemporary technological change on the division of labour, on the nature and content of work, and on the scale of unemployment is to promote still further the individuation and particularization of the special interests of labour and of labour organizations. The old world of mass production and full employment generalized market appropriation and corroborated its value-system; a new world now being determined and reshaped by technologically-induced mass unemployment, and by increasingly advanced machine-design and information systems, threatens the potentiality of a labour opposition to it far beyond what was previously achieved by labour's historic acquiescence in the market. A combination of high technology on the one hand, and 'second-class' or 'surplus' millions with their state-subsidized purchasing power on the other, cannot possibly provide the social constituency for a unified 'consciousness' and organization, where the old technological order for two centuries failed to do so; and neither can a slowly shrinking domestic workforce combined with a market founded upon multinational microefficiencies and increasingly specialized private labour interests. Instead, the newly emerging industrial forms, with their complex social effects, are in all senses moving beyond labour's political grasp. For the circumstances in which great technical changes took place at the beginning of the nineteenth century are not now being repeated, even though labour's just fears of change and of job losses, the present attacks on the trade unions, and deepening economic divisions among working people are reminiscent of the first industrial revolution. Why are the circumstances distinct? Because two centuries ago, new machine power and mass labour power were being yoked together, power with power, in the forces of production. And for over a century and a half, despite the continuing survival of artisanal production, the relation between these powers epitomized the relation between capital and labour.

Today's new technologies possess no such characteristic, nor can they. Rather, labour's social or collective strengths have contracted precisely because the scale and range of their functions in the division of labour have diminished in the face of new technical powers of production and destruction. Indeed, the very refinement and force of the latter puts their social control, as well as social progress itself, into profound question. But the articulation (and organization) of a new 'moral economy', capable of withstanding and reordering these effects, depends upon countervailing forces which are themselves being sundered by the technical division of labour, social insecurity and unemployment. Worse still, the acceptance of the ends and interests of the market, by the overwhelming majority of working people, is an acceptance of ends which are best served by exactly those forms of technical innovation whose social impact has been so drastic upon labour's collective strengths and organization. We should also note that the narrow institutional interests of established labour organization are one thing, and the wider, 'freer' or more desperate private market interests of labour's constituents are another. And *when they are in conflict*, it is the first which has been increasingly subordinated by the 'rank and file' to the second; the declining ideological status of labour institutions, and the otherwise puzzling data of 'disapproval' even among trade unionists for the actions of their own trade unions, reveal it as clearly as ever. Moreover, even at the best of times for labour, it is the internal politics of the labour movement which has itself constituted the most formidable historical obstacle in the struggles of a small left minority to move beyond the mere seeking of 'recognition', from capital, for purposes of bargaining in the political and economic market. In the worst of times, this merely becomes plainer. Thus, it is the organizations of the labour movement themselves which have historically defeated such socialist opposition as there has been, whether inside or outside the movement, to the narrow politics of private labour interest. That Labour's own constituency should have increasingly seemed to reject the economic and political organizations created to express and advance them, is merely a last irony, but also with its own logic.

In fact, the Labour Party was itself founded upon a precarious and unsustainable bargain, whose true history has never been candidly written on the left. It is not surprising that this should be so, even if such a history would reveal the source of many of the Labour Party's present dilemmas. In the last two decades of the nineteenth century, it was a minority of (mainly middle-class) socialist intellectuals, with a disproportionately pervasive influence on contemporary left debate and with their own political ambitions, who secured funds from the trade union movement for the creation of a new political party. It was a party which, at the time, most trade union leaders did not really want, and many of whom for a long time did not believe in. But the collective bargain on which it rested offered the trade unions, in return for their funds, a 'party of their own', in which the particular labour interest of the trade unions – not the *socialist* interest – would be represented in Parliament by (mainly middle-class) socialist spokesmen. Indeed, throughout the period of the formation of 'a political Labour Party'[67] – and far beyond – the political and social identity and interests of such spokesmen, and the social identity and interests of the leaders of the trade unions, remained remarkably distinct from each other. This is because it was, as ever, an arm's-length voluntary bargain, its style and character shaped by the market; but this time a bargain not between capital and labour, but between labour and its parliamentary agents. Subsequent and ever more complex crises in the party (in which the bargain has been tested to near breakdown) simply cannot begin to be understood unless this context shapes analysis of their causes. The repetitious description of the Labour Party as, for example, a 'broad church' or, more truly, as an 'association of socialist faith and trade union interest',[68] cannot do justice to the nature of the bargain which upholds and divides it. Indeed, like the greater bargain between capital and labour, of which it is a reflection, it requires continuous private brokerage and renegotiation in the political labour market to sustain it. Furthermore, to reconcile 'socialist faith' and 'trade union interest' by bargain – when the meaning of each is separately ambiguous, and when on both hands there are equivalently deep differences of purpose and direction – is made possible in practice only by subordinating principle to the imperatives of horse-trading of one kind or another. And if we were to raise again here the further problems caused to this 'association' of interests by the middle-class socialist intellectual of 'the left' who vicariously dons the guise of the proletarian, or by the working-class labour movement activist of 'the right' who aspires to high parliamentary status, it would serve merely to multiply every confusion. However, the basic outlines of the political truth remain relatively clear in the light of the Labour Party's own history, from its foundation. They reveal, above all, that the party's attempt to fashion a coherent political project, let alone a socialist one, has been persistently handicapped by the historically ambivalent relation of its constituent parts; that the complex combination of the economically disparate private interests of the trade unions, with the equally various political purposes of the representatives of the Labour Party, constitutes 'the interest' of the labour movement; and that this interest acquires the real homogeneity it possesses *only* through the wide common acceptance, on all sides, of the political and economic bargain with the market system.

'The Labour Party', Tawney wrote hopefully, 'sprang from a profound popular movement.'[69] But this is not, to put it mildly, the whole truth; such truth as it contains excludes all sense of the 'precarious bargain' which serves as its political basis. Paradoxically, Trotsky knew more than Tawney of it, describing the Labour Party's 'doctrine' as 'a kind of amalgam of Conservatism and Liberalism, partially adapted to the needs of the trade unions'.[70] It is a bold and well-enough informed analytical stroke. But then Trotsky thought that the Labour Party was 'itself only a brief stage in the revolutionary development of the working class', which Tawney, at least, never believed. 'A great deal less time will be required', Trotsky continued, even more hopefully than Tawney, 'to turn the Labour Party into a revolutionary party than was needed for its creation.'[71] In fact, less than forty years, from 1880 to 1918, were needed for its creation. More than sixty-five years of political market bargains have passed since then, yet working people are now no more – arguably much less – involved in party organization and parliamentary representation, to say nothing of revolution, than they were at the beginning. However, this is itself a relatively minor fact, when set against the intransigent political and ideological form which the narrow pursuit of labour movement realpolitik, inside and outside Parliament, has taken. Despite this, the stereotype of the staunchest non-socialist, and even socialist, ideologues of labour's market interests has never been adequately identified. He – for the model figure is always male – will be a militant defender of the trade unions' 'rights' and traditions; a chauvinist of class, but not (in the Marxist sense) class-conscious; hostile to middle-class

intellectuals alike of left or right, for their privilege and ambition; a
xenophobe, often, and capable at worst of sexual, racial and
national animus; a Labour Party loyalist, for whom to be stalwart
is the highest political virtue; and a moral puritan with a sense of
'respectability' and self-reliance which will normally be deeply
authoritarian. In so far as these are set out as model attributes
only, the political character of the real individuals who man the
non-socialist ranks of labour can only approximate to them, or to
some of them. Nevertheless, the scale of the absence throughout the
labour movement of a critical temper in political response to 'things
as they are' owes at least part of its explanation to the particular
qualities – *not* weaknesses – which are fostered in the culture of the
labour movement itself. Indeed, its very virtues, in general promoted
without ulterior moral purpose, are not only politically self-
consuming; they are also destructive of socialist hopes of 'other ways
of living'.

Hence, it is not possible to hold, with Tawney, that 'the
trade union basis has . . . ensured that Socialism in this country
rests on broad popular foundations'.[72] And not merely because
such 'broad popular foundations' do not exist; nor because a
powerful case can be made out against trade union leaders'
entrenched privileges, against their (historic) financial control
over the Labour Party, or against the anti-democratic misuse of
their command of the bloc vote and its 'dead souls'[73] at Labour
Party conferences. Even the increasingly instrumental trade
union perception of the Labour Party's purpose, as the latter's
political status falters in the country at large, is relatively
unimportant. (In any case, it was always an implicit risk of the
unequal bargain made between unions and party.) Much more
crucial, historically, is that the parliamentary pursuit of labour
movement interests, largely funded by the trade unions, has
demanded of the Labour Party a politics that must satisfy specific
sets of demands which are, in practice, irreconcilable with each
other. Thus, the Labour Party was expected from the outset to
advance essentially non-socialist vested trade union interests in
the labour market, yet oppose the market with whatever it
possessed of its own socialist purpose, while defending the
'national interest' against particular labour interests as a national
party! In the event, the strength of the trade union movement's
commitment to its bargaining relation with the capitalist market
came to dominate (without significant resistance) Labour's

domestic economic programmes. Moreover, the political and moral influence of the narrow values of the trade union movement, carried over into the party, has served for decades to inhibit Labour's more radical and innovative social impulses, such as they have been. In fact, just as the plebeian economics of the trade union bargain invites a monetarist response from the right, while at the same time impeding every form of left economic planning, so the trade unions' own Tammany politics have encouraged the right's instinct for anti-trade union legislation. Together, it can be argued that they have taken a heavy moral toll of Labour's claims to offer the nation a politics of general social renewal. To found a 'movement' upon the bargain of 1918 was itself to ask for future political trouble. But where fundamental and unresolved conflicts of political and economic interest – masked by false distinctions between 'theoretical' socialists and 'practical' or 'hard-headed' trade unionists – become the basis of cabals and factions which destroy policy and threaten to break up organization, the sense of direction of the whole 'movement', always problematical, comes into even deeper question.[74]

On the one hand, the political capacity to make sense of immediate and urgent issues – whether, for example, of the Common Market, or wages policy, or planning agreements[75] – has been consistently sacrificed to decidedly non-class sectarian labour interests. On the other, pugnacity without perspectives, whether socialist or any other, tends to become a poor but inevitable substitute for coherent political purpose. The world of Labour ought to be, and is, more than merely a world of vested labour interest, yet party determination is more readily aroused to the stone-walling defence of the political *status quo*, or the lowest common denominator of labour's private interests, than it has ever been to political or economic offensives against the existing order. Likewise, the trade union movement's cabalistic rule-books and masonic internal procedures, taken over into the party, have for decades exerted a stifling influence upon its policy-making, particularly in periods of party crisis. [76] Here the political cost to the Labour Party of the bargain which underpins it cannot be understated. For it is not just a cost to be measured in political energies spent and misspent upon the relation between party and trade unions. Nor, obviously, can the dead weight of trade union conventions be entirely blamed for the party's history of ideological immobility in the face of social and political challenge.

Nevertheless, the cumulative impact on the Labour Party of the increasingly narrow scope of trade union concerns can be measured by the disastrous fact that the real social underclasses – the old, the poor, the jobless and those suffering from racial and sexual injustice – have gained no greater political franchise from the Labour Party than they have from the trade unions. (The institutionalized racism and sexism of the trade unions I shall here pass over in silence, since its scale beggars description.) Apologists may seek to argue, for their own purposes and at the current nadir of trade union influence, that 'in the last decade the trade union movement has developed enormously as a political force. It has moved far beyond the confines of wage negotiation to intervene extensively in economic policy formation and in legislation on a wide range of subjects.' They may similarly insist that the trade union movement has 'gained enormously in the range and sophistication of its thinking on economic and social policy'.[77] But the exact opposite is the truth. With its century of unconcern for the political education of its members it could not be otherwise. It is because the trade union movement has *not* 'gained enormously in the range and sophistication of its thinking' that political action on the most imperative social and political issues of the day – for example, that of nuclear disarmament, or the defence of fundamental human rights or the redistribution of the world's resources – is monopolized throughout the world of Western capitalism by the moral concerns of the liberal middle classes.[78] Nor can it be otherwise, since, as I have argued throughout, it is the private interests of labour, not public interest nor the common welfare, which must be the trade unions' prior concern, given the determining effect upon their role, their principles and their organizations of their unshakable bargaining relation with the market.

But because this is so, even the basic moral claims of trade unionism, as the sole substantial means of its members' self-defence against the arbitrary exercise of capital's power over labour, are diminishingly able to hold their ideological ground in the culture. That the interests of labour, unlike the interests of capital, are expected (by what is itself a double moral standard) to be socially and not competitively perceived and pursued, merely adds to the labour movement's burdens. But, in consequence, what is ethically just in their actions is now seen, rightly or wrongly, to be more than balanced by what is ethically suspect or even indefensible. Indeed, the trade union movement shows increasing unconcern and lack of engagement – position papers and rhetorical gestures notwithstanding – with social and moral issues which lie outside the realm of immediate labour interests. Yet this has itself begun seriously to marginalize the political influence of the labour movement, as the focus of major social issues widens far beyond its own world of production for the market. Thus, the social organization and representation of the jobless falls essentially on the wrong side of the historical demarcation line separating the interests of employed from unemployed labour. Despite intermittent efforts, past and present, by a small minority of trade unions to cross it, it is a line which has held firm for the most obvious of reasons: that trade union bargaining power in the market, trade by trade and union by union, derives from its social capacity to command the 'right' to negotiate with capital, on behalf of a collectivity of individuals, the price of their labour and the conditions under which they will perform it. The unemployed, who can contribute nothing of substance to the trade union once they fall outside the division of labour itself, must also therefore fall outside the main concerns of labour organization. But that the reach of the trade union movement cannot, in these and other circumstances, extend far beyond the factory gate is itself a source of many of its dilemmas. Circumscribed in their funds and functions, simultaneously decried both for overstepping and not overstepping the boundaries of their historically-given role in the labour market and at the point of production, the trade unions are morally disabled by both success and failure, strength and weakness, as they attempt to carry out their obligation to defend the private interests of labour.

It is these which are the true 'contradictions' of trade union function, contradictions which have remained largely hidden from socialist theory. Moreover, because the problems which they pose have for decades been (unavoidably) carried by the trade unions into the wider labour movement, their impositions can be followed to the very heart of the Labour Party's own permanent political dilemmas. They are dilemmas which it has been neither willing nor able to resolve. Thus, the Labour Party has been constrained by just obligation to serve the trade unions' historical purposes in the labour market. At the same time, it has itself been politically handicapped by the public odium attached, however unjustly, to the (necessary) pursuit by the trade unions of their market purposes. But it is the labour movement as a whole – party and trade unions – which has suffered from what are in fact deeply-shared common commitments to the market system. In the last analysis, therefore, allocations between them of historical responsibility or blame for the political consequences of such shared commitment can serve no practical purpose.[79] Nevertheless, the years of attrition in Labour's moral impulse, and the low level of general political education in the culture, are truly failures of the trade union movement; as is, also, the lack of dynamism and invention in Labour's political, economic and social thinking. Indeed, it would be a much simpler matter if it was intellectual incapacity, or poor organization, or bad advice which had compromised moral purpose, political education and the tasks of theoretical renewal together. Instead, the cause is far more fundamental: the inherent and chronic ambivalence, left, right and centre, as to the true interests of labour in its relations with the existing order. Moreover, the movement's long internal struggles – never bitterer than in the recent period – to secure the party to 'progressive' or 'new' political and social positions, have always been fought out against, and been sapped by, a majority sense of commitment to its bargained engagements, political and economic, with the market. And it is these engagements which have proved sufficiently powerful, since the party's foundation, to resist all comers; able, always, to repel the political challenge of innovation, whether on the right or left of the party.

The style and substance of it, however, are the very opposite of inertia. For the movement is capable of mobilizing, under threat, the strength of real political convictions against every form of radical ardour. That the most heroic political effort is sometimes reserved to the most demeaning of political purposes is a merely incidental matter, once the 'soul of the party' or the 'survival of the movement' have been put at issue, most often in causes where neither is in question. Yet behind the movement rhetoric of left and right, entirely other processes, deeply understood and accepted, are always simultaneously at work. Taken over from the relation itself between capital and labour, they are those of the bargaining away of 'extremes' to find the inner party centre, or still point of equilibrium, where competitive interests can receive their quietus by mutual accommodation. The 'heavy moral toll' suffered by the labour movement is to be found here also, and perhaps here above all. For the cumulative consequence of the

internal bargaining away of principle has usually been the
absence of a sense of direction, particularly in times of economic
and social turmoil. Indeed, it is for this reason that such periods
are also times of additional danger and weakness for the labour
movement's collective social interest. In the ideological vacuum
left by the long history of barter and exchange of one labour
interest for another, it is in general the strongest physical or
numerical force which prevails in crisis; in which the regression of
moral purpose in the labour movement can fully match that
elsewhere in the culture. Thus, when its own fortunes are most
threatened, we can sometimes see labour and trade union politics
beat an historical retreat to the low ground of working-class
reaction; observe the surfacing of a 'class consciousness' which
has more to do with class (and at worst, race) origins than ethical
principles, whether socialist or any other; and be confronted with
a labour economics which has less to do with morality than with
muscle. But if these tendencies are latent in labour politics even at
the best of times, it is the market which demands and trains them.
Above all, the trade unions have learned – because they have had
to learn – how to make market virtues of the most partial of their
interests; and especially of those, the narrowly economic, in which
the convenience of being able to split the difference, make a cash
settlement or trade off one market advantage against another is
their strongest recommendation. More 'abstract' issues of moral
principle or social justice, lacking an economic exchange value,
clearly pose different and much more awkward challenges to
trade union purposes, shaped since the industrial revolution by
the need to defend only those practical interests which can be
practically defended.

Yet the limiting expertise which such practicalities demand is
one thing. What the trade unions have made of it organizationally
is another. 'The conservative bureaucrats of the trade unions',
Trotsky wrote in the year before the General Strike, 'represent at
the moment the most counter-revolutionary force of Great
Britain, and perhaps of all the world's development.'[80] But this
was, and is, a gross exaggeration, deep in the disdain of the
socialist intellectual for labour's market institutions, whose functions and structures invariably express their interrelation with the
capitalist mode of production. Arnold, addressing himself (in
his own way) to the same issue, lumped the leadership of the
Victorian trade unions into his category of 'philistines' – a term for

the middle class, it should be noted – complaining that 'its thoughts' were filled with 'external goods' rather than with 'inward perfection'.[81] But a market order is socially a hard taskmaster, and 'inward perfection' can no more flourish in the labour movement, least of all in its bureaucracies, than anywhere else in the organization of the market. Indeed, this becomes particularly clear, as I have pointed out, at the very time when a disproportionate virtue – political, cultural, moral – is most expected of the movement in times of social and economic crisis. For it is then that the trade unions have historically been looked to, generally in vain in our culture, for leadership in the Manichean battle with the forces of market darkness; more important, looked to as the potential source of an alternative social principle to that of the law of the jungle or the survival of the fittest. But in each phase of capitalist crisis, the more severe the more obvious, the same kind of social Darwinism has always been discovered – with the same concealed dismay in each historical period – to be the cultural hallmark of the politics of both capital and labour. Moreover, in crisis, neither revolution nor counter-revolution has ever been seriously at issue; just as neither class conflict, nor Marx's 'much vaunted community of interests',[82] can ever adequately characterize the nexus between them. Instead, a market relation has been at work since the industrial revolution whose legitimacy through thick and thin has had a tendency to carry everything before it, including adherence to principle. And this has remained true whether the principle be that of class solidarity, of unity in adversity – both much stronger in the ranks of capital than of labour – or of the defence of the weakest in the market. Indeed, in labour politics, it is faction which dominates in social crisis. Or, put another way, *the crisis of capital becomes the crisis of labour, precisely because of the inextricable relation between them.* At its most banal, particular factional interest becomes party schism and 'subversion'; while rival internal tendencies can come to be perceived as 'cuckoos in our nest', a 'different species who wish to take us over' or even a source of 'terror' to 'solid' – that is, more orthodox – labour interests.[83] These are the battle-cries of vested movement interests under challenge, when internal political bargains can no longer hold under external pressure.

But the conventional socialist charge of 'labourism', directed against this politics of the labour movement, cannot itself hold. For it is a charge normally grounded in intellectual privilege, and armed with an ideal notion of socialism drawn from speculation. It also knows too little of the market, too little of the relation between capital and labour in it, and too little of the effects of this relation upon the labour movement as a whole, left, right and centre. Nevertheless, socialist critics of the movement have persisted with moral expectations and castigations of it which have always been rooted in error. Thus, Tawney was wrong to insist, against unavoidable contrary truths, that the 'sentiments of human dignity, justice and equality' to which 'British socialism . . . appealed' had 'transcended' its lower-level appeal to 'economic interests'.[84] It is a reading false to an historical circumstance, two centuries old, in which the prior market relation between capital and labour, institutionalized first in the trade unions and later in the Labour Party, governs such 'appeals' and at the same time prevents their 'transcendence'. Likewise, the judgement that 'labourism' – the non-socialist politics of labour – is a 'weak, sickly and pathetic ideology' which has 'dominated the British working class' and which 'must be displaced if we are to move forward',[85] is mistaken on all counts. It is neither 'weak' nor 'sickly'; indeed, its strength, correctly identified, is the very cause of the inability of rival versions of socialism to 'displace' it and 'move forward'. And far from having 'dominated' the British working class, it is itself the authentic historical expression of real working-class interests in the labour market.

Some left socialists of course compensate for these unconceded truths with anticipations of a future socialist transformation of the Labour Party, often coupled with political abuse of its present 'cowardice' and past 'betrayals'.[86] But this is mere intellectual gymnastics; an ultimate (socialist) 'triumph' for the Labour Party, which would be based – in imagination – upon 'generating a tremendous political counter-charge, capable of exploding the colossal weight of centuries [*sic*] of sanctified, sedimented authority and custom',[87] is a rank inflation of political possibility. Why? Because this same 'authority and custom', inhering in the labour movement's political and economic relations with the market, is its vindication and *raison d'être*. Nor can today's left optimists reasonably look to the trade union movement to 'provide a far more positive and constructive leadership than its critics believe is possible'.[88] For the trade unions' relation to the realm of 'civil society' in general, as well as to the state and its powers, is governed by and subordinated to the trade unions' relations with

the market. Indeed, it is because of the need for the relation
between labour and capital (and Labour and capital) to be secure
– and, in turbulence, to be re-secured by negotiation and accommodation – that the greater issue of state power, and the
working-class conquest of it, cannot become a serious political
object of the labour movement. At best, the historical purpose of
even the most militant action taken by it against the state, its laws
and institutions has been ultimately directed not to securing
political power, but to reasserting the private interests of labour in
the eyes of its opponents. Hence, struggles to affirm and reaffirm
trade union freedoms, against capital's attempts to impose
through the state legal restrictions on labour organization in the
former's market interest, are themselves struggles to restore
labour's market position. At issue is labour's right freely to
bargain in the market, and the protection of particular (sometimes very particular) bargaining strengths. But this is a very
different matter from a political challenge to the existing market
order – despairing left rhetoric to the contrary, notwithstanding.
In consequence, the central institutions of state power – the
police, the army, the established church, the courts, the civil
service mandarinate, the City and the press and broadcasting
media – have for a century and more remained fundamentally
immune from labour movement action, and even from serious
criticism. Moreover, they will remain so, provided always that it
remains broadly possible to pursue the private interests of labour
in the limited ways that labour perceives and organizes them.

Labour leaders, whether of party or trade union, have themselves insisted on the priority, particularly in times of crisis, of
maintaining the market relation with capital over whatever
internal pressures have seemed to threaten it. Thus, every
prospect of expansion of the party and trade union role beyond the
sphere of the political and economic bargain – whether negotiated
in Westminster or Whitehall, the public sector boardroom or the
factory manager's office – has been successfully resisted not by
state coercion or denial, but (in effect) by capital and labour
acting in conjunction. Because this is so, the objective confinement and subjective self-confinement of labour movement purpose to the dimensions of the market is in essence the history of the
labour movement. To 'convert' the trade unions, as Crosland put
it – not merely more right than left, but more right than wrong –
'from wage bargaining organizations mainly concerned to adv-

ance the interests of the workers . . . into organizations primarily concerned with national economic policy . . . could only be to deprive them of the confidence and loyalty of their members.'[89] But if national economic policy be considered as outside the 'bread and butter' scope of trade union action – and it is so considered, covertly, throughout the trade union movement – it is no surprise that 'political power' represents for the Labour Party no more than an opportunity for stewardship by labour of capital's interests, and the shifting of market advantage marginally towards the former while it is in office.

'A Labour Government . . . utterly devoted to the interests of the proletariat would . . . be compelled to break up the old state apparatus', Trotsky declared in 1925.[90] 'We in England', Tawney wrote blandly twenty-four years later, 'have repeatedly re-made the State, and are re-making it now.'[91] Both were wrong: the first, however correct in theory, because in political practice the 'interests of the proletariat' have been held by working people themselves to be in essence coterminous with the interests of capital; and the second, because the state was no more being 're-made' in 1949 than at any other time in the 300 years since the English Revolution. But it is socialist impatience with the 'displacement' of labour and Labour purposes, from hostile engagement with state and class power to largely benign engagement with the market and the market bargain, which is most thoroughly mistaken. As a result, critics have superficially perceived the labour movement to be 'overawed by the privilege of saluting [the] established proprieties',[92] or engaged upon a long act of 'class betrayal'. But what such critics are in fact observing is a small part of a much larger complexity: the political and economic brokerage of private labour interests in a socio-economic order whose fundamental legitimacy was long ago accepted. And accepted not only by most British working people, but *sub rosa*, by most British socialists also.

6   Avoiding Utopia

The dependency of an ostensibly oppositional social theory and political movement upon an economic order whose laws, values and institutions it does not seriously intend to challenge can no longer be compensated for by radical wishful thinking, however ingenious. The urge to seek asylum from this dilemma in utopia, during a period of social and economic crisis – in our time, the utopia is that of 'participation' – merely extends the dominion of politically disenfranchising illusion. Yet, although such ideological castles-in-the-air can offer no refuge from the implications of the commitment of the labour movement to the world of market appropriation, it is no deterrent to their continuous reconstruction. For radical and radical-seeming hopes justly spring eternal; even if a century of their failure to make any political headway in the movement, crisis or no crisis, should long ago have taught the greater political reach (and political significance) of the bargain struck between capital and labour. Instead, 'old' left, 'new' left and a new left newer still has each in its own ways displaced, glossed over or miniaturized the historic evidence which has decade on decade revealed the rejection, by the majority of working people themselves, of socialist intention. And, decade on decade, the left has pushed on regardless into its own political limbos. In consequence, fundamental issues of liberty (above all), of welfare, justice and progress – and questions as to the very validity of the terms 'left' and 'right' – cannot now be adequately engaged with, as long as they are confined to the perspectives of the labour movement. Castles-in-the-air the left's intellectual sanctuaries may be, some soaring and cloud-capped, others dungeons of the mind and spirit. But they are also so structured as to have prohibited all those thoughts and actions which might once have been able to provide relief from ideological failure. Thus, although labour is the largest contributory part of that 'social force' which, in tandem with capital, not only reproduces but *needs and seeks* to reproduce the existing 'social relations of production' – capitalism, in short – such a truth seems doomed to an eternal socialist taboo. The prospects for the advance of socialism in our culture are doomed along with it. To translate this truth more concretely: the majority of working people, even when organized within the trade union movement and voting for the Labour Party, do not subscribe, and cannot be expected to subscribe, to those socialist and social causes which left intellectuals consider central to the preservation of a civilized order. And particularly not, as long as such causes are seen to threaten present or future employment, the right to bargain in the market, and the priority of private appropriation.

Hence, the spirit of a renewed political creativity – like the will to associate with political interests beyond the immediate concerns of labour – cannot reasonably be looked for in the ranks of the labour movement. This is especially the case where expectation of renewal takes the rejection of the capitalist or market system as its basic premise. Yet, despite the fact that all this has long been so, left illusion must continue hotly to deny that it is the labour movement itself which has historically constituted the most powerful cultural obstacle to socialist aspiration. By now it deserves to be regarded as an unremarkable truth, and so settled as to be of relative insignificance as a contemporary political issue. Moreover, in the absence of a mass movement of class opposition to the existing social and economic dispensation, it is the defence of civil liberties and democratic institutions – not the illusory prospects for socialism in a period of further decline in manufacturing production – which demands the redirection of radical energies dangerously misspent upon compensatory utopian fancies.[1] Indeed, such change of perspective has never been more urgent. For these are times when the individual's capacity for self-identification as a citizen, possessed of commonplace but fundamental citizen-rights, has arguably never been so reduced in our culture, particularly among working people.[2] In addition, we must face the fact of the practical impossibility of reviving an alternative moral economy to that of capital around the narrow constituency of labour's private interests. But the implication of this for the defence of democratic entitlement is equally serious. For the pursuit of their market interests by labour organizations has served to narrow the ideological perception of their members as to what constitutes the full scope of citizen-rights in the political system. The right to bargain, the right of individuals and trade unions to struggle to bargain, and the right privately to appropriate the rewards of the bargain are of course themselves civil rights, and valuable (though limited) forms of market freedom. However, the trouble is that they have become, for many in the labour market, the institutionalized expression of what organized labour essentially *means* by democratic freedom. And it is this ideological reduction – coupled with the labour movement's century of neglect of political education – which has itself reduced the movement's capacity for collective response to the steady contemporary erosion of civil liberties; that is, unless they bear directly upon the exercise of its economic interests in the market.[3] No doubt, current left advocacy of new (and old) utopias of 'democratic participation'[4] is an unadmitted compensation for the knowledge of how frail and relatively undefended are our wider political freedoms; particularly when working people and their organizations do not themselves accord such freedoms the ideological status which attaches to the right to bargain. But it has become all too obvious that 'bourgeois democratic' rights can be restricted or imperilled – as by the extension of arbitrary police powers – without the risk of that militant labour response which is intermittently aroused by capital's assaults on the balance of negotiating advantage between capital and labour. In such circumstances the socialist prospect of 'reversing the hierarchy of power'[5] established by the capitalist system can never have been remoter. In particular, the political concerns of the mainly middle-class civil libertarians inside and outside the Labour Party do not evoke even the short-lived pugnacity and solidarity which are brought by the labour movement to the defence of the trade unions' bargaining powers. Instead, struggles over the conditions of, and the rewards for, production or the assertion of job property rights, take – and in economic crisis are bound to take – ideological precedence over resistance to changes in the Judges' Rules, to the forms of emergency rule in Northern Ireland, or to the increase of police surveillance of individual behaviour. Yet, ultimately, civil liberties cannot be adequately defended, let alone extended, unless the institutions of state and police power are thought to be the legitimate object of challenge by the labour movement.

But these state and para-state institutions are themselves the very guarantors of the order with which the labour movement long ago made its ideological peace; an order to which it is bound now by deep structural ties of political and economic allegiance, ties both voluntary and reinforced by one kind of mortgage and another. In consequence, labour's and Labour's conceptions of the limits of civil liberty cannot radically outrun the (shifting) parameters which capital and its state themselves prescribe for them. Thus, the left utopian may call upon the trade union movement, until he is hoarse, to 're-think its own vision of its role in much bolder terms, if it is to widen its appeal to those beyond its ranks'.[6] But 'beyond its ranks' stand, among others, those whose notions of civil and human rights are less bounded or determined by the market. They include those who – whether from class privilege or moral choice (or both) – set the cause of universal physical survival, racial and sexual equality, or the liberation of 'Third World' peoples from neocolonial domination, ahead of the defence of the British industrial revolution's division of labour. Indeed, they include large numbers of individuals to whom the values of the labour movement can make only a limited and uneasy appeal; and precisely because such individuals do not so exclusively derive their sense of political and social identity from the capitalist system itself, unlike the labour movement. Moreover, any radical political action – taken, say, against military exports to South Africa or Chile, or against the manufacture of weapons of mass destruction, or against the discharge of radioactive effluent onto public beaches – which threatens the 'competitiveness' or security of domestic industrial enterprise, and is literally counterproductive, threatens the fortunes of capital and labour together.[7] These latter compose a nexus so strong that even the worst of threats to our collective well-being, that of terminal annihilation, has proved incapable of shaking it; so strong that it possesses the historic power to resist (in the world of 'real' socialism also) every claim whose argument is 'merely' moral. For the organizations of labour inescapably embody, despite all the exceptions, the same aspirations as capital to defend and enhance not cross-class citizen-rights in general, but particular interest. And whether in competition or collusion with capital, national and multinational, they do so within the same range of ideological assumptions. That the trade unions 'do *nothing*' to 'move men away from their image of themselves as ... appropriators'[8] is exaggerated, and therefore untrue. But that the classless universality of moral concepts of human and civil rights, and the domestic defence of specific economic interests within an international division of labour founded upon exploitation, are incompatible with each other can hardly be questioned. Unable, in addition, to deal with the newly emerging technical forces of production, the labour movement's 'essentially defensive values'[9] in protection of producer interests nevertheless pose questions quite different from those traditionally raised by the left utopian. Thus what has to be asked is whether, lacking a clear moral prospectus, though lacking ready popular support in capitalism's own crisis, and lacking an active commitment to those civil liberties which stand beyond the world of the market bargain, the labour movement's 'bedrock ethics' – those grounded in anti-collectivist notions of self-help, self-reliance and economic independence – nevertheless might provide a democratic bulwark broader and deeper than can be coopted to capital's purpose.

Certainly, we can see that the trade union struggle to preserve its 'right' and powers to bargain, as for example through the closed shop, may offend capital's own rights to a prior or greater freedom to bargain in its own market. But is there more to such a struggle than a recalcitrant form of conflict, which defends labour's market interest in ways that capital cannot always assimilate? The political denunciations of the closed shop as a denial of market freedoms are, of course, no more than an expression of the clashing interests of capital and labour in the market; just as the insistence upon labour's 'right' to retain a particular balance of market forces, or to maintain the price of labour's skill and effort within it, pits labour's (anti-socialist) self-interest against capital's otherwise unchecked domination of the labour market. But the deeper issue we must raise is whether this form of market competition between the self-interest of capital and the self-interest of labour – a parody of the 'class struggle' – might be said to offer in its various expressions, including in the unfettered right to strike, an earnest of democratic and anti-market purpose. If not socialist in intent, as it plainly is not in most cases, could not such action at least be held to be in radical breach of market conventions? Posed thus, the answer is not reassuring. For such actions, militant as may be, are themselves almost always governed by the market, by its purposes and customs, above all that of restoring, defending or amending in detail, not substance, the essential relation between capital and labour. Moreover, the political scope of the 'struggle' to preserve this relation tends continuously to be diminished and narrowed, as technological change in some cases constricts, and in others destroys, the existing division of labour; the particularity of the labour interests which are being defended itself has a tendency to shrink in compass. Such 'struggles' may of course be ideologically dignified by perceiving them in terms of 'principle', and sometimes justly so. But from a wider non-market perspective, the issues often resist such generalization – whether socialist or democratic – confined as they often are to socially regressive forms of special concern within the division of labour. This is because the contraction of the market, and the contraction of labour (and Labour) actions and perspectives, in general proceed together; the horizons and limitations of capital become the horizons and limitations of labour. Moreover, we should remember that the theoretical effort of left radicals to formulate a 'socialist manifesto' which will escape these bounds is conducted at one political level;[10] but the practical struggle for labour's market interests is conducted at another, and one which is ideologically much more decisive. Had this not been the case, and had the market system not earned overwhelming ideological approval in the world of Western capital, then our epoch – of the fascist defence of capital's national interests, of two world wars between capitalist nations, of intense neocolonial exploitation, of phases of mass unemployment, and now of the threat of universal annihilation – would not also have been marked by such persistent failures of socialist theory and practice.

Yet renewed left invitations to utopian escape from this predicament, as for example into the romantic consolations of the past or into a Nirvana of nuclear disarmament and the unlearning of nuclear knowledge, must more than ever be resisted. Today, the essential rejection of socialist aspiration by working people in Western capitalism must also be taken as settled. New principles of social justice must be discerned and extrapolated, for they are there, from the general cultural acquiescence in the legitimacy of individual appropriation in the market. Furthermore, the (essentially middle-class) project for the 'winning of the working class to socialism' must be abandoned for realizable political aims; aims themselves deeply threatened as never before by utopian distractions of one kind and another. Above all, the cause of the defence of basic human and civil rights, in particular those relating to the physical integrity of the person, must now be seen to be intellectually and politically wider than existing socialist articulations of purpose. Therefore, at the most immediate practical level, the reconstruction of notions of what is 'progressive' demands a drastic clearing of the decks: that is, if working people in our culture do not in sufficient numbers find, and have never in sufficient numbers found, the (feigned) economic egalitarianism and market rejections on the part of middle-class socialists to be politically acceptable, then such socialists – after two centuries of the experience – will have to begin to learn how to live with it. What is involved is nothing less than the rejection of the political 'bad faith' upon which, for decades, their own socialist expectations have rested. Indeed, the deeper purposes served by left utopianism – as source for intellectual production or as hope of universal redemption – have first to be recognized, if they are to be rejected. But this is easier said than done. For, among the utopian left, the intellectual displacement of the incorrigible realpolitik of the labour movement has created a deep emotional dependency upon figments of its own political imagination; arbitrary constructs which, for many, give life its meaning and purpose. But waiting and working, against the will of the majority, for the radical transformation or overthrow of the Western market order, a transformation which has come no nearer in two centuries of expectation, now represents much more than a tragic existential dilemma. It is itself an independent obstacle, most strenuously defended by those who know inwardly that their own beliefs have no real foundation, to every reformulation of progressive social purpose. It is not simply that 'they know there are alternatives, but cannot believe that they will live to see them'.[11] Rather, it is that the 'utopian impulse' itself ('there can be no question of dispensing with it')[12], in an historic period of social crisis, serves to mask political verities which illusion prefers never to encounter. Such impulse may, for example, still call upon Labour to 'prepare for that great day: the day when we set about rescuing [sic] our country'.[13] But that no such 'great day' is dawning – nor, in those messianic terms, ever will dawn – for an act of 'rescue' by Labour, is a difficult and demanding truth for those who have committed their lives to a self-sustaining structure of political fancies; fancies powerful enough, in addition, to withstand the evidence which refutes them.

The internal content of such fancies does however fluctuate historically, even if only back and forth through a limited range of illusion. Yet each compensates, in its own way, for truths whose discomforts must at all costs, even the cost of political and intellectual defeat, be avoided. 'Socialists' will thus gird themselves to 'take over the Labour Party' – though they cannot, for all the reasons this book has examined – 'with only a few more modifications to the transmission, and drive it past the winning post before 2000'.[14] Or a fondly imagined world 'free of nuclear weapons' has the power to dissolve, by wishful thinking alone, not only the permanent human capacity to manufacture those weapons, but also the determinate (and competing) economic and political interests which demand them.[15] And 'real power' is discerned, and rediscerned in every social crisis, to lie in the 'grass roots'[16] of the social order, where political 'bases' can be rebuilt 'from the bottom up',[17] as if on newly-excavated foundations. Indeed, the appeal that 'we've got to go back to where the power is . . . on the shop-floor, in the rank and file. We do need to operate there, in the rank and file'[18] exactly expresses, in ideological stereotype, the urge to such imaginary 'renewal'. But it is also a direct compensation for political failures suffered precisely 'on the shop-floor' and 'in the rank and file' of the labour movement. Thus, the currently clamant left demand, in defeat, for ever 'more democracy' has itself taken a characteristically utopian and distracting form, as history should have taught us to expect of such forms of reaction. Typically, in Raymond Williams's words, 'the principle is, and the practice should be' – how? where? when? and with whose support? – 'that *all* decisions are taken by *all* those who are directly concerned with them'.[19] That no real social or political institution could fulfil this imaginary nostrum, the product of nothing more than armchair speculation, is no deterrent to such thinking. Far from being a real initiative capable of translation into the actual practices of the labour movement, it is itself the clearest symptom of the scale of the left's political and intellectual failure. This is not merely a question of a defensive reaction to socialism's crisis: it is part of that crisis. For it avoids and disguises, in ways I have already discussed, not only the real nature of the relation between capital and labour, but also the increasingly complex and contradictory nature of labour interests, out of which no utopian 'general will' can be constructed. Such thought-processes also conceal the fact that economic regression, social decline and above all educational failure are not a politically promising basis for 'new' schemes of 'maximising' democracy or 'devolving' power to 'the people'. And, worst of all, left utopianism of this kind presumes that 'the people' can somehow 'take back their rights of self-government'[20] under capitalist conditions. Certainly, their overthrow is not the premise of the argument; indeed, the fundamental legitimacy of these conditions has itself long ago been accepted.[21]

Paradoxically, it is the subterranean knowledge that these political dilemmas are in fact insoluble by utopian prescription which drives the left further into its intellectual ghetto. At any rate, if the truth were not being arbitrarily cancelled, the advocacy of 'maximum self-management', or of 'new kinds of co-operative and collective institutions',[22] could not be so blandly insisted upon in the teeth of a labour movement which neither wishes them, nor can now be their bearers. Moreover, to argue (a-historically) that it was labour organization which 'invented the social forms of modern participatory democracy and practised them in union branch and co-op meeting',[23] is to ride ideologically roughshod over dense complexities in the history of the labour movement's means and ends. By implication it makes of collective social action a false synonym for progressive purpose, confusing the historic desire for market self-organization, and labour solidarities expressed in closed and often competitive self-defence of specific interest, with democratic impulse. 'Centralization' may be 'not English', as Mr Podsnap roundly declares in *Our Mutual Friend;* but its 'devolved', 'communal' or 'grass-roots' alternative can in turn lay no claim to a genuine popular authenticity, socialist or democratic, as long as it is itself driven mainly by desperate compulsions to rescue socialism (and socialists) from the dangers of further 'grass-roots' rejection. 'Low [levels of] participation and social inequity' may indeed be 'bound up with each other',[24] as some democratic theorists argue. But it does not make a 'popular participatory democracy . . . in which parliament would remain at the centre, but [in which] people at all levels would be directly involved in decision-making or in running their lives'[25] any the less an intellectual refuge from all those intractable political truths, including truths of simple political logic, which deny it. We know very well now that the Victorian broadening of the franchise did not have the democratic political consequences, especially not that of an enhanced level of participation and political awareness, which John Stuart Mill anticipated from it. Nor, likewise, can an 'anti-elitist' or 'new' democratic practice make much headway against a capitalist order whose basic social and political institutions – including those of the monarchy – are accepted by the mass of the people to whom the invitation to 'run their own lives' is directed. But this is not the main political objection to such seemingly radical proposals; it is, rather, that ultra-democratic illusion-mongering, under largely accepted capitalist conditions, flees the materiality of the real into realms of politically idle fantasy. And, in so doing, it not merely undermines our sense of the truth but, by politically vacating to the left's opponents the actual world inhabited by incorrigibly real individuals, invites further political disaster. 'A great new movement for reform is building up', it was urged in 1974; but no such movement was 'building up', and a decade later, to our political cost, we know it. 'People are learning', it was asserted, 'from the shop workers and the students and the miners and the women, the railwaymen and the dockers that if you want to get things changed, you've got to do something about it yourself. This is a rebirth of our national self-confidence.'[26] It was no such thing. Rather, it was itself political hyperbole; spirited, radical (but Jacobin, not socialist) and, above all, quite untrue.

Yet it is this kind of falsehood, with its many left variants, which is the more sedulously defended the more politically embattled. With its terrible rhetoric and 'mindless passion',[27] it measures lie with lie against the right, and joins it in political subversion of a just knowledge of what Marx called the 'this-sidedness',[28] the actuality, we inhabit. 'In less than a generation, we *can* see, if we wish it' – or if we have the correctly-tinted spectacles – 'the beginning of a new style of men [*sic*], who will have miles to grow and universes to subdue, but who will never [what, never?] have taken an order, or been afraid of other men, or done an action without knowing why.'[29] But this is not a possible world, and in its very impossibility unhinges political reason itself. It is neither socialism nor democracy, but 'impossibilism'; and demands, especially in times of crisis, intellectual resistance. And what, too, of that illusory 'socialism' which 'only acquires a *real* content with the withering away of *all* state power, and the self-management of the *entire* society'?[30] Or again, that revolution which consists in the '*immediate* establishment of a system of political power which is *directly* exercised by the majority, and then rapidly by the *totality* of citizens in *all* spheres and at *all* levels'?[31] Or that '*real* task' of 'freeing civil society from the dominion of capital' through the 'liberating activity of the party in the quick of social existence . . . present at *every* contradiction and conflict in the society, and at

every effort at invention and creation'?[32] Is it not, instead, required
of us that in the name of political and intellectual progress such
manias be fought and rejected?

For when the 'real' comes to be thus absurdly defined, in the
name of freedom, there occurs a truly drastic destruction (at the
hands of illusion) of the saving graces of meaning, purpose and
reason. Moreover, to charge unimaginary human beings with the
task, say, of *'liquidating* governmental powers' – 'without which',
Lenin argued in 1919, bewilderingly begging every question, 'real
democracy, that is to say equality and liberty, cannot be
achieved'[33] – is to make absolute political impossibility into
equally absolute political virtue. Similarly, to posit as an attainable objective of human effort and sacrifice, as did Rosa
Luxemburg, *'unlimited* political freedom', *'unlimited* democracy'
and 'the most active, *unlimited* participation of the mass of the
people',[34] is to invite us to pursue mere chimeras. No politics can
survive it without the coercion of mind and body. Nor can the
'structure of the socialist movement' be 'married' to 'the contours
of civil society';[35] working people, or people of any kind, cannot
'manage the whole of social life by themselves, directly';[36] and
'what touches all' cannot be 'approved by all',[37] even if socialist
theory, decade upon decade, insists upon it. Such propositions do
not merely begin in familiar kinds of intellectual desperation, and
inevitably end in familiar kinds of political failure. Each new
failure must in turn be compensated for, often with even direr
forms of theoretical and practical unreason. But it is this cerebral
game-playing which itself permits the left's ideological opponents,
armed with their own error, to advance the more surely over the
ruins of socialist endeavour. In political reprisal, it invites the
right to deny that 'popular rule' or 'the participation of the
masses' can be any 'guarantee of political liberty'[38] whatever,
when the left adversary posits as desirable an impossible 'destruction . . . of the *principles* of authority, hierarchy, subordination and
dualism'.[39] And who could not refute the socialist prospectus of a
'liberty for all' based upon *'all equally* having access to control over
productive property'?[40] Rationally considered, a schema of this
kind is a sitting target to every scepticism about the socialist
project.

The urgency of avoiding such utopianism, whether of left or
right, grows daily in a world menaced as never before by the
historic pursuit of ends which are unattainable. Moreover, it is a

pursuit conducted in the name not only of impossible virtues, but of illusory concepts of 'the real' which a Lewis Carroll would have best appreciated. Under their terms, recalcitrant hedgehogs and flamingos become, by dint of intellectual and political violence, the croquet balls and mallets of ideological struggle; a struggle to bend men and nature into moral shapes which often threaten to wring the flamingos' necks, and dash out the hedgehogs' brains, in their own interests. In a culture dominated by intricately-bargained relations between capital and labour, and by the legitimacy of individual appropriation, the scale of the moral revolution imagined for its citizens under such 'alternative' projects has the clear mark of hallucination about it. The thought is as ever mistaken for the deed, and the pipe-dream for the political programme. Thus 'full' or 'grass-roots' democracy, 'popular administration and control',[41] 'mass participation' and the 'reversal of the hierarchy of power' become the (glib) benchmarks of 'new' theory, or new glosses on old devices; but a new practice, under accepted capitalist conditions, is an entirely different matter. Yet the paradox is that behind many of these supposed innovations in left theory stand new forms of political unease, unrecognized and unacknowledged. It is an unease, now universal in its reach, not simply with the political and economic failures of state socialism or with the effects of public provision under capitalist conditions, but with the socialist project itself in all its guises. In fact, today's left critiques of capital's hierarchies and exclusions, in the name of 'self-management' or 'participa-tion' – for all their Jacobin flourishes and socialist declarations of purpose – are merely *left-seeming*. They contain an unadmitted liberal democratic and utilitarian recoil from precisely that 'comprehensive direction of the social process' without which socialist ends could not be attained in the first place. It is no coincidence that the 'left' now shares with the 'right', without admitting it, a wide area of common political concern, whose issues each side debates with itself, but using an increasingly similar political language whose meanings are also increasingly convergent.

Questions of statism, bureaucracy, freedom, alienation and self-determination stand at the centre of this 'left' and 'right' convergence, in which the left's 'self-management' and the right's 'self-reliance' are twin expressions of what is essentially a single thought and a single preoccupation. Put another way, it is probable that today's left espousal of the virtues of 'grass-roots' democracy, of the accountability of political organization (of state and party) to 'the people', and of the need for the latter's 'participation' in decisions which affect it, even contains an unconscious anti-socialist impulse. The left radical's search for an 'unfettered expression of the popular will' in a 'free society'[42] is not only a mirror-image of the basic themes of the 'libertarian right', for all the differences of economic philosophy which underpin them. It also expresses a reaction against the 'over-governed society',[43] whether overgoverned in the name of capital or labour. Thus, it is not necessary to believe that a free market is a 'necessary condition for political freedom'[44] in order to see that the right's advocacy of 'standing on one's own two feet' – with the state 'off our backs' – and the left's decentralist or community-participant politics have a great deal ideologically in common, even if their ulterior purposes are (ostensibly) different. For they are variants on the same theme of 'voluntary co-operation among free individuals to achieve our several objectives', and of the desirability of 'co-ordination without coercion'.[45] Indeed, these are not the left's terms, but Milton Friedman's. And for all that the special interests of capital plainly lurk within his concept of the 'free individual', the left's own libertarian politics of an equally 'uncoerced' grass-roots 'coordination' of labour interest now shares a common political logic.

But there are far more serious potential embarrassments for the left than the right in the former's shift of emphasis away from the orthodox forms and goals of state socialist centralization to a politics which would seek to devolve popular authority, under capitalist conditions which are commonly accepted. For such cross-class 'libertarianism' is being espoused, from the right, in the cause of the political and economic market interests of capital; and, from the left, in the political and economic market interests of labour. It is no more and no less, in either case, than an expression of aspirations which are shared across a common culture: but for an enhanced degree of economic and social autonomy to be provided to the market contestants within the capitalist order, and not for its socialist transformation. Nevertheless, in labour's case, such a demand also has its own historic logic. For by 'extending democracy' in the labour interest, the reach is also extended of that particular kind of non-socialist independence in the market to which labour's self-organization has always aspired.

But where the 'new right', in pursuit of capital's private interest, negatively (and often destructively) demands 'less government', less bureaucracy, less intervention and the elimination of restrictions on private enterprise and private profit, the libertarian left's 'democratic spirit'[46] – running parallel, with its own charter of autonomies and freedoms – stalks a much more serpentine path towards utopia. That there is no 'free' market, and that the interests of capital themselves could not prosper if there were, is one thing. But that a freer, self-managed world for participant labour can really be constructed, against Labour's general will and within the constraints of a capitalist order whose economic values and political institutions are generally accepted, is quite another.

Nevertheless, in what Friedman accurately calls a 'changed intellectual climate'[47] of libertarian opposition, honest and dishonest, to denials of individual and social freedom, the 'new right' and newer left have begun increasingly to share certain beliefs in the priority of citizen-rights against the state, beliefs which contain significant values. Ambiguity or hypocrisy may often be their most distinctive mark, particularly on the right; after all, it espouses the claims of free trade unionism under socialist, but not under capitalist, conditions. However, any form of ideological preoccupation with the 'protection of the citizen against the state', or against the 'tyranny of government'[48] – whatever special and even potentially oppressive pleading may underlie it – can be held to keep alive a humane politics in this period of the general dissolution of Western socialist prospects. But the trouble for the left, given socialism's loss of ideological coherence, is that it is the right which has thus far benefited most, politically, from a spreading concern with the 'threat to human freedom' posed by 'concentrations of power' in the hands of government, monopoly capital or (allegedly) organized labour.[49] Worse, so ideologically unpersuasive in our own culture have socialist conceptions of liberty become, that the right has been able to argue its case for greater individual freedom even in the teeth of the free market's destructive effects on basic forms of human equity and social justice. Moreover, it is the negative impact of 'real' socialism together with Western socialist confusions of purpose which have between them helped to ratify the unfreedoms of the market; but it is the left itself which cannot see this.[50]

What is at issue, in fact, are the most fundamental ideological challenges to the integrity of socialist conceptions of freedom.

They run as deep as, or even deeper than, those which vitiate the
'new right's' claims to a monopoly of libertarian virtue. The most
obvious intellectual fissure can be detected, once more, in Marx's
own writings. On the one hand, 'only the proletarians of the
present day', he wrote (with Engels) in 1845, 'are in a position to
achieve a complete . . . self-activity, which consists in the
appropriation of the totality of productive forces.'[51] (That such an
appropriation, and the 'free self-activity' which would accompany
it, is now impossible given the very nature of these technical
forces, I shall for the moment pass over.) On the other hand, Marx
told the central committee of the Communist League five years
later, in March 1850, 'the workers . . . must not only strive for a
single and indivisible German republic, but also within the
republic for the most determined *centralization of power* in the hands
of the state authority. They must not allow themselves to be
misguided by the democratic talk of freedom for the communities,
of self-government.'[52] Left casuistry about 'transitional' demands, or about the difference between proletarian dictatorship
and communist freedom notwithstanding, every contemporary
socialist uncertainty and division as to the rival claims of
'self-activity' and concentration of power is inscribed here, both
on and below the surface. And two years later, in an article in the
New York Daily Tribune, Marx innocently raised, very early in the
socialist canon, another issue which was subsequently to become
the site of an ideological battlefield among Marxists. 'Universal
suffrage', he wrote in 1852, 'is the equivalent of political power for
the working class of England, where the proletariat forms the
large majority of the population . . . Its inevitable result is the
political supremacy of the working class.'[53] He was wrong.
Indeed, to Trotsky, writing *Where is Britain Going?* seventy-three
years later, universal suffrage had proved to be 'simply hypocrisy', 'asses' gates erected by the bourgeoisie . . . so constructed
that it is impossible to pass through them'.[54] But the long socialist
argument had had more than to do with the defeat of political
expectation. It went to the very heart of the saga of socialist means
and ends in Western capitalist conditions, of which the panacea of
a devolved participation is merely the latest democratic instal-
ment. Indeed, the whole political terrain of 'democratizing'
capitalism in the socialist interest has been historically criss-cros-
sed with polemic and contradiction. Thus, the same Trotsky for
whom universal suffrage was an 'asses' gate' could also believe

(ten pages later) that 'a real democratization of the administration', carried out by a Labour government, 'would quicken a mighty [*sic*] flood of enthusiasm in the working masses, and – since appetite comes with eating – would inevitably set in train more and more radical reforms.'[55] But only fifty pages on in the same text, the 'left wing of the Labour Party', which would have helped earlier to unleash the 'mighty flood' of Trotsky's expectation, has become in turn a 'monstrous illusion'; 'their leftism . . . opportunist throughout' and 'not capable of leading the masses to the struggle'.[56]

These bewilderments, which are rooted in the political settlement between capital and labour, are organic to the Western socialist tradition. In France in May 1968, for example, the determination to renew this cross-class bargain decisively worsted (with the support of the communist movement) the struggle to breach it. In fact, the 'taking of power, from the periphery to the centre', by means of an 'initiative of the masses' and through the 'rise of self-organized popular forces',[57] was defeated politically by the much greater ideological strength of the institutionalized market relation between the classes. 'Self-determination from below' – precisely that 'misguided' 'freedom for the communities' or 'self-government' against which Marx had warned in 1850 – had given way to another form of self-determination entirely: that of labour's private interest in negotiating with capital and its state, under the pressure of a general strike, an improved market bargain, both political and economic. Once more, the true political meaning of labour's liberties, and the liberties of labour organization, was expressed in the voluntarist (but intransigent) form of advancing a particular claim within, and not against, the labour market. What was ultimately at issue was not, for all the temporary fright in French ruling circles at factory occupations, the political supremacy of the working class nor the appropriation of the productive forces. Indeed, two European decades (without change) later, our own demands for the greater accountability of power-holders, for 'open government',[58] and for enhanced levels of popular participation, remain in essence demands for a wider range of political goods and services. And no more now than then is a radical transfiguration of the system of class power really being sought by the majority of the protagonists, in their exertion of a collective or social pressure upon the political market. The rhetoric of it may sometimes suggest otherwise; but the substance of it is not in question. More often, the expression of the demands indicates their political-market nature. Thus, typically, 'people have had no say over the form or allocation of the benefits and services of the welfare state. The welfare state has not been ours. Like the old poor law, it is theirs.'[59] It is itself a proprietary objection. But much more serious for the integrity of the socialist 'alternative' is that the demand for these political goods and services confuses the enhancement of liberty with the modest extension of special interest in the existing political market; and in so doing, permits the avoidance of all challenge to political power. Moreover, the capitalist system is wholly incapable of being managed by 'popular initiative' – the suggestion is absurd – while the spurious 'democratization' of an economically and socially unjust order, founded upon exploitation, can serve only to mask even further the 'real location' of its powers.[60] Instead, there lurks here the politics of the 'responsible' self-government of labour; a politics, as John Stuart Mill well understood (and advocated through the mid-Victorian legitimation of trade union functions), which has always recommended itself to utilitarians of left and right as the best means of securing a politically sufficient equilibrium between capital and labour.

Certainly, the freeing of the human-as-worker from the economic compulsion to sell his or her time and skill in the market – that is, the 'suppression of the proletarian condition'[61] – even if it could be achieved, is not at all what is at issue in the 'self-management' of the labour interest. And this remains so, however extensive the latter's bargained autonomies, both real and imagined. For self-determination at the point of production (whether of political or economic goods) is at best an illusory promise under capitalist conditions, particularly when those conditions are themselves legitimated by cross-class acceptance. Moreover, to attempt to proceed, as if by gradual attrition, from an ever-wider participation in the labour market to out-and-out refusal and – by refusal – domination of it, is to discount labour's own historically non-socialist purposes in the self-organization of its interests. In addition, a capitalist (and socialist) world governed increasingly by technical systems of 'esoteric knowledge',[62] as well as by the means of mass destruction, can be challenged only in the head by schemes of purely libertarian endeavour. (And that it can be challenged by no other means, without the prospect of self-destruction, completes the circle of our dilemmas.) 'Socialism',

Poulantzas wrote, 'will be democratic or it will not be at all.'[63] That it will, therefore, 'not be at all', in the heart of Western capitalism, the utopian impulse must instantly deny; summoning up images and experience of past popular struggle, present capitalist 'contradiction', the law of dialectics and a succession of models for socialist theory and practice. And all this is to set at bay two centuries of capitalist development, in which class interest, class consciousness and even notions of class freedom have so expressed and institutionalized themselves that socialism could now be achieved – especially in the utopian forms announced by socialist theory and historiography – only by dint of a struggle with the *combined* forces of capital and labour. Furthermore, a politics of purely libertarian means and ends, left or right, remains a utopian 'escape from brute fact'[64] as long as the actual means and ends of real power, and of real vested interest, are so systematically discounted. That 'self-sufficiency' and 'self-regulation', whether as means or ends, have been historically part of nearly every ideal alternative order itself signifies the scale of our intellectual crisis. Indeed, to repeat formulaically, but yet with a sense of discovery and invention, what has been endlessly repeated in the history of political theory, is not *prima facie* a symptom of renewal! Such ideas are for ever, and most typically, 'utopias of simplification',[65] predicated on dreams of cooperation in a natural order, ultimately conflict-free or classless, and self-ruled in peace and justice. From Campanella's *City of the Sun* to the 'parallelograms' of Robert Owen, from Fourier's 'pha-lanxes' to Marx's 'freely associated producers', from Nozick's 'minimal state' to Marcuse's 'erotic liberation' or the 'total revolution' of Jayaprakash Narayan,[66] the attempt to 'conceive imaginatively a better ordering of human society'[67] has run through its gamut, not merely short-ranged but essentially unvarying also.

Counter-factual 'possible worlds'[68] are necessary both to human speculation and human action, but they are not as politically or intellectually necessary, least of all now, as facing the true nature of this one. 'Such phrases as "self-government" and "the power of the people over themselves"', John Stuart Mill wrote (remarkably) in 1859, 'do not express the true state of the case.' In a sentence, Mill passes beyond our slogans. 'The "self-government" spoken of', he argued – in his own terms, but at least critically – 'is not the government of each by himself, but of each by all the rest.'[69] In fact, it is the fantasy of a complete self-command, whether of the individual or the collective, to which Mill directs our attention. His are not Burke's strictures against democracy, in which 'the restraint of men is to be reckoned among their rights'.[70] Rather, Mill justly reproves those historically persistent illusions, always inviting ideological defeat, which posit a 'directly exercised' power, decisions 'made by the people as a whole' or a world in which 'all equally have access to control over productive property', and so on. It is not simply that the conditions for political order and social progress in the real world – of capitalism and socialism together – and among real human beings, are materially unyielding beyond a certain degree. Even less does it deserve a charge of philosophical resignation to direct attention to them. The issue, rather, is that the idle or rhetorical promise of the revolutionary breach of these conditions, for ever unrequited, has itself helped to promote in our culture that conservative liaison between capital and labour which has sealed Western socialism's fate in the eyes of the class for which it was intended. Thus, the 'proletarian state', where socialist theory demands that 'to the greatest extent public offices must be elective', or insists that there be a 'right of recall' and the 'permanent and extensive control by the people over those exercising state power, with as small a separation as possible between those who exercise state power and those over whom it is exercised',[71] exists nowhere. No real society corresponds to it, because none can, in practice. Hence, those forms of political knowledge and prescription which anticipate the eternal disappointment of utopian expectation ought in principle to be accorded a higher intellectual status than the empty reiteration of impossible prospects, whose historical defeat is clearly inscribed *ab initio* in the projects themselves. Instead, the historical tendency of the left is to relegate the caution itself to the domain of a tawdry realpolitik, or to the category of the 'pessimism' of the 'petit bourgeois'; while, behind the back of the prospector, the real for ever asserts its demands against the utopian, hurrying him to defeat, or (if he chooses to resist it) into coercion of the sceptic and unbeliever.

Indeed, most utopianism, whether of left or right, has philosophically been more despairing – whether the despairs have pointed to 'unlimited political freedom' in the one case, or, say, to the 'thousand-year Reich' in the other – than are realist objections to its worlds of false promise. Moreover, and worse, ultimates of class, race or nation best serve to distract our capacities to apprehend the priority of recurring and basic human needs: above all, for immediate and direct protection from cruelty and persecution, from neglect, disease and hunger, and from degrading forms of punishment and exploitation, whether such punishment and such exploitation be carried out in the name of capital or labour. The impulse of utopianism, right and left, is instead to postpone such attentions to the day after the revolution, and until old scores have been settled; to that day of revelation in which a discoverable social harmony, whose latency the imperfections of the existing order are held to conceal from our knowledge, will at last be manifested to us. Even parochial or local forms of such expectation are often tainted by the grandiose, or by political and social delusions just as absolute: whether in false readings of the popular will, say, or of its propensities to concerted class action, or of the imminence of liberation from the market bargain between capital and labour. In the ideological confusion, the humanly necessary and possible, the directly and practically achievable, becomes for some – and grotesquely so – a concession to the immediate, a 'pragmatic' compromise, a limitation of political perspectives, an obstacle to political progress. For others, that which is not the political *all*, is itself *nothing*. Yet real political 'democracy' in the real world of real human beings, whether under capitalist or socialist conditions, can mean not much more (and not much less) *in practice* than that all citizens should have 'equal access, at least in the formal sense, to public office . . . [be] eligible to join political parties, to run for elective positions, and to hold places of authority'.[72] But such a proposition will, in turn, be refuted by every left utopian as beneath notice; not, as could well be, for its own unreality, but for its insufficient absolutism, its prerevolutionary innocence, or its cynical lack of grandeur in conception. In the meantime, other varieties of left suspicion – often wedded to their own sectarian or vested interest – can detect in the most benign (and banal) schemes of 'grass-roots' or 'shopfloor' participation hidden designs to subvert the established representation of trade union interests;[73] or see them as mere forms, whose true purpose is to exclude the participants from a genuine influence on 'decision-making'. In consequence, the more awkward arguments about representation and order are rarely reached, or avoided. Similarly, the evidence can be discounted that modern systems of industrial production, whether organized in the name of capital or labour, are barely able to function at all without a substantial degree of involuntary and demeaning subordination. Indeed, in this respect – as in many others – the 'workforce' of capitalist accumulation, and the 'working masses' of socialist construction, have everything in common. But absolutist obsession, left or right, is in general a poor basis for a technical critique of the existent or the given. In particular, the left's archetypal ideal of a direct democracy can be found at the tangled root of its objections to a materiality which has yielded to nothing.

Moreover, so despairing has been the search of some on the left for 'democratic socialist' alternatives to the havoc wrought to their prospects by the political record of 'real' socialism, that they have in effect been driven backwards, politically, into (for them) anachronistic forms of speculation and exploration. Here, the real confusion for socialist theory lies in the fact that a socialist utopia has been silently sacrificed for a democratic one, but without acknowledgement (or self-knowledge) of the radical shift in perspective. Today, therefore, the 'deformed workers' states' are increasingly being countered with a politics, *in vacuo,* of 'democratic self-administration in the workplace', combined with 'democracy in all spheres of social relations' and even with 'global self-management'.[74] Likewise, the spectre of Soviet bureaucracy is being set to rest with the 'democratic participation of producers and citizens in the management of the economic, political and social life of the country'.[75] But there is no *necessary* connection between all this and 'socialism', whether in its final state or in 'transition' to it. Indeed, such formulations, self-perceived by their begetters as revolutionary political innovation, precisely repeat the oldest utopian models of social organization. Furthermore, the left's present intellectual uncertainty is such that behind even the most radical democratic schemata stand deeper confusions of ultimate purpose, in which revolutionary rhetoric and cautious utilitarian intention can (and do) rub shoulders together. Thus, strident demands made to capital and its state for the maximum accountability of power can astonishingly turn out to be justified merely in terms of 'maintaining confidence in our system of government', or of 'reflecting the desires of the people expressed through the ballot-box more rapidly than is now the case'.[76] Or the 'system of self-management' can even be advocated, in the most extreme terms and from the left, as 'the best way of raising the productivity of labour'.[77] And behind the gaudy mask of the ultra-democrat, the old Adam of a plain, common-or-garden authoritarianism can often be found hiding. It was Thomas Carlyle who, with consummate cynicism, believed that most people prefer to be ruled, especially if they are encouraged to believe they are ruling themselves. But a leading democratic socialist of today can also be found quoting Lao Tzu with uncritical approval: 'when the best leader's work is done', Lao Tzu wrote, 'the people say, "we did it ourselves".'[78] They did not in fact 'do it themselves', but in believing that they did lies at least one authoritarian vindication of the principles of 'accountability' and 'participation'.

But all these ambivalences are no more than surface reflections of the deepest political dilemmas, which it has been my task in this book to explore. Not the least of them, in conditions where labour's bargain (and desire to bargain) with capital is hegemonic, is that democratic institutions are both the most effective means of maintaining the rule of capital – by humanizing the facts of political power – and also the most favoured means in the culture of representing the private interests of labour.[79] And there is no escape from this except into utopia. It is not surprising, therefore, that 'participation' in practice should become merely another means of 'man-management'; that in the real world enlightened Benthamism should overtake the left's dreams of sovereign self-organization; and that the intended beneficiaries of a democratic emancipation from the rule of capital and its state should themselves resist the invitation. Worse still for such dreams, more not less state and central control over a-social industrial and technological powers is a precondition for their socialization. In addition, no industrial society with its presently constituted productive forces can be a participant one at anything more than a token level. It is wishful thinking, too, which adamantly refuses the knowledge that the existing structure of the division of labour, and the class and sexual divisions which are rooted in it, despite contemporary technical changes, are *not* in fundamental dissolution: that capital and labour, bourgeoisie and working class, is none of them disappearing. But it is not simply the case now that 'autonomous' workers' power, whether under advanced capitalist or socialist conditions, has become incompatible with the forms of manufacture which are promoted in them. Instead, labour, through every phase of the modern industrial revolution, has been their captive. Indeed, in Western capitalism well over a century has passed since the time when it could be said that 'workers were not yet fully subject to capitalist command, and found in their own skills and self-organization the basis for an alternative economic system'.[80] And today, as Andre Gorz has put it, 'it is impossible to imagine that telephones, video-machines, microprocessors . . . or photo-electric cells . . . could be produced at the level of a family, a group, or a local community'.[81] To deny it is obscurantism; as it is obscurantist also to deny that, in the shadow of such technologies and the social system based upon them, self-management, the minimal state, unlimited participation and erotic liberation are all in similar ways utopian.

Nevertheless, in the name of democracy, the search (largely in the head) continues for new 'socio-technical' structures and systems of planning, which might somehow combine direct control by the producers with the efficient regulation of resources and output in a modern industrial order.[82] The empirical absence in the real world of any such combination has once again proved no deterrent to the quest for it. Instead, the belief, utopian in entirely familiar ways, persists undaunted that there might some day, or somewhere, exist 'a "real" socialist democratic planning system which could dispense simultaneously with market, bureaucracy and hierarchy, based upon some undefined form of mass democracy'.[83] Hence, to the statelessness and marketlessness of the classical socialist utopia must be added the phantasm of a rational but non-authoritarian regulation of economic allocation and distribution in bewilderingly specialized technical conditions. There can be no such solution, in theory or in practice; logic in the one case, and experience in the other, refutes it. Despite this, further confusions related to this 'solution' pursue the Western democratic socialist in the capitalist here and now, as well as into the utopian hereafter. On the one hand, 'strong powers of government' are required to 'deal with entrenched private interests' – that is, capital's state must somehow be democratically turned against itself by political legerdemain. But on the other hand, there must be 'increased participation in policy-making at national and local levels'.[84] Each is separately fraught with difficulty; together, in the imaginary form of 'a strong government to protect us [which is] fully democratic in character',[85] or, worse, as 'a powerful society with a minimal state',[86] they are politically and intellectually incoherent. But, repeats the utopian, unabashed, 'a socialist must reconcile two principles. The first is the need for the powers of government to be strong in the face of entrenched private interests. The second is the need to preserve, indeed improve, the means whereby all those in authority can be scrutinized and held to account in public.'[87] Each principle may be desirable in itself, but to insist (on paper) upon their 'reconciliation' is to demand no less than the squaring of the political circle. Yet such contradiction itself points us back clearly to the oldest and deepest of dichotomies in socialist thinking, that between *dirigisme* from above and control from below, whose bland combination could be the political programme only of a sophist.

The truth is that it is only in armchair theory, not in practice, that such a dilemma can be resolved. The real world is too stubborn. Moreover, in common with most of the other issues raised in this book, its honest exploration lies as much beyond the intellectual reserves of existing socialist thought, as it also stands beyond the bounds of labour's (and Labour's) interests and resources. It is not simply that the libertarian anti-statist of the left or right can do nothing with the intractable fact that in our societies 'no consumption, production, communication, transportation, illness, health care, learning or exchange' – or hardly any – 'occurs without the intervention of professional agencies or centralized administrations'.[88] Rather, on the very ground of labour, where the technical forces of production and destruction are harnessed, the universality of the problems which these forces pose to mankind transcends the interests of class and the labour movement. Moreover, they are problems whose scale escapes the confines of merely socialist theory. Thus, even if it were not the case that Western labour is as deeply implicated as Western capital in the reproduction of these forces, the rejection of exhausted forms of socialist theory and practice – for their complicities with capital in some cases, and their utopianism in others – would have become an objective historical necessity. Indeed, it is a necessity as imperative as any commanded in the past by the 'science of the dialectic'. Against the theoretical prospect of a 'workers' control over society at large',[89] which would be asserted as the result of a subjective (or imaginary) rejection by Western labour of its bargain with capital, stand increasingly formidable obstacles in practice, which now more than ever dwarf socialist effort. They include cross-class anti-socialist popular will, the rejection of the 'real' socialist example, the forms of technical development, and the objective necessity of the latter's centralized state organization. But even if these obstacles could be overcome, and the notion of 'the working class ruling in its own right'[90] be made politically intelligible beyond the narrow circle of the middle-class socialist intelligentsia, an internal revolt against the world of Western technology, and its means of mass production and destruction, would itself be dominated by the instruments of production themselves, and by the divisions of labour and organization which they impose upon the social order.

In fact, we can observe all this in microcosm to the extent that 'participation' under today's technological and state conditions – those of technocracy and mass unemployment – may superficially 'democratize', but yet brings to the participators no accretion of real powers.[91] In this respect it is on all fours with earlier progressive extensions of political democracy under Western capitalist conditions. For they too, as we can now clearly see, brought socialism (in whichever of its meanings) not one step nearer. More significant still, the 'newer' radical politics of local or 'community self-defence', albeit slowly growing in reach, has nothing specifically to do with socialist aspirations, nor with existing forms of labour organization either. Merely to socialize the means but not the ends of defending immediate and particular self-interest is certainly not synonymous with socialist purpose. Nor is there any reason why it should be, even if long-established left error in understanding the nature of earlier forms of social self-organization insists upon their connection. What such a politics signifies, instead, is that *organized individuals,* the better organized the better, can exert more influence in their own behalf than can the unorganized. Yet the (socialist) assumption that socially-organized individuals – whether in a trade union, a community group or a 'self-managing' cooperative – are *prima facie* likely to possess, merely by virtue of organization, ulterior socialist intentions has historically proved a costly political misjudgement. Indeed, it is a classical form of socialist error to mistake, as non-socialist Victorian moralists did not, social form for socialist content. Wishful thinking combines them; but it was political education, conducted by the labour movement, which would have been required to make the conjunction a real one. Moreover, the failure has been fatal; it can no longer be made good in the culture. In consequence, 'full democratic planning', the 'social control of capital' or 'an advanced democracy led by the working class'[92] which would be anti-authoritarian and anti-statist, desirable as they all may be in the abstract, are not merely unattainable under today's technical conditions. For to have been in a position today to have attained them would have required a prior and continuous 'cultural revolution' in moral purpose, social education and ideological perception. Yet these are the very tasks which the labour movement, mistaking its old strength of numbers for socialist commitment, avoided fro:1 its beginnings. As a result, Labour's present social policies are largely designed only to restore collapsed forms of social commitment to a system of state provision which has lost moral touch with its beneficiaries, and vice versa. It is a mutual disconnection whose repair is itself now beyond the capacity of socialist inspiration. Indeed, the state management of capital, technocracy and welfare under capitalist conditions can make little room, even with the best of intentions, for socialist purpose. But more clearly still, the ideological primacy of private appropriation, and the acceptance of economic inequality which goes with it, are directly at odds with vicarious middle-class socialist beliefs as to the existence of a popular will – which does not exist – to exercise a participant social control from below over capital's fortunes.

Only the socialist utopian of a political generation trying to seek refuge from every dilemma in a 'participatory democracy' could ignore the truth that 'the qualifications for making it real are far greater than the capacities being promoted in the culture'.[93] Neither Ruskin nor Morris (and certainly not Carlyle, Mill and Arnold) would have recoiled from such a judgement. On the contrary, they would almost certainly themselves have been urging it today, as each in his own way and in his own day urged it. Yet it is a measure of the contemporary left's lack of seriousness about the high premium placed upon public 'capacities', especially under a system of democratic accountability and partici-pation, that the fundamental issue of the quality of popular education can be so entirely discounted. It is brushed aside – often by self-conscious and dishonest middle-class scruple – as if it contained an implied insult against the people; or as if the (plebeian) *vox populi*, unconfined, were the best guarantor of our moral and social progress. Thus it is that left populism can argue that 'we must *never* accept that democracy can be limited by the educational qualifications of the rank-and-file'.[94] (What, never?) Yet, for such a proposition to be generally accepted, and in the name of socialism no less, is to bring to an end a century and more of cultural assumptions about the preconditions of social advancement. It is also to mock the very purpose of establishing the ideological legitimacy of the principle of popular accountability in the first place. Worse still for such reactionary populism, the forms of knowledge which are required to exert a genuine (as distinct from a token) social control over today's technics and their organization, now demand much more than a popular spirit of democratic scepticism, even if such existed. To attempt to foster it by merely administrative or managerial means is wholly insufficient. Illusion may, if it wishes, attempt to 'envisage a *reform of government* which will ensure that people know what is really happening, are free to express their own views, and by debate as well as by election, are able to determine the conduct of government nationally'.[95] But experience of the real political world declares something entirely different: that a 'self-confident community', both able and willing in significant numbers – let alone large and active numbers – to exercise such democratic rights and freedoms, cannot be spirited into being by populist incantation. Nor could a community, if it existed, acquire the political authority and power to 'determine the conduct of government nationally' (whatever this means), without precisely those skills which the educational system has failed to furnish to the overwhelming mass of the people. Indeed, as I pointed out earlier, the increasing scarcity of appropriate knowledges is merely one – but here the most drastic in its effects – of the poverties of our culture; 'deskilling' is more than a 'mere' technical matter, or one confined to the technical division of labour.

In its present form, the (essentially middle-class) utopia, or ruse, of a more fully participatory democracy under capitalist conditions can at best be no more than a Benthamite device for giving vent to powerless political feeling. At worst – as a populist playing to the gallery, or 'rank and file', for opportunist and ill-considered ends – such a politics fatally lacks the anchorage of the kind and quality of working-class constituency to which Victorian social and moral purpose made its appeal. As such it could only take us yet one more pernicious step in the reactionary plebeianization of our political culture. There is in any case, as I have already argued, a strong cultural tendency at work (as the labour movement weakens in conditions of mass unemployment) towards the ideological suffusion across class boundaries of the crudest plebeian values – precisely those values which the (truly) popular press speaks to and so clearly expresses. In such conditions, to confuse a populist left demagogy with socialist progress is to confuse the plebeian with the proletarian revolution; is to risk pandering, for socialist or pseudo-socialist purpose, to a-social plebeian impulses dangerously free of 'educational qualification'; and, again riding a tiger, to follow (rather than to lead) social forces capable of consuming, not redeeming, the social order. After all, in contrast with the mass scale of popular and plebeian support for the monarchy or the armed forces, there has been no comparable majority enthusiasm, to which the calls for 'wider democracy' would have been a just response, for the accountability to 'the people' of these and other institutions of political power. In such circumstances, the utopian magnification of such limited pressures as there are for a greater degree of 'participation', and the left populist rhetoric which expresses these pressures, become no more than political cant. It is cant, moreover, which serves only to disguise the regressive nature of much 'grass-roots' or 'rank and file' political opinion in the culture. No wonder, then, that this cant of 'domination from below' contains its own rhetorical excesses, when the powers of political and social hierarchy themselves rest more securely than ever upon a 'grass-roots' and cross-class bargain between capital and labour. There could be no greater irony than that it is precisely at the levels to which the ideologist of self-management, or of workers' control, or of local devolution, looks for social renewal that the existing political dispensation is most deeply rooted! And it can be no more uprooted in the interests of a putative proletarian emancipation, and of the left's rescue, than the development of new forces of production can be reversed or broken. It is not in question that the gap between what new technology could provide to meet human needs, and what it provides in practice, is growing; nor that the wastage and misuse of material resources, human creativity and skill – technical and social – have never been greater. But it is in the reaction to such phenomena that illusion weaves its spells: in the face of capitalist conditions which are socially accepted, inscribing on the left's political drawing-boards 'alternative' technologies, or an 'alternative' division of labour, or an 'alternative' distribution of power.[96] Yet, closely examined, they are no more than today's blueprints for yesterday's, and the day before yesterday's, utopias.

Like them, the newer left's fantasies of 'disconnecting the motor of monopoly competition' or of bringing to an end 'the boundless need to valorize capital, to make value with more value'[97] – a need as characteristic of 'real' socialist as it is of capitalist economy – are idle daydreams. So too is the left fancy of programmatically 'halting'[98] economic growth, and of 'restructuring' this or that part of the social order, when the forces of ostensible opposition to what must be 'restructured' do not in essence oppose it. Instead, real tendencies to monopoly, the relentless 'valorization' of capital, irresistible patterns of growth and decline under capitalist conditions, and authoritarian changes in the technical forces of production, all stand beyond the reach of pure speculation. The testing of hypotheses may be an integral part of scientific discovery and technical invention, but theoretical experiment in the world of economy and political organization has always, sooner or later, been historically defeated by real process. It is in the pages of *The German Ideology*, but not in the real world, that the proletariat can 'appropriate the instruments of production' and make them 'subject to each individual, and property to all'.[99] And it is in the *Anti-Dühring*, not in the lives of real men and women, that producers become 'masters of their social relations, labour is no longer a commodity to be bought and sold, and the government of persons is replaced by the administration of things, and by the direction of the processes of production'.[100] The state may wither away in the head; in the real world, it is a colossus. Today's 'emancipatory abolition of work',[101] the anatomizing of a 'post-industrial' civilization, and those utopias of scarcity and conservation which we have exchanged for previous utopias of infinite production and plenty, possess no greater intellectual status; and that they appeal to our fancies is no earnest of it.

But even if the prospects for such a politics were not founded upon wishful thinking, the need which they express to combat the 'destructive side'[102] of technology, to share work and to disarm states of their nuclear weapons could not now be merely 'tacked on', by force of intellectual expectation alone, to the concerns of the labour movement. On the contrary, all the problems to which they are remedies are themselves the outcome of what Walter Benjamin called the 'illusion of positivism', and of forms of scientific and technical development which 'occurred behind the back of the last century'[103] but with the full and necessary complicity of labour. Today's competitive manufacture of universally annihilatory arms is, after all, also the work of the world's 'class-conscious' proletarians, whether under the rule of capital or (nominally) labour. Indeed, every intellectual project for a 'non-violent economy', self-sufficiently husbanding and renewing its resources, and foreswearing the 'rape of the earth'[104] in the name of progress, encounters – and must fail politically in the encounter – historically equally progressive forms of struggle. These are the struggles of real working human beings, for survival, for security, for appropriation (whether individual or social) and for the improvement of their conditions. They are struggles which ride roughshod, and always will, over the claims of nature. Moreover, 'the ecology crisis' will not 'force the end of capitalism';[105] insisting that it must, out of a just desperation, is not proof of the proposition. It is of course true that 'increasing quantities of energy are required to sustain the artefacts . . . and to control the debris and pollutants' which flow unchecked out of today's systems of production; true, too, that the world of technical artifice, much of it objectively useless, has become not only 'accessory to that provided by nature',[106] but is also deeply threatening to it. It is equally true that the traditional forms of organization which most authentically express, and the moral philosophy which now predominantly underlies, labour interests, grow ever closer to those of the protection racket. Yet these interests, determinate and real as they are, must also take precedence over the protection of the physical environment of labour, since it is within and against this environment that production must be carried out, and on it that production (and labour) will always depend for most of its resources, whether infinite or finite. The demands of peace, the cause of nature, the rights of women – in so far as they fall outside, or themselves threaten, the perceived labour interest under capitalist or socialist conditions, and whatever ideological lip-service be paid to them – are in every sense beyond labour.

In such circumstances, the left's emphasis upon the present prospect of an apocalypse, real as it is, has much in common with the histories of past political or social movements which have come to the millenarian end of their tethers. Moreover, the horsemen of the left apocalypse seem always to carry suicidally two-edged swords, as if uttering menaces alone could persuade the sceptic. Certainly, to address today's electorate so armed, and for the ideological want of other means of making an equivalent impact upon it, is itself a symptom of the left's own political exhaustion. It is true, but a truism, that 'general emancipation will never come about if we destroy the earth itself';[107] yet truer still that the politics of the holocaust cannot provide a renewed sense of direction for a disoriented socialism, lost in its own wildernesses. Defeat by local secular events – economic, political, ideological – can be made good neither with an eschatology of destruction nor in dreams of utopia. And simply because schemes for the rational conservation of resources, or for the rational management of the system of production, are claimed by the left intelligentsia in aid of socialist prospects ('both the peace and ecology movements belong to the Left'),[108] the failures of socialism as a movement and politics of labour cannot be redeemed by them. That the socialist project can regain purpose, at any rate on paper, in conditions of scarcity and with the aid of 'alternative' technical resources, may be a valid hypothesis, even if Marx would not have recognized it. But in practice, and in the real world, the ideal of self-sufficiency is not that of the labour movement, and there is little or no evidence, despite the crisis of capital, to suggest that it could become so. For that which 'terrifies the bourgeois' terrifies the 'proletarian' also, but not sufficiently in either case to break the relation between them. Moreover, the plainest local prospect is that 'as long as economic decline continues . . . there is not going to be an upsurge of progressive politics among the working class in Britain, a politics which is pacifist, anti-racist, anti-sexist, or even liberal democratic, let alone socialist.'[109] 'Life', Alexander Herzen declared, 'is under no obligation to realize such ideas and fantasies';[110] and British life no more than any other.

In any case, the nature of the 'progressive' itself requires redefinition – and is redefined – in every epoch; it can be even less confined to socialist rubrics now than ever. Moreover, the actual content of democratic practice has for over a century been as much governed by popular valuation of desirable and undesirable political means and ends as by the prescriptions of class interest. Indeed, it is precisely this historic pragmatism which should put us on our guard against conventional left illusion as to the allegedly thwarted democratic temper of 'the masses'. There is no real sign of it. Yet to act as if such a temper existed can do nothing in the real world to promote the popular defence of practically threatened civil freedoms. Similarly, the merely intellectual displacement, in left fancy, of actual popular demands and desires by others which are abstractly preferred by progressive opinion, can do nothing to assist the left to a true judgement of its prospects. In fact, such left wishful thinking about 'the people', as was amply revealed in the interwar period in Europe, is itself a threat to democratic freedoms. For there can be no guarantee (in any circumstances anywhere) of the survival of democratic institutions, and especially not in periods of economic decline and the social disorder which has historically accompanied them. Better by far, because a precondition for the political realism which would be required of the left if it were to cope with it, is to grasp the actual direction of today's social and economic tendencies under Western capitalist conditions: of continuing mass unemployment without popular rebellion, in an increasingly degraded environment, and accompanied by the increasing risk of mass destruction. Moreover, these are circumstances in which we are likely to see the development of a non-socialist and post-socialist politics of economic, political and social 'discipline', both in defence of 'national interest' and in search of efficiency and order in the use and distribution of resources. Similarly, there can be no real nuclear disarmament of the nuclear powers without alternative supranational sanctions to those provided by nuclear weapons; and there are none, nor will any be created. We can no more conjure up 'alternative defence' proposals out of (very) thin air, and in total disregard of the real interests and powers which demand and sustain the 'balance of terror', than we can base alternative economies and polities on the neglect – by illusion – of the real nature of the relation in Western capitalist societies between capital and labour.

Thus, it is not a deepening 'class struggle' which will accompany the deepening of social crisis; on the contrary, the latter's logic, already clearly visible to those who wish to see it, is one in which the failure of Western socialist purpose is merely one political coordinate among others. No, the relation between capital and labour is such that a 'new politics' in Western capitalism is much more likely to be presided over by increasingly

authoritarian forces and persons; forces recruited – as is already
the case – across today's political and class spectrum, including
from the ranks of labour and its organizations, and acting in joint
defence of perceived common interests. Moreover, the economic
and political reach of international financial agencies and multinational corporations, as well as the implications of the power of
nuclear forces of production and destruction, are beyond the
scope of any national labour movement to supervise or oppose;
even if they showed – as they do not – any coherent will to do so.
But, in addition, the spirit of labour internationalism, always
threadbare in our own culture, must increasingly become the
victim of the intensifying struggle being conducted with the
primary producer-nations of the poor world for secure supplies of
the 'First World's' basic material requirements. For this is a
struggle to maintain systems of production and consumption in
which the interests of Western capital and Western labour are
invested in common. There is nothing here which is exceptional.
Rather, it is hibernating left expectation, for over a century
pleading (against phenomena like these) for time and the
unfolding of the dialectic, which continues to insist upon truths
whose political and intellectual life is exhausted. Yet, in our
present circumstances, the cost of idle socialist belief in a general
human emancipation to be secured through the 'self-activity' and
'self-organization' of the working class, national or international,
is an always higher one. To emerge from this (largely middle-
class) dream of proletarian virtue into our world as it is, is to enter
a world sustained by capital and labour acting together. It is a
world of the necessary state and of its necessary forces of
production, now globally distributed; of state secrecy and increasing state surveillance; of permanent nuclear armament and
permanent unemployment; of advanced information systems and
increasing scarcity of real knowledge; and of fiercely competitive
forms of technical progress whose applications and powers are
profoundly undemocratic.[111] And since the new technics cannot
be unlearned, not even the shadow of nuclear annihilation can
now recede from our culture. Moreover, such unchained natural
powers are the historic outcome, and late triumph, of the
innermost rationality of the scientific and industrial revolutions.
In fact, the very whistling-in-the-dark which for three decades
and more on the left has greeted these technical developments
must be added to our dangers. For it has persistently denied us a

true sense of the feasible, in times when the democratic, let alone socialist, control of our 'destinies' has itself become a utopian prospect.

'To stop this tide sweeping all of us aside', says an innocent voice, 'will take a labour movement . . . willing to offer a genuine and radical alternative.'[112] That is, a labour movement, radical as none has ever been in the history of industrial progress, will conquer the powers – and the few who (alone) can command them – of nuclear fission and fusion, and the new industrial revolution's optical fibre conduits, 'storage chips' and semiconductors, and 'fifth generation' micro-electronic computers. But to this world there *is* no real 'radical alternative', and perhaps least of all one discoverable by the labour movement. Instead, the political price of left illusions about the prospects for 'technological freedom' – in which, for example, 'advances in computer technology . . . might make it possible to achieve direct democracy at the required million-fold level'[113] – is itself now increasing. The social order abhors a 'steady state' as much as nature abhors a vacuum; yet it can neither find an 'escape through growth' into the 'realm of freedom',[114] nor discover the secret of social harmony in the fear of its destructive capacities and the waste of its human and material resources. And, as we have seen, alternative worlds inscribed on paper merely re-draw the ground-plans for the most ancient of utopias. This politics of illusionary deliverance from the weapons of mass production and mass destruction serves only to obstruct a just perception of the real political tasks which confront the 'left movement'. Thus, it remains the greatest of all heresies on the left that a 'complete reorganization of life by, and for, the collective producers'[115] – even supposing that the 'collective producers' desired it – is now as much beyond the reach of a socialist as of a capitalist order, under our technical conditions. But the very energy misspent on the vain refutation of this heresy blinds the left to the principal political battle of our age: that for the rearguard protection of the physical and mental integrity of the individual person, and of his or her fundamental rights as a human being. Indeed, the paradox of all left paradoxes is that such concerns could ever have come to be regarded as peripheral or merely 'liberal' matters. Yet the political defence of individual human rights against authoritarian coercion from whatever source, a politics of relief and amnesty from state cruelties and the use of increasingly inhuman methods of 'social control', now

claims a political and moral precedence over all others. It is not
political eugenics, not further experimentation, right and left, in
the name of the long-suffering people, and not vainglorious
designs to make the whole world safe – by suicidal means –
whether for capital or labour, which now summon our allegiance.
It is, rather, the values of individual or collective resistance to lies,
cruelty and political violence, in whatever cause, and however
rhetorically ennobled, which alone can give meaning now to the
notion of social progress.

But the political practice of labour movements under modern
capitalist conditions does *not* embody a coherent will to set such
ends above those of private economic interest, or above public
political accommodation with its nominal opponents. Hence, the
Western labour movement as a whole is effectively a junior
partner with capital in the economic subjugation of 'Third World'
peoples of 'the South': an a-moral 'First World' enterprise which
has nothing at all to do with economic progress or social justice.
For however oppressed itself, Western labour – with Soviet labour
comprising the labour of 'the North' – knowingly colludes with
capital in a (competitive) system of universal economic domination, armed to the teeth and world-destroying. Human 'emancipation', of whatever kind, cannot be promoted by such collusion. More concretely, the left notion of a moral, let alone a
political, revolution of the Western working class is entirely
incompatible with the real economic vested interests of labour
forces which sustain, and are sustained by, social systems founded
upon the economic and political exploitation of other nations.
Indeed, it is Amnesty International, for instance, not international
capital nor the Third or Fourth Internationals, which expresses
(against the greatest odds in degrading forms of state violence)
that impulse to human freedom which, from the seventeenth to
the nineteenth centuries, was looked for from the democracy of
advancing capital; and in the nineteenth and twentieth centuries
from the democracy of the 'vanguards' of labour. Today, however,
the Western idealist's belief in a subjectively necessary revolution
in the moral perception of 'ordinary people', whether from 'above'
or 'below', is overwhelmed by the sheer scale of the a-social
organization of popular economic interests; while the materialist's
confidence in the objectively demanded political and economic
revolution of the working class against the existing order, is
ideologically driven to the wall by the relation between capital

and labour.

The consequences for the cause of universal human rights have been drastic. It is the domestic 'curtailment of people's rights as labour-power'[116] in the 'free' market, and not the denial or atrophy of civil rights and human dignities, which has taken ideological precedence as a democratic grievance in our own culture. It is little wonder, then, that particular class or economic interests, whether of capital or labour – and however narrow or demeaning – prevail, for their protagonists, over what are now global human interests in physical survival. The world's present geopolitical crisis is decisively not a merely class crisis; and a merely class politics, even if disguised by a rhetoric of universality, will not meet it. Nor can 'labour tradition', trade union purpose, class mobilization and even the triumph of the producer class over all others any longer address the erosion, by state violence and technological oppression, of the truly human rights – beyond those of mere appropriation – of the individual. And despite the fact that 'the proletarian' under Western capitalist conditions does not recognize himself merely as a proletarian, it has nevertheless not served to arouse that classless form of organized vigilance which alone can protect the integrity of the individual person; and against which the regimes of 'real' socialism have been amongst the greatest historical offenders. Yet, so deep are the dilemmas now facing Western (and British) socialism, and so remote from the assumptions and concerns of traditional socialist theory of all kinds, that it is necessary to ask further new questions of the anti-socialist and non-socialist politics of labour which I have been exploring. Among them, as I have already indicated, is whether reactionary forms of labour solidarity, in stubborn defence of particular interest in the labour market, themselves constitute a democratic bulwark against the rise of undemocratic social and political forces, especially in economic crisis. That is, we must reconsider the simplistic proposition, established by left orthodoxy, that it is the 'powerful labour movement with its democratic traditions'[117] which should be placed in the political scales against the anti-democratic weight of its ostensible class opponents. Instead, we must inquire whether it is labour's (and Labour's) very commitment to the capitalist order, and its overriding determination *come what may* to strike a bargain with it, which provides the true source of the stability of the socio-economic system, particularly in periods of crisis. For this is a commitment of labour interests to capital and its state, not only stronger than that of the latter to labour, but much more jealous of those articles of bargaining faith and convention (the 'fair deal') which regulate the relation between them. And behind this stand other mutant issues, far removed from the socialist 'problematic', and thus never raised by socialists. They include the question whether the dogged pursuit of labour's socially-organized interests in the market, together with the (sometimes) militant objections of trade unions to encroachment on their economic independence and 'right' to bargain, might themselves represent safeguards *against* the 'corporatism' which is generally diagnosed in the convergence of the interests of capital and labour. And if, by way of recapitulation, we were to add to all this the primacy of the individual freedom of appropriation, the hidden resistance in the working class to welfare provision, the growing scale of the cultural refutation of 'proletarian' identity, the labour ethic of self-reliance, and what Gorz has called the 'yearning' among working people for 'individual autonomy' and an 'independent existence',[118] then what political total might we have arrived at? Certainly, there is much more here than a new, or old, model of the 'Tory working class'. Rather, we could argue, these are in outline the historical characteristics of the non-socialist working class, whose beliefs and values contain elemental resistances to the authoritarian; resistances which could in future be reread by the left, if it is wise, as the vital components of a new kind of democratic theory and practice.

Moreover, in the making of this theoretical equation, we must also seriously reckon with labour's desire to escape both its condition and the point of production altogether. That is, in the working-class aspiration for greater individual independence may lie its point of closest potential contact with that struggle for the 'defence of human rights against authoritarian coercion from whatever source', and for the protection of the physical integrity of the person, which I described earlier. And we would set against it, in a contradiction unknown to socialist theory, labour's institutionalized bargain with capital and its acceptance, over all other ends, of the legitimacy of narrow individual appropriation; a bargain which serves to circumscribe (as well as to promote) the economic independence of the individual. Yet this complication is itself only part of those increasingly contradictory working-class interests which this book has examined; the struggle to preserve, and the aspiration to escape, an industrial system in decline is merely one more among them. But whatever democratic interests, newly defined, might ultimately be served by the historic incompatibility of labour aspirations and interests with the means and ends prescribed by socialist theory and practice, the strongest present tendency of such aspirations is to make these democratic speculations themselves utopian. For the labour movement's interests are institutionally wedded, understandably enough, to the defence of the present production and welfare systems, in the name of nineteenth-century conceptions of progress. Moreover, as matters stand, their conservative objectives are reconcilable neither with a socialist transformation of the existing order, nor (in practice) with a coherent redefinition, in rapidly changing circumstances, of the meanings of human freedom. Instead, in Britain, even if further economic contraction and decline may spare us the worst of the negative social consequences of industrial growth and technological innovation, yet in the accompanying fall in the marketable value of the powers and interests of traditional working-class producers and their organizations, a further contraction of political perspective much more probably lies in waiting. Such developments, together with others I have discussed, potentially contain a further relentless unravelling of the dialectic of events as Marxists have hitherto understood it. For they do not only promise an increasingly 'necessary' authoritarian control, throughout the world of Western capital, over material resources and human conduct. They also portend an even greater protectiveness on the part of the *employed producers*, of the benefits, both real and imagined, to be derived from the domestic production system and the international division of labour. Such a politics would clearly furnish further imperatives, in practice, of a force to make nonsense of a theory of deepening class contradictions; employed labour and concentrated capital alike 'mechanically worshipping their fetish of the . . . increase of manufactures', as Arnold put it, 'and looking neither to the right nor left so long as this increase goes on'.[119] In such darkening circumstances, the protection of human rights from violent coercion – not the revival nor intensification of class struggle – would become, even more urgently, the principal constituent of a 'left' politics of progress and social justice. As it is, a politics of opposition to the physical degradation of the person and to the physical misuse of resources, not a simple production-

and producer-based theory of human 'emancipation', already stands at the heart of every truly democratic resistance to the iniquities committed (in the name of this or that abstraction) by the world's great powers.

That this should be so is for the simplest of reasons: there is no present or foreseeable alternative to it. The fundamental legitimacy of the capitalist system in the eyes of the majority of Western labour – and its corollary, the basic rejection of the socialist project – is an essentially incorrigible feature of each national political culture. Moreover, there can be no prospect, in practice, of new socialist concepts of moral entitlement, human rights and social justice being accorded any real ideological status in such cultures, unless socialists themselves accord to *individual private appropriation* the overwhelming status as a right which it presently possesses. No doubt it can be argued that it is precisely this right, under capitalist conditions and their excesses, which gives rise to the denial of the selfsame (as well as other) rights in others. But a democratic or socialist politics which itself flies in the face of the general will of the people, and simultaneously takes ideological refuge in an egalitarian utopia which the majority of working people themselves do not wish to inhabit, has even less prospects of success now than ever. So that even if it can be shown that erosions of citizen rights are themselves the direct or indirect consequence of the cultural primacy of private appropriation and the competitive defence of special interest in the market, far from this giving socialism its future tasks and programmes, it is a truth which represents its past and irredeemable failures. Indeed, any future socialist programme which seeks to provide yet further 'substitute satisfactions' – through enhanced social provision – for Hayek's 'individual moral judgement and action', Bahro's 'genuine self-development' or Rawls's individual 'life-plan',[120] can itself only enhance certain liberties which are not preferred in the culture, at the expense of others which are.

Instead, for the left, the issue of the relative values of such liberties must be wholly *reopened*. And if it were, it would represent, as I have pointed out, an urgently necessary resumption on the left of the late-eighteenth and early-ninteenth centuries' revolutionary debates about the true nature of freedom. It would quickly show us that it is the Benthamite antidote to the 'rights of man' – that antidote discovered in the pseudo-democratic 'obligation to minister to the general happiness' and taken over into the politics of Labour – which must itself be rejected. The times demand it. Moreover, to do so is a precondition for the left's reclaiming from the right, as its historical entitlement, the latter's ideological appropriation of the whole ground on which the old arguments about the 'rights of man' rested. It is not, now, to justify a right to property – a right which cannot in any case be overturned – but to rediscover the left's own ideological origins in pre-socialist and non-socialist conceptions of individual freedom. What is at stake, in our irreversible technological conditions and given the authoritarian state forms which necessarily accompany them, may seem, to left orthodoxy, to be 'confined' to the defence of basic human dignities. Or such a politics may seem to be 'limited' to the moralities of resistance to worldwide state violence against the integrity of the individual person. But the truth of it is that such resistance transcends the limitations of class interest and every socialist illusion. And in so doing, it comes closer to a truly libertarian impulse than the nuclear-armed megalith of 'socialism' on the one hand, or the competitive self-defence of labour interests in the domestic market on the other, could ever come. Moreover, the recovery of our pre-socialist and non-socialist sense of the worth, dignity, skills and rights of the individual, offers some opportunity of ideological rescue from that modern degradation of vision which sees human beings as dispensable, unwanted or 'surplus'; and thus invites them to the worst forms of maltreatment. To resume the debate about individual freedom at the historical point (at the end of the eighteenth century) where socialist theory interrupted and overtook it, would also be to find the deepest roots for our objections to the plebeianization of our political culture, that of the labour movement included. It would enable us to understand better the cultural significance of the universal scarcity of real knowledge about the societies we inhabit; and to recover a truer sense of the principles of justice, restored from their equation with material self-interest under capitalist conditions on the one hand, and with a 'social union'[121] imposed and/or maintained by force in the name of socialism, on the other.

Indeed, it is because the worlds constructed in the name of 'free' enterprise and in the name of the 'free' association of producers are unfree worlds, and unfree in increasingly similar fashion, that the meaning of freedom itself must be searchingly re-examined. For the pressure on personal rights of all kinds, on rights both 'self-regarding' and 'other-regarding', across the whole range of the moral spectrum and in every society, is mounting. The pressure on human dignities is mounting with it. Their common effects have even become politically more important than their causes, economic and non-economic, technological, cultural, sexual, racial; coercing in the same ways populations, classes and individuals, but always in the service of special truths and partial interests. Moreover, these effects upon human life overshadow in priority any conventional political categorization – into 'right' and 'left' – *of those who resist them*. Above all, the protection of the integrity of the person against degrading and oppressive treatment, and the safeguarding of basic human rights as an imperative which knows no political nor moral boundaries, cannot be achieved merely by productive development and material ameliorations, however enlightened, and critical as they are to human welfare. Rather, it is in their name, and on behalf of capital and labour alike, that the greatest historical assaults have been carried out by states on the truth, and on human bodies. It is in the overwhelming of human daily life, by the industrial and political process, that lost but true conceptions of citizen-rights have been buried; and they can no more be resurrected by the repetition of 'real' socialism's errors, than by doctrines of the survival of the fittest. But neither can the arbitrary, secretive and oppressive abuse of political and industrial powers – an abuse which has accompanied the march of technological progress in intensifying forms decade by decade, and state by state – be met by fantasies of a paragon commonwealth on earth, any more than it can be found in heaven.

Instead, the issue, with all its limitations, remains exactly the one which was debated in the new French National Assembly on 20 August 1789. It rests, now as then, in that 'ignorance, neglect or contempt of human rights' which was held on that day to be the signal, and even sole, cause of 'corruption and public misfortune'.[122] These human rights were termed the 'sacred rights of citizens', and there was not a whisper of socialist theory about them.[123] Moreover, at their philosophical heart, and as their organizing principle, was not 'bourgeois right' – as the left falsely argues – but a politics of *resistance to oppression*. Indeed, the capacity for such resistance was correctly seen, in 1789, to be founded upon the securing to each individual citizen of such 'inalienable' means, both political and material, as could hold in check that coercion of the economically and politically vulnerable upon which political power rests in every social order. It is a power which, experience tells us, can be held in check not by the 'social ownership of the means of production' – nor by self-management in utopia – but by the countervailing powers of the 'collective individual'. Such sufficient powers, which exist within neither of the two worlds whose state and industrial interests now dominate the rest of the planet, were also never secured to the citizens of the revolutionary French Republic. Nevertheless, to reconsider their formulation is also to direct our attention to those conceptions of individual human rights which now struggle for expression the world over: in every act of citizen resistance to state oppression, every act of dissent from official dogma and superstition, and every act of refusal of thought-control, censorship and police violence, whether organized in the name of the 'bourgeois' state or the state of the 'proletarian'. There is reassurance, too, to be gained from the fact that 'with respect to his own feelings and circumstances', as Mill wrote in his essay *On Liberty*, 'the most ordinary man or woman has means of knowledge immeasurably surpassing those that can be possessed by anyone else';[124] and not even the institutionalized denial of information, which passes for state education in the worlds of capital and labour, can suppress those sources of truth to which Mill appeals, and which are beyond the reach of any censor.

But socialist theory cannot, and does not, really address itself to these matters. Indeed, the question of the moral and political sustainability of *any* form of civil society, in the epoch of newly tyrannical technological and political powers over the individual, of 'overkill' and 'surplus' labour, of 'police socialism' and a capitalism of war and violence, transcends socialist categories of analysis. Why? Because ideological engagement with such issues now depends, more than it has ever done, upon the status which is accorded in theory and in practice to respect for fundamental human rights, to humane public treatment of the individual, and to the protection of the integrity of the human body from assault and degradation, above all as the result of officially authorized torture and cruel forms of incarceration. By some criteria – such as those which are compelled by the needs of industrial output (capitalist or Stakhanovite), or are demanded by the struggle for national or class prowess – these are, for left and right alike, minimal concerns. By other criteria, which the left must come to

share or abandon all title to the 'progressive', they are the very
preconditions of human survival. Certainly, glib historical
assumptions that there is a necessary connection between socialist
aspiration and a humane regard for the physical integrity of the
individual have been desperately refuted: whether in the name of
military self-defence, the removal of class enemies or the gross
national product. Tragically, it is as if socialist endeavour can
moralize its means and ends only in its most local and 'spontaneous' forms of expression; or as if the institutionalization of the
means were incompatible with the ends of 'emancipation'. Worst
of all, the history of socialism itself has taught us that 'fascism' –
far from being merely a symptom either of recurring capitalist
crisis, or of the dementia of individuals – is a permanent tendency
of the relation between power and the politically defenceless. For
the realpolitik of the left and right at their most ruthless has
everything in common. Against it, there is no defence in paradisal
prescriptions for universal equality and freedom ('either all men
are free or none are'), the spiritual transformation of hearts and
minds, or the redemptive powers of this or that agency of human
'liberation'. Instead, the refusal of illusion, socialist as well as any
other, alone makes possible a grasp of the dire necessities and
contemporary limits of political action: in which the socially and
politically organized self-defence of the most basic human and
citizen rights, within the social orders created in the service and
name of capital and labour, is the most practically urgent.
Without theory, as a socialist would understand it, and impelled
by human solidarities of the most fundamental kind, it is in any
case already the politics and morality of citizen struggles the
world over; struggles which have no common name, nor common
organization, nor common position in the political spectrum.

Silently predicated on a rejection of the exclusive claims-to-
truth both of capitalist and socialist definitions of freedom, they
constitute precisely that 'resistance to oppression' which the
French Revolution sought to express. It is, of course, socialism's
universal tragedy that Marx should have denied as 'bourgeois'
(and Marxists as 'petit-bourgeois') exactly those conceptions of
human rights which occupy the very centre of such actions; that he
should so drastically have confined his definition of 'what
individuals *are*' to 'what they produce' and to 'the material
conditions determining their production'.[125] Indeed, Marx holds,
in the name of socialism, that the concept of 'the interests of

Human Nature, of Man in general who belongs to no class' has 'no reality' and 'exists only in the misty realm of philosophical fantasy'.[126] It was a fatal reduction. For it came to license – however unwittingly – those socialist denials of freedom, in the name of socialist freedom, which themselves have helped in this half-century to earn for the brutal conduct of Western capitalist interests otherwise incomprehensible immunities from ideological rejection, even by its own victims. In consequence, the authoritarian proposition that the working class, as a precondition for further human progress in general, 'should obtain the possibility of dictating its will to all society'[127] now has little remaining ideological status even in the socially most devastated regions of the 'free' market; less status, perhaps, than Mussolini's fascist *pronunciamento* that 'the more complicated the forms of civilization, the more restricted must become the freedom of the individual'.[128] Moreover, that 'the chief end of socialism is the raising of the economic might of the people'[129] is one thing, and capable of being fully justified in theory. But that, in practice, 'the whole of society will . . . become a single office and a single factory', as Lenin put it in *The State and Revolution*, 'with equality of work and equality of pay',[130] is another. It is a prospect which has proved, for obvious reasons, no match even for capitalism's most blatantly false forms of ideological self-justification. Hence it is less surprising still, if Lenin's is the alternative to it, that the right's own utopia of a 'free' market, 'shaped by the enormously varied and diverse objectives of its citizens',[131] should come to be seen as a truly libertarian prospect – and this, ironically, in a period of the steady erosion in Western capitalist states of their collective safety and of every individual freedom. Indeed, not even capitalism's 'reckless plundering of nature', as Tawney described it in 1949, its 'callous exploitation of human energies' and its 'dissipation of resources in superfluous, futile or even mischievous ventures to the prejudice of objects of urgent importance'[132] can be confined, as a critique, to the capitalist economic process. Instead, the existence of such universally a-social phenomena – 'in present-day society, and it is only with this one has to deal', as Marx reminded us – has served to blur, and even to cancel, many otherwise legitimate distinctions between 'left' and 'right' and between progress and reaction. In consequence, we are confronted even more sharply and justly with the centrality of the relation between the state and the citizen, a relation which has nothing any longer to do with a world bounded by the categories of bourgeois and proletarian.

In fact, a supreme paradox is that the historical result of pursuing a socialist utopia has become gradually less costly to the ideological (or material) fortunes of Western capital than to those of its left opponents. What have been crucially damaged, above all, are collective definitions of the 'good and the just'; definitions which were expected to have been the historical antidotes to, and supersession of, liberal democratic – or 'bourgeois' – conceptions of individual well-being, founded upon self-interested aspiration. Moreover, Western socialist problems have been compounded by the left's myopic insistence, itself deeply authoritarian, that 'individual particularities and their selfishness'[133] have *exclusively* to do with the narrow defence of special privilege and the maintenance of the capitalist system. It is a belief as absurd as holding that there is little difference between individual freedom and the law of the jungle; yet many on the left hold it. Hence, concepts of individual rights of every kind can disastrously be caught up in the same reflex of left rejection. The most extreme statment of the error is arguably to be found in Marx himself. 'The so-called [*sic*] rights of man', he declared in 1843, 'are nothing but the rights . . . of egoistic man, of man separated from other men and from the community.'[134] But this can now be seen as a morally impoverished (and analytically unconvincing) reading of historical demands which expressed a desire not simply for selfish and objectionably exclusive forms of appropriation and licence, but for citizen-rights and citizen means to resist tyranny and coercion. Indeed, they are rights and means which either inhere in the individual, or do not exist at all. And more clearly still, they are rights which cannot be forestalled to the day after the socialist millennium. Moreover, 'individualism' itself, as a moral and philosophical category, has more dimensions than either socialist theory or socialist practice has been capable of encompassing. In consequence, the left rejection of many of the concerns of 'humanism' as 'bourgeois' has itself been a large part of social-ism's ideological failure. The failure has, of course, been deepened in turn by the fact that the 'fulfilment of democracy',[135] in the forms anticipated by socialist theory, has not come about in any existing socialist order.

Instead, we stand at the end of an historical epoch for the left, since the struggle for freedom and the struggle for socialism are no longer capable of being considered as necessarily connected, let

alone as synonymous. In fact, it is because all this is so that
socialist theory has even been gradually disarmed from making
that most crucial of all political and moral distinctions: between
the freedom of the individual as a merely entrepreneurial means,
and the integrity of the person as a fundamental human value.
Moreover, the inviolability of the sentient human being – whether
expressed as the right to 'use and interpret experience in [the
individual's] own way',[136] or as a moral and legal *cordon sanitaire*
drawn around the physical body of the individual 'which even the
welfare of everyone else cannot override'[137] – can hardly be
claimed to be the special virtue of any particular form of social
order. For each of them is historically steeped in gross forms of
disrespect for the 'inherent worth and dignity'[138] of the irreplaceable individual person. But this is also precisely what lends a *real*,
not abstract, universality to the 'rights of man', Marx's strictures
notwithstanding. Indeed, even if it could be shown that their form
was determined by 'bourgeois' purpose, and their content by
'bourgeois' interest, they nevertheless speak directly to today's
oppressions. The question of the moral and political worth of the
individual, together with the citizen-rights required to uphold it,
is after all not an issue which can be held to be bounded by the
terms and circumstances of the eighteenth century's particular
struggle over it. Yet left error has tragically succeeded in
surrendering to the right the 'problematic' of 'respect for the
autonomy of individuals'; and, by ideological default, has permitted the realism of the right, however self-serving, to perceive a
towering truth entirely refused to left illusion – that 'this is the first
century in which moral scruple has been the only guarantee of
freedom'.[139]

Moreover, that the right in its turn displays a profound moral
indifference, without any such scruple, to the economic causes of
unfreedom, and to demands for political reliefs from economic
oppression, can no longer provide the left with an alibi for moral
failure. Its own relative unconcern for socialism's moral delin-
quencies – from petty privilege to bureaucratic and party stasis,
from mass exploitation of powerless labour to state killing – has
been too deeply disabling. And it is surely no relief that crime on a
vast scale has been an integral part of the histories both of
capitalist accumulation and of socialist construction. Mass
human slavery and the extirpation of peoples, arbitrary arrest and
physical seizure, the surveillance and suffocation of resistance,

and the state's misuse of its ever-growing technical powers, have truly been part of a continuum of the 'historical process'. But it is this process, crossing centuries, continents and 'modes of production' together, which has also consumed most of what we know of the socialist project; and consigned the further building of the socialist alternative to the architects of utopia. Instead, we must look to the soldier Schweik's, or Galileo's, ingenuities of refusal; to the mutineers of Invergordon or Kronstadt, Gdansk or Treblinka; or to the worker's strike against coercion, whether under capitalist or socialist conditions. For they each represent the means of resistance to arbitrary power, means which in the last analysis require no theory to explain them; and which also escape, as universal acts of human rebellion, the bounds of the class-specific. Furthermore, most socialists – bounded and morally blinkered by taboo – are unable fully to come to terms with the ('right-wing') proposition that 'it is the individual in whom all that is good must be realised'.[140] Indeed, the left is fatally compromised by its refusal to acknowledge that the defence of the human rights of the individual – to life and safety, to physical integrity, to free speech and knowledge, and to basic protection from cruelty, neglect, persecution and the fear of annihilation – is a correlate of the effective expression of all other political and economic rights, whether democratic, socialist or any other. At the same time, the ideological failure of 'welfare democracy' under capitalist conditions has been such that the individual's own sense of his or her *political* rights, and of the moral entitlements (and duties) of citizenship, has arguably never been so diminished as it is now in our culture, particularly among working people. The just demands of a Paine have been usurped by the false satisfactions of a Bentham; and further distracted by decades of political and economic illusion, whether of infinite plenty, national superiority or (for a minority) of socialist transformation. But the logic of British industrial decline, of the debility of the working-class movement, and of the slow recession of unreal expectation is necessarily to bring us back, at last, to those non-socialist issues and causes which preceded the long haul of factory industrialization and the 'creation of the modern proletariat'.[141] And in the light, especially, of 'real' socialism's infirmities, the democratic aspiration of the French Revolution, above all in respect of the non-class and pre-socialist conceptions of civil and civic rights which informed its struggles, remains the only practical – that is, culturally viable – basis for today's arguments for citizen protection against the state's powers.[142]

Thus, in the absence under Western capitalist conditions of massed forces of class-conscious, socialist or socialist-inspired proletarians, and the impossibility of their future appearance, what Paine bitterly called the 'government of conquerors' can only be assailed – if it can be assailed at all – by the 'common interest of society',[143] particularly in its own survival. This common interest is no utopian abstraction. But neither can it be a classless or simple harmony of purpose, despite the strength of those shared cross-class assumptions which sustain the capitalist system, assumptions to whose reproduction both capital and labour are habituated. For such common interest is, at best, a constellation of interests of particular individuals, but which they hold in common as citizens of the same body politic. Moreover, they are precisely those practical common interests to which the right lays monopoly claims of ideological representation, as the 'national' or 'public' interest. Hence, they are the very interests whose potential range the left, avoiding utopian fancy, must re-explore, reinterpret and at last begin to articulate in its own 'address to the people'. 'Can then Mr. Burke produce the English Constitution?' Paine asked his adversary in the *Rights of Man*. 'If he cannot, we may fairly conclude that though it has been so much talked about, no such thing as the Constitution exists, or ever did exist; and, consequently, that the People have yet a constitution to form.'[144] Today, the constitution, still mystically unwritten, can no more be produced before us than it could two centuries ago; and the 'rights of man' are no more secure – indeed, a good deal less – now than then, after two centuries of intervening 'democratic progress'. But the greatest political irony of all is that the right, in its inarticulate and self-interested demands to 'get the state off our backs', should now itself have begun to take ideological charge of the very cause of freedom; while the left, for ever pursuing its phantoms, continues on the long march of its historic failure in our culture. Burke, resurrected, would doubtless enjoy (in ways that he could never have anticipated) the spectacle of the forces of citizen-progress so worsted. Yet even he might pause in the face of what has happened: that Paine's libertarian case has, almost in its entirety, been suffocated by the combined deadweight of the nexus between capital and labour, socialism's false prospectuses and the unchecked powers of the state together.

'A King in France', Paine wrote in 1791, 'does not, in addressing himself to the National Assembly, say "my Assembly", similar to the phrase used in England, of "*my* Parliament"; neither can he use it consistently with the Constitution, nor could it be admitted.'[145] Indeed, the left movement might well remind itself, in a monarchy with an hereditary peerage, of how little a political distance it has travelled in two centuries of British industrialization, 'class organization' and 'class struggle'. But the more urgent need is to recognize that its present incapacity, historically deep-rooted, to articulate a non-utopian politics of common democratic rights and safeguards, has lost it the very constituency to which a left radicalism of the real world might now be making its mass appeal. Instead, it offers, and is beset by, a strange combination of ideological burdens: those of fantasy *and* humdrum accommodation with the existing order. It is not simply that the governing institutions of the established system, monarchy included, gain their legitimacy from popular cross-class approval; but that Bentham's old argument that 'it is we that understand rights . . . while you, poor simple souls, know nothing about them',[146] still retains its force in the vacuum created by domestic socialism's ideological failures. The extent of this failure, and of the damage wrought by illusion to left prospects, needs also to be measured against what Tawney (hopefully) called the 'sensitivity' of the British to 'such subjects as personal liberty, freedom of speech and meeting, tolerance, the exclusion of violence from politics, and parliamentary government – what, broadly, it regards as fair play and the guarantees for it'.[147] Discounting the hypocrisies of it, which include acceptance of the selective use of police violence against those who disrupt the bargain between capital and labour, the left has paid dearly for its refusal of Tawney's general knowledge. 'The only version of socialism', he argued, which had 'the smallest chance of winning mass support' in Britain was one which accepted his diagnosis.[148] Today, Tawney's argument points directly to that resumption of a politics of rights of which I have been speaking.

The cost of taking a path which instead leads deeper into the labyrinth of socialist illusion, its every political thought confined within categories which are exhausted, will be the further surrender of ideological ground already lost; and lost, above all, to the right's claims to be the real legatee of past struggles for individual freedom. Yet the left, if it properly reconstrued the libertarian features of the history of the British working-class movement, would see that it is itself a history rooted in popular voluntarist conceptions of social justice, economic independence and individual freedom. It is a history which cannot be accommodated in practice to any of the current versions of the socialist project; and it raises no question, in Britain, of a revival of Jacobin fury – after all, not even the threat of nuclear annihilation has aroused it. Nevertheless, this historic legacy cannot be talked down by the left as no more than a body of 'labourist' or 'reformist' political vices inherited by the socialist movement. Moreover, the absolute cultural primacy across class boundaries of these voluntarist notions of individual rights to life, liberty and (yes) property is not a latent, but a fully live, force in the culture. Indeed, if they were not so vainly discounted in the name of a utopian version of progress, the left might see that there resides in the unshakeable commitment to such rights the ground of every necessary resistance to coercion; and, above all, coercion by those forms of dangerous power, political and technological, which have already gone so far to usurp the fundamental rights of the individual. In addition, it is not a single class, or class fraction, but the vast majority of the population which lacks the power over, and the means of refuge from, forces which now threaten human and citizen rights together. These rights, in essence and in potential, are more than mere rights of possession. They are, historically, rights of self-protection against oppression, and must once again become so. Indeed, the necessity of this rests in the very fact that it is 'the absence or severe restriction of civil and political liberties' which, 'relatively autonomously' of the particular form of socio-economic order, now does most to diminish individual rights the world over.[149] But at least in our own culture, the general belief in the legitimacy of such rights, of which the right to private appropriation is merely one, makes possible a politics of commitment to an irreducible minimum of individual freedoms, entitlements and protections. It is a politics which the left must espouse, however incomplete or imperfect such freedoms are to the utopian. If it does not, the right will do it instead, while the left, collapsing the universally valid into the 'bourgeois', will be doomed to go on chasing its tail for ever.

In turn, Labour's own realpolitik ought openly to concede that, though the laws and ethics of the market certainly diminish the claims and 'rights' of labour, working people themselves overwhelmingly accept, as well as sustain, the market system. And since this is so, the Western left has no ideological choice but to make the centre of its own political concerns the 'free development of the individual'. To begin with, this must mean resisting the forever unquestioned logic of social provision, as well as rejecting both the 'servile belief in the state' and the 'democratic belief in miracles', under capitalist conditions, which Marx excoriated; refusing them automatic elevation over the historically much deeper-rooted, pre-socialist logic of commitment to the cross-class defence of the political and human rights of the individual. And the left must itself see that its long failure to take up this commitment has been a failure of political vigilance, a neglect of constitutional reform and, above all, an historic indifference to political education. Indeed, the degree to which those who protest against the threat of nuclear destruction, police brutality, sexual harassment or racial prejudice *attract increasing popular odium,* is the precise degree to which the 'sacred citizen rights' of the French Revolution have been lost; and they will not be regained in a utopia of 'self-management' or through the 'common ownership' of production. The truth is, rather, that so far from being superseded by modern forms of social development and industrial organization, every pre-socialist and pre-industrial argument for citizen-rights and democratic entitlements, culturally approved as they may be, is now more than ever threatened. So that to by-pass, in Britain particularly, the tasks of the far from complete 'democratic revolution', and to press on regardless to grandiose forms of popular self-determination (in a monarchy and under monopoly capital!) is to miss every true political turning. For the 'social questions on the agenda of advanced capitalist countries' are decidedly *not* 'who will govern the machines? . . . who will select the range of products to be made? . . . who will establish the priorities in the use of the productive forces at society's disposal?'[150] No doubt it would be agreeable, in true utopian fashion, if they were; but the issues which actually confront us, in the real world we now inhabit, are quite different. And so, therefore, are the questions we must ask of it: how shall the present erosion of existing individual freedoms be halted? how shall the present spread of arbitrary state and police powers be resisted? and how, above all, shall the citizens be made aware of the present extent of their political disenfranchisement?

These are not inaccessible questions of idle teleological speculation, like so much of Marxist metaphysics. Instead, despite the frailty of an unequal opposition to state and technological power, all three are of practical and immediate importance. Moreover, the 'right' is only capable of asking the first question, and that from an ideological perspective which is deeply partial. The second and third, and many others related to them, only a revitalized 'left' is capable of asking and answering. But this requires more than a *theoretical* recognition that events have overtaken the left's 'good old cause' of proletarian emancipation; or that social progress now depends upon organized citizen resistance to the otherwise irresistible subversion of our civil and political freedoms. The practical problems of renewal facing the left lie much deeper, above all in the scale of its politically reactionary commitments; the chief of which is to be found in its self-destructive adherence to exhausted welfare notions of social-ist progress. For it is by 'welfarism', as much as from any other cause, that the individual will to assert the political rights of the sovereign and rational citizen has been corrupted and subverted. Equally clearly, what Bahro calls the contemporary 'revolt of individuality'[151] – not a revolt of 'class' – cannot any longer be abandoned to the right, without posing always greater dangers to the social order. After all, we know only too well that a politics of unleashed personal self-determination, if combined with a ruth-lessly competitive 'mode of individuation', can mean little more than a politics of the violent survival of the fittest. But the protection of individual moral worth, and of the individual citizen-rights which express and alone can defend it, is an entirely different matter. Indeed, it is *this* 'individualism' – not the right's political and moral 'freedom of the individual' to exploit the market and the other actors in it – which can now alone provide the left with its *raison d'être*; an individualism which demands the defence of the individual's political and moral sovereignty from assault and dispossession. The left must also at last face the fact that under Western capitalist conditions it no longer has any other (non-utopian) politics open to it; just as it must at last recognize that the movement of organized labour, for all the reasons I have examined, can play only a minor and hesitant role in the defence of those freedoms which are not specific to its own market interests. It is this which is the true, illusion-free prospect; and not the idealist reiteration of 'confidence in the historically inevitable rise of labour' or in the 'overcoming of capitalism'[152] by a class-conscious proletariat.

Instead, there is another dialectic at work, which is largely concealed by Marxists. Under it, the strengths of the right's political theories, even in the depths of capital's economic crisis, are themselves the effects of socialism's ideological failures. But more than this is the hard truth that, politically, the labour movement is going nowhere; and Labour, whether a defeated or renascent force at the hustings, is going nowhere with it. However, it is a truth preferable to that Oedipean self-blinding, a century and a half old, which has continued – against the evidence – to dictate the possibility of 'the working class' in Western capitalism generating within itself a will to power. It has continued, against the evidence, to insist that working people, allegedly fighting for their own homogeneously-perceived class interests, possess now (or will come to possess) the purpose of mastering the capitalist state and its productive processes, as the ruling class of the future. 'I advise looking closely into the question', Alexander Herzen wrote as long ago as 1850, 'whether the masses are really moving where we think they are moving.'[153] And it is no answer to such an old question, when all other left illusion fails, to threaten ourselves (in the name of a false realism) with Marx's warning of the 'common ruin of the contending classes',[154] should such a revolutionary 'class will' be 'lacking' during a period of dire social and economic crisis. For the Western working class – whether 'self-organized', democratically-participant or party-led – does not only now lack the will, but also the power, to overcome the existing forces of multinational production and the existing means of world destruction. And this remains true whether such an imaginary will were to exert itself for its own immediate benefit, or, even less likely, for the benefit of Western industrialism's 'Third World' captives. No such assertion of class purpose, unasserted in the nineteenth century, and unasserted for the first eighty years of the twentieth, can possibly be now ascribed (in however mystically latent a form) to the present condition and direction of Western labour and labour organization. Indeed, the latter's complicity with the interests of Western capital has arguably never been greater. It is, in consequence, an even bitterer truth for Western socialists that neither the closer association of left political parties with their trade union movements, nor the keeping of a greater political distance from them,[155] can radically alter the political consequences of labour's Western-wide commitment to the capitalist system. 'Labour', Tawney wrote of the Labour Party in 1931, 'needs behind it the temper, not of a mob, but of an army.'[156] Nearly sixty years later, and in the midst of another economic crisis, it still has neither.

The reasons, complex as their analytical explanation here may have been, are in essence simple: in their overwhelming majorities, neither the 'working class' nor the trade union movement nor (therefore) the Labour Party, constitutes or wishes to constitute an opposition to the existing order. Thus, within their own ranks and given the dominant ideological estimation of the legitimacy of this order, there is not even any felt need for such an 'army'. Moreover, the locus of state and economic power in Britain has remained basically untouched for two centuries, precisely because there has been such little desire to touch it. Indeed, if we should reserve the term 'socialism' for whatever challenges in theoretical fundamentals the rights of capital, and in practice seeks to mobilize labour against them, then the prospect for a socialism so defined no longer exists in the Western capitalist system; and perhaps least of all in Britain. In short, it is the Marxist conception of capitalism as itself the premise, or basic precondition, of socialism which has been falsified throughout the whole period of Western industrialization. It is not negation, but corroboration, which has been the leading form of the relation between capital and labour. Furthermore, it is this main feature of our social and political evolution which must throw into question every confident categorization of what is, and is not, 'progressive'. It is this which must cast doubt on every certain left meaning which is given to the notion of 'emancipation' or 'liberation'; and justify our deepest agnosticism about the socialist project. Above all, it is the global reach of fundamental socio-economic problems, the growing risk of universal destruction, and the consequent convergence of radical democratic ideologies across opposed political systems, which constitute the principal elements of a new dialectic unknown to Marxism. The parallel and growing strength of states, and the parallel cultural disorientation of civil societies, together with common imperatives to moral action which can acknowledge no boundaries between one political order and another, have now clearly transcended the politics of class contradiction.

These phenomena, in the very width of their reach, also forbid the seeking of refuge in a new Atlantis. Thus, in our own culture a new political theory of needs, a new economics of 'zero' growth, a new sociology of permanent unemployment, and a new (or old) moral philosophy of the irreducible integrity of the person can none of them afford to displace the given. But in particular, it is the liaison between capital and labour which most successfully resists the efforts of left imagination to dispel it. In the face of the false hopes, and even falser theories, which left wishful thinking has in general created, it would even be intellectually preferable to go back to the empirical surface of things, and modestly learn there how to recognize and reread their most immediate meanings.[157] Certainly, a plain integrity insists upon it, if the only alternative which the left can offer is the further transcendence of the real, and the further elaboration of illusion, in the search for a final truth of social and economic organization. The continuous recession of political promise demands not more resistance by the left to actualities which threaten its purposes; not more 'speculative hypotheses' and 'waking dreams . . . with which men warm their own heads' and whose 'foundation' is 'in their own fancies';[158] but 'accurate practical observation'[159] of that stubborn materiality of real circumstance and real behaviour which has served to defeat every socialist theory. 'The task of philosophy', Ludwig Feuerbach exclaimed in his *Principles of the Philosophy of the Future,* 'consists . . . not in turning away from . . . real things, but in turning towards them.'[160] And however disconcerting to the left may be discoveries of the true nature of the relation in our culture between capital and labour, and of much else besides, such a 'turning towards real things' remains a precondition for our own avoidance of utopia.

Notes and References

Chapter 1

1. Cf. e.g. 'Utopianism invariably gets a bad press . . . yet a sheer pedestrian absence of imagination or vision is one of the things which has harmed the cause of Socialism in this century', A. Arblaster, 'Socialism and the Idea of Science' in B. Parekh (ed), *The Concept of Socialism* (London, 1975) p.151; and 'all creative socialist thought is likely to possess a utopian dimension', P. Anderson, *Arguments within English Marxism* (London, 1980) p.175n; also p.205. In 'An Open Letter to Leszek Kolakowski', E.P. Thompson declares that since 1956 he had sought to 'rehabilitate the utopian energies within the socialist tradition', R. Miliband and J. Saville (eds), *The Socialist Register* (London, 1973) p.1. For a useful recent discussion, see B. Goodwin and K. Taylor, *The Politics of Utopia* (London, 1982). G. Kitching refers to the 'weak-minded utopianism' of the Labour left in *Rethinking Socialism* (London, 1983) p.ix. On the 'utopian mentality', K. Mannheim, *Ideology and Utopia* (London, 1966) pp.173–236.

2. The recent literature of British decline is itself rich and thriving; see, e.g., A. Gamble, *Britain in Decline* (London, 1981); W. Beckerman (ed), *Slow Growth in Britain* (Oxford, 1979); J. Alt, *The Politics of Economic Decline* (Cambridge, 1979); F. Blackaby (ed), *De-Industrialisation* (London, 1979); S. Pollard, *The Wasting of the British Economy* (London, 1982). It also has an extensive pedigree; cf. L. Trotsky, *Where is Britain Going?* (1925) (London, 1970): 'from the eighties [sc. 1880s] onward an obvious weakening of Britain set in. New States entered the world arena, Germany being in the first rank . . . The displacement of Great Britain from the position of world domination . . . thus came to be openly revealed during the fourth quarter of the last century', p.2. On p.8, Trotsky calls Britain a 'second-rate power'. A century earlier (*Quarterly Review*, June–August 1826), 'the manufacturing industry of England', could be 'fairly computed as four times greater than that of all the other continents taken collectively, and sixteen such continents as Europe could not manufacture so much cotton as England does', cited M. Beer, *A History of British Socialism* (1919), vol. 1 (London, 1953) p.283.

3. Cf. 'It is in any case obvious that the "old working class" or "the classical proletariat", at whatever dates these are supposed to have existed, did not vote "socialist" in the way that many interpretations presume or infer', R. Williams, *Towards 2000* (London, 1983) p.155; cf. his *The Long Revolution* (Harmondsworth, 1965) pp. 354–5.

4. A. Crosland, *The Future of Socialism* (London, 1956) pp. 22–3, 25–6, 28–9, 37, 95; and 'it is manifestly [*sic*] inaccurate to call contemporary Britain a

256

capitalist society', ibid., pp. 62, 517. The perils of prophecy are more manifestly exemplified at pp. 22–3 ('the future is more likely to be characterized by inflation than by unemployment'), and at pp. 60–1, where 'a wholesale counter-revolution' among Conservatives is held to be 'rather unlikely' since their party 'lacks . . . a faith, a dogma, even a theory'. At pp. 20–1, Crosland declares that Marx has 'little or nothing to offer the contemporary socialist'. Cf. 'He [sc. Crosland] had the rare satisfaction of reading the judgement of Professor Anthony King that he was the greatest British socialist thinker of all time – greater than Robert Owen, William Morris and R.H. Tawney', D. Leonard, 'In Memoriam', in D. Lipsey and D. Leonard (eds), *The Socialist Agenda* (London, 1981) p. 9; 'I was one of many for whom Tony Crosland was a kind of political prophet', G. Radice, ibid., p. 117. For a disturbing contrast between the morale of Labour in Jarrow in the 1930s and Labour now, see E. Wilkinson, *The Town That Was Murdered* (London, 1949): 'In 1932 . . . the town was down and out. The shops were closing one by one. But the old Labour rooms, nearly falling round our heads, were the centre of a vivid, intense communal life', p. 192. For Crosland's revisionism modestly revised, A. Crosland, *Socialism Now* (London, 1974).

5. R. Williams, *The Long Revolution*, p. 12; and 'it seems clear that industrial development is a powerful incentive to new kinds of democratic organization', ibid., p. 11. In *Towards 2000* ('The Analysis Reconsidered', pp. 83–174), Williams fails to do real justice to these earlier themes, or their false optimism and defeated expectation.

6. In 'Resources for a Journey of Hope', ibid., pp. 243–69, the vague teleology of a 'long march' (towards an unknown destination) in the earlier text persists; indeed, it has become even vaguer.

7. R. Williams, *The Long Revolution*, p. 12.

8. R.H. Tawney, *Equality* (London, 1964) p. 125; but cf. his rejection of the notion of 'social development as an automatically ascending spiral with Socialism as its climax', in *The Radical Tradition* (Harmondsworth, 1966) p. 178.

9. E.g. M. Arnold, *Culture and Anarchy* (1869), ed. J.D. Wilson (Cambridge, 1960) p. 54. cf. R. Williams, *Towards 2000:* 'it is necessary to insist that a decline in manufacturing is not a decline in "industrialism", and certainly not in industrial capitalism', p. 93. Instead, it is 'not weakened, but in its immediate terms strengthened, when smaller and smaller numbers of workers are required to operate it [sc. the 'system of rationalized production']', ibid. This seems to have no real meaning.

10. A. Ure, *The Philosophy of Manufactures* (1835) (London, 1967) p. 18.

11. B. Goodwin and K. Taylor, *Politics of Utopia*, p. 45.

12. J. Bellini, *Rule Britannia* (London, 1982) p. 7; and 'British industry is dying . . . [it is] the end of an era for industrial working man and woman', p. 80. Also, 'by the year 2000 a further 2 million jobs will have evaporated giving Britain an industrial strength of just over 5½ million . . . Industry will have all but died', p. 17. Cf. 'this hair-raising crisis', A. Benn, *Arguments for Democracy* (Harmondsworth, 1982) p. 108.

13. This is discussed more fully in Chapter 5, pp. 180–2.

14. P. Anderson, 'Origins of the Present Crisis', in P. Anderson and R. Blackburn (eds), *Towards Socialism* (London, 1965) pp. 15–29. The

consequence is held to be the 'subordination of the working class movement within British capitalist society', p. 26.

15. This is discussed more fully in Chapter 6, pp. 207–28.

16. R. Williams, *The Long Revolution*, p. 176.

17. For the 'decomposition' and 'recomposition' of the British labour movement, and 'popular' discussion of its political implications see, e.g., E. Hobsbawm, *Marxism Today* (Oct 1982) pp. 8–15; (Oct 1983) pp. 7–13, and (March 1984) pp. 8–12; M. Jacques and F. Mulhern (eds), *The Forward March of Labour Halted?* (London, 1981); S. Hall, *Marxism Today* (Nov 1982) pp. 17–19; M. Rustin, *New Socialist* (March–April 1982) pp. 29–33; I. Crewe, 'The Disturbing Truth Behind Labour's Rout', *Guardian*, 13 June 1983, and R. Miliband, *Socialist Register* (1983) pp. 103–21. Also, R. Taylor, *Workers and the New Depression* (London, 1982) and from a wider perspective still, A. Gorz, *Farewell to the Working Class* (London, 1982).

18. R. Taylor, *Workers and the New Depression*, p. 200.

19. R. Krooth, 'America Reconstructed' in *Economic and Political Weekly* (5 March 1983).

20. Ibid.

21. Cf. S. Hall, *Marxism Today*, p. 17.

22. R. Williams, *Culture and Society, 1780–1950* (Harmondsworth, 1961) p. 12 and *The Long Revolution*, p. 319 ('the cultural expansion, again with new technical developments, continues').

23. This form of compensatory argument has been most often reiterated by R. Miliband; see, e.g., *The State in Capitalist Society* (London, 1973) pp. 162–5, and *passim*, and *Capitalist Democracy in Britain* (Oxford, 1982) pp. 54ff.; cf. N. Poulantzas, *Political Power and Social Classes* (London, 1973) pp. 137–41, 221 ff.

24. See, e.g., B. Taylor, *Eve and the New Jerusalem* (London, 1983) for a recent (if unintended) account of the evidence for this; and cf. 'by this time [sc. the late 1820s] British capitalism was so firmly in the saddle that to overthrow it must mean also overturning the State', V.J. Kiernan, 'Socialism: The Prophetic Memory [*sic*]', in B. Parekh (ed), *Concept of Socialism*, p. 26.

25. E.g. I. Crewe, B. Särlvik and J. Alt, 'Partisan Realignment in Britain, 1964–74', *British Journal of Political Science*, vol. 7, no. 2 (1977) 129–90; 'the most serious loss of faith in labour principles has . . . occurred amongst those who should be its firmest adherents: solid Labour supporters amongst the organized working class', p. 156. The continuous refrain is the 'crumbling of labour partisanship', ibid., p. 158; also see *Economist*, 11 March 1978, p. 24, *Observer*, 22 April 1979, *Guardian*, 13 June 1983, B. Särlvik and I. Crewe, *Decade of Dealignment* (Cambridge, 1983) and P. Whiteley, *The Labour Party in Crisis* (London, 1983) pp. 24–51.

26. P. Anderson, 'Problems of Socialist Strategy', in *Towards Socialism*, p. 261.

27. D. Hayter, *New Socialist* (March–April 1982) p. 13; P. Whiteley, *The Labour Party in Crisis*, pp. 6–10, 53–79. Also, 'it is extraordinary that in Sweden, with one seventh of our population and in Austria, with one eighth, the socialist parties should each have twice as many individual members as the Labour Party', D. Lipsey and D. Leonard (eds), *Socialist Agenda*, p. 54.

28. I. Crewe, *Guardian*, 13 June 1983. Cf. K. Coates (ed), *What Went Wrong* (Nottingham, 1979) pp. 28–9; S. Hall, *Marxism Today* (Nov 1982) p. 17; E. Hobsbawm, *Guardian*, 20 Dec 1982; P. Whiteley, *The Labour Party in Crisis*,

pp. 81–107, 208–19. And cf. 'the British working class . . . has in fact never voted solidly Labour . . . It is an extraordinary misunderstanding of politics to suppose that a man [*sic*] necessarily votes for a proletarian party because he was born in a proletarian position. The building of the Labour movement . . . has been a continuous struggle', R. Williams, *The Long Revolution*, pp. 254–5. But in 1959, over 70 per cent of trade unionists voted Labour, and only 17 per cent Tory; see P. Anderson, 'Problems of Socialist Strategy', *Towards Socialism*, p. 262.

29. E.g. 'Revisionism . . . drastically weakened [Labour's] political programme and undermined the credibility of socialist values' and 'revisionism was . . . the cause of Labour's long-term loss of vitality and support', F. Cripps, J. Griffith, F. Morrell *et al.*, *Manifesto: A Radical Strategy for Britain's Future* (London, 1981) pp. 105, 112. That is, the fact that Labour's policies had drawn closer to the political preferences of an increasing proportion of its own working-class constituency is blamed by the authors for Labour's defeat. Yet, at p. 107 – between the two objections to 'revisionism' – the text admits that, by 1979, 'fewer Labour supporters believed in extending nationalization, or in spending more on social services, or even in retaining close ties with the unions'. It is therefore impossible to make head or tail of the argument. Cf. P. Whiteley, *The Labour Party in Crisis*, pp. 1–2, 12–18, 69–79 ('failures of policy performance are at the heart of the crisis') and A. Benn, *Arguments for Democracy*, pp. 213–16, for a discussion of 'anti-socialist revisionism'.

30. P. Anderson, *Towards Socialism*, p. 282.

31. The literature of dissent (and disarray) on the question of what British socialism is, or should be, is now vast. See, e.g., F. Bealey (ed), *The Social and Political Thought of the British Labour Party* (London, 1970); K. Coates, *The Labour Party and the Struggle for Socialism* (Cambridge, 1975); D. Kavanagh (ed), *The Politics of the Labour Party* (London, 1982); S. Holland, *The Socialist Challenge* (London, 1975); and P. Sedgwick, 'Varieties of Socialist Thought', in B. Crick and W.A. Robson (eds), *Protest and Discontent* (Harmondsworth, 1970). Cf. 'the left has not presented a clear vision of a socialist future. Labour has not explained what a socialist society would actually be like', P. Hain, *The Democratic Alternative* (Harmondsworth, 1983) p. 11; described as a 'socialist response to Britain's crisis', it is less successful than most. For a distinction between the left's 'windy generalizations' and the more workmanlike 'building the new Jerusalem brick by brick', see R. Hattersley, *Guardian*, 9 July 1983. Also G. Stedman-Jones, 'Why is the Labour Party in a Mess?' in his *Languages of Class: Studies in English Working Class History, 1832–1982* (Cambridge, 1983) pp. 239–56.

32. G. D. H. Cole, *A Short History of the British Working Class Movement* (London, 1948) p. 287 (this is Cole's view of Keir Hardie's view of the matter); cf. 'I think we shall come nearest to the essence of Socialism by defining it as the advocacy of communal ownership of land and capital', B. Russell, *Roads to Freedom* (1918) (London, 1966) p. 21.

33. F. Hayek, *The Road to Serfdom* (London, 1944) p. 213.

34. N. Kinnock, *New Socialist* (March–April 1983) p. 13.

35. T. Ali, *New Socialist* (March–April, 1983) p. 12.

36. G. D. H. Cole, *A Short History of the British Working Class Movement*, p. 22.

37. Quoted in Y. Kapp, *Eleanor Marx*, vol. 2 (London, 1976) pp. 483–4.

38. F. Engels to L. Schorlemmer, 29 April 1893, K. Marx and F. Engels, *Collected Works*, vol. 39, p. 70.

39. Cf. F.A. Hayek, *Road to Serfdom:* 'It [sc. socialism] may mean . . . merely the ideals of social justice, greater equality and security . . . but it means also the particular method by which most socialists hope to attain these ends . . . There are many who call themselves socialists although they care only about the first',p. 24.

40. M. Peston, 'Liberty and the Left', in D. Lipsey and D. Leonard, *Socialist Agenda*, p. 192.

41. T. Nairn, 'The Nature of the Labour Party', in P. Anderson and R. Blackburn, *Towards Socialism*, p. 166.

42. Ibid., p. 200.

43. R. H. Tawney, 'British Socialism Today' (1952), *The Radical Tradition*, p. 176.

44. R.H. Tawney, 'Social Democracy in Britain', p. 150.

45. E. Hobsbawm, *Marxism Today* (Oct 1982) p. 15; also *Guardian*, 27 Sept 1982.

46. Interview in *New York Herald*, 3 Aug 1871, in S.K. Padover (ed), *The Essential Marx* (New York, 1979) pp. 93–5.

47. L. Trotsky, *Where is Britain Going?*, pp. vii, 11, 38. Cf. 'Only the blind [*sic*] can fail to see that socialism is now [1908] growing rapidly among the working class in England, that socialism is once again becoming a mass movement in that country, that the social revolution is approaching in Great Britain', V.I. Lenin, 'Speech to Meeting of the International Socialist Bureau', Oct 1908, *Collected Works*, vol. 1 (Moscow and London, 1963) p. 237. In October 1913, Lenin again referred to 'the growth of a deep going revolutionary movement among the working class of England. No eloquent orator, no Liberal charlatan', he added, 'can stop this movement', 'The Liberals and the Land Problem in Britain', *Collected Works*, vol. 19, p. 442. Lenin also refers in his 'Constitutional Crisis in Britain' (1914) to 'the torpor of the British proletariat approximately between the 1850s and 1900s', *Collected Works*, vol. 20, p. 228. Today's socialist historians, who have fetishized this period for their own purposes, would no doubt disagree with Lenin.

48. K. Marx and F. Engels, *The Communist Manifesto* (Harmondsworth, 1967) pp. 86–94, 120–1.

49. K. Marx, 'The Class Struggles in France', in K. Marx and F. Engels, *Selected Works*, vol. 1 (Moscow, 1969) p. 289.

50. L. Trotsky, *Where is Britain Going?*, pp. viii, 128, 112 (emphases added); and 'the inevitable hour will strike for American capital too . . . the American proletariat will ultimately fulfil their revolutionary function', ibid., p. ix.

51. C. Crouch, 'The Place of Public Expenditure in Socialist Thought', in D. Lipsey and D. Leonard, *Socialist Agenda*, p. 158.

52. For an example of this absurdity – but helpfully made manifest – see G. Kitching, 'the central task of the left in the current situation is to help restore boom conditions as quickly as possible, but to do so in ways which, whilst simultaneously helping capital to restructure itself, also provide real political and economic gains for the working class', *Rethinking Socialism*, p. 29. Also, 'advances towards socialism are much more likely to occur in capitalist booms', ibid., and pp. 22–7, 31–2 ff.

53. D. Coates, 'Labourism and the Transition to Socialism' in *New Left Review*, 129 (Sept–Oct 1981) p. 14 ('at this stage of late capitalism at least').

54. T. Nairn, in P. Anderson and R. Blackburn, *Towards Socialism*, p. 195.

55. A. Crosland, *The Future of Socialism*, pp. 517, 520.

56. D. Lipsey, 'Crosland's Socialism', in D. Lipsey and D. Leonard, *Socialist Agenda*, p. 29 (for Crosland, 'growth was a necessary condition for achieving the socialist objective of greater equality', ibid., p. 27); and A. Crosland, 'rising consumption increases the fact and the consciousness of social equality . . . higher consumption [should be] an important socialist objective', *The Future of Socialism*, p. 292. Cf. 'Labour gets a higher percentage of the total vote in the period of washing machines and television than in the period of high unemployment', R. Williams, *The Long Revolution*, p. 358. He then describes this as 'too complicated for any single explanation', ibid.

57. R. H. Tawney, *Equality*, p. 39.

58. R. H. Tawney, 'Social Democracy in Britain' (1949), *The Radical Tradition*, p. 163.

59. A. Freeman, *The Benn Heresy* (London, 1982) p. 51; this is described as the 'traditional Bevanite view', ibid.

60. R. Williams, *The Long Revolution*, p. 330; ('the systems taken into public ownership . . . have reproduced . . . the human patterns, in management and working relationships, of industries based on quite different social principles', ibid.). Two pages earlier, 'socialism . . . has almost wholly lost any contemporary meaning', ibid., p. 328.

61. A. Benn, *Arguments for Democracy*, p. 170; cf. his *Arguments for Socialism* (Harmondsworth, 1980) p. 60.

62. A. Benn, *Arguments for Democracy*, pp. 6, xi.

63. Ibid., pp. 6–7; and on p. 17 he repeats his call for a 'liberation struggle to end our colonial status'.

64. Ibid., p. 123 ('loving thy neighbour as thyself'), p. 126 ('the teachings of Jesus'), p. 142 ('decent human values and fair play'), and p. 176 ('social justice'). Cf. A. Crosland, *The Future of Socialism*, p. 85 ('fellowship, altruism, service') and p. 113 ('relief of . . . distress' and 'elimination of squalor').

65. A. Benn, *Arguments for Democracy*, pp. 6, 43.

66. A. Benn, quoted in A. Freeman, *The Benn Heresy*, p. 186. Yet, elsewhere, 'our democratic rights' have been 'taken from us', *Arguments for Democracy*, p. 16. Cf. F. Cripps *et al.*, *Manifesto*: 'In Britain, we live in a democracy, and yet we do not govern ourselves', p. 9. It is a proposition worthy of a Socratic dialogue.

67. Cripps *et al.*, *Manifesto*, pp. 18, 77.

68. A. Benn, *Arguments for Democracy*, pp. 43, 19.

69. Ibid., pp. 17, 49; and cf. 'it is essential that the machinery of government at all levels should be capable of reflecting the desires of the people expressed through the ballot-box more rapidly than is now the case. Indeed, it must be if we are to maintain the stability of our society', ibid., p. 67. So much for the 'national liberation struggle'!

70. F. Cripps *et al.*, *Manifesto*, p. 105; and '[Thatcher's] ideological victory was due in part to the Labour leadership's own weakened commitment to the ideals of the welfare state', ibid., p. 75.

71. A. Benn, *Arguments for Democracy*, pp. 7, 35, 130 ('the link between the Labour Party and socialism is so tenuous').

72. A. Benn, 'Spirit of Labour Reborn', *Guardian*, 20 June 1983 (on Labour's 1983 general election defeat); 'socialism has reappeared once more upon the national agenda . . . the establishment . . . still fears us, not because the Labour Party has changed, but because – after all – the Labour Party has *not* changed' (emphasis in original), ibid.

73. A. Benn, *Arguments for Democracy*, p. 194; and 'the Labour Party [is] the main democratic instrument of working people and their families', ibid., p. 38; also E. Hobsbawm, *Marxism Today* (March 1984) p. 8. Cf. P. Anderson, 'Problems of Socialist Strategy', *Towards Socialism*, p. 266. ('The Conservative Party is the oldest major working class party in Britain'.)

74. B. Goodwin and R. Taylor, *Politics of Utopia*, pp. 232–3.

75. P. Anderson, *Towards Socialism*, p. 225.

76. Ibid., pp. 225–7.

77. See, e.g., M. Raptis, *Socialism, Democracy and Self-Management* (London, 1980) pp. 17–34.

78. P. Anderson, 'Origins of the Present Crisis', in P. Anderson and R. Blackburn, *Towards Socialism*, p. 12.

79. T. Nairn, 'The Nature of the Labour Party', ibid., pp. 212–13.

80. See, e.g., H. Pelling, *The Origins of the Labour Party*, 2nd edn (Oxford, 1965) p. 116.

81. See A. Barnett, 'Iron Britannia', *New Left Review*, no. 134 (July–Aug 1982) p. 36; where, referring to the Second World War, Barnett argues that then too 'Labour . . . suffered from its inability to transform its "moral equaliy" into an equivalent ideological hegemony over the national war effort that Churchill exercised', ibid.

82. R. H. Tawney, *The Radical Tradition*, p. 183.

83. M. Arnold, *Culture and Anarchy*, pp. 104–5. cf. 'Through the sixties and seventies [sc. 1960s and 1970s], the Labour movement was able to take advantage of high levels of employment to consolidate its strength – *unmatched in any other industrial country* – both nationally and at the shop-floor level' (emphasis added), CSE London Working Group, *The Alternative Economic Strategy* (London, 1980) p. 3.

84. J. S. Mill, *Principles of Political Economy* (1848) (London, 1920) p. 756.

85. Cf. R. Bahro, *Socialism and Survival* (London, 1982): 'this industrial system does not create the basic conditions for socialism', p. 129. (There is more than a hint of this heresy in E. Hobsbawm, *Marxism Today* (Oct 1982) pp. 10–11.) The more orthodox Marxist view is that 'the same epoch of groping and confusion that gave birth to modern capitalism was also giving birth to its antithesis, modern socialism', V.J. Kiernan, in B. Parekh (ed), *Concept of Socialism*, p. 19. But cf. 'In England, popular mobilizations were becoming less widespread and less radical by the time that Marx, Engels and others were giving the theory of working class radicalism its decisive formulation', C. Calhoun, *The Question of Class Struggle* (Oxford, 1982) p. 214.

86. For a contradictory (and characteristically mannered) discussion of the theme of agency, see P. Anderson, *Arguments within English Marxism*, pp. 16–58; cf. H. Marcuse, *An Essay on Liberation* (Harmondsworth, 1972) p. 82 ('the search for specific historical agents of revolutionary change in the advanced capitalist countries is . . . meaningless'). He also refers to the

'absence of a class basis' in a 1960s 'radicalism' which was opposed to the 'society organized by corporate capitalism', ibid.
87. S. Hall and M. Jacques (eds), *The Politics of Thatcherism* (London, 1983) p. 10.

CHAPTER 2

1. I. Crewe, 'The Disturbing Truth Behind Labour's Rout', *Guardian*, 13 June 1983.
2. See, e.g., A. Gamble, 'New Toryism', *New Socialist* (Jan–Feb 1983) pp. 7–14: 'the intention is not to revive British capitalism immediately but to destroy the power of organized labour and the institutions of social democracy, so as to create a more secure basis for a future capitalist expansion', p. 12.
3. D. Blunkett, *Guardian*, 10 Jan 1983; he refers to the 'pieces of the jigsaw' which 'have begun to fall neatly into place', ibid.
4. *Observer*, 22 April 1979.
5. CSE London Working Group, *Alternative Economic Strategy*, p. 64.
6. A. Gamble, 'New Toryism', p. 11; cf. 'what is really happening is that people are extremely frightened, and when they are frightened they swing to the right. Really what we're witnessing is pressure for the formation of a corporate state', A. Benn in A. Freeman, *The Benn Heresy*, pp. 160–1.
7. Freeman, *The Benn Heresy*, p. 109; but cf. 'the fact that the political battle today [sc. 1955) is waged mainly on ground chosen by the left is remarkable evidence of the change in national ideology', A.Crosland, *The Future of Socialism*, p. 61. The right's 'bankruptcy' notwithstanding, the same cannot be said thirty years later.
8. D. Keys, G. Asher *et al.*, *Thatcher's Britain: A Guide to the Ruins* (London, 1983) p. 3.
9. *Observer*, 6 Sept 1964.
10. R. Samuel, *New Statesman*, 21 Jan 1983.
11. A. Crosland, *The Future of Socialism*, pp. 60–1.
12. P. Anderson, 'Problems of Socialist Strategy', in P. Anderson and R. Blackburn, *Towards Socialism*, p. 265.
13. R. H. Tawney, *Equality*, p. 207.
14. P. Anderson, 'Origins of the Present Crisis', in P. Anderson and R. Blackburn, *Towards Socialism*, p. 31; cf. T. Nairn who, in 'The Nature of the Labour Party' refers to the 'systemized indifference to ideas' of British 'empiricism' and its 'basic stupor of outlook', ibid., p. 197.
15. J. Rawls, *A Theory of Justice* (Oxford, 1973) pp. vii–viii. The intellectual failure of left critics to engage with contemporary political ideas of which they disapprove continues. For a recent example, see D. Coates and G. Johnston (eds), *Socialist Arguments* (Oxford, 1983). 'We have asked [our contributors]', say the editors (p. 4), 'to lay out and then to answer the most complex as well as the most vulgar of the arguments they are attacking.' The book then fails to set out adequately, or to answer, the right's case.

16. K. Marx, *Capital*, vol. 2, trans. E. and C. Paul (London, 1933) p. 671. Marx further describes him as 'insipid' and 'pedantic', a 'genius in the way of bourgeois stupidity', and as a 'purely English phenomenon', ibid.

17. T. Nairn, 'The Nature of the Labour Party', p. 197.

18. R. Samuel, *New Statesman*, 21 Jan 1983.

19. R. H. Tawney, *The Radical Tradition* p. 174; it is, he adds, a matter not of quantity of possessions, but of quality of life'.

20. See also B. Goodwin and K. Taylor, *Politics of Utopia*, pp. 230–1, 241.

21. J. Ruskin, *The Stones of Venice*, 3 vols (London, 1907) p. 151.

22. R. H. Tawney, *The Radical Tradition*, p. 178. 'Discreetly termed "relativism"', he adds, it 'falsifies ethical standards', ibid; cf. 'To describe English life, thought and imagination in the last three hundred years simply as "bourgeois" is to surrender reality to a formula', R. Williams, *Culture and Society*, pp. 272–3.

23. L. Trotsky, *Where is Britain Going?*, p. 105.

24. P. Anderson, 'Problems of Socialist Strategy', in P. Anderson and R. Blackburn, *Towards Socialism*, p. 288. But only a few lines later, socialism itself is meaninglessly defined as a 'promulgation of human freedom across the entire existential space of the world', ibid.

25. C. B. Macpherson, *The Life and Times of Liberal Democracy* (Oxford, 1977) p. 1.

26. M. Arnold, *Culture and Anarchy*, p. 75; also 'our prevalent notion is . . . that it is a most happy and important thing for a man merely to be able to do as he likes. On what he is to do when he is thus free to do as he likes, we do not lay so much stress', ibid., p. 74. The title of the chapter (ch. 2) is 'Doing As One Likes'.

27. See M. Wiener, *English Culture and the Decline of the Industrial Spirit, 1850–1980* (Cambridge, 1981) esp. pp. 81–97. Cf. 'Freedom is not obtainable through industrialization, but only through the rejection of industrialization', R. Bahro, *Socialism and Survival* (London, 1982) p. 150.

28. J. Westergaard, 'The Withering Away of Class: A Contemporary Myth', in P. Anderson and R. Blackburn, *Towards Socialism*, p. 110.

29. It is not a new dilemma; cf. e.g. G. Rudé's discussion in *The Crowd in the French Revolution* (Oxford, 1967) of the 'panic fear, propagated by rumour', which broke out intermittently during the revolution: 'It arose from the threat, real or imaginary, to three matters of vital moment – to property, life and the means of subsistence . . . The panic fear of an attack on property . . . particularly affected the bourgeoisie, substantial farmers and peasant proprietors, but it also vitally concerned the small property owners among the *sans-culottes*', pp. 221–3. For a counter-example of misunderstanding of these matters at its ideological ripest, 'Chartists . . . wanted to resettle the people on the land, giving each family a farm of its own. *This seems strangely atavistic*, considering how long it was since most Englishmen had possessed any land', V. Kiernan in B. Parekh (ed), *The Concept of Socialism*, p. 26 (emphasis added).

30. P. Green, *The Pursuit of Inequality* (Oxford, 1981) p. 240 (emphasis added).

31. E.g. Leon Brittan, *Guardian*, 23 Sept 1982 ('the refusal to face uncomfortable facts and disagreeable alternatives is one of the major causes of our present problems').

32. P. Green, *Pursuit of Inequality*, p. 81 (emphasis added).

33. A. Benn, *Arguments for Democracy*, p. 16; and we have been 'reduced to colonial status', ibid.

34. Ibid., p. 117; 'we do not have a free press', ibid., p. 102, and 'the role of the BBC and the consensus media is similar to the role of the medieval church', ibid., p. 110. Cf. A. Scargill, who 'promised . . . to nationalize television, radio and the press at a single stroke', Labour Party Conference 1982, *Guardian*, 29 Sept 1982.

35. F. Cripps *et al.*, *Manifesto*, p. 10 ('Britain's subjection' is also referred to, ibid., p. 9).

36. H. J. Laski, *Liberty in the Modern State* (London, 1930) p. 14 (emphasis added); cf. F.A. Hayek, 'some security is essential if freedom is to be preserved', *Road to Serfdom*, p. 99.

37. J. S. Mill, *Principles of Political Economy*, p. 210.

38. J. S. Mill, *On Liberty* (London, 1859) p. 26; and see J. Rawls, *Theory of Justice*, pp. 407–16.

39. Cf. J. P. Sartre, 'there is no difference between the being of man and his being free', *Being and Nothingness*, trans. H. Barnes (London, 1957) p. 57.

40. B. Parekh, *Contemporary Political Thinkers* (Oxford, 1982) p. 115; M. Oakeshott, *On Human Conduct* (Oxford, 1975) pp. 31–46, 234–42.

41. A. Gorz, *Farewell to the Working Class*, p. 90.

42. K. Marx, *A Contribution to the Critique of Political Economy* (Chicago, 1913) p. 268.

43. A. Gorz, *Farewell to the Working Class*, p. 93.

44. B. Goodwin and K. Taylor, *Politics of Utopia*, p. 107.

45. A. Smith, *An Inquiry into the Nature and Causes of the Wealth of Nations* (1776), ed. R.H. Campbell, A.S. Skinner and W.B. Todd (Oxford, 1976) vol. 1, p. 341.

46. F. A. Hayek, *Road to Serfdom*, p. 13; and cf. 'the idea that the promptings of individual self-interest will tend towards the interest of society as a whole was never very plausible . . . greater freedom and a greater sense of responsibility cannot be assumed automatically to go hand in hand', I. Crowther, 'Mrs Thatcher's Idea of the Good Society', *Salisbury Review*, no. 3 (Spring 1983) pp. 41–3.

47. H. Fink, *Social Philosophy* (London, 1981) p. 65; cf. 'the lean and barren individualism of the bourgeois view of man', B. Parekh (ed), *The Concept of Socialism*, p. 7, in a discussion in which 'selfishness' and 'individualism' are coarsely conflated. Also, 'it is private privilege, not public liberty, that they yearn after', P. Green, *Pursuit of Inequality*, p. 222.

48. M. Friedman, *Free to Choose* (Harmondsworth, 1980) p. 47; and cf. Hayek's definition of 'individualism': 'the respect for the individual man [*sic*] qua man, that is, the recognition of his own views and tastes as supreme in his own sphere, *however narrowly that may be circumscribed*, and the belief that it is desirable that men should develop their own individual gifts and bents', *Road to Serfdom*, p. 11 (emphasis added). Also, L. von Mises, *Socialism* (London, 1957) pp. 191–5.

49. Hayek, *Road to Serfdom*, p. 44; cf. 'people do buy electric ice-crushers. One can argue that they should not want such things, but one cannot argue that they do not in fact want them', K. Joseph and J. Sumption, *Equality* (London, 1979) p. 81. Also see N. Bosanquet, *After the New Right* (London, 1983) pp. 31–5.

50. A. Benn, *Arguments for Democracy*, p. 135; cf. N. Bosanquet, *After the New Right*, pp. 92–102.

51. F. A. Hayek, *Road to Serfdom*, p. 11.

52. E. H. Carr, *The Twenty Years' Crisis, 1919–1939* (London, 1946) p. 135.

53. ' . . . whatever may have been the case in the hey-day of Victorian capitalism, or even in the 1920s, British society and industry today, so far from being a breeding-ground for aggressive self-assertion, are psychologically oriented towards security, group solidarity, safe markets, and a quiet life with long weekends, regular golf, and a place in the country', A. Crosland, *Future of Socialism*, p. 223.

54. W. von Humboldt, *The Sphere and Duties of Government*, trans. J. Coulthard (London, 1854) cited by J. S. Mill as the epigraph to *On Liberty* [p. 4].

55. R. H. Tawney, *The Radical Tradition*, p. 183: 'what men [*sic*] want . . . is not merely a fair deal in pecuniary matters . . . but security, decent conditions . . . the right, subject to getting their job done, to do it in their own way, without being badgered and bossed about; the consideration for their convenience and respect for their opinions which makes a man [*sic*] feel that he counts; and an equal chance, irrespective of income, for themselves and still more for their children, to make the most of what is in them', ibid.; cf. 'there is no such thing as freedom in the abstract, divorced from the realities of a particular time and place . . . It means the ability to do, or to refrain from doing, definite things at a definite moment, in definite circumstances, or it means nothing at all', R. H. Tawney, *Equality*, p. 228.

56. E.g. K. Joseph and J. Sumption: 'the slave is a slave; you do not set him free by feeding him', *Equality*, p. 52.

57. Unlike Milton Friedman, who barely admits monopoly into his world of the 'freedom to choose', Hayek gives the subject significant, if contradictory, attention. Thus, in *The Road to Serfdom*, the extent of monopoly is 'often greatly exaggerated' (p. 32); just over 100 pages later, however, 'the impetus of the movement towards totalitarianism comes mainly from . . . organized capital and organized labour . . . through their common, and often concerted, support of the monopolistic organization of industry', ibid., pp. 144–5.

58. A. Smith, *Wealth of Nations*, vol. 1. pp. 26–7.

59. A. Crosland, *Future of Socialism*, p. 65.

60. M. Friedman, *Free to Choose*, p. 30, and *Capitalism and Freedom* (Chicago, 1962) p. 10; cf. C.B. Macpherson, *Democratic Theory: Essays in Retrieval* (Oxford, 1973): 'political freedom was a necessary condition for the development of capitalism', p. 148.

61. M. Friedman, *Free to Choose*, p. 29; and cf. F. A. Hayek, *Road to Serfdom*, p. 10, where he describes 'that freedom in economic affairs without which personal and political freedom has never existed in the past'. But cf. 'political liberty was preserved by abandoning full economic liberalism. The idea that democracy can be preserved only through adherence to minimum government is false', I. Gilmour, *Britain Can Work*, p. 179.

62. P. Green, *Pursuit of Inequality*, p. 242; cf. 'the increase in the freedom of ordinary men and women during the last two generations has taken place, not in spite of the action of Governments, but because of it', R. H. Tawney, *The Radical Tradition*, p. 169.

63. M. Friedman, *Free to Choose*, p. 29; cf. 'recent experience in Cambodia tragically illustrates the cost of trying to do without the market entirely', ibid., and 'communist governments . . . have been unable to eliminate market forces', ibid., p. 44.

64. Ibid., p. 46.

65. P. Green, *Pursuit of Inequality*, p. 245.

66. M. Friedman, *Free to Choose*, p. 20; cf. 'egalitarians rely for the achievement of their objects on the coercive power of the State, as they are bound to do', K. Joseph and J. Sumption, *Equality*, p. 42; and 'ultimately coercion destroys equality itself', ibid., p. 52.

67. Ibid., p. 47.

68. Cf. M. Peston, 'Liberty and the Left', D. Lipsey and D. Leonard, *Socialist Agenda*, p. 193, 'their free system depends on the maintenance of the most stringent restraints on . . . economic and political behaviour'; alternatively, 'the use of the market system does not imply a lack of reasonable human autonomy', J. Rawls, *Theory of Justice*, p. 281. Also, R. H. Tawney, *Equality*, pp. 117, 164: 'freedom for the pike is death for the minnows'.

69. M. Friedman, *Free to Choose*, pp. 180–1; 'these achievements have made available to the masses conveniences and amenities that were previously the exclusive prerogative of the rich and powerful', ibid., p. 181.

70. F. A. Hayek, *Road to Serfdom*, p. 13 (despite 'the discovery of very dark spots in society', ibid., p. 12).

71. 'Nor is the preservation of competition incompatible with an extensive system of social services', F. A. Hayek, ibid. p. 28; cf. 'high individual incomes will not purchase the mass of mankind immunity from cholera, typhus and ignorance', R. H. Tawney, *Equality*, p. 126.

72. P. Green, *Pursuit of Inequality*, p. 85.

73. R. H. Tawney, *The Radical Tradition*, p. 167; such a society 'may have virtues of its own, but freedom is not one of them', ibid. At p. 166, Tawney also refers to the 'tranquil identification of liberty with the arrangements congenial to a favoured minority'.

74. A. Benn, *Arguments for Democracy*, p. 170.

75. R. H. Tawney, *The Radical Tradition*, pp. 169–73; hitting the émigré Hayek below the belt, Tawney calls his 'hysterics' the 'product of an authoritarian nightmare', p. 172.

76. J. Habermas, 'What Does A Crisis Mean Today? Legitimation Problems in Late Capitalism', *Social Research*, vol. 40, no. 4 (1973) p. 661; and allegedly, 'the market has been losing its credibility as a mechanism for distributing rewards based on performance', ibid.

77. P. Green, *Pursuit of Inequality*, p. 224 ('the answer was made clear by Marx over a century ago', ibid.).

78. K. Marx and F. Engels, *The German Ideology* (London, 1965) p. 483.

79. Cf. 'Our compulsion is applied by a workers' and peasants' government, in the name of the interests of the labouring masses', L. Trotsky, *Terrorism and Communism: A Reply to Karl Kautsky* (London, 1921) pp. 29–30.

80. Keir Hardie, 13 Jan 1893, quoted in H. Pelling, *Origins of the Labour Party*, p. 119.

81. R. H. Tawney, *Equality*, p. 233.

82. A. Crosland, *The Future of Socialism*, pp. 504–5; 'and even if he were not, the principle of individual liberty would still require that he should be left free

to spend it', ibid.

83. E.g. 'the aim of socialism is to give greater freedom to the individual', C.
     R. Attlee, *The Labour Party in Perspective* (London, 1937) p. 139. Cf. K.
     Harris, *Attlee* (London, 1982): '"Most of our friends are Conservatives . . .
     Clem was never really a socialist, were you, darling?" Attlee . . . made a
     mildly dissenting noise. "Well, not a rabid one", she said', p. 56; this is
     Harris's report of a conversation between Attlee and his wife, at which
     Harris was present.

84. R. Titmuss, introduction, R. H. Tawney, *Equality*, p. 9; and 'by 1960 . . .
     the climate of majority opinion [was that] . . . it was high time that he [sc.
     the 'common man'] was led into the larger market-place of choice', p. 11.

85. R. H. Tawney, *The Radical Tradition*, p. 162.

86. C. B. Macpherson, *Democratic Theory*, p. 16; but Macpherson himself is
     more tentative, suggesting that there 'may be . . . a value judgement'
     among 'voters' to this effect, ibid.

87. Ibid., p. 17.

88. A sense of the deep-rootedness of these notions and of their essentially
     defensive and conservative nature can be found in G. Rudé: 'at every
     important stage of the Revolution the *sans-culottes* intervened, not to
     renovate society or to remodel it after a new pattern, but to reclaim
     traditional rights and to uphold standards which they believed to be
     imperilled . . . by innovations . . . This defensive reaction to events is a
     characteristic feature of each one of the great *journées* that led up to or
     marked the progress of the Revolution', *The Crowd*, p. 225. Cf. e.g. E. P.
     Thompson, *Whigs and Hunters* (London, 1975) pp. 21–4, 81–115 on an
     eighteenth-century British struggle over customary property rights.

89. For a different view of this, see A. Gorz, *Farewell to the Working Class*, p.24.

90. E.g. see J. Benson, *The Penny Capitalists* (Dublin, 1983) a recent study of
     nineteenth-century working-class entrepreneurs: 'full-time and nearly
     full-time penny capitalism . . . was determined, not so much by self-
     defence, as by the desire to attain independence from wage labour . . . It
     was part of [a] mid-life search for independence, for freedom from the
     increasingly severe restraints of factory and other work discipline', p. 131.
     The literature of this, from the nineteenth-century autobiographical
     accounts of it to today's academic analyses, is now voluminous. But the
     necessary social and political conclusions to be drawn from it all are much
     less obvious in socialist theory. Also see, e.g., E. Roberts, 'Working-class
     Standards of Living in Barrow and Lancaster, 1890–1914', *Economic
     History Review*, vol. 30, no. 2 (1977); J. Foster, *Class Struggle and the Industrial
     Revolution: Early Industrial Capitalism in Three English Towns* (London,
     1974); R. J. Morris, 'Whatever Happened to the British Working Class,
     1750–1850?', *Bulletin of the Society for the Study of Labour History*, no. 41
     (Autumn 1980). And cf. 'the strong social sense of "working" = "lower"
     class, with inferiorities and deprivations *to which nobody in his senses wants to
     return*' (emphasis added), R. Williams, *The Long Revolution*, p. 362.

91. R. H. Tawney, *The Radical Tradition*, pp. 155–6.

92. T. Paine, *Rights of Man* (Part 2, 1792) (London, 1906) p. 198.

93. H. Ireton, quoted in A. S. P. Woodhouse (ed), *Puritanism and Liberty*
     (London, 1938) p. 73. Cf. Sir T. Aston, *A Remonstrance Against Presbytery*
     (1641), quoted in C. Hill (ed), *The World Turned Upside Down* (Harmond-

sworth, 1975): 'True liberty is knowing by a certain law that our wives, our children, our servants, our goods are our own', pp. 347–8. Alternatively again, *'meum et tuum* divide the world into factions, into atoms; and till the world return to its first simplicity, covetousness will be the root of all evil', P. Chamberlen, *A Voice in Rhama* (1647), quoted in Hill, p. 115.

94. K. Joseph and J. Sumption, *Equality*, p. 10.
95. I. Crowther, 'Mrs Thatcher's Idea of The Good Society', p. 43.
96. A. Crosland, *The Future of Socialism*, p. 419.
97. K. Marx and F. Engels, *The Communist Manifesto*, p. 96; and 'communism deprives no man of the power to appropriate the products of society; all that it does is to deprive him of the power to subjugate the labour of others by means of such appropriation', ibid., p. 99; cf. 'property in capital . . . inflated and emancipated . . . is most properly to be regarded, not as freedom, but as a franchise', R. H. Tawney, *Equality*, p. 169.
98. K. Marx and F. Engels, *The Communist Manifesto*, p. 97: 'we by no means intend to abolish this personal appropriation of the products of labour, an appropriation that is made for the maintenance and reproduction of human life, and that leaves no surplus wherewith to command the labour of others'. cf. J. Rawls, *Theory of Justice*, who argues that the 'basic liberties of citizens' include 'freedom of the person along with the right to hold (personal) property', p. 61. But the issue of property is barely discussed in the book, and the word does not appear in the index.
99. J. Strachey, *Why You Should Be a Socialist* (London, 1944) p. 64.
100. J. Seabrook, *Unemployment* (London, 1982) p. 37; cf. A. Crosland, who in discerning 'socialist grounds' for according greater status to the goal of 'higher personal consumption', argues that 'whether this case is accepted or not by writers and intellectuals, the people themselves are quite determined on a rapid improvement in their living standards; and governments will have to attend to their wishes', *The Future of Socialism*, p. 378.
101. A. Crosland, *The Future of Socialism*, p. 293; and cf. his *Socialism Now*, pp. 75–80.
102. A. Gorz, *Farewell to the Working Class*, p. 80.
103. G. Lukacs, *History and Class Consciousness* (London, 1971) p. 80; cf. W. Reich, *What Is Class Consciousness?*, Socialist Reproduction No. 1 (London, n.d. (c.1968)) pp. 36–43.
104. R. Bahro, *Socialism and Survival*, p. 127.
105. R. H. Tawney, *Equality*, p. 173.
106. Abbé Sieyès, *What is the Third Estate?* (1789), trans. M. Blondel (London, 1963) p. 58.
107. J. Rawls, *Theory of Justice*, pp. 542–3 ('once a certain level of wealth has been attained' and once 'basic liberties can be effectively exercised').
108. Ibid., p. 93 ('each individual has a rational plan of life drawn up subject to the conditions that confront him'), and pp. 407–16; for its motives, ibid., pp. 178 ff., 424–33, 440 ('perhaps the most important primary good is that of self-respect'). Despite Rawls's strenuous disclaimers, the *Theory of Justice* is essentially a long-winded restatement of the classical positions of liberal utilitarianism; there is nothing in it with which Mill would have disagreed, and little of substance that he did not say himself.
109. B. Russell, *Roads to Freedom*, p. 7.

110. C. B. Macpherson, *Democratic Theory*, pp. 14–15. I shall resume discussion of this issue in Chapter 6.

111. K. Marx, *Capital*, vol. 3 (Moscow, 1959) pp. 245, 252.

112. K. Joseph and J. Sumption, *Equality*, p. 39: and on the subject of 'real' socialist aspirations for equality, 'we are entitled to be guided by the failure of these attempts', ibid., p. 42.

113. Ibid., pp. 11–12.

114. Ibid., p. 122.

115. J. S. Mill, *Principles of Political Economy*, pp. 209–10.

116. M. Raptis, *Socialism, Democracy and Self-Management*, p. 18; cf. R. H. Tawney, on what he calls the 'police collectivisms': 'the pretence' that they are a 'shining example for Western socialists to follow, when not mere cynical bluff, is either ignorance or a credulity so extreme as to require . . . a doctor', *The Radical Tradition*, p. 178. The doctor is available; ' . . . which had to erect a wall to pen in its citizens? which must man it today with armed guards, assisted by fierce dogs, minefields, and similar devices of devilish ingenuity in order to frustrate brave and desperate citizens who are willing to risk their lives to leave their communist paradise for the capitalist hell on the other side of the wall?', M. Friedman, *Free to Choose*, p. 78.

117. M. Raptis, *Socialism, Democracy and Self-Management*, intro. C. Goodey, p. 8.

118. Thus, 'what is repulsive is not that one man should earn more than others . . . [but] that the fact of human fellowship, which is ultimate and profound, should be obscured by economic contrasts which are trivial and superficial', R. H. Tawney, *Equality*, p. 113. This is met head on by 'brotherhood is not necessarily destroyed by inequality, but it is necessarily destroyed by the abrasive measures which are required to make men equal', K. Joseph and J. Sumption, *Equality*, pp. 11–12. Cf. A. Crosland, 'I have never been able to see why high consumption and brotherly love should be thought incompatible – why should not the brothers be affluent, and the love conducted under conditions of reasonable comfort?', *The Future of Socialism*, p. 287.

119. Cf. A. Benn, 'our whole programme is . . . characterized by a broadly libertarian and democratic spirit which will include *absolute equality for women*' (emphasis added), *New Socialist* (March–April 1983) p. 10; and for a recent socialist utopia where 'all people are free to fulfil themselves *in whichever way they choose*' (emphasis added), P. Hain, *The Democratic Alternative* (Harmondsworth, 1983) p. 179.

120. S. Holland, 'Capital, Labour and The State', in K. Coates (ed), *What Went Wrong*, pp. 242–3.

121. K. Marx, 'Critique of the Gotha Programme', in K. Marx and F. Engels, *Selected Works*, vol. 3 (Moscow, 1970) p. 16.

122. L. Trotsky, *Where is Britain Going?*, p. 13; 'socialism is not at all concerned with the creation of an anatomical, physiological and psychical equality', ibid.

123. See J. Rawls, *Theory of Justice*, pp. 14–15, where inequalities are justified if they 'result in compensatory benefits for everyone, and in particular for the least advantaged'; and, e.g. p. 179, where Rawls discusses 'inequalities for reciprocal advantage'. Bentham's 'felicific calculus' is writ large across this balancing of interests. For further such calculation, see, e.g., A.

K. Sen, 'Rawls versus Bentham: An Axiomatic Examination of the Pure Distribution Problem' in N. Daniels (ed), *Reading Rawls* (Oxford, 1975) pp. 283–92. On the 'inevitability' of inequality, see J. Rawls, 'Distributive Justice' in P. Laslett and W. G. Runciman (eds), *Philosophy, Politics and Society*, Third Series (Oxford, 1967); also, C. B. Macpherson, *Democratic Theory*, pp. 89 ff. and S. Lukes, 'Socialism and Equality', *Essays in Social and Political Theory* (London, 1977) pp. 111–17.

124. C. B. Macpherson, *Democratic Theory*, p. 90.
125. Ibid., p. 93.
126. K. Joseph and J. Sumption, *Equality*, p. 82; and 'redistribution is unwise. But it is also morally indefensible, misconceived in theory and repellent in practice', p. 19.
127. Ibid., p. 30; for an entirely more profound (and contrary) argument on the *appearance* of equality, and the illusion of freedom, in market and money transactions, K. Marx, *Grundrisse*, trans. M. Nicolaus (Harmondsworth, 1973) pp. 240–51.
128. K. Joseph and J. Sumption, *Equality*, p. 102, p. 121, pp. 54–5, p. 99. Friedman's cosmology ('life is not fair') is of the same fatalistic order, *Free to Choose*, p. 168.
129. R. H. Tawney, *Equality*, p. 168.
130. Ibid., pp. 39–44, 56.
131. F. A. Hayek, *Road to Serfdom*, p. 76.
132. M. Friedman, *Free to Choose*, p. 167.
133. Ibid., pp. 175–6.
134. F. A. Hayek, *Road to Serfdom*, p. 115.
135. F. Cripps *et al.*, *Manifesto*, p. 125 (emphasis added).
136. K. Marx, 'Critique of the Gotha Programme', p. 28.
137. *New Socialist*, editorial (Jan–Feb 1983) p. 4.

CHAPTER 3

1. M. Arnold, *Culture and Anarchy*, pp. 69–70 ('the ordinary popular literature is an example of this way of working on the masses').
2. Cf. 'The positing of the individual as a *worker*, in this nakedness, is itself a product of history'. K. Marx, *Grundrisse*, p. 472 (emphasis in original). Cf. 'many theories of socialism, but also and more specifically the forms of trade unionism itself, which were centred not only on the working man but on the man *at work*, often amounted in practice to the *isolation* of this one powerful form', R. Williams, *Towards 2000*, p. 168 (emphasis in original).
3. For the outlines of an uneasy Anglo-American discussion of this term, e.g. E. P. Thompson, *The Making of the English Working Class* (Harmondsworth, 1968) pp. 9 ff.; J. Foster, *Class Struggle and the Industrial Revolution*, pp. 1–6, 43, 123–4; E. P. Thompson, *The Poverty of Theory* (London, 1978)

pp. 298–9; P. Anderson, *Arguments within English Marxism*, pp. 39–43; C. Calhoun, *Class Struggle*, pp. 23–33.

4. C. Calhoun, *Class Struggle*, pp. 204 ff. Also see R. Glen, *Urban Workers in the Early Industrial Revolution* (London, 1984) which helps to confirm Calhoun's scepticism about the relation between factory organization and 'collective consciousness'; for a recent populist restatement of socialist orthodoxy, P. Foot in P. Hain (ed), *The Crisis and the Future of the Left* (London, 1980): 'the important units are industrial, where people spend most of their active lives, where they co-operate most together, where they contribute most together, and where, because they produce there, they have the power', p. 39.

5. P. Green, *Pursuit of Inequality*, p. 241.

6. R. Williams, *Culture and Society*, pp. 312–13; cf. C. Calhoun, *Class Struggle*, who argues that 'the working class' has 'a thousand genetic inheritances', is not a 'singular entity', and that the greater truth is the 'diversity and disunity of workers', pp. 6–7. And 'where Marx appears to have gone wrong was in arguing that the class must supersede all other collectivities for the worker, that those interests which they had in common as members of the working class must become their exclusive interests, and that therefore it was individually rational for each worker to participate in the collectively rational overthrow of capitalist domination . . . Workers have sought other, less radical, ends', ibid., p. 229.

7. This is unconsciously revealed, e.g., in B. Taylor, *Eve and the New Jerusalem*, where discussing the mid-Victorian literary theme of the 'ruin' of the poor working girl by the 'dastardly blue blood' of the upper classes, she remarks that this is 'a clear evasion of *the reality of sexual power* within the working class itself' (!), p. 201 (emphasis added).

8. G. Sims, in *How the Poor Live and Horrible London* (London, 1889) was prescient; referring to the London poor and outcast, 'they have become natural curiosities, and to this fact they may have *the honour in store for them*, of dividing public attention with the Senanas, the Aborigines and the South Sea Islanders', p. 3 (emphasis added). This could serve as an epigraph for today's school of 'socialist history' – or social anthropology – of working-class life and labour.

9. R. Williams, *Culture and Society*, p. 263.

10. R. Plant, 'Democratic Socialism and Equality', in D. Lipsey and D. Leonard, *Socialist Agenda*, p. 135, Cf. 'Many working-class militants and still more some middle-class people who have espoused the workers' cause, feel their whole status and psychological security to depend on preserving a political proletarian philosophy of class struggle . . . in order to be accepted as a good comrade, to win the approval of the workers', A. Crosland, *The Future of Socialism*, p. 98. And cf. R. Hoggart, *The Uses of Literacy* (London, 1957) pp. 16–17.

11. G. Radice, 'Crosland has a respect, almost a reverence, for his working-class constituents and their needs', in Lipsey and Leonard, *Socialist Agenda*, p. 118. This recalls a visit to Ruskin by Charles Parker, the BBC producer, who, tape-recorder in hand, told a startled and irritated Ruskin student that he 'worshipped the working class'; cf. J. Seabrook, *Unemployment*, p. 105.

12. K. Marx, 'Introduction to a Critique of Hegel's Philosophy of Law', in K.

Marx and F. Engels, *Collected Works*, vol. 3 (London, 1975) pp. 186–7; F. Engels, preface (1888), *Communist manifesto*, p. 63.

13. Cf. R. Bahro, *Socialism and Survival*, pp. 64–5.
14. J. P. Sartre, *The Communists and Peace* (London, 1969) p. 260; 'nevertheless I knew that man has no salvation [*sic*] other than the liberation of the working class . . . I know that our intellectual interest lies with the proletariat', J. P. Sartre, *Literary and Philosophical Essays* (New York, 1967) p. 221.
15. P. Anderson, 'Problems of Socialist Strategy', in P. Anderson and R. Blackburn, *Towards Socialism*, p. 216; and ibid., p. 264.
16. P. Anderson, 'Origins of the Present Crisis', ibid., pp. 29, 26; T. Nairn, 'The Nature of the Labour Party', ibid., p. 188.
17. L. Trotsky, *Where is Britain Going?*, p. xv.
18. Ibid., p. 37 (and 'poor, miserable, silly Fabianism, ignominious in its intellectual difficulties', ibid., p. 57). By p. 59, Fabianism has become a 'mental abomination'.
19. T. Nairn, 'The Nature of the Labour Party', p. 68.
20. D. Lipsey in D. Lipsey and D. Leonard, *Socialist Agenda*, p. 31.
21. A. Crosland, *The Future of Socialism*, p. 290; Crosland calls this mixture 'curiously common', ibid.
22. L. Trotsky, *Where is Britain Going?*, pp. 42–4. He also refers to 'the dim past' when 'the radical intelligentsia went to live in the working class districts of London in order to carry on cultural and educational work', ibid. (The 'dim past'?) Also, B. Hindess, *The Decline of Working Class Politics* (London, 1971), T. Forrester, *The Labour Party and the Working Class* (London, 1976) and F. Parkin, *Middle-class Radicals* (Manchester, 1968).
23. Quoted in J. Halperin, *Gissing: A Life in Books* (Oxford, 1982) p. 163.
24. G. Gissing, *The Private Papers of Henry Ryecroft* (New York, 1961) p. 49.
25. J. Seabrook, *Unemployment*, p. 35 (and 'the working class has been gutted of much of its substance, and dependency on commodities has been substituted for it', ibid., p. 8); cf. R. Hoggart's warnings against the alleged dangers of working people accepting a 'mean form of materialism as a social philosophy', *Uses of Literacy*, p. 264, where he also refers to the 'hypnosis of immature emotional satisfactions'.
26. G. Lukacs, *History and Class Consciousness*, p. 74.
27. W. Reich, *What is Class Consciousness?*, pp. 28 ff; G. Lukacs, *History and Class Consciousness*, p. 80; and R. Sennett and J. Cobb, *The Hidden Injuries of Class* (Cambridge, 1972).
28. P. Anderson, 'Problems of Socialist Strategy', in P. Anderson and R. Blackburn, *Towards Socialism*, p. 245 (emphasis added); for the widespread use of precisely the same term 'dumb millions' by Congress Party leaders during the 1975 Indian Emergency, see D. Selbourne, *An Eye to India* (Harmondsworth, 1977) p. 88.
29. A. Benn, quoted in A. Freeman, *The Benn Heresy*, p. 175; and cf. 'last night I was speaking at a steel strike committee in South Wales and when we were talking about the media, one of the steel workers said "And when we have a Labour paper, let's have a nude on page 2 and page 3 in order to boost the circulation", *without realizing what he'd said and not meaning it*', in P. Hain (ed), *The Crisis and the Future of the Left*, p. 44 (emphasis added). This

is a combination of middle-class ventriloquism and middle-class apologia.

30. H. Lefebvre, *Everyday Life in the Modern World*, trans. S. Rabinovitch (London, 1971) p. 94 (emphasis added).

31. W. Reich, *What is Class Consciousness?*, p. 19.

32. Ibid., p. 22.

33. E.g. 'negative factors obstructing class consciousness are notably pub life and all-male cliques', ibid., p. 40; and 'football in particular . . . promotes reactionary tendencies', ibid., p. 31; cf. L. Trotsky, '[sc. working-class fervour] has been drawn off into artificial channels with the aid of boxing, football, racing and other forms of sport', *Where is Britain Going?*, p. 134.

34. See C. Calhoun, *Class Struggle*, pp. 17, 122.

35. P. Corrigan, *New Statesman*, 3 Dec 1982.

36. Thomas Cooper, *Life* (London, 1877) p. 393.

37. R. Taylor, *Workers and the New Depression*, p. 196; but cf. Λ. Benn's puzzlement about the adoption by Labour ministers of a 'campaign against scroungers', *Arguments for Democracy*, p. 214.

38. See H. Pelling, *Origins of the Labour Party*, pp. 132–44.

39. E.g. M. Thatcher, quoted in the *Guardian*, urging striking water workers to 'respect the puritan work ethic', 29 Jan 1983. (This is one of many examples of such homilies.)

40. R. Samuel, *New Statesman*, 21 Jan 1983 (emphasis added); the article also contains sallies on 'Victorian philanthropy'. But cf.: 'the Labour Party's opposition to philanthropy and altruism . . . has done it grievous harm. For . . . the party, trade unions, and the co-op. movement were all a hundred years ago inspired by a profound and passionate altruism . . . a conviction that it was an essential part of socialism to practise what one preached by volunteering to help comrades in distress', R. H. S. Crossman, 'The Role of the Volunteer in a Modern Social Service', in Λ. H. Halsey (ed), *Traditions of Social Policy* (Oxford, 1976) p. 278.

41. R. Samuel, *New Statesman*, 17 May 1983; the article is entitled 'Soft Focus Nostalgia'. But cf. 'Thatcherism . . . may be seen, in one aspect, as the revenge of business and commerce against the servile middle-class – i.e. those in the liberal professions and public sector employment', R. Samuel, *New Socialist* (Jan–Feb 1983) p. 36.

42. J. Cunningham, 'The Victoria Line Started Here', *Guardian*, 10 June 1983; the 'thrust' of the Thatcher/Roberts family's 'working-class Toryism' is described as 'self-reliance', ibid.

43. S. Smiles, *Self Help* (1859) (London, 1958) p. 35; also, 'Heaven helps those who help themselves', and 'the spirit of self-help is the root of all genuine growth in the individual', ibid.

44. Ibid.

45. J. S. Mill, *Principles of Political Economy*, p. 757.

46. S. Bamford, *Walks in South Lancashire*, p. 21.

47. S. Smiles, *Self Help*, p. 35.

48. Keir Hardie, *British Weekly*, Jan 18 1894, quoted in H. Pelling, *Origins of the Labour Party*, p. 140.

49. M. Arnold, *Culture and Anarchy*, p. 79.

50. Cf. V. I. Lenin, who thought in 1908 that working-class racism – or

'colonial chauvinism' as he discreetly called it – 'can only be a passing phenomenon', in *British Labour and British Imperialism* (London, 1969) p. 64; and cf. 'Twenty-five per cent of our parents . . . is producing 50 per cent of the next generation. This can hardly result in anything but national deterioration; or, as an alternative, in this country gradually falling to the Irish and the Jews', S. Webb, *The Decline in the Birth Rate*, Fabian Tract no. 131 (London 1907) pp. 16–17; also P. S. Gupta, *Imperialism and the British Labour Movement, 1914–1964* (London, 1975) esp. pp. 1–17, 275–302, 349–86.

51. R. Samuel, *New Statesman*, 28 Jan 1983.

52. R. H. Tawney, *The Radical Tradition*, p. 188; and cf. V. J. Kiernan in B. Parekh (ed), *The Concept of Socialism*, 'in the working class there has always been a dose [*sic*] of individualism', p. 33, a particularly foolish understatement.

53. R. H. Tawney, *The Radical Tradition*, p. 187; cf. 'I don't want workmen even temporarily to look upon a swell club as a desirable thing . . . I ask them to think that the good life of the future will be as little like the life of the present rich as may be', W. Morris, *The Society of the Future* (1887), in A. L. Morton (ed), *Political Writings of William Morris* (London, 1973) pp. 193–4.

54. R. Williams, *Culture and Society*, pp. 310–11 ('one should not be too quick to call this vulgar materialism', ibid.). On the question of 'envy' – always a hot potato, and much exploited as an argument by the right – cf. A. Crosland, who alleged that the working class was 'embittered' by 'envy and resentment' at the high incomes and status of the upper classes, *The Future of Socialism*, p. 250; also R. Nozick, *Anarchy, State and Utopia*, pp. 239–46. But one of the (unobtrusive) premises of John Rawls's main argument is that unequal citizens 'in a well-ordered society . . . take little interest in their relative position as such . . . they are not much affected by envy', since they are of course too busy with their 'life plans', *Theory of Justice*, p. 544. cf. S. Bamford, in the manner of Carlyle, 'They [sc. the 'commonalty of England'] want none of your fineries, nor your sumptualities, nor your knackeries of big babyism; they rather contemn these things, but they do want what they have a right to have, a good living for their right good labour', *Walks in South Lancashire*, p. 21.

55. R. Hoggart, *Uses of Literacy*, p. 15.

56. K. Marx, 'The Holy Family', in K. Marx and F. Engels, *Collected Works*, vol. 4, p. 37. cf. K. Marx, '[sc. in modern English society] the stratification of classes does not appear in its pure form, even there. Middle and transition stages obliterate even here all definite boundaries, though much less than in the rural districts. However, this is immaterial for our analysis', *Capital*, vol. 3, p. 862; an authoritarian proposition which, if adopted as true, would prohibit all further knowledge of real circumstance. But cf. the 'other' Marx: 'Is it not the first duty of the seeker after the truth to proceed directly at it, without glancing to the right or left? Do I not forget to speak about the substance if I must never forget to state it in "a prescribed form?"', 'Comments on the Latest Prussian Censorship Instruction' (1842), in K. Marx and F. Engels, *Collected Works*, vol. 1, p. 111; or, say, 'man must prove the truth, that is the reality

and power, the this-sidedness of his thinking, in practice', 'Theses on Feuerbach', K. Marx and F. Engels, *Selected Works*, vol. 1, p. 13. See D. Sayer, *Marx's Method* (Brighton, 1979) pp. 88–103.

57. A. Herzen, *From the Other Shore* (Oxford, 1979) pp. 35, 104, 136; and 'on one side, you have the logical consistency of thought, its successes; on the other, its complete impotence before a world deaf, mute, powerless to grasp the idea of salvation in the form in which it is expressed', ibid., p. 31.

58. J. Locke (letter to W. Molyneux , 1 Nov 1692), quoted in K. Dewhurst, *John Locke: Physician and Philosopher* (London, 1963) p. 309.

59. J. Locke (letter to W. Molyneux, 20 Jan 1693), in K. Dewhurst, ibid., p. 310.

60. Ibid., p. 309; and 'I see it is easier and more natural for men to build castles in the air of their own, than to survey well those that are to be found standing', p. 310.

61. Ibid., p. 310; cf. 'Where does experience lead? What consciousness does it generate? What action does it inspire? No reply comes packaged [*sic*] together with it – alone, the word remains dumb before these questions. For explanatory purposes, the term is an ambiguous void' (!), P. Anderson, *Arguments within English Marxism*, p. 80; similarly, 'Origins of the Present Crisis', in P. Anderson and R. Blackburn, *Towards Socialism*, pp. 31–2. Cf. A. Arblaster (on the 'tradition of British empiricism' in politics): 'it has taken the myopic form of treating people's present and expressed desires, habits and inclinations as an irreducible, unalterable datum of policy', in B. Parekh (ed), *The Concept of Socialism*, p. 150. What logically follows from this left disparagement of 'empiricism' is the allegation that 'the left has abstracted itself from experience everywhere', and that 'Marxist dogma' is a 'defiance of experience', I. Gilmour, *Britain Can Work*, pp. 103, 107.

62. J. Locke, quoted in K. Dewhurst, *John Locke*, p. 310; and letter to N. Thoynard (20 Feb, 1681), ibid., p. 159.

63. L. Trotsky, *Where is Britain Going?*, p. 36.

64. R. H. Tawney, *Equality*, p. 200.

65. That is, it is not merely the 'innermost secret' or 'hidden foundation' of capitalism, as Marx described it in *Capital* (vol. 3) p. 772, but the characteristic form of the economic process in general; cf. 'it is stupid to wish that exchange value would not develop into capital, nor labour which produces exchange value into wage labour', K. Marx, *Grundrisse*, pp. 249, 283–4. Quite so; but Marx did not anticipate that such a law would apply in socialist economies also. For the division of labour in 'real' socialism, see R. Bahro, *The Alternative in Eastern Europe* (London, 1978) pp. 140 ff. and e.g. G. Konrad and I. Szelenyi, *Intellectuals on the Road to Class Power* (Brighton, 1979) pp. 145 ff.

66. K. Marx, *Capital* (vol. 3) p. 245.

67. A Smith, *Wealth of Nations*, vol. 1, p. 49.

68. K. Marx, *Capital*, p. 800.

69. E.g. see R. Hyman, 'Andre Gorz and his Disappearing Proletariat', in R. Miliband and J. Saville (eds), *Socialist Register* (London, 1983) pp. 272–95, and cf. S. Carrillo, *Eurocommunism and the State* (London, 1977) esp. ch. 6, a thesis subsequently disowned – it seems – by its begetter.

70. E.g. F. Braudel, *The Wheels of Commerce* (London, 1982) pp. 297 ff; and see J. Day, 'Fernand Braudel and the Rise of Capitalism', *Social Research,* vol. 47 (1980) pp. 507–18.

71. E.g. V. I. Lenin, 'Imperialism, Highest Stage of Capitalism' (1916) in *Collected Works,* vol. 22, pp. 193–4, 246 ff; 'and England's monopoly . . . yields super-profit . . . out of this super-profit the capitalists are able to devote a part . . . to bribe *their own workers,* to create something like an alliance . . . between the workers of the given nation and their capitalists *against* the other countries', 'Imperialism and the Split in Socialism' (Autumn 1916), *Collected Works,* vol. 23, p. 114 (emphasis in original); for a wider historical discussion of the ideological significance of 'third worldism' see, e.g., E. Said, *Orientalism* (London, 1978); for a view of it in microcosm, D. Selbourne, *Through the Indian Looking Glass* (Bombay and London, 1983) pp. 143–53.

72. R. Bahro, *Socialism and Survival,* p. 112.

73. M. Allaby and P. Bunyard, *The Politics of Self-Sufficiency* (Oxford, 1980) p. 86.

74. Cf. 'Capitalist development has produced a working class which, on the whole, is unable to take command of the means of production and whose immediate interests are not consonant with a socialist rationality', A. Gorz, *Farewell to the Working Class,* p. 15; cf. W. Benjamin's prophetic judgement, subsequently a commonplace: 'the development of technology made it more and more difficult for the proletariat to take possession of it', 'Edward Fuchs, Collector and Historian', in *One-Way Street* (London, 1979) pp. 357–8.

75. B. Goodwin and K. Taylor, *Politics of Utopia,* p. 38.

76. A. Gorz, *Farewell to the Working Class,* p. 21.

77. K. Marx, *Capital* (vol. 1) p. 403; cf. K. Marx and F. Engels, 'The bourgeoisie, during its rule of scarcely one hundred years, has created more massive and more colossal productive forces than have all preceding generations together. Subjection of Nature's forces to man, machinery, application of chemistry to industry and agriculture, steam-navigation, railways, electric telegraphs, clearing of whole continents for cultivation, canalization of rivers, whole populations conjured out of the ground . . .', *The Communist Manifesto,* p. 85. There is a vicarious breathlessness in this which points, *inter alia,* to a middle-class mixture of fear and awe of labour.

78. J. Bentham, 'A Table of the Springs of Action' (1817), quoted in A. Clayre, *Nature and Industrialization,* p. 20 and see D. Baumgardt, *Bentham and the Ethics of Today* (New York, 1966) pp. 374–95.

79. J. Fielden, *The Curse of the Factory System* (London, 1836) pp. 56, 68–9.

80. Though the assertions are often convoluted; e.g. in the *Grundrisse,* Marx takes issue with Adam Smith's view of work as always in part unpleasant, yet concedes 'he is right, of course, that in its historic forms as slave-labour, serf-labour, and wage labour, labour always appears as repulsive', p. 611; and, even in its (utopian) form as 'self-realization', it 'in no way means that it becomes mere fun, mere amusement, as Fourier, with *grisette*-like naivete, conceives it', ibid. And to add to the complexity of Marx's views, 'the proletarians, if they are to assert themselves as individuals, will have to abolish the very conditions of their existence

hitherto . . . namely labour', K. Marx and F. Engels, *The German Ideology*, pp. 85, 236.

81. J. Bentham, 'A Table of the Springs of Action'; Marx sees a greater virtue in the 'suspension of tranquillity', *Grundrisse*, p. 611. And cf. L. von Mises, *Socialism*, on the 'disutilities and satisfactions of labour', pp. 163–81.

82. K. Marx, *Grundrisse*, p. 611.

83. W. Morris, 'Useless Work Versus Useless Toil' (1884) in A. L. Morton (ed), *Political Writings*, p. 87; and 'we must feel while we are working that the time will come when we shall not have to work', ibid., pp. 87–8. But there are ambiguities in Morris too; cf. 'Art and Socialism' (1884), where he refers to 'pleasure in daily work' as a 'birthright', and argues without qualification that 'labour should be a real tangible blessing in itself to the working man, a pleasure even as sleep and strong drink are to him now', ibid., pp. 115, 119. For a different and wry view of nineteenth-century middle-class attitudes to working-class labour, 'the *gemütlichkeit* of the bourgeoisie', in Walter Benjamin's phrase, stemmed from a 'vague satisfaction at never having had to experience at first hand the development of the forces of production', *One-Way Street*, pp. 357–8.

84. O. Wilde, *The Soul of Man Under Socialism* (1891) (London 1895), p. 40.

85. R. Southey, *Sir Thomas More: or, Colloquies on the Progress and Prospects of Society* (1829), quoted in R. Williams, *Culture and Society*, p. 41. Cf. J. London's harsh descriptions of the East London working-class poor in 1902 as 'dirty', 'dull and unimaginative', 'brutalized and degraded'; 'as they grow older, they become steeped and stupefied in beer. When they have nothing else to do, they ruminate as a cow ruminates. They are to be met with everywhere, standing on the curbs and corners, and staring into vacancy', *The People of the Abyss* (1903) (London, 1977) p. 94.

86. K. Marx, quoted in Y. Kapp, *Eleanor Marx*, vol. 1, p. 208; and, as his daughter protested to a 'luridly red critic', 'Heaven save Karl Marx from his friends', ibid., p. 539.

87. K. Marx and F. Engels, 'Circular Letter' to A. Bebel, W. Liebknecht and others, 17–18 Sept 1879, in D. Fernbach (ed), *Karl Marx: The First International and After*, vol. 3 (Harmondsworth, 1974) pp. 373–4; 'hence there are among these gentlemen as many viewpoints as there are heads; instead of clarifying anything, they only produce arrant confusion – fortunately, almost always only among themselves', ibid., p. 374.

88. K. Marx and F. Engels, *The German Ideology*, p. 52; 'for the mass of men, i.e. the proletariat, these theoretical notions do not exist, and hence do not require to be resolved' (!), ibid.

89. K. Marx, *The Class Struggles in France* (Moscow, 1979) p. 123, originally written in 1850.

90. B. Tillett, 1893, quoted in G. D. H. Cole, *British Working Class Politics, 1832–1914* (London, 1941) p. 141; these 'magpies' were 'continental revolutionists'. He compared them with the 'solid, progressive, matter-of-fact, fighting trades unionism of England', ibid. Tawney's 'futility' attached to the 'gibbering' controversies of 'dialecticians', at which 'the semi-political public merely shrugs its shoulders . . . it sees little advantage in voting for a parrot-house', *Equality*, pp. 197–202.

91. E.g. P. Anderson, 'Origins of the Present Crisis', in P. Anderson and R.

Blackburn, *Towards Socialism*, p. 19; these terms allegedly denote a truth about changing class relations in mid-nineteenth century Britain. 'The end-result of these convergent mutations was the eventual creation of a single hegemonic class, distinguished by a perpetually recreated virtual homogeneity and actual – determinate – porousness i.e. exactly what Sartre calls a "detotalized totality"', ibid., p. 20 and p. 20n. This is the kind of extravaganza which arguably denoted the intellectual alienation, not the renaissance, of British Marxism in the 1960s. But for a description of the achievement of the 'new left' from 1969 to 1975, cf. 'the most searching and at the same time the most scholarly kind of enquiry that has taken place since before the First World war. The benefits of this in the long run are going to be very considerable', R. Williams, in B. Parekh (ed), *The Concept of Socialism*, p. 236.

92. P. Anderson, 'Problems of Socialist Strategy', in P. Anderson and R. Blackburn, *Towards Socialism*, p. 256.

93. T. Nairn, 'The Nature of The Labour Party', ibid., pp. 164–5; cf. (for its like arrogance) 'the secret Gaitskell was searching for, but had not the political intuition to uncover, was how to insert [*sic*] the movement into the new fabric of capitalist relations *without* appearing to do so', ibid., p. 206 (emphasis in original).

94. P. Anderson, 'Origins of the Present Crisis', ibid., p. 36.

95. T. Nairn, 'Nature of the Labour Party', ibid., p. 182.

96. Ibid., p. 208.

97. P. Anderson, 'Problems of Socialist Strategy', ibid., pp. 221–2; with 'a range and depth that can stand comparison with any period in this century', ibid. The judgement of the future is likely to be more sober.

98. The subtitle of P. Hain (ed), *The Crisis and the Future of the Left* (London, 1980) a transcript of a somewhat unnoteworthy debate held at Central Hall, Westminster, 17 March 1980; also, D. Coates, 'Labourism and the Transition to Socialism', *New Left Review*, no. 129 (Sept–Oct 1981); T. Ali and Q. Hoare, 'Socialists and the Crisis of Labourism', *New Left Review*, no. 132 (March–April 1982); G. Hodgson, 'On the Political Economy of the Socialist Transformation', *New Left Review*, no. 133 (May–June 1982); and D. Coates, 'Space and Agency [*sic*] in the Transition to Socialism', *New Left Review*, no. 135 (Sept–Oct 1983). They all debate, in essence, the dilemma of whether the left should now be inside or outside the Labour Party – after two decades of 'revolutionary struggle'.

99. Editorial, *New Left Review*, no. 134 (July–Aug 1982) p. 3.

100. A. Freeman, *The Benn Heresy*, p. 46; and at p. 141, there is reference to the 'revolutionary socialist tradition in Britain', of which there is, objectively, barely any trace whatever.

101. Ibid., p. 14.

102. T. Ali and Q. Hoare, *New Left Review*, no. 132 (March–April 1982) p. 74; cf. T. Ali in the 'debate of the decade', where he called for a 'revolutionary party which can mobilize the majority of the working people in this country . . . a new type of party . . . a mass revolutionary party', in Hain, *Crisis and the Future of the Left*, pp. 73–4. (Within a short period he had applied to join the Labour Party.) For a similar inflation of vocabulary and expectation – psychotic in its intensity – cf. L. Trotsky, *Where is Britain*

Going?, pp. 133–4: in 1925, he announced, the way was being prepared for a *'gigantic* development and strengthening in the British proletarian revolution'; it would be 'one of the greatest dramas in the world's history', etc., ibid. The misuse of words like 'mass' and 'massive' for the relatively diminutive, and 'central' or 'seminal' for the relatively peripheral and insignificant, deserves a study on its own. For the continuing vitality of the 'massive', see, e.g., P. Anderson, 'Class Struggle in the Ancient World', *History Workshop Journal*, no. 16 (Autumn 1983) p. 57, where even the 'atlas of Marxist historiography in Britain' is 'massively' altered by a new publication; but cf. S. Holland, who in the 'debate of the decade' alone drew attention to the contrast between the 'degree of realism among working people', and 'left rhetoric', *Socialist Challenge*, p. 22. And, 'any Labour Government that was foolish enough to commit itself to revolutionary action would lose the electoral support on which it had been formed, would have to fight without an army to lead, and would become a sorry company of deluded Jacobins fighting a people', E. J. M. Durbin, *The Politics of Democratic Socialism* (London, 1940) pp. 277–8. For an intellectually dishonest retrospect, see *New Left Review*, no. 134 (July–August 1982) which now refers disparagingly to the 'rhetoric of post-sixties radicalism', and 'outworn jargon', p. 1, while continuing to deal in both.

103.   For an attempt at an answer, itself inadequate, 'class membership [has] come to be lived as a contingent and meaningless fact. It is no longer a question of winning power as a worker, but of winning the power no longer to function as a worker', A. Gorz, *Farewell to the Working Class*, p. 67; and a 'non-class of non-workers is coming into being', ibid.

104.   A. Herzen, *My Past and Thoughts*, ed. D. MacDonald (London, 1974) pp. 659, 662. Cf. E. Wertheimer, who refers to 'proletarian snobbery' and its 'tenderly wistful interest in the vacuous doings of the upper ten thousand', *Portrait of the Labour Party* (London, 1929) pp. 138–9.

105.   R. H. Tawney, *Equality*, pp. 41–2; and cf. J. Benson, *Penny Capitalists*, *passim*.

106.   E. Bernstein, *Evolutionary Socialism* (1899) (New York, 1961) p. 219.

107.   E. Toller, *I was a German: An Autobiography* (London, 1934) p. 253; and 'they imitated ways of living that only direst necessity had thrust upon the working classes. One . . . went about in a coat full of holes which he had made himself. "Why on earth did you do that?" I asked? "It is my duty to live like a true member of the proletariat", he answered', ibid., pp. 253–4. Cf. Mao Tse-Tung, *Talks at the Yenan Forum on Literature and Art* (2 May 1942): 'I came to feel that compared with the workers and peasants the unremoulded intellectuals were not clean and that, in the last analysis, the workers and peasants were the cleanest people, and even though their hands were soiled and their feet smeared with cow-dung, they were really cleaner than the bourgeois and petty-bourgeois intellectuals' (Peking, 1967) p. 78.

108.   A notable exception: 'all the decisive pressures of a capitalist social order are exerted at very short range and in the very short term. There is a job that has to be kept, a debt that has to be repaid, a family that has to be supported', R. Williams, *Towards 2000*, p. 254. He calls them 'binding

relations', ibid.; and in *The Long Revolution*, he refers to 'a system of usury . . . [which is] the old exaction, by the propertied, from the needs of the unpropertied', p. 351. But the ideological implications of the credit system are not followed through in either work. Also W. Reich, *What is Class Consciousness?* where he describes the 'everyday difficulties' affecting a form of 'class-consciousness' which is 'of an entirely personal nature', p. 22.

109. K. Marx, 'Wage-Labour and Capital', in K. Marx and F. Engels, *Selected Works*, vol. 1, p. 163.

110. K. Marx, 'Speech on Poland' (29 Nov 1847), in K. Marx and F. Engels, *Collected Works*, vol. 6, pp. 388–9.

111. L. Trotsky, *Where is Britain Going?*, p. 26.

112. J. Seabrook, *Unemployment*, p. 104.

113. Report of the First Conference of the Independent Labour Party, Jan 1893, p. 6, quoted in Y. Kapp, *Eleanor Marx*, vol. 2, p. 530; cf. Engels's bluff remarks about the 'ineradicable suspicion' among workers 'against any schoolmaster, journalist and any man generally who was not a manual worker as being an "erudite" who was out to exploit them', 'On The History of Early Christianity', in K. Marx and F. Engels, *On Religion* (Moscow, 1955) p. 322.

114. Y. Kapp, *Eleanor Marx*, p. 531.

115. See H. Pelling, *Origins of the Labour Party*, pp. 208–9; the resolution was defeated by amendment.

116. J. O'Grady, quoted *Guardian*, 17 February 1983; and 'Hate Mail Persists for Tatchell', *Guardian*, 3 March 1983. Also, P. Tatchell, *The Battle for Bermondsey* (London, 1983). Cf. J. Golding MP, *The Democrat* (Nov 1982), for disparagement of 'middle-class CLPs'; and, referring to Golding, 'nothing so exasperates him as the left intellectual, whether smart polytechnocrat or bedsit in style. His own image is unselfconsciously proletarian', D. Brown, *Guardian*, 28 September 1982. For a preliminary discussion of some of this, see D. Selbourne, *New Statesman*, 2 July 1982 and 22 October 1982.

117. But cf. T. Nairn, 'The Nature of the Labour Party': 'It is quite wrong to think that the leadership has "betrayed" socialist principles . . . "Betrayal" was always an integral part of it', p. 185; for 'elitist' politicians, D. Selbourne, 'Talking About Labour', *New Society*, 12 November 1981.

118. E.g. P. Shore ('conspirators') and R. Hattersley ('parasites'), on the subject of the 'Militant Tendency' at pre-Labour Party conference meeting, Blackpool, 26 Sept 1982, quoted in *Guardian*, 27 September 1982.

119. For the intellectual riding of a political tiger, L. Trotsky, *Where is Britain Going?*, referring to the 'Fabian intelligentsia and liberals. . . at the head of the Labour Party': 'we must firmly hope that sooner or later the workers will sweep out this rubbish [*sic*] with a housebroom', p. 47.

120. It has a long pedigree; cf. V. I. Lenin, writing on 'English Democracy' in 1897: 'the proletariat alone can be . . . a consistent and complete democrat . . . alone capable of bringing about the *complete* democratization of the social and political system', *British Labour and British Imperialism*, p. 46 (emphasis in original).

121. K. Marx, 'The Eighteenth Brumaire of Louis Bonaparte', in *Surveys from Exile*, ed. D. Fernbach (Harmondsworth, 1973), where he describes the 'brothel keepers, porters, pen-pushers, organ grinders, rag and bone merchants, knife-grinders, tinkers and beggars' of Paris in 1848 as an 'indeterminate fragmented mass' and 'the scum, the leavings, the refuse of all classes', p. 197. Also see E. P. Thompson, 'Patrician Society, Plebeian Culture', *Journal of Social History*, vol. 7, no.4 (1974) pp. 382–405.

122. Examples of the genre are to be found in the research publications of Birmingham University's Centre for Contemporary Cultural Studies; see, for instance, T. Jefferson, 'Cultural Responses of the Teds: The Defence of Space and Status', J. Clarke, 'The Skinheads and the Magical Recovery of Community' and P. Willis, 'The Cultural Meaning of Drug Use', in *Working Papers in Cultural Studies*, nos. 7–8 (Summer 1975, University of Birmingham) pp. 81–6, 99–102, 106–18. Also, R. Johnson, 'Three Problematics [*sic*]: Elements of a Theory of Working Class Culture', in J. Clarke, C. Critcher and R. Johnson (eds), *Working Class Culture* (London, 1979) pp. 201–37.

123. In the case of India, for example, see D. Selbourne, *An Eye to India*, pp. 286–7, 300 ff.

124. See J. Seabrook, *Working-Class Childhood* (London 1982) pp. 69–72.

125. E.g. J. Seabrook, *Unemployment*, p. 115; and for the loss of 'shared purposes' and 'collective projects', ibid., pp. 160–1.

126. E.g. 'the traditional character of the working class movement . . . is not a culture which has ever seemed capable of assuming a national popular leadership or of refashioning bourgeois culture in its image . . . it remains essentially non-hegemonic', S. Hall, *Marxism Today* (Nov 1981) p. 20. For an equivalent failure of comprehension, see e.g., M. Davis, 'Why the U.S. Working Class is Different', *New Left Review*, no. 123 (Sept–Oct 1980) pp. 3–44, and cf. W. Sombart, *Why is there no Socialism in the United States?* (1906) (London, 1976). The supposed 'enigma' of the *actual* American working class, together with the *ideal* working class from which it 'differs', are both of them the left's intellectual constructs. A brief and quickly abandoned glimpse of an alternative truth ('it has not been lack of class consciousness but – in one sense – excess of it which has been the obstacle to the commitment of the working class to socialism') can be found in P. Anderson, 'Origins of the Present Crisis', p. 34.

127. J. Bellini, *Rule Britannia*, p. 82 ('the mass of unemployed, under-employed and the deskilled . . . this mass of unwanted labour').

128. See C. Calhoun, *Question of Class Struggle*, p. 231.

129. As in A. Benn, *Arguments for Socialism*, p. 146 ('democratic socialism . . . is very much a home-grown British product which has been slowly fashioned over the centuries. Its roots are deep in our history'.)

130. C. Hill, *Guardian*, 12 March 1983 ('this calls for a fuller Marxist analysis than it has yet received').

131. A. Barnett, 'Iron Britannia', *New Left Review*, no. 134 (July–Aug 1982) p. 54; cf. 'when we started out, there were the waverers and the faint-hearts, the people who thought we could no longer do the great things we once did, those who believed our decline was irreversible, that we could never again be what we were, that Britain was no longer the nation that had

built an empire and ruled a quarter of the world. Well, they were wrong',
M. Thatcher, quoted *Guardian*, 20 December 1982.
132. R. H. Tawney, *Equality*, p. 201; Trotsky had a different view of it, referring
to the 'consciousness of large circles of the working class' being 'tightly
bound' to the 'conservative-national traditions and discipline of the
bourgeois order', *Where is Britain Going?*, pp. 40–1.
133. R. H. Tawney, *Equality*, ibid.
134. M. Arnold, *Culture and Anarchy*, p. 109.
135. F. Cripps *et al.*, *Manifesto*, pp. 43–4.
136. P. Anderson, 'Problems of a Socialist Strategy', p. 259; cf. R. H. Tawney,
Equality, p. 43; R. Williams, *Culture and Society*, pp. 318 ff., and R.
Williams, *The Long Revolution*, pp. 363 ff. For another view of the 'common
culture', see K. Joseph and J. Sumption, *Equality*: 'television has finally
killed off a distinctive working class culture and produced an almost
homogeneous national civilization (if that is the right word for it) for the
first time since the medieval church held undisputed sway over the minds
of millions', p. 13.
137. S. Bamford, *Walks in South Lancashire*, p. 21.

CHAPTER 4

1. The limits of left discussion here are usually quickly reached; see, e.g., P.
Thane, 'The Working Class and State Welfare, 1880–1914', *Bulletin of the
Society for the Study of Labour History*, no. 31 (1975) pp. 6–8; H. Pelling,
Popular Politics and Society in Late Victorian Britain (London, 1968) pp. 1–18;
or J. Hains, 'Did British Workers want the Welfare State? G. D. H. Cole's
Survey of 1942', in J. Winter (ed), *The Working Class in Modern British
History* (Cambridge, 1938) pp. 200–14. Also see M. Bruce, *The Coming of
the Welfare State* (London, 1961); D. C. Marsh, *The Future of the Welfare State*
(Harmondsworth, 1964); and P. Thane, *Foundations of the Welfare State*
(London, 1982).
2. A. Benn, *Arguments for Democracy*, p. 169.
3. R. Grantham, Labour Party Conference, Blackpool, 1982, quoted
Guardian, 30 September 1982.
4. See, e.g., R. M. Titmuss, *Essays on the Welfare State* (London, 1963) pp.
35–9, where the issues are avoided; and, likewise, nearly twenty years
later, F. Field, *Inequality in Britain: Freedom, Welfare and the State* (London,
1981). In F. Field, *Poverty and Politics* (London, 1982), there is the briefest
discussion of '"the incentives to work" question', pp. 85–7.
5. A. Benn, *Arguments for Democracy*, pp. 7–8, where such 'building' appears
as entirely unproblematical; or cf. the crude propositions in P. Hain,
Democratic Alternative, where it is held that 'Labour's task is to go back to
basics', chief among them the commitment to a 'welfare society' [*sic*], p.
41. The instances of this almost always unexplored position are now
innumerable.
6. F. Cripps *et al.*, *Manifesto*, p. 60; and see P. Townsend, *Poverty in the United*

Kingdom (London, 1979), pp. 893 ff.

7. R. H. Tawney, *Equality*, pp. 134, 219; and, 'to the mass of the population, who must obtain the benefits in question through public action or not at all, such services mean the difference between health and sickness, knowledge and ignorance and, sometimes, life and death', ibid., p. 219.

8. A. Crosland, *The Future of Socialism*, p. 154. (He refers, as 'special cases', to the fields of mental health, and the treatment of alcoholism and drug abuse, ibid.)

9. E.g. M. Friedman, *Free to Choose*, pp. 118–58; but cf. 'the welfare state is a thoroughly Conservative institution – which is why Conservatives did so much to bring it into existence – and its roots go deep in British history', I. Gilmour, *Britain Can Work*, p. 225.

10. Cf. 'there was never any way in which the genuinely new ideas and provisions for a caring society could persist as an exceptional sector, contradicted by systematic inequality and competition everywhere else', R. Williams, *Towards 2000*, p. 100; yet the correctness of this statement is characteristically blurred, one page earlier: 'in the provision of public education and health services . . . [and] in the extension of benefits to citizens rather than only to workers, the crude market principle has already been refined', ibid., p. 99. But cf. 'the welfare state . . . has degenerated into a system which perpetuates poverty in the very act of partially relieving it', F. Cripps *et al.*, *Manifesto*, p. 59.

11. M. Friedman, *Free to Choose*, p. 203.

12. E.g. F. Field, *Inequality in Britain*, pp. 19–67; or J. Westergaard, 'Income, Wealth and the Welfare State' in D. Coates and G. Johnston (eds), *Socialist Arguments*, pp. 146–63.

13. R. H. Tawney, *The Radical Tradition*, p. 46.

14. Ibid., p. 116; and 'the community should be offered the best service technically possible at the lowest price compatible with adequate payment to those who provide it', ibid.

15. Ibid., p. 126; cf. A. Crosland, *The Future of Socialism*, pp. 475–6.

16. Cf. 'The basic fact is [that] the large corporation, facing fundamentally similar problems . . . [acts] in fundamentally the same way, whether publicly or privately owned', A. Crosland, *The Future of Socialism*, p. 479. Also, 'in the end a detailed attempt to plan the output of different industries is bound to fail unless backed by direction of labour; and this no one [is] willing to countenance as a permanent measure', ibid., p.501.

17. Coal Industry Commission, 1919, *Reports* (HMSO, London, 1919) Cmd. 845, 210 and R. H. Tawney, *The Radical Tradition*, pp. 127–43.

18. See C. B. Macpherson, *Democratic Theory*, p. 131 ('the rise of the welfare state has created new forms of property and distributed them widely', ibid.).

19. C. Crouch, in 'The Place of Public Expenditure in Socialist Thought', in D. Lipsey and D. Leonard, *Socialist Agenda*, denies it: 'it is only by a verbal conceit that the "public" arena can be regarded as a genuine communal property in any sense of the term', p. 179.

20. K. Joseph and J. Sumption, *Equality*, p. 23.

21. R. H. Tawney, *Equality*, p. 223 (emphasis added).

22. C. B. Macpherson, *Democratic Theory*, p. 12.

23. P. Green, *Pursuit of Inequality*, p. 192.
24. K. Woodroofe, 'The Making of the Welfare State in England', in H. R. Winkler (ed), *Twentieth Century Britain: National Power and Social Welfare* (New York, 1976) p. 161.
25. A. Briggs, 'The Welfare State in Historical Perspective', *Archives Européennes de Sociologie*, vol. 11, no. 2 (1961) p. 228, quoted in K. Woodroofe, 'Making of the Welfare State in England', p. 167; cf. 'Socialism in practice has meant limiting, controlling or replacing market forces as the main determinant of human activity', A. Benn, *Arguments for Democracy*, p. 169.
26. Lord Beveridge, reported in *Hansard*, House of Lords (1953), vol. 182, col. 675–6.
27. Cf. 'If the object of the social services is the abolition of want, then an income test to establish the existence of want is a logical corollary. If, on the other hand, payment of benefit regardless of means is elevated into a principle, then the object cannot be simply the elimination of want', A. Crosland, *The Future of Socialism*, p. 120.
28. Ibid., p. 142.
29. S. Holland in K. Coates (ed), *What Went Wrong*, pp. 243–6; also the 'right to socialised planning', ibid., p. 245.
30. R. H. S. Crossman, 'The Lessons of 1945', in P. Anderson and R. Blackburn, *Towards Socialism*, pp. 153–4; cf. the disparaging definition of post-war socialism as 'wartime controls, combined with welfare benefits paid for with the proceeds of Britain's world leadership', A. Freeman, *The Benn Heresy*, p. 104.
31. R. Titmuss, 'Goals of Today's Welfare State', in P. Anderson and R. Blackburn, *Towards Socialism*, p. 357.
32. F. A. Hayek, *Road to Serfdom*, p. 101.
33. K. Kautsky, *The Social Revolution*, trans. A. M. and M. W. Simons (Chicago, 1916) p. 81.
34. F. Cripps *et al.*, *Manifesto*, p. 182.
35. P. Wintour and F. Wheen, *New Statesman*, 15 October 1982.
36. D. Blunkett, *Guardian*, 10 January 1983.
37. F. A. Hayek, *Road to Serfdom*, p. 44.
38. Ibid., pp. 79–80.
39. K. Joseph and J. Sumption, *Equality*, p. 121.
40. Ibid.
41. A. Crosland, *The Future of Socialism*, p. 152.
42. R. H. Tawney, *The Radical Tradition*, p. 77.
43. M. Friedman, *Free to Choose*, p. 120.
44. A. Smith, *Wealth of Nations*, vol. 1, p. 27.
45. M. Friedman, *Free to Choose*, p. 149.
46. Ibid., p. 135; cf. the discussion between general practitioners I reported in *New Society*, 3 December 1981, reprinted as 'At the Doctor's', in P. Barker (ed), *The Other Britain* (London, 1982) esp. pp. 155–7.
47. M. Friedman, *Free to Choose*, p. 158.
48. Ibid., pp. 135, 220.
49. J. Bentham, 'A Critical Examination of the Declaration of Rights' (1816), in B. Parekh (ed), *Bentham's Political Thought* (London, 1973) p. 269.
50. F. A. Hayek, *Road to Serfdom*, p. 99.

51. R. H. Tawney, *The Radical Tradition*, p. 149.
52. J. S. Mill, *On Liberty*, p. 198, as the result of the 'interference of government'. Its extension would be a 'great evil', and 'the evil would be greater the more efficiently and scientifically the administrative machinery was constructed', ibid., pp. 198–9. 'A state which dwarfs its men, in order that they may be more docile instruments in its hands even for beneficial purposes, will find that with small men no great thing can really be accomplished; and that the perfection of machinery to which it has sacrificed everything, will in the end avail it nothing, for want of the vital powers which, in order that the machine might work more smoothly, it has preferred to banish', ibid., p. 207. These are the concluding words of Mill's essay.
53. C.Crouch, 'Public Expenditure in Socialist Thought', p. 164; cf. R. Titmuss, 'the "welfare state" has no meaning unless it is positively and constructively concerned with redistributive justice and social participation', 'Goals of Today's Welfare State', p. 365 (emphasis added); and 'it is not by bureaucratic regulation – but only by *direct communal administration* that an idea of common welfare can become actual', R. Williams, *Towards 2000*, p. 100 (emphasis added).
54. C. Crouch, 'Public Expenditure in Socialist Thought', p. 182.
55. M. Thatcher, quoted in R. Samuel, *New Statesman*, 28 Janury 1983 ('it reads very much like . . . "looking after No. 1"').
56. See A. Benn, *Arguments for Democracy*, p. 214.
57. S. Smiles, *Self Help*, p. 35; and 'the healthy spirit of self-help created amongst working people would more than any other measure serve to raise them as a class', ibid., p. 284.
58. Ibid., p. 35.
59. Ibid., p. 36.
60. Cf. 'working class activists . . . are more "instrumental" in their approach to politics than the middle-class; that is, they are more concerned with achieving concrete material benefits from policies than are middle-class activists, who are more concerned with idealistic and symbolic questions', P. Whiteley, *Labour Party in Crisis*, pp. 14, 57–61, esp. p. 61; and F. Parkin, *Middle-Class Radicals*, pp. 34–40.
61. R. Titmuss, 'The Irresponsible Society' (Originally Fabian Tract 323, 1960), in his *Essays on the Welfare State*, p. 229; and 'the major beneficiaries of the high-cost sectors of social welfare' – i.e. health and education – 'are the middle and upper-middle classes. The poor make more use of certain services (for instance, public assistance), but these tend on a *per capita* basis to be the low-cost sectors', R. Titmuss, 'Goals of Today's Welfare State', in P. Anderson and R. Blackburn, *Towards Socialism*, p. 360.
62. S. and B. Webb, *Our Partnership* (London, 1948) p. 479.
63. R. H. Tawney, *Equality*, pp. 147–8.
64. R. Williams, *Culture and Society*, p. 332; and 'with an assumption of virtue, we seek to lay hands on others and, from our own constructions, determine their course', ibid. (How the left agrees with the right, but always seeks to deny it!)
65. D. Blunkett, *Guardian*, 10 January 1983.
66. K. Marx, 'The Communism of the *Rheinischer Beobachter*' (Sept 1847), in

K. Marx and F. Engels, *Collected Works*, vol. 6, p. 231.

67. K. Marx and F. Engels, *The Communist Manifesto*, p. 93.
68. K. Marx, 'Critique of the Gotha Programme', in K. Marx and F. Engels, *Selected Works*, vol. 3, p. 28; see also, e.g., R. Miliband 'Marx and the State', in R. Miliband and J. Saville (eds), *Socialist Register 1965*, pp. 278–96, and L. J. Macfarlane, 'Marxist Critiques of the State' in B. Parekh (ed), *The Concept of Socialism*, pp. 167–91.
69. R. H. Tawney, *Equality*, p. 154.
70. Ibid., pp. 230–1.
71. R. Bahro, *Socialism and Survival*, pp. 29, 151.
72. A. Gorz, *Farewell to the Working Class*, p. 40.
73. L. Trotsky, *Where is Britain Going?*, p.7.
74. Ibid., p. 119.
75. J. Bellini, *Rule Britannia*, p. xiv.
76. J. S. Mill, *On Liberty*, p. 126.
77. F. Cripps *et al.*, *Manifesto*, p. 75.
78. Ibid.
79. Cf. J. Seabrook, *Unemployment*, p. 69.
80. M. Arnold, *Culture and Anarchy*, p. 70; and 'culture has a rough task to achieve in this country. Its preachers have, and are likely to have, a hard time of it', ibid., p. 49.
81. Ibid., intro. J. D. Wilson, p. xxxvi.
82. F. Cripps *et al.*, *Manifesto*, p. 69; and 'only 0.01 per cent of young women from unskilled working homes went to university', ibid., p. 68. The authors call this 'the statistic which reveals most plainly the enduring disadvantages of class and sex which are built into British society', ibid.
83. K. Marx and F. Engels, *The Communist Manifesto*, p. 105.
84. K. Marx, *The Class Struggles in France*, pp. 121–2 (emphasis added).
85. K. Marx, 'Instructions for Delegates to the Geneva Congress', in D. Fernbach (ed), *The First International and After*, vol. 3, p. 89 (emphasis added).
86. *Minutes of General Council of the First International*, 10 August 1869, quoted in S. Padover (ed), *The Essential Marx*, p. 224 (emphasis added).
87. K. Marx, 'Critique of the Gotha Programme', p. 28 (emphasis added).
88. Labour Party, *The Old World and the New Society* (London, 1942) p. 11.
89. Labour Party, *Labour's Programme* (London, 1982) p. 115.
90. Ibid.
91. N. Kinnock, *New Socialist* (March–April 1983) p. 13.
92. R. Titmuss, intro. to R.H.Tawney, *Equality*, p. 11; but, confusingly, the purpose of education is also to 'make them . . . more capable of fulfilling their personal differences', ibid., p. 15.
93. J.Westergaard, 'The Withering Away of Class: A Contemporary Myth', in P. Anderson and R. Blackburn, *Towards Socialism*, pp. 90–2; cf. R. Titmuss, 'earning power, life chances, achievement, position and class, and even the level of pension in old age depend on education and training', 'Goals of Today's Welfare State', ibid., p. 358.
94. R. H. Tawney, *The Radical Tradition*, p.53.
95. R. H. Tawney, *Equality*, pp. 144–5.
96. J. Seabrook, *Unemployment*, p. 54.

97.   M. Arnold, *Culture and Anarchy*, p. 65.

98.   J. Seabrook, *Unemployment*, p. 74.

99.   T. Burgess, 'Democratic Socialism and Education', in D. Lipsey and D. Leonard, *Socialist Agenda*, p. 204.

100.   R. Titmuss, intro. to R. H. Tawney, *Equality*, pp. 11–12.

101.   R. Titmuss, 'Goals of Today's Welfare State', p. 362.

102.   R. Williams, *The Long Revolution*, p. 364.

103.   R. Williams, *Culture and Society*, p. 317.

104.   Cf. A. Crosland, 'it would be absurd from a socialist point of view to close down the grammar schools, while leaving the public schools still holding their present commanding position', *The Future of Socialism*, p. 275; but it was precisely this 'absurdity' which was achieved by the Labour Party in office.

105.   J. S. Mill, 'Coleridge' (1840), in *Mill on Bentham and Coleridge* (London, 1950) p. 105.

106.   R. H. Tawney, *The Radical Tradition*, pp. 60–1.

107.   A. Crosland, *The Future of Socialism*, p. 275; cf. 'the provision of free and universally available services will not enhance social equality if they are much inferior to the corresponding private services', ibid., p. 146. Also, 'the social values of a public school background would become worthless in a country where popular education was successfully installed', J. Bellini, *Rule Britannia*, p. 168; he bluntly (and correctly) calls the 'rise of popular education' a 'confidence-trick', ibid., p. 98.

108.   A. Crosland, *The Future of Socialism*, p. 265 (emphasis added).

109.   R. Titmuss, 'Goals of Today's Welfare State', p. 359.

110.   R. H. Tawney, *The Radical Tradition*, pp. 63–4.

111.   A. Crosland, *The Future of Socialism*, p. 277; 'the gap in standards remains very wide, and the private schoolboy in fact enjoys an incomparably superior education', ibid., p. 144.

112.   Ibid., p. 260.

113.   Ibid., p. 262.

114.   R. Williams, *Culture and Society*, pp. 18, 311; 'with the extension of education, the distribution of this culture [sc. as 'a body of intellectual and imaginative work'] is becoming more even' (!) ibid., p. 311.

115.   F. Cripps *et al.*, *Manifesto*, p. 214.

116.   Ibid.

117.   A. Sofer, SDP member of the GLC, quoted in the *Guardian*, 12 October 1982.

118.   F. Cripps *et al.*, *Manifesto*, p. 214.

119.   Ibid., p. 148 ('we envisage a reform of government which will ensure that people know what is really happening, are free to express their own views and, by debate as well as by election, are able to determine the conduct of government nationally').

120.   A. Benn, *Arguments for Socialism*, p. 178.

121.   A. Smith, *Wealth of Nations*, vol. 2, pp. 781–2; cf. 'the uneducated state of the "lower orders" . . . is the dark den of incendiarism and misrule . . . which, if not cleared out, will give birth ere long to disastrous corruptions in every province', A. Ure, *The Philosophy of Manufactures*, p. 404. Engels also refers to 'factory work' as in general inducing 'stupefaction', but says that '[cotton] operatives have, nevertheless, not only rescued their

intelligence, but cultivated and sharpened it more than other working men', *The Condition of the Working Class in England in 1844* (London, 1950) p. 177.

122. K. Marx, 'The Holy Family', in K. Marx and F. Engels, *Collected Works*, vol. 4, p. 131.

123. F. de Tocqueville, *Journeys to England and Ireland* (1835) (London, 1958) p. 108.

124. D. H. Lawrence, 'Nottingham and the Mining Country' (1929), in *Selected Essays* (Harmondsworth, 1950) p. 119; 'the great crime which the moneyed classes and promoters of industry committed in the palmy Victorian days was the condemning of the workers to ugliness, ugliness, ugliness: meanness, and formless and ugly surroundings, ugly ideals, ugly religion, ugly hope, ugly love, ugly clothes, ugly furniture, ugly houses, ugly relationship [*sic*] between workers and employers', ibid., p. 120. (Interestingly, Lawrence has plagiarized this passage from G. Gissing's description of Dickens' times as 'a time of ugliness: ugly religion, ugly law, ugly relations between rich and poor, ugly clothes, ugly furniture', *Charles Dickens: A Critical Study* (London, 1904) p. 14.)

125. J. S. Mill, *On Liberty*, pp. 190–1.

126. Ibid., p. 191.

127. K. Joseph and J. Sumption, *Equality*, p. 60.

128. M. Friedman, *Free to Choose*, pp. 157–8.

129. Ibid., p. 192.

130. Ibid., p. 204.

131. K. Joseph and J. Sumption, *Equality*, p. 94; described as an 'enormity', ibid.

132. M. Arnold, *Culture and Anarchy*, p. 196; also, 'vast, miserable, unmanageable masses of sunken people', ibid., p. 193.

133. J. Seabrook, *Unemployment*, p. 136; he also refers to 'the lack of common cause' between them, and argues that the 'old epic of labour' is 'surely finished as far as the young are concerned', p. 139.

134. A. Crosland, *The Future of Socialism*, pp. 527–8; cf. P. Townsend, *Poverty in The United Kingdom*, pp. 413–542, on the forms and scale of deprivation in Britain, including the environmental.

135. Home Office, *Criminal Statistics: England and Wales* (London, 1982) Cmnd. 9048, and Home Office, *Criminal Statistics* (1982), *Supplementary Tables*, vol. 4, pp. 10–22.

136. R. H. Tawney, 'Social Democracy in Britain' (1949), *The Radical Tradition*, p. 162; but cf. 'they [sc. the 'members' of a 'well-ordered society'] do what seems best to them as judged by their own plan of life without being dismayed by the greater amenities and enjoyments of others', J. Rawls, *Theory of Justice*, p. 544.

137. Cf. R. H. Tawney, *The Radical Tradition*, p. 173.

138. Cf. I. Crowther, *Salisbury Review* (Spring 1983) p. 41.

139. R. Williams, *The Long Revolution*, p. 234.

140. M. Arnold, *Culture and Anarchy*, p. 130.

CHAPTER 5

1. Cf. 'Private interest is itself already a socially determined interest, which

can be achieved only within the conditions laid down by society and with the means provided by society; hence it is bound to the reproduction of these conditions and means', K. Marx, *Grundrisse*, p. 156; cf. 'what has then really failed, inside the labour movement and in the whole society, is any accepted concept of the general interest', R. Williams, *Towards 2000*, p. 165.

2.   C. Calhoun, *Question of Class Struggle*, p. 126.

3.   K. Marx, 'The Poverty of Philosophy', in K. Marx and F. Engels, *Collected Works*, vol. 6, p. 210, and see R. Hyman, *Marxism and the Sociology of Trade Unionism* (London, 1971) pp. 4–14.

4.   K. Marx and F. Engels, *The Communist Manifesto*, p. 90.

5.   K. Marx, *Wages, Prices and Profit* (Moscow, 1974) pp. 54–5.

6.   F. Engels, *The Condition of the Working Class in England*, pp. 219, 224.

7.   F. Engels, letter to E. Bernstein, 17 June 1879, in K. Marx and F. Engels, *Selected Correspondence* (Moscow, 1953) p. 386; two years later, the 'worst type of British trade unions' were 'led by men who have been bought by the capitalists, or at least are in their pay', F. Engels, letter of 11 August 1881, quoted by V. I. Lenin, *Imperialism, The Highest State of Capitalism*, in *Collected Works*, vol. 22, p. 284.

8.   V. I. Lenin, 'On Strikes' (1899), *Collected Works*, vol. 4, p. 317.

9.   V. I. Lenin, 'What is to be Done?', *Selected Works*, vol. 1 (Moscow, 1947) pp. 175, 177.

10. V. I. Lenin, 'Lecture on the 1905 Revolution' (1917), *Collected Works*, vol. 23, p. 242; and see T. T. Hammond, *Lenin on Trade Unions and Revolution, 1893–1917* (New York, 1957) esp. pp. 90–122.

11. A. Gramsci, *L'Ordine Nuovo*, 8 November 1919, in *Selections from Political Writings, 1910–1920*, ed. Q. Hoare (London, 1977) p. 110.

12. L. Trotsky, 'The Unions in Britain' (1933), in *Leon Trotsky on the Trade Unions* (New York, 1969) p. 54; but cf. 'the Chartist epoch . . . gave us . . . the whole gamut of proletarian struggle – from petition in Parliament to armed insurrection . . . the British proletariat may and must see in Chartism not only its past, but also its future . . . Chartism is not by any means liquidated . . . There you have the original national tradition of the British Labour Movement', L. Trotsky, *Where is Britain Going?*, pp. 99–100. He calls this 'the truly proletarian, revolutionary tradition', ibid., p. 99.

13. P. Anderson, 'The Limits and Possibilities of Trade Union Action' in R. Blackburn and A. Cockburn (eds), *The Incompatibles* (Harmondsworth, 1967) p. 264.

14. S. Bamford, *Walks in South Lancashire*, p. 21.

15. Cf., e.g., Lenin's abrasive objection that 'industrial workers cannot fulfil their world historical mission of liberating humanity from the yoke of capital if they . . . self-contentedly restrict themselves to improving their sometimes tolerable *petit-bourgeois* position', in *British Labour and British Imperialism* (London, 1969) p. 67; B. de Jouvenel, *Problems of Socialist England* (London, 1949) pp. 134–45; and note I. Gilmour's mordant observation that 'trade unionism . . . must be permitted to indulge in its own capitalism if it so chooses. Of course, ordinary capitalists and trade union capitalists [*sic*] have different objects and different functions, and so

are likely not to agree; hence some machinery and special efforts are needed to weave them together' (!), *Britain Can Work*, p. 204. Also, 'the movement of so many trade unions and so many wage-earners towards the principle of economic competition has radically weakened the idea of an alternative . . . what *will now happen* is either the final incorporation of the labour movement into a capitalist bargaining mechanism . . . or the wide remaking of a social movement', R. Williams, *Towards 2000*, p. 172 (emphasis added). But it is not a question of what 'will now happen'; the former has happened, and long ago.

16. J. Meade, 'The Fixing of Money Rates of Pay' in D. Lipsey and D. Leonard, *Socialist Agenda*, pp. 78–9 (and, of course, 'keeping ahead of the Joneses', etc., ibid., p. 83).

17. R. H. Tawney, 'The Conditions of Economic Liberty', *The Radical Tradition*, pp. 107–8; in order that workers can exercise 'their corporate power to control the *conditions* upon which their livelihood depends', ibid. (emphasis added).

18. R. H. Tawney, *Equality*, p. 119; that is, the trade unions are merely perceived by Tawney to 'set limits to the ability of one group to impose its will, by economic duress, upon another, and thus soften inequalities of economic power', ibid.

19. L. Trotsky, *Where is Britain Going?*, pp. 104–5.

20. C. Attlee, *The Labour Party in Perspective*, p.141.

21. Cf. 'while the trade union movement may contain political reaction, cultural inertia or bureaucracy, it also contains – block votes or no – a greater element of democracy than any other organization within working class life', and 'more democratic involvement of more working class people than any other experience', P. Corrigan, *New Statesman*, 3 December 1982. The same point seems to be made, obscurely, in 'the union introduces the worker into a new ideological and relational universe [*sic*], however minimally. It creates its own loyalty . . . and its own logic – a logic which leads to Labour allegiance', P. Anderson, 'Problems of Socialist Strategy', p. 263; but cf. 'logic is fatal to Labourism', T. Nairn, ibid., p. 202.

22. P. Green, *Pursuit of Inequality*, p. 234.

23. Cf. A. Gramsci, 'in many respects a union leader represents a social type similar to the banker . . . a banker of men', *L'Ordine Nuovo*, 30 October 1921, in *Selections from Political Writings, 1921-1926*, ed. Q.Hoare (London, 1978) p. 77.

24. W. Lovett, *The Life and Struggles of William Lovett*, vol. 1 (London, 1920) p. 42.

25. L. Trotsky, *Where is Britain Going?*, p. 111.

26. A. Smith, *Wealth of Nations*, vol. 1, p. 85, and 'workmen . . . very seldom derive any advantage from the violence of these tumultuous combinations', ibid. Cf. 'Labour . . . responded to the challenge of capitalism in a way that Adam Smith did not anticipate . . . and combined into trade unions to defend their interests by collective wage bargaining', A. Benn, *Arguments for Socialism*, p. 143. This is precisely what Adam Smith anticipated.

27. H. Pelling, *Origins of the Labour Party*, p. 199.

28. A. Scargill, *Guardian*, 26 October 1982; the National Coal Board was also referred to as 'the bosses', ibid.

29. Cf. M. Friedman, who describes the trade unions as 'conservative investors in job property', *Free to Choose*, p. 280. C. B. Macpherson takes a more positive view: to think of 'the workers' main property as his right to the job' is 'to see (or to come close to seeing) as one's property a right of access to some of the existent means of labour, that is, to some of the accumulated productive resources of the whole society, no matter by whom they are owned', *Democratic Theory*, p. 135.

30. R. Bahro, *Socialism and Survival*, pp. 48, 20.

31. K. Marx, 'Wage-Labour and Capital', in K. Marx and F. Engels, *Selected Works*, vol. 1, p. 171; 'the workers do not only compete by one selling himself cheaper than another; they compete by one doing the work of five, ten, twenty', ibid. But despite the organic relationship between such labour competition and the market system itself, the ingenuousness of left responses and reproaches never abates; e.g. 'you [sc. trade unionists] have allowed yourselves to be presented to the public as if you actively favoured the conservative philosophy of personal acquisitiveness', A. Benn, *Speeches*, ed. J. Bodington (Nottingham, 1974) p. 285. Similarly, R. Williams complained (in 1961) of the 'visible moral decline of the labour movement . . . a set of men playing the market in very much the terms of the employers they oppose', *The Long Revolution*, p. 328; this 'crisis' was 'not yet permanently resolved', ibid., p. 319.

32. K. Marx and F. Engels, *The Communist Manifesto*, p. 90; 'the organization of the proletarians into a class, and consequently into a political party, is continually being upset again by the competition between the workers themselves, But it ever rises up again, stronger', ibid. In the meantime, this is a world of 'wages drift', 'differentials', 'special cases' and so on.

33. A. Benn, *Arguments for Democracy*, p. 131.

34. R. H. Tawney, *Equality*, pp. 40–1.

35. G. Rudé, *The Crowd*, pp. 139–40; cf. undaunted by the tumbrils, 'a maximum income limit would be the most important step towards a general narrowing of inequality of incomes and raising low wages and benefits', F. Cripps *et al.*, *Manifesto*, p. 187. Two hundred years ago, such a limit took a revolution to secure and a counterrevolution to remove.

36. 'The Cotton Lords of Preston' (1853), a strike ballad quoted in A. Clayre, *Nature and Industrialization*, pp. 168–9.

37. J. Ruskin, *Stones of Venice*, vol. 2, p. 149.

38. K. Marx, 'Inaugural Address to the First International' (1864), in D. Fernbach (ed), *Political Writings*, p. 79.

39. J. Ruskin, *Stones of Venice*, p. 149.

40. R. H. Tawney, *Equality*, pp. 42, 177.

41. W. (Lord) McCarthy, 'Socialism and Incomes Policy', D. Lipsey and D. Leonard, *Socialist Agenda*, p. 112.

42. Ibid., pp.112, 114; McCarthy calls the 'going-rate' a 'fascinating [*sic*] but elusive concept', p. 112.

43. S. Holland, in K. Coates (ed), *What Went Wrong*, pp. 219–20; 'in other words, even at the sub-structure of the system, trades union bargaining is marginalized under present conditions', ibid., p. 220.

44. A. Benn, *Arguments for Democracy*, p. 165; cf. 'the annual pay round is not a battle against capitalism but an ugly competitive struggle within the working class itself', B. Pimlott, *New Society*, 23 and 30 December 1982.

45. A. Freeman, *The Benn Heresy*, p. 90.

46. Cf. C. Calhoun's account of the essentially defensive policies of early trade unionism, *Question of Class Struggle*, e.g. pp. 42 ff.

47. R. Luxemburg, *Social Reform or Revolution* (1900) (London, n.d.) p. 53.

48. M. Friedman, *Free to Choose*, p. 276; and 'the gains that strong unions win for their members are primarily at the expense of other workers', ibid.

49. R. Bahro, *Socialism and Survival*, p. 81; 'the word "lost" shows how we socialists are trapped by the logic of capital', ibid.

50. Ibid., p. 82.

51. Cf. K. Marx and F. Engels, *The Communist Manifesto*, p. 86.

52. F. Engels, quoted in Y. Kapp, *Eleanor Marx*, vol. 1, p. 207.

53. For the archaism of British institutions see T. Nairn, *The Break-up of Britain* (London, 1977) *passim*, but esp. pp. 14–44, 291–302; cf. 'there is a . . . mismatch between our ancient political institutions, which are geared to a modified *laissez-faire* economy, and the political activities which are necessary both to deal with the "interests" and to guide the economic affairs of the nation', I. Gilmour, *Britain Can Work*, p. 220.

54. F. A. Hayek, *1980s Unemployment and the Unions* (Institute of Economic Affairs, London, 1980) p. 52.

55. N. Tebbit, Tory Party Conference, 1982, quoted in *Guardian*, 8 October 1982; but such a view is not confined to the right of the Tory Party, Cf. '. . . Britain has probably the most legally privileged unions in the world', I. Gilmour, *Britain Can Work*, p. 107.

56. F. A. Hayek, *1980s Unemployment*, p. 52.

57. M. Friedman, *Free to Choose*, p. 271; 'today [in the US] fewer than one worker in four is a member of a union', ibid., p. 270.

58. Ibid., p. 286. Strangely, a specialized version of this contradiction is also to be found in Lenin; in May 1899 he refers to 'the enormous strength of the organized trade unions' in Britain as one of the factors which 'weaken [*sic*] the antagonism between the British employers and workers', in *British Labour and British Imperialism*, p. 25; but, in 1916, he protests that 'it cannot be seriously believed that it is possible to organize the majority of the proletariat under capitalism', ibid., pp. 148–9.

59. M. Friedman, *Free to Choose*, p. 271 ('a throwback . . . to the guilds').

60. M. Alison, Tory Party Conference 1982, quoted in *Guardian*, 6 October, 1982 ('a new spectre is stalking the corridors of power of the British trade union movement. That spectre is democracy, and it is democracy they fear.')

61. M. Friedman, *Free to Choose*, p. 280.

62. F. A. Hayek, BBC2 interview, 23 September 1982.

63. P. Carter (midlands region organizer, UCATT), *Marxism Today* (Nov 1982) p. 36; also 'the closed shop . . . has not necessarily increased member commitment to trade unionism: it has "depoliticized" the idea of union membership', P. Hain, *Democratic Alternative*, p. 23; cf. 'freedom for a group of workers to associate in order to press jointly a claim to a given rate of pay is one thing. Freedom for that group of workers to insist that no

other workers shall be employed in that occupation without their permission is a totally different and objectionable privilege', J. Meade, 'The Fixing of Money Rates of Pay', in D. Lipsey and D. Leonard, *Socialist Agenda*, p. 95.

64. K. Marx, *Capital* vol. 3, p. 800.

65. E.g. see P. Kahn and A. Scargill, *The Myth of Workers' Control*, Occasional Papers no. 5 (Leeds/Nottingham, 1980) p. 9.

66. C. Calhoun, *Question of Class Struggle*, p. xii; indeed, his general argument is that such foundations, being essentially communal, were undermined rather than strengthened by industrial development and factory organization. Cf. 'Labour socialism . . . has steadily increased [*sic*] its political strength ever since the class structure of our society polarized under the impact of industrialization', F. Cripps *et al.*, *Manifesto*, p. 168.

67. 'To organize and maintain in Parliament and in the country a political Labour Party', *Labour Party Constitution*, (26 Feb 1918), clause 3a; cf. 'Most of the non-Socialist trade union leaders would have been happy to stay in the Liberal Party . . . if the Liberals had made arrangements for a larger representation of the working class among their Parliamentary candidates', H. Pelling, *Origins of the Labour Party*, p. 272. Also see F. Bealey (ed), *The Social and Political Thought of the British Labour Party* (London, 1970), R. McKibbin, *The Evolution of the Labour Party, 1910–1924* (Oxford, 1974), and J. Hinton, *Labour and Socialism: A History of the British Labour Movement, 1867–1974* (Brighton, 1983).

68. H. Pelling, *Origins of the Labour Party*, p. 227; and 'the early components of the Labour Party formed a curious mixture of political idealists and hard-headed trade unionists: of convinced Socialists and loyal but disheartened Gladstonians', ibid., p. 225.

69. R. H. Tawney, *Equality*, p. 206.

70. L. Trotsky, *Where is Britain Going?*, p. 34.

71. Ibid., pp. 8, 35.

72. R. H. Tawney, 'British Socialism Today' (1952), *The Radical Tradition*, p. 177.

73. T. Nairn, 'The Nature of the Labour Party', p. 180.

74. Cf. 'the powerful labour movement' – unproblematically perceived – 'with its democratic traditions', A. Benn, *Arguments for Democracy*, p. 181 (after the contrary imputation at p. 166); and see F. Cripps *et al.*, *Manifesto*: 'the paradox of union leaders, subject to periodic re-election, voting against the same principle for MPs as representatives of the Labour Party, is only equalled by that of union leaders, elected or appointed for life, who are advocates of mandatory reselection', p. 172. Alternatively, 'the Party has begun to throw off the stifling, Tammany Hall, narrow politics of the past', P. Hain, *Democratic Alternative*, p. 9.

75. For the lack of trade union interest in planning agreements, see, e.g., CSE London Working Group, *Alternative Economic Strategy*, pp. 67 ff.

76. Cf. 'He [Michael Foot] pleaded with the conference to believe that the best guide to conduct in the present critical situation was a defence of the party's constitution, which he described as a very precious instrument. Many other socialist movements had come to grief in sectarian struggle because they lacked such a sheet anchor', Labour Party Conference,

Blackpool, 1982, quoted in *Guardian*, 29 September 1982. Also see S. Hall, *Marxism Today* (Nov 1982) p. 20.

77. CSE London Working Group, *Alternative Economic Strategy*, pp. 6–7. But cf. e.g. Commission for Racial Equality, *Massey-Ferguson Perkins Ltd: Formal Information Report* (London, Dec 1982). Published after a four-year inquiry, it reported (p. 2) on the 'apathy and inertia' of the AUEW and TGWU in the face of discrimination against blacks at Massey-Ferguson, Coventry; the mere tip of the iceberg of trade union racism.

78. Cf. F. Parkin, *Middle-class Radicalism*, pp. 40–59, on the 'middle-class basis of CND'; for another view, B. Pimlott, *New Statesman*, 8 October 1982 on the commitment of some trade unions to unilateralism, and B. Pimlott and C. Cook (eds), *Trade Unions in British Politics* (London, 1982).

79. E.g. 'Labourism . . . has imprisoned socialism instead of liberating it, and deformed its whole development', T. Nairn, 'The Nature of the Labour Party' , p. 188; for an extended diatribe on 'labourism', see R. Miliband, *Parliamentary Socialism* (London, 1973) pp. 272–349.

80. L. Trotsky, *Where is Britain Going?*, p. 58.

81. M. Arnold, *Culture and Anarchy*, p. 105.

82. K. Marx, 'Wage-Labour and Capital', in K. Marx and F. Engels, *Selected Works*, vol. 1, p. 163.

83. At 1982 Labour Party Conference, Blackpool, *Guardian*, 27 and 28 September 1982.

84. R. H. Tawney, 'British Socialism Today', *The Radical Tradition*, p. 176.

85. T. Ali, in P. Hain (ed), *Crisis and The Future of the Left*, p. 74; and 'the Labour Party cannot deliver the goods', ibid., p. 73.

86. E.g. T. Nairn, 'The Nature of the Labour Party' ('realism turns, in Labour leaders, into mere cowardice . . ., practicality . . . into wilful shortsightedness . . . to exorcise the sort of theoretical thinking socialism requires').

87. P. Anderson, 'Problems of Socialist Strategy', p. 285.

88. A. Benn, *Arguments for Democracy*, p. 171; 'and there is no reason to think that it will not respond to the challenge', ibid. (except that the double negative itself belies such confidence).

89. A. Crosland, *The Future of Socialism*, p. 459.

90. L.Trotsky, *Where is Britain Going?*, p. 71; and 'if a real Labour Government came to power in Britain even in the most ultra-democratic manner, a civil war would be inevitable', ibid.

91. R. H. Tawney, *The Radical Tradition*, pp. 171–2 ('that the state is the executive of the capitalist class . . . is a pessimistic bluff'); cf. 'men do not burn down the house which they intend to occupy, even though they regard its existing tenant as a public nuisance', R. H. Tawney, *Equality*, p. 98.

92. R. H. Tawney, ibid., p. 41; the 'bearing' of the 'leaders of the working class movement . . . not infrequently recalls less the tribune than the courtier', ibid., pp. 40–1.

CHAPTER 6

1. But cf. 'the *connections* between . . . the defence of civil liberties and

Against Socialist Illusion

illustration [*sic*] of utopian virtues are where collective work is now most
wanting and most necessary', P. Anderson, *Arguments within English
Marxism*, p. 205 (emphasis in original); what this means – if anything – is
unclear, but at least it points towards the correct 'problematic'.

2. Also see B. Hindess, *The Decline of Working Class Politics* (London, 1971);
and P. Whiteley, *Labour Party in Crisis*, pp. 61–4.

3. A notable exception is E. P. Thompson, *Writing by Candlelight* (London,
1980) pp. 94–133, 149–256, which contains some of the finest adversarial
prose written since Hazlitt.

4. Cf. 'The case for an educated and participatory democracy has again to be
made', R. Williams, *Towards 2000*, p. 104; for a characteristic recent
example of the genre, see P. Hain, *Democratic Alternative*, pp. 40 ff.:
'devolution must be given real teeth', ibid., p. 45, 'involving ordinary [*sic*]
people themselves', p. 46. He also calls for an 'alternative state', pp. 41–3,
based upon 'full participation', p. 83.

5. F. Cripps *et al.*, *Manifesto*, p. 121; yet, three pages earlier, 'the Labour
Party of the future must adopt again a class strategy', ibid., p. 118.

6. A. Benn, *Arguments for Democracy*, p. 164.

7. Hence, 'the trade union bureaucracy is itself heavily implicated in
defending Britain's state, both at home and abroad', A. Freeman, *The
Benn Heresy*, p. 108; this is in particular true of the TUC's International
Department.

8. C. B. Macpherson, *Life and Times of Liberal Democracy*, p. 105 (emphasis
added); cf. 'what a theoretical blindness, seeing *nothing* outside the factory
gates', R. Bahro, *Socialism and Survival*, p. 64 (emphasis added).

9. C. Calhoun, *Question of Class Struggle*, p. 48.

10. E.g. cf. M. Rustin, *New Socialist* (March–April 1982) p. 31.

11. R. Williams, *Towards 2000*, p. 13.

12. Ibid., p. 14; cf. E. P. Thompson's view that utopianism is 'not beyond the
criticism of sense and feeling, although the procedures must be closer to
those of creative literature than those of political theory', *William Morris:
Romantic to Revolutionary* (London, 1977) p. 793; also P. Anderson,
Arguments within English Marxism, pp. 157–75.

13. M. Foot, Labour Party Conference Blackpool 1982, *Guardian*, 29 September 1982.

14. T. Nairn, *Guardian*, 13 January 1983; the irony is directed at Tony Benn.

15. D. Selbourne, in L. Mackay and D. Fernbach (eds), *Nuclear-Free Defence*
(London, 1983) pp. 103–6.

16. The term, particularly in the form of 'grass-roots democracy', has become
an incantation; cf. P. Hain who calls for 'state policies designed to mesh in
[*sic*] with a wider grass-roots strategy for social mobilization', *Democratic
Alternative*, p. 54; 'the industrial grass roots', P. Jenkins, *Guardian*, 27
September 1982; the term approved of, R. Williams, *Towards 2000*, p. 124;
and 'grass-roots democracy' as a means of 'facilitating social learning', R.
Bahro, *Socialism and Survival*, p. 34. And even, D. Berry, *The Sociology of
Grass Roots Politics* (London, 1970).

17. E.g. P. Foot, who calls for the 'transformation of society into an egalitarian
democracy . . . from the bottom up', P. Hain (ed), *Crisis and the Future of the
Left*, p. 41.

18. Ibid., pp. 33–4; cf. 'the odious label of the "rank and file"', T. Nairn, 'The Nature of the Labour Party', p. 177.

19. R. Williams, *Towards 2000*, p. 124.

20. A. Benn, *Arguments for Democracy*, p. 17.

21. Cf. V. I. Lenin, at the end of 1907, on British 'municipal socialism', which he describes as a 'specific trend [to be found] chiefly in England'. Its preoccupation with 'minor questions of local government' – including 'tramways' – is 'extremely opportunist'; it is also, he argues, 'philistine', 'reactionary' and 'particularly hopeless'. Why? Because, according to Lenin, 'as long as it rules as a class, the bourgeoisie cannot allow any encroachment, even from the "municipal" point of view, upon the real foundation of its rule . . . Any attempt on the part of socialist municipalities' – as at the GLC or in Sheffield! – 'to go a little beyond the boundaries of their normal i.e. petty activities . . . is invariably and absolutely vetoed in the most categorical fashion by the central government of the bourgeois state', in *British Labour and British Imperialism*, p. 91.

22. R. Williams, *Towards 2000*, pp. 123–5; ('it is my belief that the only kind of socialism which now stands any chance of being established, in the old industrialized bourgeois-democratic societies, is one centrally [!] based on new kinds of communal, cooperative and collective institutions', ibid., p. 123); cf. M. Raptis, who describes 'self-management' as 'express[ing] essentially the deep desire of the broad masses of people . . . to manage their labour and their entire social life directly. In this respect, self management is a new aspiration', *Socialism, Democracy and Self-Management*, p. 177. In fact, it is one of the oldest themes of political theory.

23. A. H. Halsey, *Change in British Society* (Oxford, 1978) p. 85.

24. C. B. Macpherson, *Life and Times of Liberal Democracy*, p. 94; but cf. the view that there is 'little warrant for the widespread belief that increased political participation leads to a more equitable distribution of income', I. Adelman and C. T. Morris, *Economic Growth and Social Equity in Developing Countries* (Stanford, 1973) p. 187.

25. A. Freeman, *The Benn Heresy*, p. 24; cf. 'as long as inequality is accepted the non-participatory political system is likely also to be accepted by all those in all classes who prefer stability to the prospect of complete social breakdown', C. B. Macpherson, *Life and Times of Liberal Democracy*, p. 100.

26. A. Benn, *Speeches*, p. 38.

27. T. Nairn, 'The Nature of the Labour Party' p. 186; this 'passion' or 'neurotic subjectivity' is the 'obverse of its ideological subjection', ibid.

28. K. Marx, 'Theses on Feuerbach', in K. Marx and F. Engels, *Selected Works*, vol. 1, p. 13.

29. K. Coates, 'Democracy and Workers' Control', in P. Anderson and R. Blackburn, *Towards Socialism*, p. 316; this is called 'democratic self-regulation', ibid., p. 315.

30. M. Raptis, *Socialism, Democracy and Self-Management*, p. 194 (emphasis added).

31. Ibid., pp. 195–6 (emphasis added).

32. P. Anderson, 'Problems of Socialist Strategy', pp. 244–5 (emphasis added).

33. V. I. Lenin, 'Theses on Bourgeois Democracy and the Proletarian

Dictatorship' (1919), in *Collected Works*, vol. 28, p. 466 (emphasis added).

34. R. Luxemburg, *The Russian Revolution* (Michigan, 1961) pp. 67, 71, 76–7 (emphasis added); cf. J. Bentham, 'the more ample the extent given to any proposition or string of propositions, the more difficult it is to keep the import of it confined without deviation within the bounds of truth and reason', 'A Critical Examination of the Declaration of Rights', in B. Parekh (ed), *Bentham's Political Thought*, p. 258; and 'it is not easy to avoid a certain irritation when one hears the word "participation". Not only has it become [sc. in 1956] a catchphrase, bandied about as though it were a nostrum for every social evil, but those who preach it hardest appear to think that . . . we must all be herded into participating groups of one kind or another', A. Crosland, *The Future of Socialism*, p. 340.

35. P. Anderson, in P. Anderson and R. Blackburn, *Towards Socialism*, p. 279.

36. M. Raptis, *Socialism, Democracy and Self-Management*, p. 151.

37. R. H. Tawney, *The Radical Tradition*, p. 149; he calls this a 'venerable phrase'. Yet in his *Equality* he argues that 'inequality of power is inherent in the nature of organized society', p. 112.

38. A. Crosland, *The Future of Socialism*, p. 247.

39. M. Raptis, *Socialism, Democracy and Self-Management*, pp. 143, 147 (emphasis added).

40. P. Green, *Pursuit of Inequality*, p. 240 (emphasis added); cf. 'decisions, in a democratic society, must ultimately be made *by the people as a whole*', A. Benn, *Arguments for Democracy*, p. 101 (emphasis added); also, ibid., p. 170, and *Arguments for Socialism*, p. 60.

41. F. Cripps *et al.*, *Manifesto*, p. 167; 'people would need to have a real chance individually [*sic*] to influence, and collectively to determine, policy making at national and local level', ibid., p. 126.

42. A. Benn, *Parliament, People and Power: Agenda for a Free Society* (London, 1982) (blurb).

43. M. Friedman, *Free to Choose*, p. 43.

44. Ibid., p. 9.

45. Ibid., p. 25; and e.g. cf. E. Luard, *Socialism Without The State* (London, 1979) and D. Marquand, 'Inquest on a Movement', *Encounter*, vol. 53, no. 1 (July 1979) pp. 8–18.

46. A. Benn, *Arguments for Democracy*, p. 29.

47. M. Friedman, *Free to Choose*, p. 14.

48. Ibid., p. 22.

49. Ibid., p. 359.

50. For an example of discussions which the left does not conduct, cf. R. Dworkin, *Taking Rights Seriously* (London, 1979) pp. 184–205, 266–278.

51. K. Marx and F. Engels, *The German Ideology* (London, 1965) p. 83; three years later, this 'self-activity' was visualized in the form of an association in which the free development of each is the condition for the free development of all', *The Communist Manifesto*, p. 105. But in the next section of the *Manifesto*, Marx and Engels themselves castigate the 'utopian' socialists – St Simon, Fourier, Owen – for their 'fantastic pictures of future society' and their 'castles in the air', ibid., pp. 116–17.

52. K. Marx and F. Engels, 'Address of the Central Committee to the

Communist League' (March 1850), *Selected Works*, vol. 1, p. 183 (emphasis added).

53. K. Marx, 'The Chartists' (August 1852), in K. Marx and F. Engels, *Collected Works*, vol. 11, p. 335.
54. L. Trotsky, *Where is Britain Going?*, pp. 68–9.
55. Ibid., p. 79.
56. Ibid., pp. 129–30.
57. Editorial, *Les Temps Modernes*, 6 June 1968; also, 'the revolution will be based on the initiative of the masses, on the exercise of dual power by action committees of strikers and workers', ibid. Cf. E. Mandel, 'The Lessons of May 1968', *New Left Review*, no. 52 (Nov–Dec 1968) pp. 9–31; 'it is only a beginning. The struggle will go on', ibid., p. 31.
58. Cf. A. Benn, *New Socialist* (March–April 1983) p. 10; S. Holland in K. Coates (ed) *What Went Wrong*, pp. 246–7; also 'open press and media', ibid., pp. 247–8.
59. F. Cripps *et al.*, *Manifesto*, p. 76.
60. Cf. C. B. Macpherson, *Life and Times of Liberal Democracy*, esp. pp. 95–7; 'by giving the appearance of being democratic the system would conceal the reallocation of power and would thus enable "democratic" governments to be more autocratic than they are now', ibid., p. 97.
61. E. Mandel, *Marxist Theory of the State*, p. 29.
62. J. Bellini, *Rule Britannia*, p. 89.
63. N. Poulantzas, *State, Power, Socialism* (London, 1978) p. 265.
64. B. Goodwin and K. Taylor, *Politics of Utopia*, p. 21.
65. Ibid., p. 58.
66. See R. Nozick, *Anarchy, State and Utopia*, pp. 26–53, 88–119, and 297–334 ('a framework for utopia'); H. Marcuse, *An Essay on Liberation*, pp. 33 ff; J. P. Narayan, *Socialism, Sarvodaya and Democracy*, ed. B. Prasad (London, 1964) and D. Selbourne (ed), *In Theory and In Practice: Essays on the Politics of J. P. Narayan* (New Delhi and Oxford, 1984).
67. B. Russell, *Roads to Freedom*, p. 13; 'better . . . than the destructive and cruel chaos in which mankind have hitherto existed', ibid.
68. B. Goodwin and K. Taylor, *Politics of Utopia*, p. 210.
69. J. S. Mill, *On Liberty*, p. 12; cf. as rhetoric without real meaning, 'the human energy of the long revolution springs from the conviction that men can direct their own lives, by breaking through the pressures and restrictions of older forms of society, and by discovering new common institutions', R. Williams, *The Long Revolution*, p. 375.
70. E. Burke, *Reflections on the Revolution in France* (Harmondsworth, 1968) p. 151; in 'civil society . . . each person abdicates all right to be his own governor . . . [and] that he may secure some liberty, he makes a surrender in trust of the whole of it', ibid., p. 150.
71. E. Mandel, *Marxist Theory of the State*, p. 26.
72. J. Rawls, *Theory of Justice*, pp. 223–4.
73. Cf. A. Crosland, who (in the name of trade union 'independence') argues that 'the workers' side must have an untrammelled trade union movement to defend its claims', *The Future of Socialism*, p. 345. He calls this the unions' 'essential opposition freedom', a freedom which would be

compromised if they were 'enmeshed in, and committed to, the responsibilities of management', ibid., pp. 346–8. For a similar argument from the left, P. Kahn and A. Scargill, *Myth of Workers' Control, passim.*

74. M. Raptis, *Socialism, Democracy and Self-Management,* pp. 10, 144.
75. Ibid., p. 94.
76. A. Benn, *Arguments for Democracy,* pp. 49, 67.
77. M. Raptis, *Socialism, Democracy and Self-Management,* p. 75 ('there can be no doubt about the relatively quick returns of such an investment' (!) ibid., p. 77).
78. A. Benn, *Arguments for Socialism,* p. 179; cf. William Morris's 'society into which I would like to be reborn', a society which would have 'no consciousness of being governed', 'The Society of the Future' (1887), in A. L. Morton (ed), *Political Writings,* p. 201.
79. Cf., e.g., C. B. Macpherson's view that 'participation' is 'in the best tradition of liberal democracy', *Life and Times of Liberal Democracy,* p. 115.
80. B. Taylor. *Eve and the New Jerusalem,* p. 105; but, cf. R. Samuel, 'The Workshop of the World', *History Workshop Journal,* no. 3 (Spring 1977) pp. 6–72.
81. A. Gorz, *Farewell to the Working Class,* pp. 100–1.
82. See, e.g., H. Wainwright and D. Elliot, *The Lucas Plan: A New Trade Unionism in the Making?* (London, 1982); J. Seabrook, *What Went Wrong?* (London, 1978) pp. 246–54; M. Cooley, *Architect or Bee? The Human/ Technology Relationship* (Slough, n.d.) pp. 63–82.
83. A. Nove, 'The Soviet Economy: Problem and Prospects', *New Left Review,* no. 119 (Jan–Feb 1980) p. 7.
84. F. Cripps *et al., Manifesto,* pp. 147, 126.
85. A. Benn, *Arguments for Democracy,* p. 43.
86. F. Cripps *et al., Manifesto,* p. 164.
87. Ibid., p. 147.
88. A. Gorz, *Farewell to the Working Class,* p. 41.
89. A. Hirsh, *The French Left* (Montreal, 1982) pp. 210–11.
90. Ibid.
91. Cf. 'It is not conceivable that real political democracy could fail to lead to greater social equality and socialism', A. Benn, *Argument for Democracy',* p. xii. (But it is entirely conceivable; as the double negative again reveals.)
92. N. Poulantzas, *State, Power, Socialism,* pp. 251–65.
93. M. Levin, 'Marxism and Democracy', in G. Duncan (ed), *Democratic Theory and Practice* (Cambridge, 1983) p. 94; 'not only must we assume a highly participatory motivation as a generalized attribute of "socialist man", so also we must add to it a polymathic intelligence. As the necessary atributes mount up in terms of knowledge, ability and purpose, the result defies commonplace credibility', ibid.
94. A. Benn, *Arguments for Socialism,* p. 178.
95. F. Cripps *et al., Manifesto,* p. 148.
96. From an enormous literature, see F. Schumacher, *Small Is Beautiful* (London, 1973); G. McRobie, *Small is Possible* (London, 1981); R. Diwan and D. Livingston, *Alternative Development Strategies and Appropriate Technology* (New York, 1979); J. Galtung, *The True Worlds* (New York, 1980).
97. R. Bahro, *Socialism and Survival,* p. 24.
98. Ibid., pp. 21–2.

99. K. Marx and F. Engels, *The German Ideology*, p. 84.
100. F. Engels, *Anti-Dühring* (Moscow, 1959) pp. 386–91.
101. A Gorz, *Farewell to the Working Class*, p. 7.
102. W. Benjamin, *One-Way Street*, p. 358.
103. Ibid.
104. *Politics for Life*, manifesto of the Ecology Party, London, 1983, p. 3 ('printed on 100% recycled paper').
105. A. Bahro, *New Socialist* (Nov–Dec 1982) p. 49.
106. M. Allaby and P. Bunyard. *Politics of Self-Sufficiency*, p. 86.
107. R. Bahro, *Socialism and Survival*, p. 18; 'all those human energies involved in the evolution of civilization find themselves more or less implicated in the overall exterminist tendency', ibid., p. 152; also E. P. Thompson, 'Notes on Exterminism', *New Left Review*, no. 121 (May–June 1980) pp. 3–31.
108. E. Hobsbawm, *Marxism Today* (Oct 1982) p. 10.
109. D. Selbourne, *New Statesman*, 22 October 1982.
110. A. Herzen, *From the Other Shore*, p. 33.
111. For a recent study, see D. Burnham. *The Rise of the Computer State* (London, 1983).
112. D. Blunkett, *Guardian*, 10 January 1983; and 'we must go back [*sic*] to our tested and tried strategy of strong trade unions, closely linked to the party . . . we must work with the trade union movement; establish workplace branches . . .' A. Benn, *Arguments for Democracy*, pp. 191–2. Cf. 'what could still be achieved in Paris in 1871 by the internal class struggle, with barricades and cannons, no longer offers any human perspective at all in the conditions of today', R. Bahro, *Socialism and Survival*, p. 50.
113. C. B. Macpherson, *Life and Times of Liberal Democracy*, p. 95; that is, through 'two-way television'. But 'popular initiative could not formulate adequate questions on the great inter-related issues of overall social and economic policy . . . we cannot do without elected politicians', ibid., p. 97.
114. D. Singer, *Prelude to Revolution* (London, 1970) p. 363.
115. Ibid., p. 266.
116. R. Bahro, *Socialism and Survival*, p. 133.
117. A. Benn, *Arguments for Democracy*, p. 181.
118. A. Gorz, *Farewell to the Working Class*, p. 35.
119. M. Arnold, *Culture and Anarchy*, p. 195.
120. F. A. Hayek, op. cit., pp. 42–5; R. Bahro, *Socialism and Survival*, p. 29; J. Rawls, *Theory of Justice*, pp. 407 ff.
121. Cf. 'what binds a society's efforts into one social union is the mutual recognition and acceptance of the principles of justice', J. Rawls, *Theory of Justice*, p. 571.
122. 'Declaration des Droits de l'Homme et du Citoyen' (3 Nov 1789), preamble, in M. Williams (ed), *Revolutions, 1775–1830* (Harmondsworth, 1971) p. 96.
123. Ibid., p. 96; they were also 'natural and inalienable', ibid. But cf. '1789 may have opened the door to unrestricted capitalism, but its intentions were at least as much in harmony with socialism', V. J. Kiernan in B. Parekh (ed), *The Concept of Socialism*, p. 22; this was, allegedly, 'an individualism with higher socialist overtones', ibid.
124. J.S. Mill, *On Liberty*, p.137; cf. 'all the moral questions which arise within

human experience must be capable of illumination and clarification in the light of socialist thinking', A. Benn, *Arguments for Democracy*, p. xiii.

125. K. Marx and F. Engels, *The German Ideology*, p. 32; 'this sum of productive forces, capital funds and social forms of intercourse . . . is the real basis of what the philosophers have conceived as "substance" and "essence of man "' ibid., p. 50; cf. S. Timpanaro, *On Materialism* (London, 1975) pp. 29–71; and N. Geras, *Marx and Human Nature: Refutation of a Legend* (London, 1983) pp. 89–116.

126. K. Marx and F. Engels, *The Communist Manifesto*, p. 111.

127. L. Trotsky, *Where is Britain Going?*, p. 111.

128. B. Mussolini, *Grand Fascist Council Report, 1929*, quoted in F. A. Hayek, *Road to Serfdom*, p. 32.

129. L. Trotsky, *Where is Britain Going?*, p. 26.

130. V. I. Lenin, 'The State and Revolution', in *Collected Works*, vol. 25, p. 474; cf. E. P. Thompson's account of Robert Owen as the *'ne plus ultra* of utilitarianism, planning society as a gigantic industrial panopticon', *The Making of the English Working Class*, p. 859.

131. M. Friedman, *Free to Choose*, p. 122.

132. R. H. Tawney, *The Radical Tradition*, pp. 162–3.

133. M. Vajda, *The State and Socialism* (London, 1981) p. 14.

134. K. Marx, 'On the Jewish Question', in K. Marx and F. Engels, *Collected Works*, vol. 3, p. 162.

135. M. Raptis, *Socialism, Democracy and Self-Management*, intro. C. Goodey, p. 8 ('when we in our turn assert the synonymity of socialism and democracy, how are we to be believed?', ibid.).

136. J. S. Mill, *On Liberty*, p. 104.

137. J. Rawls, *Theory of Justice*, p. 28.

138. Ibid., p. 585; cf. C. B. Macpherson's assertion that 'current liberal democratic theory . . . still asserts the ultimate moral worth of the individual', *Democratic Theory*, pp. 176–7.

139. K. Joseph and J. Sumption, *Equality*, pp. 100, 125.

140. B. Russell, *Roads to Freedom*, p. 97.

141. For justifiably deep doubt cast on the orthodox history of this development, see C. Calhoun, *Question of Class Struggle, passim*, and R. Glen, *Urban Workers in the Early Industrial Revolution* (London, 1984); the rejected assumptions (and even methods) are those of E. P. Thompson's *The Making of the English Working Class*.

142. For an opposite (religiose) view, cf. 'it has been left to socialism to fulfil all such disappointed hopes [sc. of the French Revolution]; it is the New Testament that supersedes all old ones – though like all scriptures [*sic*], it is still a very incomplete one', V. J. Kiernan in B. Parekh (ed), *The Concept of Socialism*, p. 23.

143. T. Paine, *Rights of Man*, Part 1, p. 46.

144. Ibid., pp. 48–9.

145. Ibid., p. 70; and 'if I ask a man in America, if he wants a King, he retorts, and asks me if I take him for an idiot. How is it that this difference happens? Are we more, or less, wise than others?', ibid., p. 113. Cf. 'I am not at all convinced that in England . . . political development must proceed through a republic. The monarchy hardly interferes with the

workers there and therefore its abolition may not be a condition precedent to, but a consequence of, the triumph of socialism', G. Plekhanov, quoted in V. I. Lenin, *British Labour and British Imperialism*, p. 47.

146. J. Bentham, 'A Critical Examination of the Declaration of Rights', in B. Parekh (ed), *Bentham's Political Writings*, p. 260.
147. R. H. Tawney, *Equality*, p. 201.
148. Ibid.
149. C. B. Macpherson, *Democratic Theory*, pp. 14–15.
150. E. Mandel, 'The Lessons of May 1968', p. 29.
151. R. Bahro, *Socialism and Survival*, p. 117; cf. I. Berlin, in P. Laslett and W. G. Runciman (eds), *Philosophy, Politics and Society* (Oxford, 1962) pp. 2 ff.
152. E. Hobsbawm, *Marxism Today* (Oct 1982) pp. 10–11; 'this is no longer such a plausible prospect', ibid., a revisionist heresy if ever there was one, subsequently defended against critics in *Marxism Today* (March, 1984) pp. 8–12.
153. A. Herzen, *From the Other Shore*, p. 141.
154. K. Marx and F. Engels, *The Communist Manifesto*, p. 79.
155. Cf. A. Benn, 'we must reconnect with those people whom we were established to represent', *Arguments for Democracy*, p. 194; 'political organizations need to have relationships with the classes that they hope to represent and move', P. Corrigan, *New Statesman*, 3 December 1982; 'disengagement of the trade unions from the Labour Party threatens a disaster for the working-class movement in Britain', M. Rustin, *New Socialist* (March–April 1982) p. 32; 'it is significant that the most successful social democratic socialist governments are those which, like the Australians, the Swedes, the Germans, have close links with the unions', G. Radice, 'Labour and the Unions', in D. Lipsey and D. Leonard, *Socialist Agenda*, p. 125; and 'a party based exclusively on the working class is no longer viable or desirable – although it must, of course, always be based first and foremost, in every sense, on the working class', P. Anderson, 'Problems of Socialist Strategy', pp. 240–1.
156. R. H. Tawney, *Equality*, p. 207; 'attacking the oldest and toughest plutocracy in the world [is] . . . a pretty desperate business', ibid.
157. Cf. 'And everyone who speaks of any herb, plant, art or nature of mankind, is required to speak nothing by imagination, but what he hath found out by his own industry and observation in trial', G. Winstanley, 'The Law of Freedom in a Platform' (1652), in *The Law of Freedom and Other Writings*, ed. C. Hill (Harmondsworth, 1973) p. 347. Also, 'enough of words, come down to real things! *Show* me what you are talking about!', L. Feuerbach, 'Towards a Critique of Hegel's Philosophy' (1839), in *The Fiery Brook: Selected Writings of Ludwig Feuerbach*, ed. Z. Hanfi (New York, 1972) p. 77 (emphasis in original); and 'hitherto men have constantly made up for themselves false conceptions about themselves, about what they are and what they ought to be . . . Let us liberate them from the chimeras, the ideas, the dogmas, imaginary beings under the yoke of which they are pining away. Let us revolt against the rule of thoughts', K. Marx and F. Engels, preface, *The German Ideology*, p. 23.
158. J. Locke (1 Nov 1692 and 20 Jan 1693), quoted in K. Dewhurst, *John Locke*, pp. 309–10. Cf. 'Locke founded the philosophy of *bon sens*, common sense;

i.e. he said indirectly that no philosopher can be at variance with the healthy human senses and reason based upon them', K. Marx, 'The Holy Family', in K. Marx and F. Engels, *Collected Works*, vol. 4, p. 129.

159. J. Locke, in K. Dewhurst, *John Locke*, p. 309; cf. 'the concrete . . . is the point of departure in reality and hence also the point of departure for observation and conception', K. Marx, *Grundrisse*, p. 101.

160. L. Feuerbach, 'Principles of the Philosophy of the Future' (1843), in Z. Hanfi (ed), *Fiery Brook*, pp. 232–3; and 'things in thought should not be different from what they are in reality', ibid., p. 235.

Select Bibliography

Journal articles cited in the footnotes are not included.

M. Abrams, R. Rose and R. Hinden, *Must Labour Lose?* (Harmondsworth: Penguin, 1960).

I. Adelman and C. T. Morris, *Economic Growth and Social Equity in Developing Countries* (Stanford University Press, 1973).

M. Allaby and P. Bunyard, *The Politics of Self-Sufficiency* (Oxford University Press, 1980).

J. Alt, *The Politics of Economic Decline* (Cambridge University Press, 1979).

P. Anderson, *Arguments within English Marxism*, (London: Verso, 1980).

——, *Considerations on Western Marxism* (London: NLB, 1976).

——, and R. Blackburn (eds), *Towards Socialism* (London: Fontana, 1965).

M. Arnold, *Culture and Anarchy* (1869), ed J. Dover Wilson (Cambridge University Press, 1960).

C. Attlee, *The Labour Party in Perspective* (London: Gollancz, 1937).

R. Bacon and W. A. Eltis, *Britain's Economic Problems: Too Few Producers* (London: Macmillan, 1982).

R. Bahro, *The Alternative in Eastern Europe* (London: NLB, 1978).

——, *Socialism and Survival* (London: Heretic Books, 1982).

S. Bamford, *Walks in South Lancashire* (1844) (Brighton: Harvester, 1972).

P. Barker (ed), *The Other Britain* (London: Routledge and Kegan Paul, 1982).

D. Baumgardt, *Bentham and the Ethics of Today* (New York: Octagon Books, 1966).

F. Bealey (ed), *The Social and Political Thought of the British Labour Party* (London: Weidenfeld and Nicolson, 1970).

F. Bealey and H. Pelling, *Labour and Politics, 1900–1906* (London: Macmillan, 1958).

W. Beckerman (ed), *Slow Growth in Britain* (Oxford: Clarendon Press, 1979).

M. Beer, *A History of British Socialism* (1919) 2 vols. (London: Allen and Unwin, 1953).

J. Bellini, *Rule Britannia* (London: Abacus, 1982).

R. Benewick, R. N. Berki and B. Parekh (eds), *Knowledge and Belief in Politics* (London: Allen and Unwin, 1973).

W. Benjamin, *One-Way Street* (London: NLB, 1979).

A. Benn, *Arguments for Democracy* (Harmondsworth: Penguin, 1982).

——, *Arguments for Socialism* (Harmondsworth: Penguin, 1980).

——, *Parliament, People and Power: Agenda for a Free Society* (London: Verso, 1982).

——, *Speeches*, ed. J. Bodington (Nottingham: Spokesman, 1974).

J. Benson, *The Penny Capitalists* (Dublin: Gill and Macmillan, 1983).

R. N. Berki, *Socialism* (London: Dent, 1975).

E. Bernstein, *Evolutionary Socialism* (1899) (New York: Schocken Books, 1961).

D. Berry, *The Sociology of Grass Roots Politics* (London: Macmillan, 1970).

F. Blackaby (ed), *De-Industrialisation* (London: Heinemann, 1979).

R. Blackburn and A. Cockburn (eds), *The Incompatibles: Trade Union Militancy and the Consensus* (Harmondsworth: Penguin, 1967).

D. E. Bland and K. W. Watkins, *Can Britain Survive?* (London: Michael Joseph, 1971).

N. Bosanquet, *After the New Right* (London: Heinemann, 1983).

D. Bouchier, *Idealism and Revolution: New Ideologies of Liberation in Britain and the US* (London: Arnold, 1978).

F. Braudel, *The Wheels of Commerce*, trans. S. Reynolds (London: Collins, 1982).

M. Bruce, *The Coming of the Welfare State* (London: Batsford, 1961).

E. Burke, *Reflections on the Revolution in France* (1790) (Harmondsworth: Penguin, 1976).

D. Burnham, *The Rise of the Computer State* (London: Weidenfeld and Nicolson, 1983).

C. Calhoun, *The Question of Class Struggle* (Oxford: Blackwell, 1982).

E. H. Carr, *The Twenty Years' Crisis, 1919–1939* (London: Macmillan, 1946).

D. Caute, *The Left in Europe since 1789* (London: Weidenfeld and Nicolson, 1966).

J. Clarke, C. Critcher and R. Johnson (eds), *Working Class Culture* (London: Hutchinson, 1979).

A. Clayre (ed), *Nature and Industrialization* (Oxford University Press, 1977).

H. Cleaver, *Reading Capital Politically* (Brighton: Harvester, 1979).

D. Coates and G. Johnston (eds), *Socialist Arguments* (Oxford: Martin Robertson, 1983).

K. Coates, *The Labour Party and the Struggle for Socialism* (Cambridge University Press, 1975).

—— (ed), *What Went Wrong* (Nottingham: Spokesman, 1979).

G. D. H. Cole, *British Working Class Politics, 1832–1914* (London: Labour Book Service, 1941).

——, *The History of the Labour Party from 1914* (London: Routledge and Kegan Paul, 1948).

——, *A Short History of the British Working Class Movement* (London: Allen and Unwin, 1948).

H. Collins and C. Abramsky, *Karl Marx and the British Labour Movement* (London: Macmillan, 1965).

M. Cooley, *Architect or Bee? The Human/Technology Relationship* (Slough, privately printed, n.d.).

B. Crick and W. A. Robson (eds), *Protest and Discontent* (Harmondsworth: Penguin, 1970).

F. Cripps, J. Griffith, F. Morrell *et al.*, *Manifesto: A Radical Strategy for Britain's Future* (London: Pan, 1981).

A. Crosland, *The Future of Socialism* (London: Cape, 1956).

——, *Socialism Now* (London: Cape, 1974).

CSE London Working Group, *The Alternative Economic Strategy* (London: CSE Books, 1980).

N. Daniels (ed), *Reading Rawls* (Oxford: Blackwell, 1975).

K. Dewhurst, *John Locke: Physician and Philosopher* (London: Wellcome Historical Medical Library, 1963).

R. Diwan and D. Livingston, *Alternative Development Strategies and Appropriate Technology* (New York: Pergamon, 1979).

G. Duncan (ed), *Democratic Theory and Practice* (Cambridge University Press, 1983).

E. Durbin, *The Politics of Democratic Socialism* (London: Routledge, 1940).

R. Dworkin, *Taking Rights Seriously* (London: Duckworth, 1977).

F. Engels, *Anti-Dühring* (Moscow: Foreign Languages Publishing House, 1959).

——, *The Condition of the Working Class in England in 1844* (London: Allen and Unwin, 1950).

L. Feuerbach, *The Fiery Brook: Selected Writings*, trans. Z. Hanfi (New York: Anchor, 1972).

F. Field, *Inequality in Britain: Freedom, Welfare and the State* (London: Fontana, 1981).

——, *Poverty and Politics* (London: Heinemann, 1976).

H. Fink, *Social Philosophy* (London: Methuen, 1981).

T. Forrester, *The Labour Party and the Working Class* (London: Heinemann, 1976).

J. Foster, *Class Struggle and the Industrial Revolution: Early Industrial Capitalism in Three English Towns* (London: Weidenfeld and Nicolson, 1974).

A. Freeman, *The Benn Heresy* (London: Pluto, 1982).

M. Friedman, *Capitalism and Freedom* (Chicago University Press, 1962).

—— (with Rose D. Friedman), *Free to Choose* (Harmondsworth: Penguin, 1980).

J. K. Galbraith, *The Affluent Society* (London: Hamish Hamilton, 1958).

——, *The New Industrial State* (London: Hamish Hamilton, 1967).

J. Galtung, *The True Worlds* (New York: Free Press, 1980).

A. Gamble, *Britain in Decline* (London: Macmillan, 1981).

N. Geras, *Marx and Human Nature: Refutation of a Legend* (London: Verso, 1983).

I. Gilmour, *Britain Can Work* (Oxford: Martin Robertson, 1983).

G. Gissing, *Charles Dickens: A Critical Study* (London: Gresham, 1904).

——, *The Private Papers of Henry Ryecroft* (New York: New American Library, 1961).

R. Glen, *Urban Workers in the Early Industrial Revolution* (London: Croom Helm, 1984).

B. Goodwin and K. Taylor, *The Politics of Utopia* (London: Hutchinson, 1982).

A. Gorz, *Farewell to the Working Class* (London: Pluto, 1982).

I. Gough, *The Political Economy of the Welfare State* (London: Macmillan, 1979).

A. Gramsci, *Selections from Political Writings, 1910–1920*, ed Q. Hoare (London: Lawrence and Wishart, 1977).

——, *Selections from Political Writings, 1921–1926*, ed. Q. Hoare (London: Lawrence and Wishart, 1978).

P. Green, *The Pursuit of Inequality* (Oxford: Martin Robertson, 1981).

P. S. Gupta, *Imperialism and the British Labour Movement, 1914–1964* (London: Macmillan, 1975).

P. Hain (ed), *The Crisis and the Future of the Left* (London: Pluto, 1980).

——, *The Democratic Alternative* (Harmondsworth: Penguin, 1983).

——, *Neighbourhood Participation* (London: Temple Smith, 1980).

S. Hall and M. Jacques (eds), *The Politics of Thatcherism* (London: Lawrence and Wishart, 1983).

J. Halperin, *Gissing: A Life in Books* (Oxford University Press, 1982).

A. H. Halsey, *Change in British Society* (Oxford University Press, 1978).

——, (ed), *Traditions of Social Policy* (Oxford: Blackwell, 1976).

T. T. Hammond, *Lenin on Trade Unions and Revolution, 1893–1917* (New York: Columbia University Press, 1957).

K. Harris, *Attlee* (London: Weidenfeld and Nicolson, 1982).

S. Haseler, *The Gaitskellites: Revisionism in the British Labour Party* (London: Macmillan, 1969).

M. Hatfield, *The House the Left Built* (London: Gollancz, 1978).

F. A. Hayek, *The Constitution of Liberty* (London: Routledge and Kegan Paul, 1960).

——, *The Road to Serfdom* (London: Routledge and Kegan Paul, 1944).

——, *1980s Unemployment and the Unions* (London: Institute of Economic Affairs, 1980).

A. Herzen, *From the Other Shore* (Oxford University Press, 1979).

——, *My Past and Thoughts*, ed. D. Macdonald (London: Chatto and Windus, 1974).

C. Hill, *The World Turned Upside Down* (Harmondsworth: Penguin, 1975).

B. Hindess, *The Decline of Working Class Politics* (London: Paladin, 1971).

——, *Parliamentary Democracy and Socialist Politics* (London: Routledge and Kegan Paul, 1983).

J. Hinton, *Labour and Socialism: A History of the British Labour Movement, 1867–1974* (Brighton: Wheatsheaf Books, 1983).

A Hirsh, *The French Left: A History and Overview* (Montreal: Black Rose Books, 1982).

L. T. Hobhouse, *The Labour Movement* (London: T. Fisher Unwin, 1912).

——, *Social Evolution and Political Theory* (Port Washington, New York: Kennikat Press Inc., 1911).

E. J. Hobsbawm, *Labour's Turning Point* (London: Lawrence and Wishart, 1948).

——, *Labouring Men: Studies in the History of Labour* (London: Weidenfeld and Nicolson, 1964).

J. A. Hobson, *The Evolution of Modern Capitalism* (London: Walter Scott, 1894).

G. Hodgson, *Labour at the Crossroads* (Oxford: Martin Robertson, 1981).

R. Hoggart, *The Uses of Literacy* (London: Chatto and Windus, 1957).

S. Holland, *The Socialist Challenge* (London: Quartet, 1975).

R. Hyman, *Marxism and the Sociology of Trade Unionism* (London: Pluto, 1971).

H. Jackson, *The Rise and Fall of 19th Century Idealism* (New York: Citadel, 1969).

M. Jacques and F. Mulhern (eds), *The Forward March of Labour Halted?* (London: NLB, 1981).

K. Joseph and J. Sumption, *Equality* (London: John Murray, 1979).

B. de Jouvenel, *Problems of Socialist England* (London: Batchworth Press, 1949).

J. Jupp, *The Radical Left in Britain, 1931–1941* (London: Frank Cass, 1982).

P. Kahn and A. Scargill, *The Myth of Workers' Control*, Occasional Papers no. 5 (Universities of Leeds and Nottingham, 1980).

Y. Kapp, *Eleanor Marx*, 2 vols (London: Lawrence and Wishart, 1972–6).

K. Kautsky, *The Dictatorship of the Proletariat* (University of Michigan Press, 1971).

——, *The Labour Revolution* (London: Allen and Unwin, 1925).

——, *The Social Revolution*, trans. A.M. and M.W. Simons (Chicago: Chas. Kerr, 1916).

D. Kavanagh (ed), *The Politics of the Labour Party* (London: Allen and Unwin, 1982).

W. Kendall, *The Revolutionary Movement in Britain, 1900–1921* (London: Weidenfeld and Nicolson, 1969).

G. Kitching, *Rethinking Socialism* (London: Methuen, 1983).

G. Konrad and I. Szelenyi, *Intellectuals on the Road to Class Power* (Brighton: Harvester, 1979).

Labour Party, *Labour's Programme*, (London: Labour Party, 1982).

———, *The New Hope for Britain: Labour's Manifesto* (London: Labour Party, 1983).

———, *The Old World and the New Society* (London: Labour Party, 1942).

B. Lapping, *The Labour Government, 1964–1970* (Harmondsworth, Penguin, 1970).

H. J. Laski, *A Grammar of Politics* (London: Allen and Unwin, 1967).

———, *Liberty in the Modern State* (London: Faber, 1930).

———, *Reflections on the Revolution of our Time* (London: Allen and Unwin, 1944).

H. Lefebvre, *Everyday Life in the Modern World*, trans. S. Rabinovitch (London: Allen Lane, 1971).

———, *The Survival of Capitalism* (London: Allison and Busby, 1976).

V. I. Lenin, *British Labour and British Imperialism* (London: Lawrence and Wishart, 1969).

———, *Collected Works*, vols 1–47 (Moscow and London: Lawrence and Wishart, 1960–78).

D. Lipsey and D. Leonard (eds), *The Socialist Agenda: Crosland's Legacy* (London: Cape, 1981).

J. London, *The People of the Abyss* (1903) (London: Journeyman Press, 1977).

W. Lovett, *The Life and Struggles of William Lovett* (London: G. Bell, 1920).

E. Luard, *Socialism Without the State* (London: Macmillan, 1979).

G. Lukacs, *History and Class Consciousness* (London: Merlin, 1971).

S. Lukes, *Individualism* (Oxford: Basil Blackwell, 1973).

———, *Essays in Social and Political Theory* (London: Macmillan, 1977).

R. Luxemburg, *The Russian Revolution* (University of Michigan Press, 1961).

———, *Social Reform or Revolution* (London: Merlin, n.d.)

S. MacIntyre, *A Proletarian Science: Marxism in Britain, 1917–1933* (Cambridge University Press, 1980).

L. Mackay and D. Fernbach (eds), *Nuclear-Free Defence* (London: Heretic Books, 1983).

C. B. Macpherson, *Democratic Theory: Essays in Retrieval* (Oxford: Clarendon Press, 1973).

———, *The Life and Times of Liberal Democracy* (Oxford University Press, 1977).

E. Mandel, *The Marxist Theory of the State* (New York: Merit Publishers, 1969).

K. Mannheim, *Ideology and Utopia* (London: Kegan Paul, 1936).

H. Marcuse, *An Essay on Liberation* (Harmondsworth: Penguin, 1972).

D. C. Marsh, *The Future of the Welfare State* (Harmondsworth: Penguin, 1964).

K. Marx, *Capital*, vols 1 and 2, trans. E. and C. Paul (London: Dent, 1933); *Capital*, vol 3 (Moscow: Foreign Languages Publishing House, 1959).

———, *The Class Struggles in France, 1848–1850* (Moscow: Progress Publishers, 1979).

———, *A Contribution to the Critique of Political Economy*, trans. N. I. Stone (Chicago: Chas. Kerr, 1913).

———, *Grundrisse*, trans. M. Nicolaus (Harmondsworth: Penguin, 1973).

———, *Political Writings: The First International and After*, ed. D. Fernbach (Harmondsworth: Penguin, 1974).

———, *Political Writings: Surveys from Exile*, ed. D. Fernbach (Harmondsworth: Penguin, 1973).

——, *Wages, Prices and Profit* (Moscow: Progress Publishers, 1974).

K. Marx and F. Engels, *Collected Works*, vols 1–14, 16–18, 38–9 (London: Lawrence and Wishart, 1975–1983).

——, *The Communist Manifesto* (Harmondsworth: Penguin, 1967).

——, *The German Ideology* (London: Lawrence and Wishart, 1965).

——, *On Religion* (Moscow: Foreign Languages Publishing House, 1955).

——, *Selected Correspondence* (Moscow: Foreign Languages Publishing House, 1953).

——, *Selected Works*, 3 vols (Moscow: Progress Publishers, 1969–70).

R. McKibbin, *The Evolution of the Labour Party, 1910–1924* (Oxford University Press, 1974).

D. McLellan (ed), *Karl Marx: Selected Writings* (Oxford University Press, 1977).

G. McRobie, *Small is Possible* (London: Cape, 1981).

K. Middlemas, *Politics in Industrial Society* (London: Deutsch, 1979).

R. Miliband, *Capitalist Democracy in Britain* (Oxford University Press, 1982).

——, *Parliamentary Socialism* (London: Merlin, 1973).

——, *The State in Capitalist Society* (London: Quartet, 1973).

J. S. Mill, *On Bentham and Coleridge* (1838 and 1840) (London: Chatto and Windus, 1950).

——, *On Liberty* (London: John Parker, 1859).

——, *Principles of Political Economy* (1848) (London: Longmans Green, 1920).

L. von Mises, *Socialism* (London: Cape, 1951).

W. Morris, *Political Writings*, ed. A. L. Morton (London: Lawrence and Wishart, 1973).

T. Nairn, *The Break-up of Britain* (London: NLB, 1977).

J. P. Narayan, *Socialism, Sarvodaya and Democracy*, ed. B. Prasad (London: Asia Publishing House, 1964).

A. Nove, *The Economics of Feasible Socialism* (London: Allen and Unwin, 1983).

R. Nozick, *Anarchy, State and Utopia* (Oxford: Blackwell, 1974).

M. Oakeshott, *On Human Conduct* (Oxford: Clarendon Press, 1975).

S. K. Padover (ed), *The Essential Marx: The Non-Economic Writings* (New York: New American Library, 1979).

T. Paine, *The Rights of Man* (1791–2) (London: Dent, 1906).

B. Parekh (ed), *Bentham's Political Thought* (London: Croom Helm, 1973).

—— (ed), *The Concept of Socialism* (London: Croom Helm, 1975).

——, *Contemporary Political Thinkers* (Oxford: Martin Robertson, 1982).

F. Parkin, *Class, Inequality and Political Order* (London: Paladin, 1971).

——, *Middle-class Radicals* (Manchester University Press, 1968).

H. Pelling, *The Origins of the Labour Party* (Oxford University Press, 1965).

——, *Popular Politics and Society in Late Victorian Britain* (London: Macmillan, 1968).

S. Pierson, *Marxism and the Origins of British Socialism* (Ithaca and London: Cornell University Press, 1973).

B. Pimlott and C. Cook (eds), *Trade Unions in British Politics* (London: Longman, 1982).

S. Pollard, *The Idea of Progress* (Harmondsworth: Penguin, 1971).

——, *The Wasting of the British Economy* (London: Croom Helm, 1982).

N. Poulantzas, *Classes in Contemporary Capitalism* (London: NLB, 1975).

——, *Political Power and Social Classes* (London: NLB, 1973).

——, *State, Power, Socialism* (London: NLB, 1978).

M. Raptis, *Socialism, Democracy and Self-Management* (London: Allison and Busby, 1980).

J. Rawls, *A Theory of Justice* (Oxford University Press, 1973).

J. Rée, *Proletarian Philosophers* (Oxford University Press, 1984).

W. Reich, *What is Class Consciousness?*, Socialist Reproduction no. 1 (London, n.d.) (c. 1968).

G. Rudé, *The Crowd in the French Revolution* (Oxford University Press, 1967).

J. Ruskin, *The Stones of Venice* (1851–3), 3 vols (London: Dent, 1907).

B. Russell, *Roads to Freedom* (1918) (London: Allen and Unwin, 1966).

B. Särlvik and I. Crewe, *Decade of Dealignment* (Cambridge University Press, 1983).

J. P. Sartre, *Being and Nothingness*, trans. H. Barnes (London: Methuen, 1957).

——, *The Communists and Peace*, trans. I. Clephane (London: Hamish Hamilton, 1969).

D. Sayer, *Marx's Method* (Brighton: Harvester, 1979).

F. Schumacher, *Small is Beautiful* (London: Blond and Briggs, 1973).

J. Seabrook, *Unemployment* (London: Quartet, 1982).

——, *What Went Wrong?* (London: Gollancz, 1978).

——, *Working-Class Childhood* (London: Gollancz, 1982).

D. Selbourne, *An Eye to India* (Harmondsworth: Penguin, 1977).

—— (ed), *In Theory and In Practice: Essays on the Politics of J. P. Narayan* (New Delhi: Oxford University Press, 1984).

R. Sennett and J. Cobb, *The Hidden Injuries of Class* (Cambridge University Press, 1972).

E. J. Sieyès, *What is the Third Estate?*, trans. M. Blondel (London: Pall Mall Press, 1963).

B. Simmel, *Imperialism and English Social Thought, 1895–1914* (London: Allen and Unwin, 1960).

G. Sims, *How the Poor Live and Horrible London* (London: Chatto and Windus, 1889).

D. Singer, *Prelude to Revolution* (London: Cape, 1970).

A. Smith, *An Inquiry into the Nature and Causes of the Wealth of Nations* (1776), 3 vols, ed. R. H. Campbell, A. S. Skinner, and W. B. Todd (Oxford: Clarendon Press, 1976).

W. Sombart, *Why is there no Socialism in the United States?* (1906) (London: Macmillan, 1976).

G. Stedman-Jones, *Languages of Class: Studies in English Working Class History, 1832–1982* (Cambridge University Press, 1983).

J. Strachey, *The Theory and Practice of Socialism* (London: Gollancz, 1936).

——, *Why You Should Be a Socialist* (London: Gollancz, 1944).

P. Tatchell, *The Battle for Bermondsey* (London: Heretic Books, 1983).

R. H. Tawney, *The Acquisitive Society* (London: Bell, 1921).

——, *Equality* (London: Allen and Unwin, 1964).

——, *The Radical Tradition*, ed. R. Hinden (Harmondsworth: Penguin, 1966).

B. Taylor, *Eve and the New Jerusalem* (London: Virago, 1983).

R. Taylor, *Workers and the New Depression* (London: Macmillan, 1982).

P. Thane, *Foundations of the Welfare State* (London: Longman, 1982).

E. P. Thompson, *The Making of the English Working Class* (Harmondsworth: Penguin, 1968).

——, *William Morris, Romantic to Revolutionary* (London: Merlin, 1977).

——, *The Poverty of Theory* (London: Merlin, 1978).

——, *Whigs and Hunters* (London: Allen Lane, 1975).

——, *Writing by Candlelight* (London: Merlin, 1980).

S. Timpanaro, *On Materialism* (London: NLB, 1975).

R. M. Titmuss, *Essays on the Welfare State* (London: Allen and Unwin, 1963).

A. de Tocqueville, *Journeys to England and Ireland* (1835) (London: Faber and Faber, 1958).

E. Toller, *I was a German: An Autobiography* (London: John Lane, 1934).

A. Touraine, *L'Après Socialisme* (Paris: Grasset, 1980).

P. Townsend, *Poverty in the United Kingdom* (London: Allen Lane, 1979).

P. Townsend and N. Bosanquet (eds), *Labour and Inequality* (London: Fabian Society, 1972).

L. Trotsky, *On the Trade Unions* (New York: Pathfinder Press, 1969).

——, *Terrorism and Communism: A Reply to Karl Kautsky* (London: Allen and Unwin, 1921).

——, *Where is Britain Going?* (1925) (London: New Park Publications, 1970).

D. F. B. Tucker, *Marxism and Individualism* (Oxford: Basil Blackwell, 1980).

A. Ure, *The Philosophy of Manufactures* (1835) (London: Frank Cass, 1967).

M. Vajda, *The State and Socialism* (London: Allison and Busby, 1981).

H. Wainwright and D. Elliot, *The Lucas Plan: A New Trade Unionism in the Making?* (London: Allison and Busby, 1982).

S. and B. Webb, *Our Partnership* (London: Longmans Green, 1948).

E. Wertheimer, *Portrait of the Labour Party* (London: Putnam's, 1929).

P. Whiteley, *The Labour Party in Crisis* (London: Methuen, 1983).

D. Widgery (ed), *The Left in Britain, 1956–68* (Harmondsworth: Penguin, 1976).

M. Wiener, *English Culture and the Decline of the Industrial Spirit, 1850–1980* (Cambridge University Press, 1981).

O. Wilde, *The Soul of Man under Socialism* (1891) (London: Chiswick Press, 1895).

E. Wilkinson, *The Town that was Murdered* (London: Gollancz, 1949).

M. Williams (ed), *Revolutions, 1775–1830* (Harmondsworth: Penguin and Open University, 1971).

R. Williams, *Culture and Society, 1780–1950* (Harmondsworth: Penguin, 1961).

——, *The Long Revolution* (Harmondsworth: Penguin, 1965).

——, *Towards 2000* (London: Chatto and Windus, 1983).

H. R. Winkler (ed), *Twentieth Century Britain: National Power and Social Welfare* (New York: New Viewpoints, 1976).

G. Winstanley, *The Law of Freedom and Other Writings*, ed. C. Hill (Harmondsworth: Penguin, 1973).

J. Winter (ed), *The Working Class in Modern British History* (Cambridge University Press, 1983).

Index

References to notes are given in italic numerals.

accountability, 8, 151, 212, 215, 220–1, 223, 225–7
accumulation, 167–8, 172, 220, 245, *292*
acquisitiveness, *see* appropriation
Acreland, T., 83, 112
actuality, *see* empirical, the
Adelman, I., *297*
agricultural production, agriculture, 55, 277
alcoholism, *284*
Ali, T., *279–80, 295*
alienation, 26, 50, 76, 94, 107, 138, 211, *279*
Alison, M., *293*
altruism, *261, 274*
ambition, 66, 68, 80, 188, 190
America, United States of, American, *260, 282, 293, 302*
Amnesty International, 234
anarchy, 140
Anderson, P., 6, 26, 33, *256, 262, 264, 276, 278–80, 282, 296, 303*
anomie, 107
Anti-Dühring (F. Engels), 228
anti-intellectualism, 103
anti-socialism, 34, 59, 94, 106, 167, 204, 212, 224, 235
apathy, 58, *295*
appropriation, appropriators, 45, 52–7, 59–60, 63–5, 66–7, 70, 75, 78, 84–5, 98, 101, 107–9, 112–13, 118, 120, 122, 124, 137, 139, 144, 154–6, 158, 163, 167–8, 171, 173, 175, 185–6, 201–3, 205, 211, 214–15, 225, 228–9, 235–6, 238, 244, 249, *269, 292*
see also private property
Arblaster, A., *256, 276*
archaism, 180, *293*
Arguments for Democracy (A. Benn), 24
army, armed struggle, 198, 227, 253, *290*
see also militarism
Arnold, M., 28, 38, 70–1, 83, 111, 140, 145, 154, 156, 170, 195–6, 225, 237, *264, 271, 288, 289*
artisan skills, *see* skills
Aston, T., *268–9*

Attlee, C., 51, 121, 166, *268*
austerity, 124
Austria, *258, 303*
authority, authoritarianism, 57, 59, 71, 87, 139, 150, 190, 210, 221, 225, 228, 232–3, 236–7, 239, 243–4, *267, 275*
autocracy, 61, *299*
autonomy, 80, 84, 98, 100, 132, 160, 167–9, 212, 216, 221, 236, 245, 249, *267*

bad faith, 87, 94, 169, 206
bad taste, 76
Bahro, R., 57, 238, 251, *262, 264, 293, 296, 301*
balance of terror, 231
see also nuclear arms
Baldwin, S., 102
Bamford, S., 83, 112, 163, *275*
bankers, *291*
bargaining, collective bargain, market bargain, 132, 158–99, 200 *passim, 291–2*
Barnett, A., *262*
Bavarian Soviet Republic, 99
beauty, 155
beggars, 128, *282*
Bellini, J., *257, 282, 288*
benefits, *see* social benefits, welfare
benevolence, 128, 130, 134, 149
Benjamin, W., 229, *277–8*
Benn, A., 23–5, 41, 96, 151, *259, 262–3, 270, 273–4, 283, 285, 291–2, 294, 298, 301–3*
Bentham, J., Benthamism, 14, 34–5, 94, 123, 130, 221, 226, 238–9, 246, 248, *271, 298*
Bermondsey, 103
Bernstein, E., 21, 99
betrayal, *281*
Bevan, A., Bevanites, *261*
Beverige, Lord, Beveridgeans, 114, 122, 124
Birmingham, 149
blacks, 68, 72, 105, *295*
see also race
bloc vote, 190, *291*
Blunkett, D., *263*
Bolshevik Revolution, *see* Revolution, the Russian

313

inheritance, 172
initiative, 135
Institute of Personnel Management
(IPM), 177
insurance, social, 136
see also welfare
Invergordon, 246
investment, 14, 54, 119, 135, 149, 178, *292,
300*
Ireton, H., 54
Irish, the, *275*

Jacobins, Jacobinism, 52, 174, 209, 211,
249, *280*
Jarrow, 4, *257*
Jenkins, P., *296*
Jerusalem, the new, 14, 28, 118, *259*
Jesus, *261*
Jews, the, *275*
jingoism, 111
Job Centres, 126
see also employment, unemployment
job control, 171, 183
job property, job protection, 55, 171–2,
183–4, 202, *292*
jobs, *see* employment
Johnston, G., 263
joint stock associations, 167
Joseph, K., 61, *265, 267, 270-1*
journalists, *281*
Jude the Obscure, 139
Judges' Rules, 202

Kahn, P., *300*
Kapital, Das (K. Marx), 93–4, 154
Kautsky, K., 125
Kiernan, V.J., *258, 262, 264, 275, 301-2*
King, A., *257*
Kitching, G., *256, 260*
Kronstadt, 246

labour, labour movement, working-class
movement, 9, 13, 17, 19–21, 27–30,
33–5, 45, 49–50, 53, 56, 58, 63–4, 70,
72–4, 76, 79–82, 84–5, 89, 92, 94, 96–8,
101–3, 108–12, 115, 121–2, 124–5, 132,
135–40, 143, 150, 154, 156–7, 158
passim, 200 *passim, 258, 262-3, 266-7,
269, 275-8, 289-90, 292, 303*
see also labourism, socialism, trade
unions, unwanted labour, work,
working class
Labour Church Union, 81–2
labour organization, *see* trade unions

Labour Party, Labour Government,
Labour voters, 7, 9, 12–19, 22, 24–5,
27–8, 30–3, 35, 39–41, 50, 53, 63, 80–3,
96–7, 103–4, 106, 108–10, 112, 114,
124–6, 131, 141, 143, 154, 156–9, 161,
163–4, 171, 174, 179–81, 183–4,
187–94, 197–9, 201–3, 205–7, 215, 223,
225, 235, 249, 252–3, *258-9, 261-2,
273-4, 279-81, 283, 291, 294-6, 303*
labour power, labour time, 46, 58, 71, 89,
186, 235
labour, private interests of, 132, 158–99,
201, 204–5, 212, 215–16, 221, 229,
234–5, 237, 239, 251, *289-90*
labour process, 71–2, 90, 98–100
see also production, work
labourism, 163, 196–7, 249, *291, 295*
laissez-faire, 44, *293*
Lancashire, 79, 83
language, abuse of, 41, 49
see also rhetoric
Lao-Tzu, 221
Laski, H., 41–2,
Lassalle, F., Lassallean, 142, 144, 146–7,
152
law and order, 33
Lawrence, D.H., 153, *289*
leap-frogging, 173
see also bargain, economism
Lefebvre, H., 76
legitimacy, legitimation, 49–50, 51–2, 55,
57, 63, 65–6, 69, 75, 84–5, 91, 97,
101–2, 109–10, 112, 118, 131, 134, 151,
151, 155, 159–63, 166, 168, 170, 178,
196, 199, 205, 208, 211, 216, 226, 236,
238, 248–9, 253
see also hegemony
Lenin, V.I., Leninism, 92, 160, 174, 210,
243, *260, 275, 277, 281, 290, 293, 297*
Leonard, D., *257*
Levellers, the, 110
Levin, M., *300*
liberal democracy, 'liberal',
'liberalism', 14, 27, 36, 42, 44, 49–51,
62, 85, 88, 99, 110, 192, 211, 230, 233,
244, *266, 269, 274, 281, 300, 302*
Liberal Party, Liberal, Liberalism, 37, *189,
260, 294*
liberation, emancipation, 23–4, 40–1, 53,
60–1, 73, 89, 91, 110, 203, 209, 217,
219, 221, 227–8, 230, 232, 234, 238,
242, 251, 253, *261, 269, 273, 290, 295*
liberty, libertarianism, 14, 36–7, 39, 41–8,
52, 54, 57–62, 66–8, 73, 81, 84, 109,
120, 130, 134, 137, 165–6, 168, 180,

workers' control, 183–4, 223, 227
workers' power, workers' state, 7–8, 25, 27, 220–1
workhouse, 126
working class, working people, 3–5, 6, 9–13, 15, 17–18, 19, 25–6, 28–30, 33–6, 38–40, 45, 50, 52–3, 55–6, 60–1, 63–4, 68–9, 70 *passim*, 113, 117, 128, 131–4, 136, 138, 141–2, 145, 147, 155–6, 158, 160, 162, 165–7, 170, 172–3, 175, 178–9, 181, 183–6, 188–9, 195, 197–9, 200–2, 205, 210, 214–15, 220–1, 224–6,

229–30, 232, 234, 236–8, 243, 246, 252–3, *258–60, 262, 267–8, 271–5, 277–82, 286–7, 289–95, 299, 303*
see also labour, proletariat
working-class culture, 31, 33, 56, 72, 102, 105, 139, *283*
working-class movement, *see* labour
workplace, the, 220, *301*
see also shop floor

zero growth, 253